Competition, Contracts and Electricity Markets

LOYOLA DE PALACIO SERIES ON EUROPEAN ENERGY POLICY

Series Editor: Jean-Michel Glachant, *Loyola de Palacio Professor for European Energy Policy and Director of the Florence School of Regulation, European University Institute, Italy, and Professor of Economics, Université Paris-Sud, France*

The Loyola de Palacio Series on European Energy Policy honours Loyola de Palacio (1950–2006), former Vice-President of the European Commission and EU Commissioner for Energy and Transport (1999–2004), a pioneer in the creation of an EU Energy Policy.

This series aims to promote energy policy research, develop academic knowledge and nurture the 'market for ideas' in the field of energy policy making. It will offer informed and up-to-date analysis on key European energy policy issues (from market building to security of supply; from climate change to a low carbon economy and society). It will engage in a fruitful dialogue between academics (including economists, lawyers, engineers and political scientists), practitioners and decision-makers. The series will complement the large range of activities performed at the Loyola de Palacio Chair currently held by Professor Jean-Michel Glachant (Robert Schuman Center for Advanced Studies at European University Institute in Florence, Italy, and University Paris-Sud 11.

Titles in the series include:

Security of Energy Supply in Europe
Natural Gas, Nuclear and Hydrogen
Edited by François Lévêque, Jean-Michel Glachant, Julián Barquín, Christian von Hirschhausen, Franziska Holz and William J. Nuttall

Competition, Contracts and Electricity Markets
A New Perspective
Edited by Jean-Michel Glachant, Dominique Finon and Adrien de Hauteclocque

Competition, Contracts and Electricity Markets

A New Perspective

Edited by

Jean-Michel Glachant

Loyola de Palacio Professor in European Energy Policy and Director, Florence School of Regulation, European University Institute, RSCAS, Italy

Dominique Finon

Directeur de Recherche CNRS (Centre National de la Recherche Scientifique), Centre International de Recherche sur l'Environnement et le Développement, CNRS and EHESS, Paris, France

Adrien de Hauteclocque

Coordinator, EU Energy Law and Policy Area, Florence School of Regulation and Research Associate, Loyola de Palacio Chair, European University Institute, RSCAS, Italy

LOYOLA DE PALACIO SERIES ON EUROPEAN ENERGY POLICY

Edward Elgar

Cheltenham, UK • Northampton, MA, USA

Published by
Edward Elgar Publishing Limited
The Lypiatts
15 Lansdown Road
Cheltenham
Glos GL50 2JA
UK

Edward Elgar Publishing, Inc.
William Pratt House
9 Dewey Court
Northampton
Massachusetts 01060
USA

A catalogue record for this book
is available from the British Library

Library of Congress Control Number: 2010934052

ISBN 978 1 84980 479 0

Typeset by Servis Filmsetting Ltd, Stockport, Cheshire
Printed and bound by MPG Books Group, UK

Contents

Figures

Tables

Contributors

Jacqueline Boucher, Senior Vice President Economic Modelling and Studies – GDFSuez.

Gert Brunekreeft, Professor of Energy Economics, Jacobs University Bremen and Director of the Bremer Energie Institut.

Dominique Finon, Director of the joint program LARSEN (CNRS, University Paris Sud and EDF R&D) and CNRS Senior Fellow at CIRED (Centre International de Recherche sur l'Environnement et le Développement), Paris.

Jean-Michel Glachant, Director, Florence School of Regulation and Loyola de Palacio Chair, European University Institute, RSCAS.

Leigh Hancher, Professor of European Law at Tilburg University and Counsel at Allen & Overy.

Adrien de Hauteclocque, Coordinator, EU Energy Law and Policy Area, Florence School of Regulation and Research Associate in charge of Legal Studies at the Loyola de Palacio Chair, European University Institute, RSCAS.

Petter Longva, Vice President Energy Policy, Norsk Hydro.

Frédéric Marty, French National Centre of Scientific Research Fellow (CNRS)/Research Group on Law, Economics and Management (GREDEG – University of Nice Sophia-Antipolis), Affiliate Researcher OFCE (French Economic Observatory – Sciences Po, Paris).

Richard Meade, Research Associate, New Zealand Institute for the Study of Competition and Regulation.

Guy Meunier, Post-doctoral Fellow, Département d'Économie, École Polytechnique, Paris.

Machiel Mulder, Deputy Chief Economist, Netherlands Competition Authority.

Seini O'Connor, Research Associate, New Zealand Institute for the Study of Competition and Regulation.

Julien Pillot, Research Fellow, French National Centre of Scientific Research Fellow (CNRS)/Research Group on Law, Economics and Management (GREDEG – University of Nice Sophia-Antipolis).

Fabien A. Roques, Director of European Power, IHS Cambridge Energy Research Associates and Associate Researcher to the Electricity Policy Research Group of the University of Cambridge.

Yves Smeers, Tractebel Professor of Energy Economics, Center for Operations Research and Econometrics (CORE), Université catholique de Louvain.

Acknowledgements

This book is the final result of a research program on 'Competition and long-term contracts in the electricity markets' organized by LARSEN (Laboratoire d'Analyse économique des Réseaux et des Systèmes ENergétiques), a joint undertaking of CNRS (CIRED), Paris Sud University (ADIS-GRJM) and the economic department of EDF R&D division. The chapters are mainly composed of papers presented on 15–16 January 2009 at the workshop organized in Florence at the European University Institute (EUI) by the Loyola de Palacio Chair, Florence School of Regulation and LARSEN, under a co-sponsoring. We are particularly grateful to the EUI RSCAS for having hosted this workshop.

We would like to thank LARSEN, CNRS, EDF R&D, and the Loyola de Palacio Chair for their support.

All chapters were revised after the workshop and reviewed in a process of anonymous cross-reviewing by the respective contributors. We address many thanks to each contributor for having participated to this reviewing process.

Jean-Michel Glachant,
Dominique Finon and
Adrien de Hauteclocque

Abbreviations

ACEA	Azienda Comunale Energia Ambiente (Roma)
ACER	Agency for the Cooperation of Energy Regulators
AEM	Azienda Energetica Municipale (Milano)
AES	Allied Energy System (US pure producer)
APX	Amsterdam Power Exchange
ARA	Antwerp/Rotterdam/Amsterdam coal price index
BaU	business as usual
BEB	Brigitta und Elwerath Betriebsführungs-Gesellschaft mbH
BNetzA	Bundesnetzagentur
CAPM	capital asset pricing model
CCGT	combined cycle gas turbine
CCS	carbon capture and sequestration
CDO	collateralized debt obligation
CFI	Court of First Instance
CNRS	National Centre for Scientific Research (France)
CO_2	carbon dioxide
CT	combustion turbine
DG COMP	Directorate General of Competition (European Commission)
DNO	distributor network owner
DT	Deutsche Telekom
DTe	Directie Toezicht Energie (Office of Energy Regulation in Dutch NMa)
DTI	Department of Trade and Industry
DWR	Department of Water Resources (California)
EC	European Commission
ECJ	European Court of Justice
EDF	Électricité de France
EDP	Electricidad de Portugal
EEX	European Electricity Exchange (German power exchange)
EFD	Essential Facility Doctrine
EnBW	Energie Baden-Wuerttemberg AG
ENEL	Ente Nazionale l'Energia Elettrica (Italy)
ENPV	expected net present value
ENTSO	European Network of Transmission System Operators

ERGEG	European Regulators' Group for Electricity and Gas
ESB	Electricity Supply Board (Ireland)
ETS	emissions trading system
EU	European Union
EUI	European University Institute
FAQ	frequently asked question
FCFS	First come-first served rule of access
FERC	Federal Energy Regulatory Commission
FS	Ferrovie dello Stato
FTR	financial transmission rights
GDF	Gaz de France (now GDFSuez)
GT	gas turbine
GVG	Georg Verkeorganisation Gmbh
GW	gigawatt
HHI	Herfindal–Hirschman index
ICT	information and communication technology
IEA	International Energy Agency
IP	intellectual property
IPP	independent power producer
ISO	independent system operator
ITO	independent transmission operator
kW	kilowatt
LARSEN	Laboratoire d'Analyse économique des Réseaux et des Systems Energétiques
LI	Lerner Index
LNG	liquid natural gas
LTC	long-term contract
MEIT	market economic investor test
MVM	Magyar Villamos Művek Zrt (Hungarian Electricity Works)
MVP	mean variance portfolio
MW	megawatt
MWh	megawatt hour
NBP	national balancing point (in UK gas market)
NEM	national electricity market (Australia)
NERA	National Economic Research Associates
NETA	National Electricity Trading Arrangement
NMa	Nederlandse Mededingings autoriteit (Netherlands Competition Authority)
NPV	net present value
NVE	Norges Vassdrags- og Energidirektorat (Norwegian energy regulator)

O&M	Operation & Maintenance
OECD	Organisation for Economic Co-operation and Development
OMV	Österreichischen Mineralölverwaltung
OTC	over the counter
PJM	Pennsylvania–New Jersey–Maryland regional market
PPA	power purchase agreement
PSE	Polski Sieci Elecktroenergetyczne (historic electricity utility)
PX	Power exchange
R&D	research and development
RES	renewable energy source
RPI	Retail Price Index
RSI	Residual Supply Index
RWE	Rheinisch-Westfälische Elektrizitätswerke
SAAP	State Aid Action Plan
SCBA	social cost–benefit analysis
SD	standard deviation
SEP	Samenwerkende Elektriciteitproductiebedrijven
SGEI	service of general economic interest
SO	system operator
SoS	security of supply
TCE	transaction cost economics
TEN-E	TransEuropean Energy Networks-Electricity
TFEU	Treaty on the Functioning of the European Union
TO	transmission operator
TPA	third-party access
TSO	transmission system operator
TVO	Teollisuuden Voima (Finnish nuclear reactor owner and operator)
TXU	Texas Utilities energy
TWh	terawatt hour
UIOLI	use it or lose it rule of access
URE	Urzad Regualcji Energetyki (Polish electricity regulator off)
VIU	vertically integrated utility
VOLL	value of loss of load
VPP	virtual power plant

Introduction

Dominique Finon, Jean-Michel Glachant and Adrien de Hauteclocque

This book is the second of the 'Loyola de Palacio' series in the Edward Elgar Publishers collection. It gathers different papers accessible to a range of academic and professional audiences who among others include regulatory staffs, corporate economists and business lawyers. It fills a gap in the existing literature by coping with an original issue in the complex competition developed in electricity markets, the challenge of long-term contracts, and vertical arrangements to competition policy principles while such arrangements could be needed for developing investment and an optimal mix of technologies.

This book is the result of a research project entitled 'Efficiency, Competition and Long-Term Contracts in Electricity Markets' developed between 2007 and 2009 by the Laboratoire d'Analyse économique des Réseaux et des Systems Energétiques (LARSEN), a four-year joint research programme of the French National Centre of Scientific Research (CNRS), Electricité de France research and development (EDF R&D) division and Paris-Sud University dealing with the topic of electricity markets reforms and public policies. The contributions have been presented to the workshop jointly organized on 15–16 January 2009 by the Loyola de Palacio European Energy Policy Program of the European University Institute of Florence and the LARSEN.

The electricity sector is a complex industry given the physical and economical nature of electricity. It has been liberalized in reference to the theoretical model of decentralized competition. However, this has been followed by many unexpected effects which have required several adjustments. Conventional wisdom in electricity restructuring requires limitations of long-term contracts and vertical integration between generators, retailers and large consumers. These limitations should foster market entry and development of effective competition on wholesale and retail levels. Competition authorities seek to weaken the position of dominant firms by restricting long-term contracting and vertical integration by playing down issues of investment in capital-intensive generation equipment and also seeking opportunities to lower prices in the long term. Attachment to these principles was particularly reflected in the position of the European Commission and some regulatory authorities.

However, consensus about this question is changing for different reasons. Long-term contracts and vertical integration can be a convenient way to maintain incentives to invest in all technologies of the generation mix. This converges with the objectives of European and national policies combining supply security and reduction of carbon emissions, given that they may need capital-intensive equipment. Such long-term issues of generation investments have been raised after some shortcomings. Changes are continuously made, pushing the quasi-experimental nature of market making to its limits, which involves coming and going between the definition of rules and industrial structures and the assessment of their effects, while regulators have an obligation to be consistent, reflected in the accumulation of judicial precedents. Beyond these conflicts, regulators are increasingly integrating long-term efficiency criteria in their decisions.

The book is structured in three parts. The first deals with an economic analysis of the possible efficiency of long-term contracts (LTC) and vertical integration in the opposite terms of investment development (long-term efficiency) on one side and imperfect competition (short-term inefficiency) on the other. The second part deals with this tension between long-term contracts and workable competition. The third part deals with antitrust jurisprudence concerning competition and long-term contracts in the electricity sector, with some insights into other network industries.

PART I LONG-TERM CONTRACTS, INVESTMENT AND LONG-TERM EFFICIENCY

In the first part, the chapters deal with the issue of social efficiency of long-term contracts and vertical integration in different ways. From the efficiency perspective, long-term contracts create opportunities for market players to diversify their generation investment between complementary technologies and helps approach the optimal technology mix. The optimal mix requires investment in reserve generation capacity and not focusing solely on gas generation plants as the unique efficient technology. Long-term contracts and partial vertical integration are arrangements which help investment in capital-intensive low-carbon technologies. From the perspective of producers and financial investors, long-term contracts with large wholesale buyers (fixed-price, fixed-quantity contracts or option contracts) can be efficient solutions to support investment in different technologies with high capital intensity. From the perspectives of retailers and large consumers, risks would be more manageable if they could have some long-term contracts to share risks.

Chapter 1 by Jacqueline Boucher and Yves Smeers ('Energy security and long-term arrangements') shows with a simple model that the market is not able to deliver all the types of investments to provide security of supply (SoS). Although competition is in theory able to incentivize investments in gas and electricity sectors in order to improve security of supply, it cannot currently play that role in Europe. The financial instruments necessary to tackle SoS issues in a market environment have to deal with long-term, low-probability, high-consequence risks. Investments that contribute to security of supply require contingent long-term contracts, whether financial or bilateral, that do not exist and are unlikely to exist in the real world. Moreover the tendency of governments to intervene (in case of international disruption) in favour of their national sub-systems further jeopardizes the emergence of a forward market allowing a rational risk management.

Chapter 2 by Fabien A. Roques ('Long-term contracts and technology choices in electricity markets') explores how long-term fixed-price contracts for fuel input or electricity output affect agents' power-generation technology choices in decentralized electricity markets. Investors (the so-called 'entrants') might find it difficult to find counterparties to sign long-term power contracts, and have therefore a greater incentive to choose technologies with the lowest intrinsic market-risk exposure, such as gas plant. A portfolio approach shows that fixed-price long-term power purchase contracts benefit proportionally more to capital-intensive technologies such as renewable, carbon capture and sequestration (CCS) and nuclear plants. Contractual arrangements which shift risks away from investors on to buyers or sellers change the investment risks and returns associated with different generation technologies.

Chapter 3 by Dominique Finon ('Investment and competition in decentralized electricity markets: how to overcome market failure by market imperfections?'), analyses market failures hindering a timely and optimal capacity mix. The main market failure here is with risk management, namely, the impossibility of transferring a major part of risks borne by the producer on to consumers, as opposed to the former utility regime. The chapter develops an empirical analysis of the way to secure investments in generation by vertical arrangements between generators and large purchasers, that is, suppliers (retailers) and electro-intensive consumers. Various types of long-term contracts between generators and suppliers (fixed-quantity, fixed-price contract, indexed price contract, tolling contract, financial option), as well as vertical integration appear to be instruments to allocate risk. But there is never a perfect alignment of parties' interests. The originality of the chapter is to emphasize complementary conditions for establishing long-term contracts related to new capital-intensive investment which help align interests. For generator–supplier contracts, retail competition must be sticky or limited by the legislator in order to transfer a large part of risks to consumers on different market segments. For generator–large consumer contracts, the latter must be involved in ownership and operation of the generation asset. This suggests that the impact of long-term contracts on power-generation technology choices facilitates the deployment of capital-intensive low-carbon technologies frame a new trade-off for regulators, as for competition authorities.

Chapter 4 by Richard Meade and Seini O'Connor ('Comparison of long-term contracts and vertical integration in decentralized electricity markets') proceeds to a complementary analysis of problems arising in contract markets because of transaction costs. The authors identify possible causes of hold-up as well as other contracting problems that can result in inadequate investment, less supply security and increased threat of market power. Specifically, hold-up risks arise not just from the threat of competitive retail entry, but also owing to the competition faced by industrial customers, and other factors such as generator fuel mix and fuel supply security. Additionally, contracting is further complicated by factors such as mismatches between the preferred load profiles of generators and their customers, information asymmetries regarding generator outage rates and fuel security, generator market power and strategic bargaining (in which more informed parties negotiate better contractual terms than less informed counterparties). The resulting shortcomings in electricity contract markets suggest that they are a non-robust toll to deal with market power, retail competition, investment and supply security issues. Instead, the authors argue that vertical contracts are imbalanced, often arising artificially as an imposed element of electricity liberalization reflecting initial reform priorities and concerns. High levels of vertical integration should not be a cause for concern, but may rather represent a more 'natural' structure for the electricity sector.

Chapter 5 by Gert Brunekreeft ('Vertical relations and energy networks: selected issues') focuses on vertical integration between market businesses and transport network in electricity and gas in relation to investment in transport lines. Referring to the European preference for unbundling, it compares the coordination of investments between network users and the network owner, either inside a vertical firm or in an unbundled setting in which the market should provide coordination.

The author criticizes coordination by market signals ('locational pricing') and market-friendly mechanisms ('tendering procedure'), and argues in favour of the necessity of exemption of third party access rules for the development of electricity interconnectors. Long-term capacity contracts are viewed as an institutional condition to develop the network and interconnections. One claim put forward in this chapter is that the transportation contracts, important as they are for network investment, may cause a situation of multiple equilibria. In a case of insufficient liquidity in the market for transport capacity rights, shippers will not sell to the market, but rather they will hoard their rights and thus prevent the development of the market. Conversely, if the market is sufficiently liquid, shippers will want to sell to the market (if this is profitable) precisely because they will be confident that, if needed, they can buy back the rights at market prices.

PART II LONG-TERM CONTRACTS AND IMPERFECT COMPETITION

This part focuses on the impact of long-term contracts on the efficiency of electricity markets, from the theoretical point of view and in reference to practice. Long-term contracts have been seen as foreclosing potential efficient entries on wholesale and retail markets, and the regulators' ability to monitor wholesale prices. Such prices and other key variables such as generation costs are less easily observable. A more liquid market would help for transparency. However industrial organization theory also affords new insights on contracting entries in generation: entries appear easier if entrants could be helped by long-term forward contracts, that makes market more contestable. Moreover, the theoretical approach of competition shows that forward contracts do weaken the incentives of oligopolistic firms to exert market power on short-term markets. In practical terms limiting long-term contracts to limit market power will miss its target.

Chapter 6 by Guy Meunier ('Imperfect competition and long-term contracts in electricity markets: some lessons from theoretical models') gives the state of the art in economic literature. Several streams in industrial organization provide insights to analyse long-term contracts in electricity markets. Most analyses of electricity markets have focused on forward contracts and agree on the positive effect of forward markets on the short-term efficiency of electricity wholesale markets. Such analysis of short-term forward contracts relies on the assumption of no arbitrage, the simplicity of the contract structure and the absence of bargaining between parties. The complexity of long-term contracts observed, and particularly the existence of exclusionary clauses, call for another type of analysis. Exclusive dealings are subject to controversy and are at the source of important literature on the subject. It appears that the precise structure of the market considered, the contractual environment and the bargaining process, influence the possibility of inefficient strategic use by an incumbent of exclusive agreement to prevent efficient entry. Long-term contracts can be detrimental if an adversely affected party is absent at the contracting stage (such as final consumers or entrant) or if the contractual environment is too limited. While inefficient entry deterrence can be the purpose of an exclusive agreement, it is not called for to damage all the contractual environment to prohibit only some practices.

Chapter 7 by Petter Longva ('Long-term contracts in electricity markets: long-term contracting and risk management from the point of view of a large consumer') develops a balanced view on the way competition is altered by long-term contracts. As a former manager of the risk management division of an industrial group, the author argues, first, that to secure investments in new factories, power-intensive industries need to secure long-term power prices at an affordable level, and to enter into long-term contracts for new generation equipment. He sees that the Commission's efforts to weaken the position of dominant generators by restricting long-term contracting has instead hurt the interests of power-intensive industries, while not developing market liquidity. He argues for a multi-step development of the electricity market. In an early phase, the creation of a day-ahead exchange should have top priority. Contracts may indeed contain clauses that have a negative effect on the development of market liquidity, but these clauses are more related to volume flexibility than to contract duration. Most long-term contracts with a fixed volume will improve market liquidity, since they transfer volumes from a flexible player (generator) to a less flexible player (consumer) who has to use the market to balance their portfolio. In a later phase of market development, the lack of trust in market pricing due to real or potential spot-price manipulation should be the main issue. In electricity markets, foreclosure is in most cases a less critical issue and the main 'cure' currently used to combat foreclosure does not serve this purpose. Limiting the duration of long-term contracts does not weaken the dominant players, because price transparency is not improved, and volumes for potential market entrants are available from the spot market anyway.

Chapter 8 by Machiel Mulder ('Competition and long-term contracts in the Dutch electricity market') analyses the significance of long-term contracts at different levels of a quite decentralized market – the Dutch market. How essential are long-term contracts in terms of numbers, and what is the impact on competition? On one level the chapter considers the relationship between players in the wholesale market and the infrastructure owners. On a second level, the role of long-term contracts is analysed in the wholesale markets between generators and buyers (suppliers mainly) in relation to the trading behaviour of electricity producers. It shows that in the Dutch context, long-term contracts are not systematically searched by investors to trigger investment decisions. Finally, the chapter analyses the retail market, discussing the role of long-term contracts between suppliers and consumers. It shows the limited impact of long-term contracts on competition. Although specific parties might conclude bilateral long-term contracts (between a generation company and a large industrial user, for instance), these contracts do not prevent other parties from also buying or selling electricity. In the retail market, long-term contracts might hinder competition if consumers could not easily cancel the contract. In the Dutch retail market, however, regulation has been implemented to protect consumers and to enable consumers to efficiently change contracts if needed. The main message is that for competition policy monitoring, concentration represents a more important threat than vertical arrangements.

PART III COMPETITION POLICY AND LONG-TERM CONTRACTS

The third part investigates how long-term contracts are treated under European Union competition and state aid law. The decision practice appears to evolve in the European Union (EU) because sectoral specificities in electricity and gas industries are increasingly taken into account by regulators. Antitrust authorities moderate their position, in particular concerning long-term contracts between entrants and large consumers.

Chapter 9 by Adrien de Hautecloque and Jean-Michel Glachant ('Long-term contracts and competition policy in European energy markets') starts with the statement that long-term supply contracts often have ambiguous effects on competitive structure, investment and consumer welfare in the long term. In the new market context, these effects are likely to be worsened and thus even harder to assess. Since the release of the Energy Sector Inquiry in early 2007, the portfolio of long-term supply contracts of the former incumbents has become a key target for the European Commission and national competition authorities. It is widely believed that European Competition Authorities take a dogmatic view on these contracts and systemically emphasize the risk of foreclosure over their positive effects on investment and operation. This chapter depicts the methodology that has emerged in the recent line of cases and argues that this interpretation is largely misguided. It shows that a multiple-step approach is used to reduce regulation costs and balance anti-competitive effects with potential efficiency gains. However, if an economic approach is now implemented, competition policy is constrained by the procedural aspect of the legal process and the remedies imposed remain open for discussion.

Chapter 10 by Leigh Hancher ('Long-term contracts and state aid: a new application of the EU state aid regime or a special case?') explains the way jurisprudence has been established on pre-reform long-term power purchase agreement (PPA). The standard 'test' is whether the contracts in question would have prevented efficient alternative suppliers from accessing customers, hence reducing consumer welfare. The application of this test requires complex market-based analysis. The two state aid decisions discussed here investigated how it was most efficient to allocate risk in energy markets and to some extent attempted to analyse how different forms of vertical arrangements could allow for a suitable allocation of risks. However, the decisions did not put forward any real market analysis to support the conclusion that the PPAs were inefficient. Rather, it would appear that the Commission considered that the risk should have been allocated differently, and based its conclusion on the assumption that if it had not been for these contracts, liquid wholesale markets would have developed more rapidly. This type of market structure should have delivered a better outcome.

Chapter 11 by Adrien de Hauteclocque, Frédéric Marty and Julien Pillot ('The essential facilities doctrine in European competition policy: the case of the energy sector') raises the question of the implementation of principles related to the so-called 'Essential Facilities Doctrine' (hereafter EFD) in the European energy sector. Based on a study of US and European jurisprudence, it first shows that these principles are subject to different interpretations and that the European conception is not necessarily a panacea. It then studies the evolution of European competition policy regarding essential facilities and shows that EFD principles are currently implemented with more vigour than ever before. However, the new challenges the European Union faces may lead regulatory and competition authorities to derogate from the existing doctrine. The special case of nuclear capacities in France is then analysed in the context of the EDF/Direct Energie case and a new French electricity law (the so-called NOME) which allocates drawing rights on historic nuclear assets production to competitors of the nuclear enterprise.

The conclusion of the book, a synthesis of the EUI/LARSEN workshop 'Efficiency, Competition and Long-term Contracts in Electricity Markets' (held in Florence on 15–16 January 2009), which is authored by Adrien de Hauteclocque, sums up the main economic and legal findings of this book on vertical arrangements, economic efficiency and competition policy in electricity markets.

PART I

Long-term Contracts, Investment and Long-term Efficiency

1. Energy security and long-term arrangements

Jacqueline Boucher and Yves Smeers

1 INTRODUCTION: SECURITY OF ENERGY SUPPLY IN EU POLICY

Security of supply, the mitigation of climate change and the completion of the internal electricity and gas markets are three major objectives of the European Commission in energy (EU 2006). The Commission has repeatedly invoked competition as the favorite instrument for achieving these goals (for example, EU 2007; Ungerer 2007, 2008). The statement that competition is an adequate instrument for achieving security of supply is puzzling. Notwithstanding its repeated assertions, the Commission never provided any formal support for this position. In contrast with several studies on the European Union emissions trading system (EU-ETS) and the internal energy market, no real economic analysis of security of supply, let alone of how competition can help achieve security of supply, exists today. The European project 'Coordinating Energy Security in Supply Activities' (CESSA) had security of supply on its agenda and was well staffed with economists, but it did not produce any economic analysis of the role of competition for securing energy supplies in Europe. Last but not least, security of supply has a strong flavor of public good that seems to contradict the recourse to competition: in a related area, we observe that questions about strategic oil reserves are not posed in terms of competition but rather as strategic actions with a heavy dose of public intervention. This is also the case for reliability of electricity supply (when interpreted in the sense of limited curtailments of supply but not collapse of the whole grid), which is not normally posed in the sole terms of competition.

This chapter stays away from considerations of public good or externalities and directly addresses the problem of security of supply by starting from the Commission's claim that it is induced by competition. In contrast with many discussions of security of gas supply, we abstract away from geopolitical considerations such as the EU–Russia dialogue but instead view the issue in terms of corporate risk in a competitive world.

We reason that companies are the agents operating in the competition game invoked by the Commission; they do not play the leading role in geopolitics but have to survive its consequences. The issue is then to assess what companies operating in a competitive world would do when facing low-probability, high-consequence risks of disruption of supply, whatever the origin of those risks. We assume that investing in physical capacities that prevent or mitigate disruption is the relevant action, and discard remedies like financial compensation of the consumer for a long curtailment. The question is thus whether economic agents in a competitive market will decide *ex ante* to build the necessary capacities to physically guarantee security of supply to those who demand it. Our argument is developed on a particular but important question of security of supply, namely, investments in a power sector largely driven by gas subject to a threat of disruption. We thus focus on modifications of the generation mix in favour of capacities that do not operate on natural gas. The continental EU market with its few upstream gas suppliers inspired this problem and we make no claim that our reasoning can be applied as such to all other situations of security of supply. Specifically, guaranteeing the power system against gas disruption through competition forces is much easier in a US-like market than in Europe.

We reason by contradiction and conduct a theoretical experiment backed by a quantitative model of a competitive market. Starting from the Commission's claim that competition induces security of supply, we first look at what this requires from the economy; after comparing with existing markets, we conclude that these lack the necessary instruments to achieve the goal. Competition will not induce investments that help avoid a disruption of supply or mitigate its effects because of a market failure. The payoff accruing to investors both in normal times and during a crisis plays the central role in the argument. We analyse this payoff and assess the incentive to invest for security of supply through an argument akin to Joskow's (2007a) now familiar reasoning of missing money. Joskow explains a lack of incentive to invest in peak units to insure reliability by insufficient financing of peak capacities. We similarly reason that the existing competitive markets fail to finance the investment cost of the units necessary for security of supply. The reasoning is developed on a standard capacity expansion model of the type constructed by the power industry for many decades. When properly extended to embed risk trading, this model can be interpreted as representing perfectly competitive economies with a full set of contingent markets.

We conduct the reasoning in four steps that also set the structure of the chapter. We first provide a brief introduction to the model underlying the analysis in section 2. This model deals with risk. In order to facilitate the discussion we separate risks in two groups. Security of supply (SoS) risks such as major interruptions of deliveries (here a significant reduction of gas volume available to the power system) come on top of 'business as usual' (BaU) risks such as those affecting demand growth or mild variations of fuel or carbon dioxide (CO_2) prices. Companies need to deal with both risks but the distinction between BaU and SoS risks facilitates the exposition: SoS risks are low-probability, high-consequence risks, quite different from more frequent but less catastrophic BaU risks.

Section 3 takes up the question of security of supply assuming perfectly competitive European electricity and downstream gas markets. This is the ideal environment in terms of competition: agents are price takers and there is no missing market or 'missing money'. We also assume that there is no bottleneck in the transmission of gas and electricity. We then argue that such perfect markets effectively incentivize investments that enhance security of supply. This complies with the claim of the Commission.

Perfect markets rarely exist in the real world and the question is whether existing imperfections can invalidate the above reasoning. This question is treated in section 4. In order to illustrate that competition does not always properly incentivize investments, we first briefly recall the phenomenon of the missing money and the reduced incentive to invest even in the absence of risk. We then develop an analogous reasoning that applies to investments in presence of risky supplies. We argue that the market does not trade SoS risks, which are thus not taken into account by competition: investments that contribute to security of supply in a competitive world require contingent long-term contracts, whether financial or bilateral, that do not exist and are unlikely to exist in the real world. Neither a directive nor the application of competition law can remedy this market failure because it is rooted in missing markets, not in abuses in existing markets. Insufficient contracting for risk-trading therefore makes the difference between the ideal competitive market that insures security of supply and the real one that does not. The conclusion is that competition cannot handle security of supply.

Notwithstanding the lack of *ex ante* investments, competition can play a useful role *ex post*, after the disruption has occurred. This was observed in the USA after the Katrina hurricane (Makholm 2007). This happens when competition operates the market during the crisis in order to best allocate residual resources and hence reduce damages. The tradition of member states to 'only agree to disagree' in times of stress does not suggest that this will effectively take place in the EU. Experience also reveals that member states tend to resort to national administrative solutions in situations of stress. This may result in a low cap on prices aimed at protecting the consumer. Alternatively, competition authorities may begin interpreting economically justified high prices during scarcity as embedding excessive margins compared to accounting costs. Whether originating from regulators or competition authorities, experience has created a credible threat that investors may be deprived of the revenues accruing from capacities in security of supply. Investors will rationally anticipate these possible outcomes and further reduce their incentive to build capacities for improving security of supply. We thus conclude that the lack of an *ex ante* credible commitment to letting competition operate *ex post* during a crisis is an additional deterrent to investments. This argument is made in section 5.

Summing up, our conclusion is twofold: first, the competition forces capable of *ex ante* incentivizing investments to mitigate or eliminate disruptions do not exist in real markets; second, the political willingness to let competition mitigate the impact of a disruption *ex post* will also be absent and hence deprive would-be investors from their revenue. In short, security of supply is one of these areas subject to market failure where some regulatory action is in order. This is recalled in the conclusion of the chapter.

2 THE UNDERLYING MODEL

We conduct our analysis using a capacity expansion model that we interpret as representing a perfectly competitive market in a risky environment (Ehrenmann and Smeers 2008, 2010). The following sketches the main ideas of the approach.

2.1 Scenarios and Capacity Expansion Models

Scenario analysis is the standard methodology for assessing the impact of risk, whether business as usual or security of supply. The approach is well understood and needs no reminder. Markets models are commonly used in scenario analysis to explore the evolution of endogenous variables such as capacity developments in response to exogenous evolutions of parameters such as fuel prices or demand growth. We follow suit, and reason on the basis of a capacity expansion model of a type extensively used in the power sector for many decades. These models compute the least cost development of the generation system in a given scenario over a certain period. Constructed in the early 1960s for the closed area system, they were reinterpreted after the first energy crisis in terms of risk-free, perfectly competitive markets. These models avoid market failures of the missing money type by assuming either a reserve constraint that can be interpreted as a forward capacity market or a value of lost load that represents an energy only market (Ehrenmann and Smeers 2008). Investments coming out of these models satisfy the following property that directly ties in with standard corporate practice: a new investment has a zero net present value in the sense that the sum of its discounted margins is exactly equal to its investment cost. Like a risk-free competitive market, the model selects all efficient investments; it therefore simulates investments in a perfectly competitive but risk-free market.

Scenario analysis commonly proceeds by applying a deterministic model on different scenarios. This is not sufficient for analysing security of supply in a competitive market: a standard capacity expansion model operated on a single scenario simulates a perfectly competitive market in a risk-free world but a standard capacity expansion model operated over a set of different scenarios does not simulate a competitive risky market. Something else is needed in order to describe investors confronting risk. This is what we are turning to now.

2.2 Scenarios and Event Tree

Finance and insurance markets that by nature deal with risk do not model it through scenarios; they use '(stochastic) processes' that recognize that information on risk factors progressively unfolds with time. We adopt this '(stochastic) process' view that we take in the simple form of an event tree. The distinction between scenarios and event trees is illustrated on Figure 1.1 which considers a 20-year time horizon broken into five-year periods, with a major disruption possibly occurring in each of these periods. Assuming that a disruption of supply has a low probability, the lower part of Figure 1.1 considers six scenarios; five of them represent disruption scenarios for which the date of the disruption is exactly known and represented by the vertical segment of the line (year 0, 5, 10, 15, 20). The last scenario of the lower part of Figure 1.1 supposes that we know today that there will be no disruption in the future.

In contrast, the tree depicted in the upper part of Figure 1.1 does not require that we know today whether there will be a disruption, and if so when it will arrive. The disruption may happen in any of the different five-year periods or it may not happen. A proper treatment of security of supply requires that decisions to invest account for this uncertainty and hedge against it by adapting the generation mix. This is what a perfectly competitive economy would do in the presence of a risk of disruption: it would provide the incentive to adapt the generation mix in order to hedge against a set of possible disruptions, none of which is known with certainty. It would do so by trading risks through contingent markets, that is, markets of instruments that provide rewards contingent on the occurrence of some event (here a disruption).

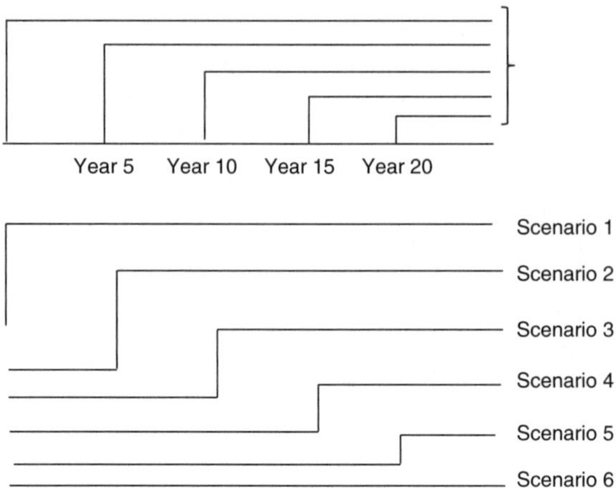

Figure 1.1 Scenario tree versus scenario analysis

2.3 Event Tree, Capacity Expansion Models and Contingent Markets

It is technically possible to adapt the standard capacity expansion model developed for a scenario analysis to one operating on a tree of scenarios. The tree reflects the unfolding of information that investors need to adapt to. This extension of the model from the scenario to the tree is referred to as a 'stochastic program' (for example, Birge and Louveaux 1997). In contrast with the standard scenario approach that considers one scenario at a time and does not explicitly rely on its probability of occurrence, a tree approach ascertains the likelihood of different futures. Special attention must thus be given to the interpretation of these probabilities and their possible relation with contingent markets if one wants to interpret the model in terms of perfectly competitive markets. Appendix 1A.1 offers two possible views of the stochastic program in terms of contingent markets and appropriate discount rates; Ehrenmann and Smeers (2008, 2010) provide technical discussions of these questions. Whatever the interpretation, the conclusion is that the model identifies all profitable investments in the following standard business interpretation: a new investment has a zero expected net present value in the sense that the expectation of the sum of its discounted margins is exactly equal to its investment cost. This implies that, like a competitive market with sufficient risk-trading, the model selects all efficient investments. The model therefore simulates investments in a perfectly competitive but risky market. This general property applies to investments aimed at security of supply if the relevant risks are properly traded. But a converse result also holds: the market will under-invest in security of supply if it does not trade the relevant risks.

2.4 Conclusion and Model Information

We simulate a perfectly competitive market through a stochastic version of a standard capacity expansion model. The calculations presented in the chapter concentrate on the Central West European market (Germany, France, Belgium, the Netherlands, Austria and Switzerland) for which individual plants of the existing generation system are represented by their capacities and technical characteristics. The model is of the linear programming type (the deterministic equivalent of a multistage stochastic program, for example, Birge and Louveaux 1997) and covers the period from 2008 to 2035. To reduce computation we use three representative years for each stage in the stochastic tree. Also, we aggregate those hours with similar residual load into 72-hour blocks per year. Assumptions regarding investment costs and discount rates are common to all scenarios. We use €1800/kW for coal units, €900/kW for combined cycle gas turbines (CCGTs) and €600/kW for gas turbines (GTs). Operational costs like fixed costs and logistic costs are also common to all scenarios. The same applies to technical characteristics like efficiencies, maintenance rates or network capacities between neighboring regions. We simplify the context and assume that new endogenous capacities can only be in gas or (capture ready) coal. The next section completes this description with additional details on the representation of risk.

3 PERFECT COMPETITION WITH COMPLETE CAPACITY AND RISK-TRADING INCENTIVIZES INVESTMENTS THAT HELP SECURITY OF SUPPLY

3.1 The Model and the Risky Environment

The stochastic capacity expansion model is constructed on the basis of the tree depicted in Figure 1.2. It embeds uncertainty on fuel prices, demand evolution, renewable development, nuclear policy and CO_2 regulation. The model classically assumes fixed demand (price insensitive) and considers both BaU and SoS risks.

The tree is structured as follows: uncertainties appear from the first branching on; data are given in Table 1.1 with prices (for example, oil and CO_2) for 2003 in euros. The assumptions depict the situation of mid-2007:

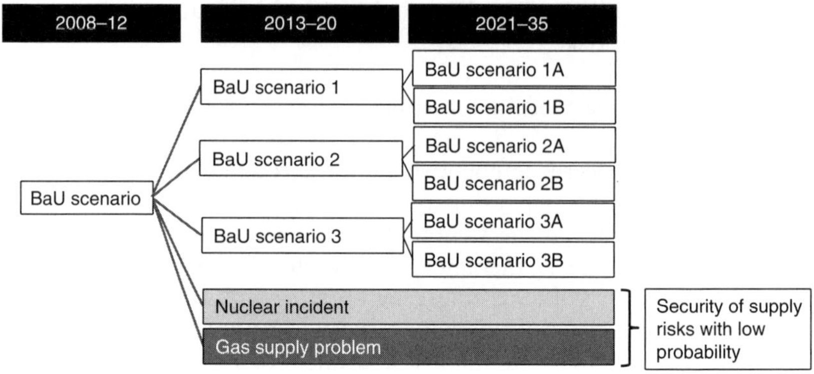

Figure 1.2 Event tree with SoS risks

Table 1.1 Hypothesis of the three scenarios

	Oil price (€/bl)	Demand	RES in 2018	Nuclear	CO_2 in 2020 (€/ton)
Scen. 1	110	.8% p.a.	343 TWh	Extension +	50
Scen. 2	75	.8% p.a.	343 TWh	Extension	35
Scen. 3	50	.5% p.a.	434 TWh	Decommissioning	25

neither fuel prices nor overall demand evolutions reflect the current economic crisis. This is of no consequence for a theoretical experiment such as the one discussed in this chapter.

The second branching of the tree only deals with the development of renewable energy by either adding an additional 100 terawatt hours (TWh) of renewable energy sources (RES) by 2030 or doubling this addition to 200 TWh. Renewable energy sources include production from wind, hydro and photovoltaic. Nuclear extension refers to the German debate on the phase out and the possible lifetime extension. The two additional branches, 'Nuclear incident' and 'Gas supply problem', are identical to the second scenario plus the branch-specific incident. In particular, the gas available to the power sector is reduced by 25 per cent, with its opportunity cost being determined endogenously by the model as a result of that reduced availability. This chapter refers only to the impact of gas supply. In order to be on the safe side in terms of incentive to invest for security of supply we assume a long disruption of three years, that is, the time length of a block in the model.

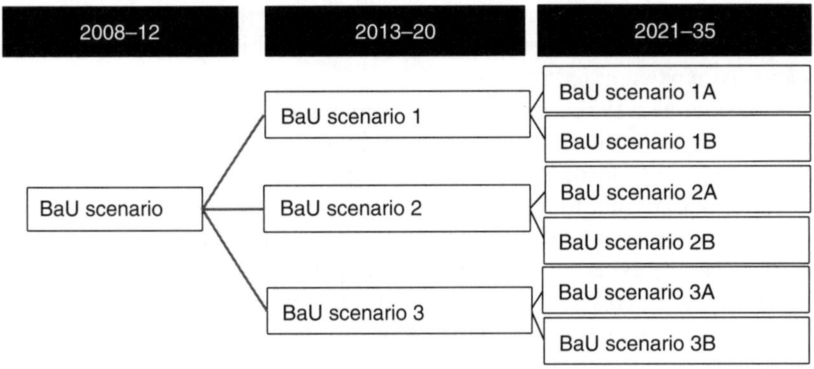

Figure 1.3 *Event tree with only business as usual scenarios*

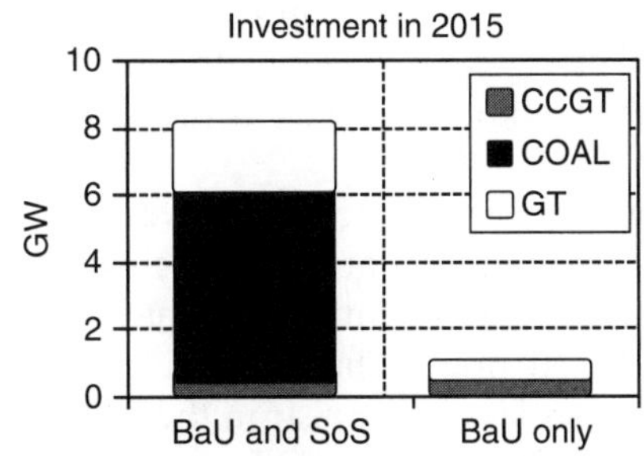

Figure 1.4 *Investments in the stochastic program with and without SoS events*

Because we are interested in identifying investments that an ideal perfectly competitive market would generate to cope with security of supply, we construct two versions of the model that differ by the underlying event tree. One embeds both BaU and SoS risks (Figure 1.2); the other represents the sole BaU risks (Figure 1.3). The comparison of the results allows one to identify investments or changes of investments justified by security of supply.

3.2 Numerical Results

A sample of results is given in Figure 1.4 summarizing the investments in year 2015. Consider first the case of the sole BaU risks, that is, without gas disruption risk. The model finds investments that balance BaU risks and investment costs in expectation, that is by assuming that BaU risks can be traded on the market. We find little investment and, not surprisingly, gas plants largely dominate these investments together with some (capture ready) coal capacities (but not in year 2015). This constitutes the BaU capacity expansion pattern.

Consider next the case where a scenario of gas disruption is added to the event tree. Computing investments again, one observes a move towards more coal units in order to hedge the gas disruption risk. The striking feature is that investments in coal capacities are quite significant and add to the total capacity of the system. This modified capacity expansion pattern can be expected in a perfectly competitive market that trades both BaU and SoS risks as we now explain. Disruption reduces the available gas and hence increases its opportunity cost. Gas plants become marginal and set the electricity price at a very high value. This in turn creates huge margins for coal plants in the disruption scenarios. Specifically, the price of base load electricity goes from €80 to €210 per megawatt hour (MWh) during the disruption with the price in peak load going to several thousands of €/MWh. The expected value of this margin justifies additional coal compared with the BaU case. This is the security of supply adapted capacity expansion pattern.

These results are easily interpreted: one invests in (capture ready) coal units as one would buy an insurance that delivers a certain amount of electricity during disruption or an option that allows one to purchase electricity at coal based price. The analysis of the results reported in Figure 1.4 shows capacities that appear in the BaU and SoS experiments but are not present in the BaU case. Their investment cost represents the insurance premium or the price of the option. The margins made by these plants in the different scenarios are the payoffs of these insurance or option products. Perfect competition models implicitly assume that the market is effectively going to pay these investments costs in order to capture these payoffs. The key question is whether this is realistic in practice; whether real markets offer these types of financial or insurance products.

In conclusion, some of the new capacities found by the model contribute to security of supply. Because the model can be interpreted as representing a perfect competition market one can claim, together with the Commission, that competitive forces induce investments in security of supply. This is not a formal proof about what could effectively be achieved in practice as there is always a distance between a model and the real world. But it can certainly support the claim that normal business conduct in a competitive market leads to investments in security of supply. The hard question is whether the assumption of perfect competition, specifically the implicit assumption of a complete set of contingent markets present in the model, is not too strong. The next section addresses this issue.

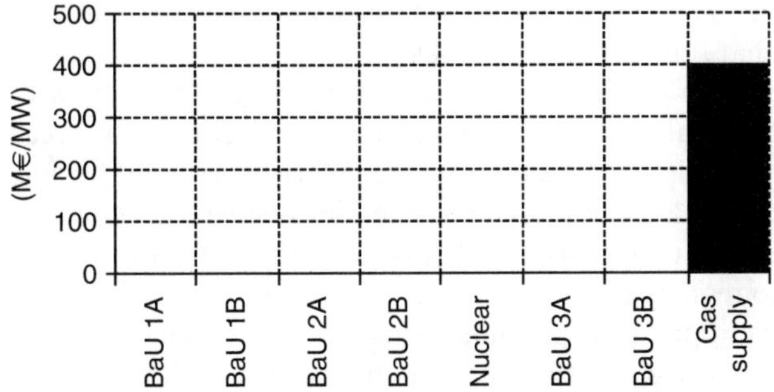

Figure 1.5 *Distribution of the present value of the gross margin of a coal plant over the eight scenarios considered in the tree of Figure 1.2 (before paying for fixed costs – horizon: 30 years)*

4 INSUFFICIENT RISK-TRADING IN REAL COMPETITIVE GAS AND ELECTRICITY MARKETS HAMPERS INVESTMENTS FOR SECURITY OF SUPPLY

While a stochastic capacity expansion model can effectively be interpreted as representing a perfect competition market capable of investing in security of supply, the implicit assumption of a complete set of contingent markets is a strong requirement that deserves further analysis.

4.1 The Risk Profile of Investments in Security of Supply and Risk-trading

Consider the risk profile of those capacities invested for reasons of security of supply. All plants, whether coal or CCGT, found in the SoS adapted capacity expansion pattern have zero expected net present value when assessed with respect to all scenarios. But coal and CCGT plants show quite different risk exposures. Specifically, the coal capacities built for accommodating SoS risks have very risky cash flows (Figure 1.5). These plants lose money (after paying for fixed costs) in all BaU scenarios because a significant part of their capacity is redundant in those scenarios. Conversely, they make a huge profit in the scenario of disruption of gas supply. Investing in those plants is thus truly speculative: these units almost certainly lose money even if there is a small chance that they make huge profits. In contrast, the gas units make small profits most of the time but do not cover their investment and fixed operating costs during disruption. These results are obtained assuming perfectly competitive markets that fully trade those risks.

The question is whether real electricity and gas markets will effectively trade the speculative cash flows of the SoS justified coal plants. Recall first that existing markets do not trade all risks, even all business as usual risks. As a trivial example, the market does not trade demand or production risks from temperature or hydro conditions. Weather derivatives that attempt to remedy the problem are still new and rather illiquid (Chincarini 2009). It is in principle possible to hedge some volume risk by a portfolio of options on electricity price but this is technically complex and even impossible in today's market because of the lack of these options. Closer to our investment concerns Finon and Perez (2008) and Finon and Roques (2008) explain that markets in the merchant restructured electricity industry do not trade risks associated with capital-intensive technologies, such as nuclear, or alternatively only trade them at prohibitive cost. This claim is in line with the fact that US policy foresees that federal support is needed to mitigate the economic risks associated to nuclear units (NEI 2008). Again, more directly related to our problem, Stern (2006) suggests that the competitive gas market in the UK does not sufficiently incentivize investments in gas storage, which creates problems of security of supply. The question is thus whether insufficient risk trading because of incomplete contingent markets is not a factor that the Commission may have overlooked in its claim that competition can handle security of supply: a competitive market under-invests in security of supply if it does not trade security of supply risks. The following reviews some characteristics of current competitive electricity systems with the purpose of identifying whether they can trade security of supply risks.

4.2 On Market Failure in Investment

4.2.1 Reasoning by analogy: from missing money in a risk-free world

The merchant system and the Power Exchange (PX) constitute the reference organization of competition advocated by the Commission for restructured electricity markets. A relevant question is whether a competitive PX can induce investments in the redundant coal plants that our theoretical experiment tells us properly handle security of supply. We begin by recalling some well-known results from the risk-free environment.

The now standard argument of 'missing money' explains that competitive markets organized as PXs do not incentivize investments in peak units even in a risk-free world (for example, Joskow 2007a). We briefly recall the essence of the reasoning before transposing it to investments for security of supply. A peak unit in a competitive PX bids for its fuel and CO_2 cost and, if retained in the auction, receives as remuneration a price of electricity equal to its fuel and CO_2 cost: its gross margin is thus zero. If unsuccessful in the auction, its revenue is also zero. Whatever the outcome, the peak plant receives no revenue for paying for capacity and fixed costs. The market therefore fails to remunerate these plant capacity costs and hence to induce investments in these units. The missing money is thus a missing market argument: the market that should collect the revenue for the capacity does not exist and needs to be supplemented by some regulatory intervention. Can one find a similar phenomenon in security of supply? Is it possible that some of the markets that should pay for the capacity of the plants meant to intervene in case of disruption do not exist?

4.2.2 To a missing market argument in a risky world

The capacity expansion model assumes away the usual missing money argument, that is, the lack of incentive to invest in peak units in a risk-free world. By implementing a reserve constraint or a value of lost load, the model remedies the missing money by either a forward capacity market or an energy-only market. We shall dwell on another facet of the reasoning: the missing money is a particular example of missing market applied to the functioning of the PX. This logic can also be applied to a different but related problem, namely the availability of a market for handling the risky cash flows accruing from the PX to the redundant coal plants. This is what we now explore.

Consider a redundant coal plant appearing in the BaU–SoS tree. This capacity remains idle or is operated at the margin in all BaU scenarios. Applying the above reasoning we find that the fraction of the coal capacity that is operating in BaU scenarios bids fuel and CO_2 cost and is paid fuel and CO_2 costs, leaving a zero gross margin. The other fraction of the coal capacity that is not generating incurs no cost but receives no revenue: the margin is thus also zero. This confirms the numerical results of preceding section: the PX gives no revenue to redundant plants built for reason of security of supply when there is no disruption. The situation is quite different during disruption; the coal units are then infra marginal in the PX because gas is scarce. Applying again the reasoning developed for the PX, these plants make huge profits because gas is expensive. This again confirms the numerical results. To sum up, the redundant plant does not collect any revenue as long as it is truly redundant; it only collects (huge) revenue when it is effectively called into service as an infra-marginal plant during the disruption. In expectation, what it collects suffices to compensate the investment cost and hence would justify the investment. Is this all there is?

A first step: uncertain revenues in the PX The above reasoning explains that security of supply creates both huge volume and price risks. This is akin to a situation already analysed by Stoft (2002) for gas turbines under BaU circumstances. Consider such a unit. It operates at the top of the load diagram and thus serves a very uncertain demand that depends on climatic risks such as exceptional cold, hot or dry years. Peak plants operate after all other plants have been called upon in the merit order; their running hours therefore also depend on the total capacity of the system and the economic conditions that drive the demand for electricity. These are unknown in the long run. Assuming that the missing money is remedied (for example, by a forward capacity market or an energy only market) investors in peak units still face a volume risk that depends on both demand and future total capacity. They may have to wait several years before their plant is called and generates any revenue. Stoft (2002) argues that economic agents are reluctant to invest in these plants, or they will under-invest so that the probability of being called is higher.

This reasoning immediately extends, with much more drastic consequences, to the redundant coal unit invested for reasons of security of supply. First, the investment cost of a coal unit is much higher than that of a peak unit. Second, the revenue of the redundant coal unit is also much more uncertain than that of the peak unit. The theoretical experiment suggests and the numerical results confirm that the redundant capacity is never used except during a disruption of supply. The revenue is thus null for several years and may indeed remain so if there is no interruption of supply. In contrast, the plant makes huge profits during the disruption. The risk exposure of the redundant coal plants is thus much worse than that of the peak units.

Extending Stoft's reasoning on peak units, economic agents will underinvest in these plants because their revenues are much too uncertain.

A second step: financing uncertain revenues Finon and Perez (2008) add a new element to the risk problem. They note that competitive electricity markets have developed the (possibly erroneous) view that plants should be assessed on the basis of their individual merits (including risk) in a competitive environment. This is the 'project finance' approach. Taking stock of that approach, they apply the argument of a risky cash flow to the financing of high-capital cost equipment such as nuclear units. Finon and Perez observe that nuclear plants cannot be project financed through non-recourse debt in merchant markets. Transpose now this reasoning to the redundant coal plant. Can one project finance a coal plant that stands idle except if Russia decides not to renew some of its contracts with Western Europe or turmoil in West Africa hinders new liquid natural gas (LNG) capacity? At least, one can claim for sure that this redundant coal plant is much riskier than a nuclear unit in base load.

4.3 Identifying the Market Failure: Insufficient Risk-trading

4.3.1 The diagnosis: missing risk markets

A natural question is why the above questions do not affect the perfect competition model that effectively invests in redundant capacities for guaranteeing security of supply. The reason is simple in principle but possibly technical in terms of exposition: the model, as well as the perfectly competitive market that it represents, implicitly assumes a complete set of financial instruments and hence full-risk trading. Risk-trading transforms the huge, but low probability, revenues accruing to coal plants during gas disruption into stable revenues that induce investment to capture them. The reality is that real markets underestimate SoS risks because they do not trade them and hence do not price SoS risks. This in turn reduces or hampers investments in redundant capacities that would alleviate them. This observation may go against the common wisdom that gives the impression that everything is possible in risk-trading provided one constructs the adequate structured products. The observation of current markets suggests that, notwithstanding the numerous 'innovations' that have led into the current crisis, markets never went as far as creating products for trading disruptions of supply: these instruments do not exist on the market and are unlikely to exist in the future.

4.3.2 Current forward and options markets do not help

We have already noted that the market does not trade volume risk. It is known that one can replicate volume risk, at least to some extent, by a portfolio of options on electricity prices. One should thus be able in principle to hedge the combination of price and volume risks through the sole price hedging. This would even be a daunting task for BaU risks. First, hedging volume risk through a portfolio of options is technically difficult because it requires information on the dependence between volume and price that goes much beyond what we know today, if not in the very short term, certainly in the long run. Second, the necessary options do not exist on the market or are at best very illiquid. Last but not least, these financial products are traded on very short maturities of maximum three years, which is totally unsuitable for hedging a plant. Transposing this difficulty from BaU to SoS risks that are much less understood, the daunting task becomes impossible. The conclusion is that the financial instruments assumed in the perfect competition model, and hence in a perfect competition market, do not exist in reality. Hedging the revenues of the redundant plant on the market goes beyond what markets offer today and will offer in the future.

4.3.3 Debt, CDOs and the non-performance of redundant capacities

Finon and Perez's (2008) non-recourse debt argument suggests another view of the problem. In order to simplify, consider financing a plant by a collateralized debt obligation (CDO) (default on CDOs in the US subprime housing market initiated the crisis!). The CDO decomposes the global revenue of the plant into tranches occurring with different probabilities. The senior tranches occur with a very high probability and are safe. They warrant a small risk premium and hence are discounted with a low rate. The junior tranches occur with a low probability and are risky; they warrant a high discount rate. Revenues of redundant plants in normal times consist of fixed costs and are thus negative; they occur with a very high probability, imply a small risk premium and hence are discounted lightly. The high revenue that only occurs during disruption has a very small probability, entails a large risk premium and hence is discounted heavily. Any reasonable marked to market valuation of the revenue of such a plant conducted with observed or extrapolated risk premiums will be negative. This interpretation suggests that our theoretical model overestimates the risk neutral probability of the disruption, or that a perfectly competitive market would not have invested in the redundant coal plants.

4.3.4 Is there a deep reason?

Current electricity markets barely trade some BaU risks in the long run. They are unlikely to trade SoS risks that are of a low-probability, high-consequence type. There may be a deep underlying reason for this. The emergence of catastrophes for instance due to climate change has emphasized the special role of low-probability, high-consequence risks and the special problems that they raise (for example, Kousky and Cooke 2009; or more generally consult the section 'Regulating risks' on 'Resources for the Future' website: http://www.ref.org/Pages/default.aspx). Catastrophic events raise new questions of fat tails, dependences between fat tails, correlations between small risks, risk perception and behavior in face of these risks. Long and deep disruptions of supply belong to that type of risk. We do not understand them well and hence understand neither their trading nor how they intervene in competitive markets. This is irrelevant in the ideal model of pure competition (the Arrow–Debreu economy) that underlies our stochastic capacity expansion model; but it matters in real markets. As a consequence, we should not simply assume that techniques that apply to high-probability, low-consequence risks carry through to high-consequence, low-probability risks.

4.4 Are There Alternatives?

4.4.1 Remedies to missing money will be ineffective

Remedies to missing money induce investments: they are now well understood in theory and experience from the market is growing. One may wonder whether they cannot be transposed or adapted here to improve the incentive to invest. Consider two of the most discussed methods that induce investments in peak units, namely, capacity markets and energy only markets (see Oren Consulting 2007 for an extensive discussion of these different methods and their implementations). Could they also incentivize investments in security of supply? First note that these methods require some regulation and hence cannot be considered as resulting from pure competition. In fact and possibly to the surprise of some, the reality is that we do not know at this stage how to induce investments in generation on the sole basis of competition whether in a risk-free or risky world. This sheds some gloomy light on the statement of the Commission that competition can handle security of supply. If we need some regulation to induce investments in a risk-free market driven by PX, how can the sole competition induce investments for security of supply? In other words, if we have difficulties dealing with BaU risks, we shall certainly have additional problems with SoS risks. We take up these points.

A first remedy for PX to induce investment is for the regulator or the transmission system operator (TSO) to introduce a forward capacity market. An auction is organized whereby the TSO or the regulator tenders a certain capacity target in the future. One ranks the submitted bids by increasing price until the target is met. The last retained offer sets the price that remunerates all installed capacities. It is obvious that this system induces investment in low-capacity cost plants, that is, gas turbines. It will not select the coal units that are much more costly in capital and necessary to overcome a disruption of supply. Therefore, the remuneration of capacity accruing from the standard capacity market will not cover coal capacity cost and hence will not induce investment in coal plants that are otherwise making a zero gross margin as we just saw. The conclusion is that the standard capacity market does not induce investments in security of supply. One can obviously plan for a special capacity market for non-gas units. This is then akin to organizations like strategic oil or gas reserves where one tries to constitute a reserve in a certain type of fuel. This is a new regulation and not the result of competition. Capacity markets are thus no competitive solution for investments in security of supply.

The energy-only market is the standard alternative to the capacity market: it allows for a very high electricity price in case of curtailment. It is the prospect of this high price that induces investments. This method requires the blanket assumption that regulators or competition authorities will not declare that the very high price prevailing during curtailment is abusive. This is far from granted in European markets. The method also requires that curtailments happen sufficiently regularly so that the investor can count on these high prices in its investment assessment. High electricity prices that occur too infrequently do not justify investments in coal units. We have tested this possibility with the model assuming an electricity price of €500/MWh during disruption; this price prevails during the whole three years of the disruption, something to which regulators and/or competition authorities would certainly object (we did not even consider allowing a €3000/MWh – the foreseen bound in European PXs – to prevail during the three years of the disruption). As expected, there was no investment in the coal units because the price is too low. In other words, the energy only markets, which offer the most competition-like solution for investments in normal conditions do not induce investments that protect against disruption.

4.4.2 Long-term bilateral or multilateral contracts unlikely to develop

One might think that long-term contracts involving generators and large consumers offer another possibility for financing redundant plants. The Finnish Teollisuuden Voima (TVO) consortium and the Exeltium arrangements are examples of bilateral contracts for the supply of electricity and provide a useful benchmark. Electricity-intensive consumers explained that they no longer wanted to be subject to the vagaries of gas prices and wished to be supplied at a fixed or properly indexed price. The TVO and Exeltium arrangements are for base load energy supplied by a fully used capacity. They resemble negotiated physical forward contracts guaranteeing a certain volume at a certain price. It thus conceptually makes sense to complete this market by contracts that resemble negotiated physical options. This is what contracts for redundant plants are: options that give access to the energy delivered by a coal plant when the price of electricity is higher than the price generated by the coal unit. Unfortunately this analogy is all that finance can offer. For reasons examined above, these contracts, even if they are of the forward or option type, will not be traded because they involve risks that the market does not trade. They will thus be negotiated bilaterally and finance cannot help determining their price.

Bilateral contracts, whether for supplies (forward) or for security of supply (options) would make quite a lot of economic sense. They correspond to securing property rights on supplies tailored to the needs of the consumer and to deliveries during contingent conditions: only those who have concluded those contracts would have access to that energy during disruption. Finon and Perez (2008) analyse bilateral long-term contracts for energy supply. They recognize the benefits accruing from these contracts but acknowledge a lot of difficulties because of diverging interests between generators and consumers. A similar analysis should be done for contracts whereby generators would secure the construction of some redundant capacity. The analysis is much more perilous though: besides the arguments pointed out in Finon and Perez (2008) for supply contracts, security of supply introduces significant adverse selection and moral hazard issues that add to the standard credit risk inherent to all long-term contracts. As the much simpler capacity markets have shown, operators in a competitive market need to be carefully incentivized by penalties on default to effectively maintain a capacity for reserve. This can be implemented for short-term reserves in a market controlled by an independent system operator (ISO); it is difficult to imagine how to transpose penalties on default for long-term capacity built against disruption. In short, even though one cannot dismiss bilateral contracts as a way to invest in security of supply, there is no evidence that this can effectively be implemented. One can only submit that these bilateral contracts for security of supply are probably much more difficult to come by than the bilateral contracts for base load energy.

In conclusion, the first step of our theoretical experiment complied with the position of the Commission. It assumed a possible gas disruption and hedged it by investing in redundant coal units. These remain idle most of the time but intervene during the gas disruption. They then make huge profits that, through the financial market, pay for the investment. Competition had effectively accomplished its task of securing investment for security of supply. The second step of the experiment argues that matters may not be that simple. Competition may require sophisticated markets to trade the risk implied by security of supply. The purpose of security of supply is to build not just to satisfy normal demand, but also to develop redundant capacity that can operate in case of disruption. In contrast with gas turbines that are built for reserve purpose in ordinary times, the plants that insure against a gas disruption cannot run on gas. They are capital-intensive coal-based units in the theoretical experiment. Generators are used to build coal plants that they expect will function most of the time but investors would certainly object to coal plants built for reserve. Companies are unlikely to ask lenders or shareholders for money to build a costly infrastructure that stands idle until a disruption occurs. An optimistic assumption is that the market provides the instruments for trading these risks (by spreading them among the public) and hence the revenue for building those plants. The reality is that it does not. This is a market failure. It results from the unusual risks caused by security of supply. The possibility of bilateral contracts remains. European authorities view them with suspicion but, even if they could commit to accept them, we know very little of this solution when it goes beyond supply contracts.

Does the above close the conversation? There is more. Suppose all these difficulties are remedied. Suppose we implement capacity or energy-only markets; assume also that the financial industry has created new instruments to trade the low probability, high risks implied by security of supply. Would everything be solved? The next section argues that the problem would remain, this time not because competition fails in the long run owing to missing markets, but because governments will prevent the market from working in the short run when the disruption occurs.

5 PAYOFF MAY NOT BE AS EXPECTED DURING A DISRUPTION

We have explained that the high revenue accruing to owners of redundant capacities during disruption finances the construction of the plants. We have argued that this requires a well-developed financial or insurance market. We here assume that these markets exist. Assuming no bottleneck of transmission infrastructure, as we did, competition can properly handle security of supply. A remaining and intriguing question is whether the large revenues expected during disruption will effectively materialize and go to those that invested in the redundant plants. We first note that the high revenues are a logical necessity. A plant is only built in a competitive system if the expected net present value of its payoffs is non-negative. Because the payoff of the redundant plant is negative in normal situation and the probability of the disruption is small, the payoff during disruption must be high. We also note that this high payoff is a normal consequence of the operation of a competitive PX during the disruption. Gas prices are high during the disruption because the fuel is scarce. Gas plants therefore move up in the merit order and set the price at a high value most of the time. Coal plants are infra-marginal and make the huge gross margins that investors expected when they built the plant. Still, even if all this seems quite logical *ex ante*, that is, before the disruption, the question remains whether this is really what is going to happen *ex post*, during the disruption. We argue here that this is not guaranteed: investors are far from being sure to collect these high gross margins that are the conditions for the market to help in security of supply.

Joskow (2007b) explains that governments in continental Europe are unlikely to let the gas market operate spontaneously during disruption and will intervene in favor of their own national system. They could do so by allocating gas or disrupting its transport, implying that the commodity would be diverted from where it is most valuable to where governments judge it is most appropriate. The *ex post* gas market could thus not operate competitively but be administrated. There are alternatives where competition has operated. The US gas market continued working competitively after Hurricane Katrina (Makholm 2007): it saw some very high gas prices but this is the logic of the competitive market for allocating the scarce resource to its most valuable use. Will the European market behave differently? We obviously do not know for sure and can note that the recent proposal of the Commission (EU 2009) wants to push a competition solution as far as possible. But what are the guarantees that the legal process will not weaken the language of the proposed regulation to a level where member states retain a lot of discretion to implement uncoordinated administrative measures? If so, a disrupted gas market could end up in a totally unpredictable state just because governments have taken over from competition and have done so in an uncoordinated and unpredictable way.

There is no equivalent to EU (2009) for the power sector but one can also expect that governments would intervene in the case of disruption. Whatever the reallocation of gas after the mix of market and political intervention during the disruption, gas prices can only be high, implying high electricity prices. This will attract attention to the gross margins made by the coal units. Will governments let it happen? The answer is probably no. The population will suffer from both high gas and high electricity prices during disruption. Public authorities will then cap the price at what they see as an appropriate level. Current and recent discussions on 'nuclear rent' and 'windfall profit' because of CO_2 illustrate the opportunistic reasoning deployed by governments when they wish to depart from the marginal cost pricing that should be the rule in the competitive market. As with nuclear rents or CO_2 costs, it is indeed quite easy to justify some average cost remuneration based on a normal depreciation (it is legally impossible to depreciate the plant in the sole year of the disruption) and the fuel (in this case coal) cost. Some governments will also emphasize the huge profits made by those plants during the disruption (the trick is to report increases of annual profits in percentage), without mentioning that these are only gross margins occurring in exceptional circumstances. Whether capping prices is fair or unfair when the population is in the cold and the dark is obviously an essential matter. But it may simply mean that fairness during a disruption invalidates using competition to induce investments in security of supply. The result is that here too the market will settle at a totally unpredictable state because competition will have been prevented from doing what it does best.

Investors rationally expect this likely intervention of governments in the market. They also anticipate that this can lead to a totally unpredictable regime, where they are unsure of ever receiving the revenue that competition promised in case of disruption. They will therefore not invest in high-risk plants, even if the market has developed the technically adequate financial instrument to do so.

6 CONCLUSION

Competition operates through markets that exist, not through those that could exist but do not. Economic theory tells us about market failure in general and missing markets in particular. Some of the benefits of competition are lost in the case of market failure and in particular when relying on markets that do not exist. Relying on competition to deal with security of supply amounts to relying on many missing markets. Security of supply, indeed, requires investing in redundant capital-intensive plants, in other words in costly assets that have no economic justification but security of supply.

The huge economic damage that occurs during deep disruption obviously fully justifies investing in redundant plants. Also, a perfectly competitive market endowed with a complete set of contingent contracts will guarantee these investments. But this does not imply that real-world markets, as we know them today or can imagine their development in the future, will do the job. The reason of this shortcoming is that the payoff of the equipment that helps security of supply is quite speculative, very poorly understood and so far non-quantifiable. The trading of the risks that they imply requires markets that may not be easy to imagine let alone to implement in today's conditions. The complexity of the high-consequence and low-probability events that affect security of supply raise the question of whether these markets will even develop on the sole basis of competition.

Last but certainly not least, current events teach us to be prudent with markets of risk that we believe we understand well, let alone with those that we have not experimented with yet.

But suppose, for the sake of the reasoning, that these necessary risk-trading markets develop according to the principles that we understand today. Casual observation of European governance teaches that national governments may opportunistically intervene during disruption at the time of settlement of these contracts. This would distort the functioning of the market and modify the payoff accruing to these capacities whose main justification is to insure or contribute to security of supply. This creates moral hazard phenomena that will further detract economic agents from entering these contracts. Recent events whether in the Russia–Ukraine gas dispute or in the financial crisis have shown that the Commission sometimes withdraws from any significant intervention in case of turmoil and hence will be of no help in restoring the competitive market that should guarantee the revenues of capacities aimed at improving security of supply. In conclusion, because the creation of appropriate markets for trading the risks entailed by security of supply seems a long way off today, competition is unlikely to effectively improve security of supply.

Because competition law can only improve competition in existing markets but is unable to create markets that do not exist, its intervention in the gas and electricity markets is also unlikely to improve security of supply.

REFERENCES

Birge, J. and F. Louveaux (1997), *Introduction to Stochastic Programming,* Berlin: Springer Verlag.

Chincarini, L.B. (2009), 'No chills or burns from temperature surprises: an empirical analysis of the weather derivatives markets', available at SSRN: http://ssrn.com/abstract=1340761 (accessed 3 February 2009).

Ehrenmann, A. and Y. Smeers (2008), 'Energy only, capacity market and security of supply: a stochastic equilibrium analysis investment risk allocation in restructured electricity markets', accepted for publication in *Operations Research.*

Ehrenmann, A. and Y. Smeers (2010), 'Stochastic equilibrium models for generation capacity expansion', accepted for publication in *Springer Handbook on Stochastic Optimization Methods in Finance and Energy.*

European Union (EU) (2006), *Green Paper on a European Strategy for Sustainable, Competitive and Secure Energy*, COM (2006) 105 final .

European Union (EU) (2007), Communication to the European Council and the European Parliament of 10 January 2007, 'An energy policy for Europe', [Com (2007) 1 final – not published in the *Official Journal*].

European Union (EU) (2009), *Proposal for a Regulation of the European Parliament and of the Council Concerning Measures to Safeguard Security of Gas Supply and Repealing Directive 2004/67/EC*, COM (2009) 363 final.

Finon, D. and Y. Perez (2008), 'Investment risk allocation in restructured electricity markets', Working Paper 17, Gis Larsen, Paris, April.

Finon, D. and F. Roques (2008), 'Contractual and financing arrangement for new nuclear build', *Competition and Regulation in Networks Industry*, **9** (3), 247–81.

Joskow, P. (2007a), 'Competitive electricity markets and investments in new generation capacity', in D. Helm (ed.), *The New Energy Paradigm*; Oxford: Oxford University Press. pp. 76–121.

Joskow, P. (2007b), 'Supply security in competitive electricity and gas markets', in C. Robinson (ed.), *Utility Regulation in Competitive Markets,* Cheltenham, UK and Northampton MA, USA: Edward Elgar Publishing, pp. 82–116.

Kousky, C. and R.M. Cooke (2009), 'Climate change and risk management:

challenges for insurance, adaptation, and loss estimation', RFF DP 09-0RV, Washington, DC: Resources for The Future.
Makholm, J.D. (2007), 'Seeking competition and supply security in natural gas: the US experience and European challenge', paper presented at the CESSA Conference 31 May–1 June, Berlin.
Nuclear Energy Institute (NEI) (2008), *Status and Outlook for Nuclear Energy In the United States*, Washington, DC: Nuclear Energy Institute.
Oren Consulting (2007), 'Program on technology innovation: alternative approaches to generating adequacy assurance', Working Paper 2007.1013774, Palo Alto, CA: EPRI.
Stern, J. (2006), 'The new security environment for European gas: worsening geopolitics and increasing global competition for LNG', working paper, Oxford: Oxford Institute for Energy Studies.
Stoft, S. (2002), *Power System Economics*, New York: IEEE Press and John Wiley.
Ungerer, H. (2007), 'Competition policy and energy security: some comments', paper presented at the Cessa Conference, Berlin, 31 May–1 June.
Ungerer, H. (2008), 'Which approach to competition in electricity and gas – are we tackling the right issues?', Paper presented at the European Competition Day, Ljubljana, 22 May.

APPENDIX: INTERPRETATION OF THE EVEN TREE IN TERMS OF MARKETS FOR RISK

The two following interpretations are common in finance.

1A.1 A First Interpretation: Agents Share a Common View of the Future and Have an Identical Cost of Capital

A first and easy economic interpretation of the stochastic programming capacity expansion model is to suppose that investors share a common view of future risk factors and of their likelihood. They also have a common cost of capital. One can show that this implies that the investments coming out of the model have zero expected payoffs, where expectations are computed using the assumed probabilities and discounting is done at the common discount rate. In other words, the expectation of the margins made by a particular plant in the different scenarios of the tree covers its investment cost. The cost of capital used in the model embeds the risk premium of investors. All this boils down to the standard capital asset pricing model (CAPM) investment criterion most commonly used in business. The simulation of the power system using the stochastic capacity expansion model is thus a valid counterfactual of a perfectly competitive market. Note that, as mentioned before, this is not the case of the scenario approach, which mixes deterministic (the scenario) and stochastic (the discount rate with a risk premium) views of the problem and is thus internally inconsistent for dealing with risk.

1A.2 A Second Interpretation: A Complete Set of Instruments for Trading Risks

Every model (and for that matter any policy statement) is based on more or less realistic assumptions. In this case, the assumption of a set of investors sharing a common view of the future and incurring a common cost of capital, even if underlying the standard and extensively used CAPM model, raises questions of realism. An alternative assumption is to admit that risk-averse investors have different views of the future but can trade risk through financial instruments on competitive markets. This involves contingent contracts, that is, contracts whose payoffs depend on the state of the world. These contracts are as old as trade itself, but their extraordinary (and, as we know today, excessive) development mainly took place during the past 20 years. There should be a sufficient number and variety of these instruments to trade risk in order for competition to work fully. Referring to the power sector, investments in generation units are financed by traded instruments (stocks, bonds, securitized debt) that embed different degrees of risk. Derivatives written on these products complete the possibilities for trading risk in the real world. Both instruments are thus part of the capacity expansion process.

A stochastic capacity expansion model embeds an implicit representation of extensive risk trading. It suffices to reinterpret the probabilities of the scenarios of the tree as 'risk neutral probabilities', or 'stochastic discount factors', that is, adapted to account for the price of risk that emerges from the trading of these securities. This statement may be somewhat technical but suffice to say here that it is a well-known result of the financial literature. Because risk-trading is now in the probabilities, the discount rate is risk-free. A stochastic capacity expansion model therefore also represents a competitive electricity market endowed with a complete set of financial products that allows agents to trade all the risks that they are exposed to. In this interpretation, investors build a plant if the expected margin accruing to this plant, computed with these risk neutral probabilities and discounted at the risk-free rate, is equal to its investment cost; in other words, if the expected net present value of the plant is zero. We fall back on the same investment criterion as before, albeit expressed in a slightly different form: the risk premium appears in the risk neutral probabilities and not in the discount rate.

2. Long-term contracts and technology choices in electricity markets[1]

Fabien A. Roques

1 INTRODUCTION

The liberalization of the power and gas industries exposes investors to greater risks than under the pre-liberalization regulatory regime. The most fundamental change affecting the value of investments is the uncertainty about electricity prices, and its interaction with fossil fuel price risk – and carbon dioxide (CO_2) emission permits in Europe. Such market risks affect technologies differently, and their impact on new investment choices will depend on the ability of investors to manage or shift part of these risks on to other stakeholders. This in turn depends on the contractual arrangements underpinning investment projects and the degree of integration downstream of the investor. The objective of this chapter is to explore how contractual arrangements for fuel inputs and power output affect technology choices in liberalized electricity markets.

A power plant investor's exposure to electricity and fuel price risk depends on the sensitivity of plant profits to electricity and fossil fuel price risks and the variability of the fuel and power prices. This chapter focuses on how the allocation of electricity and fuel price risks between the power plant investor and other parties through long-term contracts and the ability of the investor to mitigate the risk to which it is exposed affect technology choices. Gas, coal and nuclear fuel prices all have volatile spot prices, but are often secured through long-term contracts. Power generation technologies such as gas plant have a greater exposure to market risks (electricity price, fuel price, CO_2 price), while others are more capital intensive (nuclear and renewables). To what extent can these risks be shifted away from the investor through long-term fuel and power contracts, and how can such contractual arrangements affect the investment risks and returns associated with the different technologies?

The first section of the chapter reviews the financial and contractual tools available to investors in power markets to hedge power plant fuel and power price risks. The section concludes that utilities are likely to have to bear much of the cost of risk in their investment decisions, unless they can find counter-parties with complementary risk attitudes. This represents a greater issue for new entrants which are not vertically integrated or cannot leverage a diversified portfolio of generation plants to diversify their risk exposure.

The second section explores how the fossil fuel and electricity output contractual arrangements affect the risks and returns of different power generation technologies, and their attractiveness to investors. Building on a series of research publications (Roques 2006, 2008; Roques et al. 2006, 2008), we use Monte Carlo simulations of a discounted cash flow model of investment in combined cycle gas turbine (CCGT), coal and nuclear power plant to compare the impact of fuel and electricity price risks, as well as the value of contractual hedges, on these different technologies.

In the absence of long-term fixed-price power purchase contracts, we find somewhat counter-intuitively that CCGT plant is the least risky investment option as its cash flow is 'self-hedged' given the high correlation between electricity and gas prices observed in most markets. This makes CCGT particularly attractive to new entrants and more generally to investors which are not vertically integrated or do not have long-term fuel procurement contracts, as CCGT plant have the lowest intrinsic market price risk exposure. In contrast, utilities with vertical integration and/or long-term contracts – for example, fuel sourcing and power purchase agreements – are in a better position to mitigate the risks associated with investment in capital-intensive technologies such as nuclear or renewables.

The final section of the chapter discusses the policy implications of these findings. Long-term contracts and/or vertical integration have an important role to play to facilitate the deployment of capital-intensive, low-carbon technologies. The large-scale deployment of capital-intensive 'green technologies' (nuclear, renewables) necessary to meet the ambitious European environmental targets will likely best be delivered by large utilities integrated vertically and/or with a diversified generation portfolio.

The impact of the contractual arrangements and industrial organization on power generation technology choices has received little attention to date but will likely be an additional dimension to consider for regulators and competition and antitrust authorities. We recommend that competition authorities integrate the impact of contractual arrangements on technology choices and power generation investment incentives in their list of criteria when investigating mergers and acquisitions in the European power markets.

2 MANAGING ELECTRICITY AND FUEL PRICE RISKS IN LIBERALIZED MARKETS

The liberalization of the electricity industry has transformed the allocation of investment risk among the different stakeholders, as investors now bear most of the investment risks. Electricity and fuel price risks – and in Europe carbon emission permit price risk – have become key drivers of generation technology choices. The availability of financial risk management instruments and contractual hedges to mitigate and transfer some of these risks to other stakeholders therefore plays an important role in influencing investors' technology choices.[2]

2.1 Financial Risk Hedging Instruments in the Electricity Industry

Power plant investors could theoretically hedge fuel or power price risks directly by buying futures in gas (or more directly in electricity). These would pay off in high gas/electricity states of the world and compensate for the high electricity prices. However, only an extremely small number of commodities are competitively supplied and both storable and homogenous enough to support liquid futures markets. Oil products and gas satisfy these conditions in some jurisdictions (notably the USA) where there are futures markets, but gas is not sufficiently competitively traded in most of Europe to offer reliable hedges or sustain liquid futures markets. Electricity (whose value can vary each hour and across space) is not sufficiently homogenous for really low-cost liquid futures markets to take off, although some products (base and peak seasonal and annual) are traded in some markets (though with relatively low turnover/physical traded volume).

Another hedge against fuel and power price risks would be for investors to hold shares in a specialized nuclear or renewables power generating company that would earn higher profits when selling at higher electricity prices. For instance, from the time when British Energy was relisted on 17 January 2005 and the end of 2005, British Energy shares have exhibited a 91 per cent correlation to the one-year forward electricity price in the UK (see Figure 2.1). But few companies are sufficiently specialized to offer pure hedges, perhaps because their value as such is attenuated by the information costs facing individual investors. For many purposes, these information and transaction costs give an advantage to portfolio companies (or mutual funds for small investors), and as such remove the hedging options needed to reflect investors' demand for diversity.

All of this suggests that power generation investors are likely to have to bear much of the cost of risk in their investment decisions, unless they

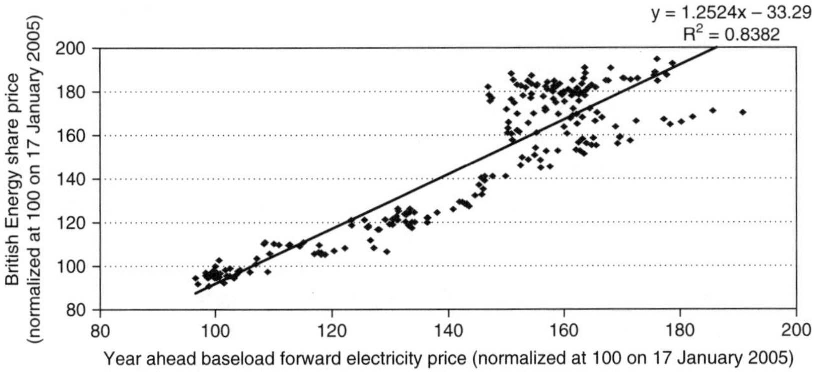

Figure 2.1 Correlation between British Energy share price and baseload forward annual power price in 2005

can find counter-parties with complementary risk attitudes willing to sign contracts and to take on some of the fuel and electricity price risks.

2.1.1 Contracts to allocate electricity and fuel price risks

Electricity producers sell their production through a combination of long-term contracts and spot market sales in various proportions depending on the production technology and the electricity company strategy. Electricity can be bought and sold (1) on the spot market, (2) through contracts that are indexed to the price of the fuel input, (3) through tolling agreements (whereby the power purchaser delivers fuel to the generator and takes delivery of the resulting power that is produced, having effectively 'rented' the use of the generation plant), or (4) through fixed-price contracts (Bolinger et al. 2006).

Power purchase agreements play a central role in allocating risks among parties in the electricity industry. The extent of risk that the plant investor, the plant operator (if different from the plant owner) and electricity suppliers bear depends in large part on how risks are allocated in these contracts (Wiser et al. 2004):

- Fixed-price electricity contracts establish a fixed and known price per MWh of delivered electricity. Such contracts allocate fuel price risk to the generator because the generator is responsible for selling electricity at fixed prices, while simultaneously dealing with an inherently variable fuel price stream.
- Indexed-price contracts generally index the price of electricity to either inflation or to the cost of another commodity, for example,

the cost of the fuel used to generate the electricity. When electricity contracts are indexed to the price of the natural gas used to generate the electricity, the fuel price risk is allocated to the buyer.

- Tolling contracts provide the buyer the right to use the seller's power plant to convert natural gas to electricity. The seller is paid not only for the use of its facility, but also for simply being available to generate. The buyer pays for the natural gas used to generate the electricity and bears the risk of fuel price variability.

2.1.2 Electricity and fuel price risks affect generation technologies differently

A power plant investor exposure to fuel price risk depends essentially on four factors: (1) the sensitivity of generation costs to fossil fuel price risk, (2) the variability of the fuel's price, (3) the allocation of fuel price risk between the power plant investor and other parties through long-term contracts, and (4) the ability of the investor to mitigate the risk to which it is exposed.

While gas costs can contribute up to 70–80 per cent of a CCGT production costs, coal costs represent between 25 and 35 per cent of the plant generating costs, and nuclear fuel costs have a small impact (less than 10 per cent) on a nuclear plant generating costs. The IEA (2006) estimates that a 50 per cent increase in uranium, gas and coal prices would increase nuclear generating costs by about 3 per cent, coal generating costs by 21 per cent and CCGT generating costs by 38 per cent.

There is little empirical data publicly available on the terms and conditions of power purchase agreements, and in particular the way in which fossil fuel price risk is allocated. Natural gas-fired generation is commonly sold through all four of the contract types described above, with gas price risk falling on the power purchaser in the first three, and the generator in the final type (Wiser et al. 2004).

Bolinger et al. (2006) point out that renewable generation, on the other hand, is typically sold through long-term, fixed-price contracts (perhaps indexed to inflation). Wiser et al. (2004) analyse a contract sample of 27 long-term (three years and longer) electricity procurement contracts signed by the California Department of Water Resources (DWR) in 2001 on behalf of the customers of California's three investor-owned utilities. They find that 41 per cent of the electricity is supplied in 'tolling' agreements, most of which give the DWR some flexibility to dispatch the facility. Fifty-nine per cent of the electricity is supplied at fixed prices; these contracts are mostly non-dispatchable. Johnston et al. (2007) discuss the theoretical benefits of take-or-pay contracts to facilitate the deployment of renewables.

Finon and Roques (2008) review the different types of contractual arrangements that underpin new nuclear build in France, Finland, the UK and the USA. A plant owner-operator might be willing to pay higher prices for nuclear megawatts if methods for mitigating price, cost and capacity risk through contracts or real assets could be found. For example, Rothwell (2006) estimates that for a new nuclear plant in Texas the owner-operator might be willing to offer long-term contracts at a risk premium of \$0.86/MWh for fixed-price, but interruptible, power.

2.2 Interruptible Contracts and Operational Flexibility Yield Significant Value

Operational flexibility is valuable in liberalized power markets. The degree of flexibility that a plant operator will have depends on factors intrinsic to the technology, as well as on the terms and conditions of the fuel supply contract. Designing contracts with flexibility, that is, with specific provision or options that allow one or both parties to respond appropriately as conditions change can save renegotiation time and be more economically efficient for both parties to allocate risks (Borison and Hamm 2005).

Gas-fired power stations' operational patterns can be expected to respond to market price signals, decreasing gas consumption when the cost of generating from other fuels is lower than the price of burning gas. But commercial interruption also depends on a number of other factors, including operational constraints and any environmental constraints (for example, SO_2) that limit the extent of running on other fossil fuels. There is a large body of literature focusing on optimal dispatch for a portfolio of plants (see, for example, Connors et al. 2004; Kahn and Stoft 1993). On a longer timescale, power generators can 'mothball' a plant temporarily if the power and fuel price projections make it uneconomic to use, and 'de-mothball' it later on if it is profitable.

Arbitrage between gas and electricity markets is of particular relevance to gas-fired power plants which are operated via tolling agreements or have flexible gas procurement contracts: operators can decide not to produce electricity and sell back the gas on the spot market if gas prices are too high relative to electricity prices to make it uneconomic to produce.[3] Many gas-fired power plants have contracted natural gas supplied on interruptible contracts. Neuhoff and von Hirschhausen (2005) analyse the changing patterns of long-term gas procurement contracts associated with the gas sector liberalization, including the evolution of the 'flexibility clause' which used to be an integral part of long-term contracts in Europe, and the 'destination clause' which remains an obstacle for competition in the European gas markets.[4]

3 THE VALUE OF LONG-TERM CONTRACTS

In order to understand in greater depth how different types of market risks and degree of contractual cover affect generation technology choices, we introduce a stylized model of investment in power generation assets under uncertainty. The model is a probabilistic discounted cash flow model of investment in CCGT, coal and nuclear plants with fossil fuel and electricity price risks and operating flexibility. We use Monte Carlo simulation to analyse the three technologies investment risk and return depending on the contracting arrangements shifting some of the fuel and electricity price risks away from the plant investor. The objective is to explore how contractual arrangements affect the competitiveness and the risk return profile of different generation technologies. We model successively the case of a new entrant without vertical integration and of a portfolio generator, and investigate in both cases the impact of long-term power contracts on optimal investment choices.

3.1 A Model to Assess the Impact of Contractual Hedges on Power Plant Valuation[5]

We concentrate on three technologies (scrubbed coal, CCGT and 'generation three' nuclear) that are likely to be the main baseload alternatives on the post-2010 time horizon. The appendix summarizes the model 'base case' cost and revenue assumptions, based on (IEA/NEA 2005) and (IEA 2006). The model is calibrated based on 2007 market conditions, but eh findings are general enough to be robust to a range or modelling inputs. For a discount rate of 10 per cent, the coal plant has a higher net present value (NPV) (€342/kW) than the nuclear and CCGT plant (respectively €74/kW and €−48/kW). With an 8 per cent discount rate, all technologies have positive NPVs, the nuclear plant NPV increasing relatively more than other technologies as nuclear is the most capital-intensive technology.

We investigate in this chapter the combined impact of both electricity and fuel price risks on the different generation technologies. Readers interested in a more thorough analysis of these risks separately are referred to Roques (2008) and Roques et al. (2008). The characterization of fuel and electricity price risks is simple as the focus is here on price risk in the medium to long term (monthly to yearly).[6] The model concentrates on lifelong discounted cash flows, and monthly fossil fuel, electricity and CO_2 emission permit price risks are modelled by random variables with a normal probability distribution whose parameters are described in the appendix. The most likely values correspond to the base case, while the standard deviation estimate is based on empirical data on five years of

UK national balancing point (NBP) term ahead forward gas prices, coal Antwerp/Rotterdam/Amsterdam coal price index (ARA) term ahead forward prices, and term ahead UK baseload future electricity prices. Each case study presents the NPV probability distribution of the three technology alternatives resulting from 100 000 simulations in the 10 per cent discount rate case with and without operating flexibility.

Two different hypotheses on the nature of the fixed-price long-term contracts will be considered. By default, it will be assumed that the long-term contracts are binding, that is, that electricity power purchase agreements require the plant to be run ('must run contracts' for electricity, or gas contracts with a 'non-resell' clause) even if it is uneconomic to do so. In the variant, it will be assumed that the contracts have some kind of flexibility clauses such that the plant owner (or operator) has the option of not running the plant if it is more economical to resell the fuel on the spot market. This latter case will be referred to as the case with *operating flexibility*.

3.1.1 The case of a new entrant: electricity and fuel price sold and bought on spot markets

In this case study, both fuels used to run the plants and the electricity produced are bought and sold from spot markets. The plant owner (or operator) therefore bears both fossil fuel and electricity price risks. The combined impact of electricity and fuel price risks on the profitability of the three different technologies depends on the degree of correlation between these prices. The impact of different degrees of correlation between electricity and gas prices is studied in detail in Roques (2008). In this chapter, an arbitrary degree of correlation of 50 per cent is assumed, as in IEA (2007).

Figure 2.2 shows that taking into account plant operating flexibility modifies the risks and expected return of the different technologies as it caps the potential downside losses of gas and, to a lesser extend, coal plant. When the CCGT operating flexibility is taken into account in the valuation, CCGT plant becomes both the most profitable and less risky investment choice. The operating flexibility not only increases the CCGT expected NPV relative to the coal and nuclear plant expected NPVs, but it also reduces the riskiness of CCGT plant by capping the likelihood of largely negative NPVs to a lower level than for nuclear or coal plant (Figure 2.2).

The combination of electricity and fuel price risks magnifies the value of operating and contract flexibility for CCGT plant, as it makes arbitrage between electricity and gas markets very profitable. While operating and contract flexibility are of relatively little value for coal and nuclear plants – from 5 to 20 per cent of total project value depending on the correlation between fuel and electricity prices – it can represent a significant part of the

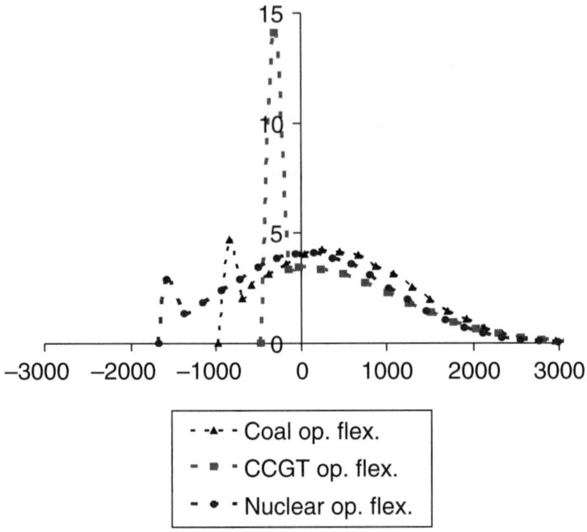

Figure 2.2 NPV distributions with operating flexibility, fuel and electricity price risks (€/kW, in 10^{-4} for 100 000 simulations)

net present value of a CCGT project. As discussed in Roques (2008), gas plant operating and contract flexibility value is very sensitive to the degree of correlation between electricity and gas prices in a particular market.

More generally, our stylized modelling results highlight the intrinsic risk mitigation advantage of technologies setting the marginal price in electricity markets (Figure 2.3). Because fuel and output price risks are strongly correlated for marginal generation technologies such as gas-fired power plants, their cash flows are paradoxically less volatile than capital-intensive technologies such as renewables or nuclear, whose cash flows vary based on the electricity price.

Gas plants play an important role in the degree of correlation between gas and power prices. Open cycle gas plants and gas boiler plants often set the marginal clearing price on power markets in peak periods, while combined cycle gas plants also play a growing role in a number of European markets to set the marginal power price during baseload periods. Arbitrage opportunities between power and gas prices, as well as the carbon price are also part of the complex dynamic between electricity and gas prices (see, for instance, Newbery 2005).

The dominance of CCGT for new entrants' investments over the past two decades can therefore be traced back to the high degrees of correlation observed in many liberalized markets between electricity and

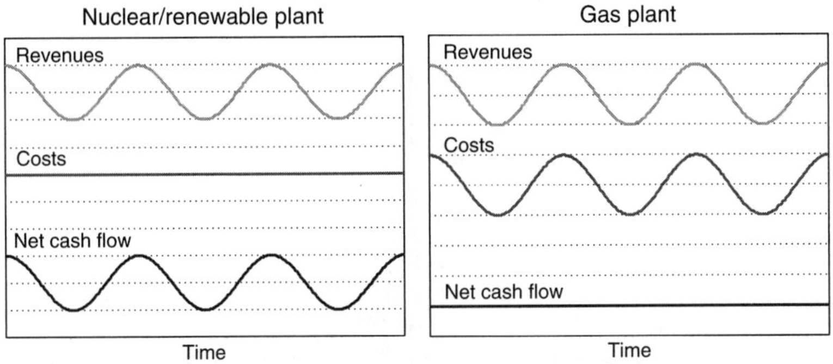

Figure 2.3 Marginal cost-setting technology faces reduced market risks in liberalized markets

gas prices, which make this technology 'self-hedged' to some extent. Gas plants benefit from a relatively more stable operating margin than coal or nuclear plants in most liberalized markets, which makes them a low-risk option for investors which cannot count on a significant retail exposure to mitigate these risks. In other words, an investor in a gas plant is likely to be proportionally less reliant on contractual hedges for fuel and power prices for the same level of risk exposure as investors in other technologies.

3.1.2 The case of a new entrant with a long-term power off take contract

In this second case study, fuels are purchased on spot markets, and the plant owner bears all of the fuel price risk. The plant electricity output is sold at a fixed price through a long-term contract, thereby shifting the electricity price risk away from the plant investor and on to electricity suppliers or consumers.

Figure 2.4 shows that the spread of the three technologies NPV distributions is very different from the previous case study (Figure 2.4), reflecting the larger sensitivity of the CCGT NPV – and, to a lesser extent, coal plant NPV – to gas and coal prices (standard deviation of respectively €1211/kW and €556/kW). The impact of operating flexibility is of relatively small magnitude and mostly valuable for gas plant. The narrow distribution of the nuclear plant NPV (standard deviation of €84/kW) illustrates the relatively small impact of nuclear fuel cost on the overall profitability of a nuclear plant investment.

Long-term power prices make nuclear power the least risky technology and change the competitiveness of the different technologies. While coal and gas plant still appears as the technologies with the highest expected

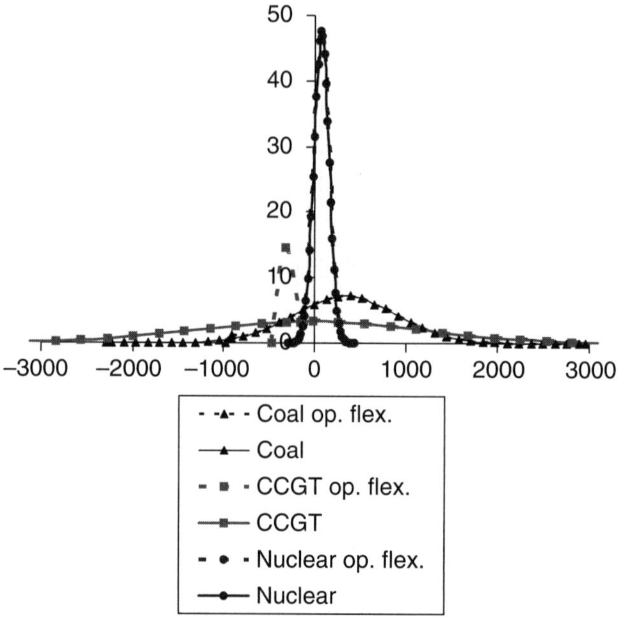

Figure 2.4 *NPV distributions with fixed electricity prices and fuel price risk (€/kW, in 10^{-4} for 100 000 simulations)*

NPV, investors might also be interested in nuclear which present the lowest downside risk.

When power prices can be locked in through a long-term contract, the main source or market risk for capital intensive technologies such as renewables or nuclear plant disappears. Long-term power purchase agreements reduce disproportionally the exposure of renewables and nuclear plant, compared with other fossil fuel technologies such as gas and coal plants which are also sensitive to fuel price risk. This is consistent with the experience, where most renewables and nuclear plants built in liberalized markets in the past decade entail long-term power off take contracts.

3.1.3 The case of a utility with a portfolio of assets[7]

The focus of this chapter so far has been on a single plant investment, a stylized representation of new entrants' in liberalized power markets, which are not significantly vertically integrated, and do not operate a large and diversified portfolio of generation technologies. We now turn to large generation companies with a diversified portfolio of technologies. These portfolio utilities have an advantage compared to new entrants to manage electricity and fuel price risks.

Portfolio utilities can leverage a diversified portfolio of generation assets to manage some of the technology specific risks and can therefore be expected to have a different attitude towards technology choices. A diversified portfolio of generation technologies is a strategy for large utilities to hedge some risks, such that intrinsic technology risk is not as important as the complementarities of a new generation risk and return profile with the existing set of assets of the utility.

In order to assess the value of contractual hedges for portfolio utilities, a different valuation framework is required which takes into account the complementarities of the risks and return profiles of different generation technologies. A recent series of papers explores the use of mean-variance portfolio (hereafter MVP) theory to optimize utilities generation portfolios, based on Markowitz's (1952) seminal work for financial securities portfolios. Bazilian and Roques (2008) present an overview of this growing literature.

Roques et al. (2008) model technology choices for a portfolio utility in the UK, with and without long-term contracts. They first run Monte Carlo simulations of a discounted cash flow model to estimate the mean and variances of the distribution of the NPV of each technology. The second step takes these and their associated correlations to determine the efficient risk-return frontier.

The returns to different generation technologies are measured by the expected net present value (ENPV) per unit of capacity (£ million/GW or £/kW) of an investment in any technology, and the risk by the standard deviation of the NPV probability distribution per unit of capacity. Similarly, the correlation between the returns of different technologies is defined as the correlation between the NPV distributions of the different technologies.

Mean-variance portfolio theory does not prescribe a single optimal portfolio combination, but a range of efficient choices, represented by the *risk-return efficient frontier* in the graph of portfolio return against portfolio standard deviation – SD). Investors will choose a risk-return combination based on their own preferences and risk aversion.

Figure 2.5 shows the risk and return of different plant portfolios based on the empirically observed average correlations between electricity, fuel, and CO_2 prices in the British market from 2001 to 2005. The right-hand triangle of lines delineates the set of possible portfolios in the case without long-term power off take contracts – its boundary made of pairs of technologies and the interior of all three. The left-hand triangle of lines delineates the set of possible portfolios in the case with long-term power off take contracts.

The set of optimal generation portfolios is very different with and without long-term power contracts. In the case without long-term power

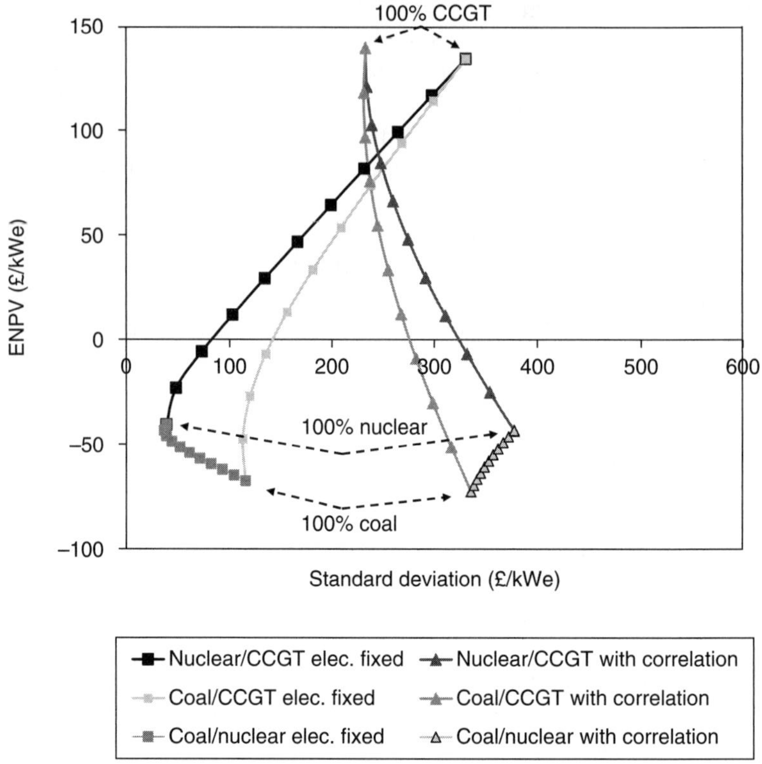

Figure 2.5 Efficient frontier for portfolios of nuclear, coal and CCGT plants with fixed and market-based electricity prices (10 per cent discount rate)

contracts, the optimal portfolio for an investor is to invest only in CCGTs, as any other portfolio would both reduce returns and increase risk. This is due to the impact of the strong empirical correlation between electricity, fuel and CO_2 prices observed in the UK market. In contrast, when the electricity price is fixed by a long-term power purchase agreement, efficient portfolios lie on the efficient frontier represented by the line with square markers, consisting of combinations of CCGT and nuclear plants in various proportions, depending on the investor's risk aversion. The more risk averse the investor, the more nuclear (or coal) plants in the optimal portfolio.

These findings are consistent with the previous case study considering a single plant investment (case of a new entrant), as long-term contracts make nuclear plant a more attractive investment option as part of a utility generation portfolio. In other words, long-term power contracts create incentives for portfolio utilities to rebalance their generation portfolios toward capital intensive technologies such as renewables and nuclear.

4 CONCLUSION AND POLICY IMPLICATIONS

Power purchase agreements, fuel procurement contracts and operating flexibility play a central role in allocating risks among parties in the electricity industry. The allocation of these risks, in turn, influences investment decisions, and thereby has a significant impact on what types of power plants are built and the overall portfolio of electricity supply.

Some power generation technologies such as gas plant have a greater exposure to market risks (electricity price, fuel price, CO_2 price), while others are more capital intensive (nuclear and renewables). The first section of the chapter discussed the financial and contractual tools available to investors in power markets to power plant investors to shift part of market risks on to plant operators, suppliers or consumers. It concluded that the lack of well-developed financial hedging instruments implies that utilities are likely to have to bear much of the cost of risk in their investment decisions, unless they can find counter-parties with complementary risk attitudes. While finding counter-parties with complementary risk attitudes might be difficult for investors in current liberalized electricity markets, recent experience with new nuclear build in Finland, or in France with the industrial consortium 'Exceltium' suggests that such long-term arrangements might interest some specific industrial consumers.

The second section explored how the fossil fuel and electricity output contractual arrangements affect the risks and returns of different power generation technologies, and their attractiveness to investors. We contrast the findings of a series of publications (Roques 2006, 2008; Roques et al. 2006, 2008), which used simulation techniques and portfolio optimization to compare the impact of fuel and electricity price risks on nuclear, gas and coal plant. We focus on the value of long-term contracts to mitigate fuel and power price risks, and how they affect technology choices, using two case studies: a single plant investment without downstream integration, reflecting the case of a new entrant, and a large utility with a diverse portfolio of power plant.

New entrants' technology choices differ from portfolio utilities as new entrants have a greater incentive to choose technologies which have the lowest *intrinsic* market risk exposure. In the absence of long-term fixed-price power purchase contracts, CCGT is the least risky option as its cash flow is largely 'self-hedged' given the high correlation between electricity and gas prices observed in most European markets. This makes CCGT particularly attractive to new entrants. This finding is consistent with the observed behaviour of investors in European power markets, which have invested heavily in CCGTs over the past two decades.

In contrast, utilities with a diversified generation portfolio are likely to consider a wider range of generation technologies as they can better mitigate the specific risks associated with capital intensive technologies. Portfolio utilities can leverage a diversified portfolio of generation assets to manage some of the risks specific to one technology. The complementarities of a new generation asset risk and return profile with the existing set of assets of the utility is more important than the risk profile of the new asset in isolation.

In both the new entrant and portfolio utility cases we find that a long-term, fixed-price power purchase agreement increases the incentives to invest in capital-intensive technologies and benefits relatively more to nuclear and renewables technologies than to gas and coal plants. While long-term power contracts do not significantly change the expected return of the different technologies, they reduce to a greater extent the exposure of nuclear and renewable technologies to electricity price. In the case of a portfolio utility, optimal plant portfolios would contain a more balanced mix of nuclear and CCGT plant when there are long-term power off take contracts.

These simulation findings can be used to inform the current policy debate about the role of government and regulators in electricity markets, as they show that if a generating company were granted a stable source of revenue through institutional or market changes (for example, long-term capacity contract or a capacity payment), or through other support mechanisms such as a feed-in tariff or credit guarantees for nuclear, then optimal generation portfolios would integrate some share of nuclear power generation.

These findings also raise new issues for antitrust policies in assessing the pros and cons of long-term contracts. Vertical integration and long-term contracts are likely to have an important role to play to facilitate investment of the scale required in capital-intensive 'green technologies' (nuclear, renewables) in order to meet the 2020 environmental objectives of the European Union. Our findings suggest that long-term contracts are critical to facilitate the deployment of capital-intensive low carbon technologies.

The impact of the contractual arrangements on power generation technology choices therefore constitutes an additional dimension to consider for regulators and competition and antitrust authorities. We recommend that competition authorities integrate the impact of contractual arrangements on technology choices and power generation investment incentives in their list of criteria when investigating mergers and acquisitions in the European power markets.

NOTES

1. This chapter is based on work that was done while the author was with the Electricity Policy Research Group of the University of Cambridge. The author would like to thank Dominique Finon, Jean-Michel Glachant, David Newbery, William Nuttall, anonymous referees, and participants of seminars at the University of Cambridge Electricity Policy Research Group and at Université Paris Sud 11 – Groupe LARSEN/Réseaux for their helpful comments on earlier versions of this chapter.
2. This section builds on Roques et al. (2008).
3. The ability to arbitrage between gas and power is, however, not restricted to those power stations that have interruptible gas transportation arrangements. For example, in the UK during the 2005–06 winter, there were occasions when firm CCGTs commercially self-interrupted while interruptible power stations continued to generate (DTI 2006).
4. Most long-term contracts between gas exporters and European gas utilities bar buyers from reselling the gas to third parties other than final private and industrial consumers within their territory. They argue that the destination clause allows gas producers to profitably price discriminate and impacts competitiveness not only through prices, but also in that it reduces liquidity in the European gas market.
5. Sections 3.1 and 3.2 draw heavily on Roques (2008) and Roques et al. (2008).
6. Commodity prices in the short term are usually modelled using complex stochastic processes to capture the impact of seasonality, daily demand variability and other operational risks (Geman 2005).
7. Section 3.1.3 draws heavily on Roques et al. (2008).

REFERENCES

Awerbuch, S. (1993), 'The surprising role of risk and discount rates in utility integrated-resource planning', *The Electricity Journal,* **6** (3), 20–33.

Awerbuch, S. (1995), 'Market-based IRP: it's easy!!!', *The Electricity Journal,* **8** (3), 50–67.

Bazilian, M. and F. Roques (2008), *Analytical Methods for Energy Diversity and Security: Portfolio Optimization in the Energy Sector: A Tribute to the work of Dr. Shimon Awerbuch,* Amsterdam and London: Elsevier.

Bolinger, M., R. Wiser and W. Golove (2006), 'Accounting for fuel price risk when comparing renewable to gas-fired generation: the role of forward natural gas prices', *Energy Policy,* **34**, 706–20.

Borison, A. and G. Hamm (2005), 'Better power contracts: using flexibility to increase value', *The Electricity Journal,* **18** (10), 64–9.

Connors, S., K. Martin, M. Adams and E. Kern (2004), 'Future electricity supplies: redefining efficiency from a systems perspective', working paper from the MIT Laboratory for Energy and the Environment (LFEE), June, available at: http://lfee.mit.edu (accessed January 2010).

Department of Trade and Industry (DTI) (2006), 'Joint energy security of supply working group', seventh report, available at: www.dti.gov.uk (accessed December 2006).

Deutch, J., E. Moniz, S. Ansolabehere, M. Driscoll, P. Gray, J. Holdren, P. Joskow, R. Lester and N. Todreas (2003), 'The future of nuclear power', an MIT Interdisciplinary Study, available at: http://web.mit.edu/nuclearpower (accessed January 2010).

Finon, D. and F. Roques (2008), 'Contractual and financing arrangements for nuclear investment in liberalized markets: which efficient combination?', *Journal of Competition and Regulation in Network Industries*, **9** (3), 147–81.

Geman, H. (2005), *Commodities and Commodity Derivatives – Modelling and Pricing for Agriculturals, Metals and Energy*, New York: John Wiley and Sons.

Girard, P., B. Barre and B. Tinturier (2004), 'Nuclear investments and markets', proceedings of the World Energy Congress 2004, available at: www.worldenergy.org (accessed January 2010).

International Energy Agency (IEA) (2006), *World Energy Outlook 2006*, Paris: OECD/IEA Publication.

International Energy Agency (IEA) (2007), *Climate Policy Uncertainty and Investment Risk*, Paris: IEA/OECD Publication.

International Energy Agency/Nuclear Energy Agency (IEA/NEA) (2005), *Projected Costs of Generating Electricity, 2005 Update*, Paris: OECD/IEA Publication.

Johnston, A., A. Kavali and K. Neuhoff (2007), 'Take-or-pay contracts for renewables deployment', EPRG Working Paper 07/07, January, available at: www.electricitypolicy.org.uk (accessed January 2010).

Kahn, E. and S. Stoft (1993), 'Analyzing fuel price risks under competitive bidding'. unpublished draft, Berkeley, CA, Lawrence Berkeley National Laboratory.

Markowitz, H. (1952), 'Portfolio selection', *Journal of Finance*, **7** (1), 77–91.

Neuhoff, K. and C. von Hirschhausen (2005), '*Long-term vs. short-term contracts: a European perspective on natural gas*', EPRG Working Paper 05, available at: www.electricitypolicy.org.uk (accessed January 2010).

Newbery, D. (2005), 'Climate change policy and its effect on market power in the gas market', EPRG Working Paper 05/10, available at: www.electricitypolicy.org.uk (accessed January 2010).

Nuclear Energy Agency (NEA) (2002), *Trends in the Nuclear Fuel Cycle*, Paris: OECD/IEA Publication.

Roques, F. (2006), 'Power generation investments in liberalised markets: methodologies to capture risk, flexibility, and portfolio diversity', *Économies et Sociétés*, Série Economie de l'Energie, **10** (Oct./Nov.), 1563–94.

Roques, F. (2008), 'Technology choices for new entrants in liberalized markets: the Value of operating flexibility and contractual arrangements', *Utilities Policy*, **16** (4), 245–53.

Roques, F., D. Newbery, W. Nuttall, R. de Neufville and S. Connors (2006), 'Nuclear power: a hedge against uncertain gas and carbon prices?', *The Energy Journal*, **27** (4), 1–24.

Roques, F., D. Newbery and W. Nuttall (2008), 'Fuel mix diversification incentives in liberalised electricity markets: a mean-variance portfolio theory approach', *Energy Economics*, **30** (4), 1831–49.

Rothwell, G. (2006), 'A real options approach to evaluating new nuclear power plants', *The Energy Journal*, **27** (1), 37–54.

Wiser, R., D. Bachrach, M. Bolinger and W. Golove (2004), 'Comparing the risk profiles of renewable and natural gas-fired electricity contracts', *Renewable and Sustainable Energy Reviews*, **8**, 335–63

APPENDIX: A PROBABILISTIC MODEL TO CAPTURE LONG-TERM CONTRACTS VALUE

We concentrate on three technologies (scrubbed coal, CCGT and 'generation three' nuclear) that are likely to be the main baseload alternatives on the post-2010 time horizon.[1] Table 2A.1 summarizes the model 'base case' cost and revenue assumptions, based on IEA/NEA (2005) and IEA (2006).

The model provides a simple yet fairly realistic description of the specificities associated with an investment in the three different technologies. The construction time is five years in the case of nuclear, four years in the case of coal, while it is only two years in the case of the CCGT plant. Nuclear plant incurs a 'nuclear waste fee' to cover the cost of decommissioning and nuclear waste treatment. When operating flexibility is not taken into account, the three plants are assumed to operate baseload with an average annual capacity utilization factor of 85 per cent (the capacity factor is endogenously determined in the case with operating flexibility).

A 10 per cent real weighted average cost of capital is used, corresponding to the cost of capital for a commercial investment in the liberalized industry.[2] Plant technical lifetimes are assumed at respectively 40 years for nuclear and coal plants and 25 years for CCGT plants.[3] Gas and coal price assumptions are based on IEA (2006), with long-term real annual fuel cost escalation rate of 0.5 per cent for the three fuels. The nuclear fuel cost includes used-fuel disposal, based on an open fuel cycle.[4] The cost of carbon emission permits within the European Trading Scheme cost is assumed to be €10/tCO_2. The electricity price is based on an average of future baseload electricity price contracts for 2009 in Europe as of early 2007 with a 0.5 per cent annual cost escalation rate.

For a discount rate of 10 per cent, the coal plant has a much higher NPV (€342/kW) than the nuclear and CCGT plant (respectively €74/kW and €−48/kW). With an 8 per cent discount rate, all technologies have positive NPVs, the nuclear plant NPV increasing relatively more than other technologies as nuclear is the most capital intensive technology. These results are consistent with recent levelized costs studies (IEA 2006; IEA/NEA 2005): the increase of natural gas prices has made coal-fired plant – and to a lesser extent nuclear plant – relatively more competitive in the USA and Europe than gas plant on a static levelized cost basis (IEA 2006).[5]

The characterization of fuel and electricity price risks is simple as the focus here is on price risk in the medium to long term (monthly to yearly).[6] The model concentrates on lifelong discounted cash flows, and monthly fossil fuel, electricity and CO_2 emission permit price risks are modelled by random variables with a normal probability distribution whose

Table 2A.1 Base case parameters

Parameters	Unit	Nuclear	Coal	CCGT
Technical parameters				
Net capacity	MW	1000	1000	1000
Capacity factor	%	85%	85%	85%
Heat rate	BTU/KWh	10400	8600	7000
Carbon intensity	Kg-C/mmBTU	0	25.8	14.5
Construction period	Years	5	4	2
Plant life	Years	40	40	25
Cost parameters				
Overnight cost	€/kW	2000	1120	520
Incremental capital costs	€/kW/yr	16	9.6	4.8
Fuel costs	€/mmBTU	0.4	2	5.8
Real fuel escalation	%	0.5%	0.5%	0.5%
Nuclear waste fee	€million/kWh	1	0	0
Fixed O&M	€/kW/year	52	40	20
O&M real escalation rate	%		0.5%	
Financing parameters				
WACC	%		10%/8%	
Government actions				
Carbon tax	€/tCO_2		10	
Carbon price escalation	%		1%	
Revenues				
Electricity price	€cents/kWh		5.5	
Electricity escalation rate	%		0.5%	

Table 2A.2 Random variables' normal distribution characteristics

Variable	Technology	Unit	Expected value	Standard deviation
Nuclear fuel price	Nuclear	€/Mbtu	0.4	0.15
Coal price	Coal	€/Mbtu	2	1.0
Gas price	CCGT	€/Mbtu	5.8	2.9
Carbon price	All	€/tonneCO_2	10	4.6
Electricity price	All	€cents/KWh	5.5	1.8

parameters are described in Table 2A.2. The most likely values correspond to the base case detailed in the previous section, while the standard deviation estimate is based on empirical data on five years of UK NBP term ahead forward gas prices, coal ARA term ahead forward prices and term ahead UK baseload future electricity prices.

Correlations between fuel, electricity and CO_2 prices are critical to assess the combined impact of such risks on the different technologies risk and return profiles. As in IEA (2007), a correlation of 0.5 between electricity and gas prices, as well as between electricity and coal prices is used as base case working assumption. CO_2 certificates prices are also assumed to be 0.5 correlated with electricity and coal and gas prices in this 'base case' simulation. The last section of this chapter provides a detailed sensitivity analysis to the degree of correlation between fuel, electricity and carbon prices.

Notes

1. Our focus on baseload generation technologies justifies the exclusion of many renewable technologies. Besides, this 2010 time horizon requires current mature technologies, which excludes many technologies (pulverized coal, small-scale modular 'generation IV' nuclear, advanced renewables) that present promising technology prospects, but that are too immature to be considered ready by 2010.
2. For a discussion of discount rates to be used in power generation investment valuations, see for example, Awerbuch (1993 and 1995), Roques et al. (2006) and IEA (2006).
3. For generating cost models with a more detailed treatment of the financing issues, see for example, Girard et al. (2004) and Deutch et al. (2003) who explore the impact of merchant project financing approaches in which the debt repayment period is shorter than the physical life of the plant.
4. For a detailed assessment of the costs of the nuclear fuel cycle, see NEA (2002).
5. Note that the advantage for coal generation is less pronounced in Europe than in the USA, because European coal prices are higher and gas prices lower.
6. Commodity prices in the short term are usually modelled using complex stochastic processes to capture the impact of seasonality, daily demand variability and other operational risks (Geman 2005).

3. Investment and competition in decentralized electricity markets: how to overcome market failure by market imperfections?

Dominique Finon[1]

1 INTRODUCTION

During the design of the market electricity reforms, the issue of investment in generating capacity generally received insufficient attention in the reference model for reforms. This model is a vertically and horizontally de-integrated industry facilitating entry and allowing effective competition on each market from wholesales to retail sales. Regulation tends to limit vertical integration and long-term contract between producers and suppliers, and between suppliers and consumers, and to incite historic producers-suppliers to divest in generation in order to limit the classical incumbents' advantages and to ease entries in view of effective competition.[2] In a number of jurisdictions in North America, Australia and Europe, it has been the reference model for defining new industrial structures and market rules and it still is for the sectoral regulators and the antitrust authorities which tend to condemn historic suppliers' long-term contracts and vertical integration as barriers to entries and restriction of potential competition.

The canonical business model in generation is the merchant plant, a stand-alone producer which sells all this production on short-term markets and without a long-term contract at a fixed price and develops its new capacities under project financing by non-recourse debt. The producer is supposed to bear all the risks (project risks, price risk, input cost risk and volume risk).

This insufficient attention was starkly highlighted by the crises on electricity markets that were partly due to inadequate capacity and by the focus of generators' investment decision on gas generation technologies which could create an excessive specialization of the technology mix. Then, after these crises, theoretical and practical considerations on generation investment largely focused on incentives to develop peak generating capacity and ensuring a reserve margin to guarantee reliability, that is, short-term security of supply. An abundant literature developed on this issue, in particular on various payments of capacity (see, for instance, Cramton and Stoft 2005; De Vries 2007; Joskow 2007; Joskow and Schmalensee 1983; Joskow and Tirole 2007; Oren 2003; Vasquez and Perez-Arriaga 2002).

But little attention was paid to the conditions for investments by entrants in baseload and semi-baseload equipments, because of a strong confidence in the quality of the price signal on the hourly markets to trigger and orient pure producers' investment decisions: their anticipation of infra-marginal rents of low variable cost equipments (hydro, nuclear, large renewable, eventually coal generation) are supposed to trigger the decision to invest in these technologies (see, for instance, Bohn et al. 1984; Hunt 2002; Hunt and Shuttleworth 1997; Oren 2003). In particular, basic principles of risk management applied by competitors end in a non-optimal technology mix distorted in favour of low capital-intensive but high and volatile fuel cost technologies as gas generation plants. For the government and the regulator their development does not present the same risks for the whole system as the inadequacy of total capacity and system unreliability risk, but their excessive development contributes to increasing the volatility of market price and moving away from the optimal technology mix.

Capital-intensive equipment, such as coal generation, nuclear and large-scale renewables which could show advantage in terms of lower expected levelized costs and higher expected net present value, could show a significant advantage for producers, but investments are more risky. They have few possibilities to allocate part of their investment risks on the suppliers or the large consumers by vertical arrangements. These arrangements, which are propitious to investments in various technologies, are impeded by regulation when they could be developed by historic operators, and undermined by the specific characteristics of competition on the wholesale and retail markets when pure producers could be candidates to develop them. The consequence is a non-optimal orientation of the overall technology mix and the non-timely development of capacities in liberalized electricity industries reformed along the referential model (Finon 2006). The long-term consequence is that because the mix of capacity is wrong and characterized by a lack of baseload equipment, the hourly market price will be unduly high during a large part of the year compared with a situation with an optimal mix; and finally it will be at the expense of the social surplus, the loss of consumers being higher than the supplement of net profit of the producers, as shown by Green (2006).

We address here the organizational unsuitability of the decentralized market model and the necessity to adapt it to long-term issues of generation investment allowing not only adequate capacity development, but also optimality of the future technology mix. The first issue of capacity adequacy has been studied in numerous publications focused on the capacity mechanisms to add to market design (see Cramton and Stoft 2005; Finon and Pignon 2008; Joskow 2007 for some overviews). We focus here on the issue of incentives to competitors' investment choices related to risk-sharing, in order to make their capacities converge towards the optimal technology mix. We introduce risk management issues as the main factor of market failures in investment in the technology mix and as central determinants for the needs of vertical arrangements. These issues cover large-scale investment hedging problems as well as 'hold-up risk' problems related to investments securitized by contracts with large buyers.

Methodologically we choose to develop the analysis of market failure in generation investment on the theoretical decentralized market model which is the referential, even if in reality the different electricity reforms are more or less as distant from this model for different reasons (political acceptability of de-integration of pre-existing utilities, resilience of performing utilities, absence of a one for all solution in a complex electricity industry). Empirical facts on generation capacity developments in 'imperfect' reforms, that is, in countries where vertical integration and horizontal concentration have not been systematically opposed by the legislator and then the regulator, will be used as elements to demonstrate the necessity of vertical arrangements and the rationale for large-size companies (and so horizontal integration) to overcome market failures.

So, in the next section, we present the premises of capacity development in the canonical model of the decentralized electricity market and we discuss each premise; their limits show theoretical and practical hurdles to investment that arise from inadequate risk allocation. The third section identifies the conditions allowing vertical or quasi-vertical arrangements to be set for workable allocations of investment risks, in particular the way that investors can meet credible counterparts in long-term contracting or by default to rely on vertical integration. The fourth section integrates this need for vertical arrangements in electricity markets to find an equilibrium between short-term efficiency by perfect competition and long-term efficiency by imperfect completion allowing equipment development on the optimal technology mix trajectory. In the fifth section we identify elements of the good balance between market imperfections (that is, vertical arrangements and horizontal integration) and long-term efficiency (that is, capacity adequacy and generation investment in the technology mix).

2 RISK ALLOCATION AS BARRIER TO INVESTMENT IN GENERATION IN THE DECENTRALIZED MARKET MODEL

It is worth remembering the simplicity of risk allocation in the former model of vertical monopoly and cost of service regulation. In this model utilities taking the decision to invest in generation were comfortably insulated from the risk associated with those decisions on a market. Given the cost-of-service regulation, their costs and risks of investment were carried on the consumers. So they built plants with debt financing at the bond-market rate and without risk premium, that is, with a low cost of capital.

In the market model, the reference business for generation, the merchant plant, is an independent generator which owns a portfolio of assorted production technologies and sells its electricity on the short-term market. It does not own a supply business and a portfolio of customers, or at the most only partly. To identify market failures which limit investment in electricity markets, we first consider the underlying four premises on generation investment by the de-integrated market players in the reference market model of a liberalized electricity industry. In the second subsection, we determine if the premises are a sound approximation of the problem to investors in electricity industry.

2.1 The Four Premises of Investment Decision and Risk Allocation in Decentralized Electricity Markets

Extending the characterization of paradigm of investment risk allocation in theoretical liberalized electricity markets by Chao et al. (2008) to financial arrangements, we stress four premises concerning the efficiency of risk management on generation investments along the chain of market activities.

First, the former vertical integration of utilities regulated in cost of service can be replaced by bilateral contracts between generators and retail suppliers or large customers, assisted by organized markets for spot trading, which are a priori the most efficient form of trade. Investment decision and technological choices will take place based on electricity price signals without regulation interferences. Energy is priced at the marginal bidder's variable cost on the hourly markets during the major part of the year, with demand-side setting the price during scarcity hours. Infra-marginal rents, as well as scarcity rents during peak periods, exactly cover fixed costs at the long-run equilibrium for the different technological plants (Figure 3.1).[3]

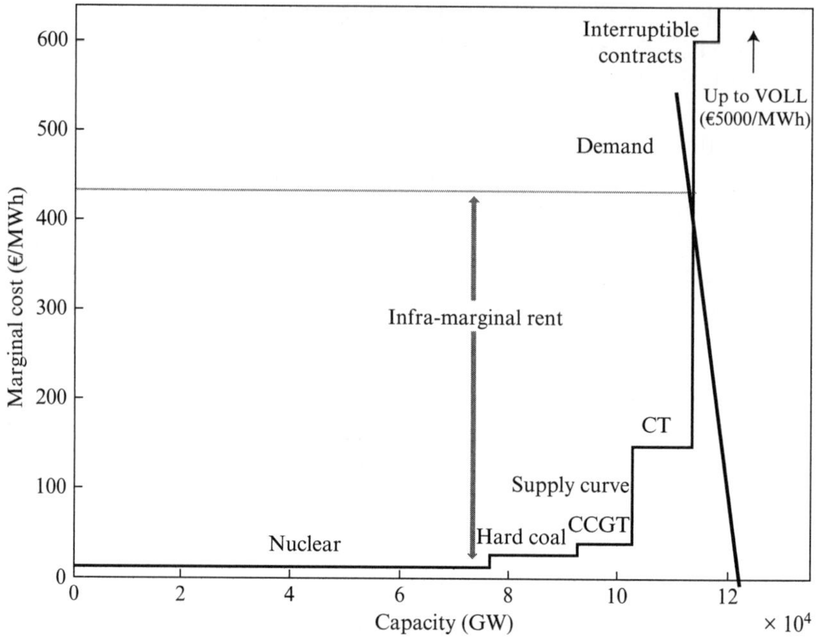

Figure 3.1 Infra-marginal rents on hourly market equilibrium with hockey stick production curve

In the new electric market paradigm, the revenues of any particular plant, the new as well as the existing ones, will be determined each hour by the market price determined by the balance between power demand and capacity, the marginal cost of the last generating equipment and eventually by the market power of competitors during peak hours for scarcity rents. The effects of such factors on prices are supposed to be foreseeable in expected value. Fixed cost recovery for new plant will be allowed by the so-called 'infra-marginal rents', that is, generation gross margins between power prices and fuel costs during each hourly market along the year, when the equipment is not among the marginal plants and hourly price is not aligned on its variable cost.

A competitive market which is cyclical by nature would give the right signal for investments in different technologies when capacity development must respond to demand growth and old plants obsolescence, and it would allow the fixed costs to be recovered with a correct return of capital. One might expect to see spot prices as well as forward prices rising well above complete cost of new equipment when operators anticipate scarcity, and to maintain this for some time after realization of some equipment by competitors.

The second premise is that consumers and intermediates compete to buy electricity by bilateral forward contracts with different generators, among which entrants on the power exchanges manage their risks by portfolio strategy. Consumers who are well informed and wish to hedge such risks are supposed to express their preference for technology and fuel diversity. They will hedge either by long-term, fixed-price contracts with specialized producers with low fuel cost equipment to limit their dependence upon the wholesale market price, or by financial contracts with gas producers to hedge risks from hourly market price determined by CCGT producers' bids. Willingness of the consumers to manage their own risks in their purchase of electricity would be expressed also for the reliability of their supply; for instance, Oren (2003) considered that bilateral financial contracts on capacity rights between consumers and producers would be sufficient to incite investment and guarantee the right level of reserve margin.

At the level of the intermediation between producers and consumers, suppliers have to manage a portfolio of different types of sales contracts with time spans and price formulas adapted to the different segment of clienteles, with volume risks inherent to their customers' switching. They are supposed to harmonize risk management between their portfolio of sourcing and their portfolio of sales contracts. Suppliers have different means with which to manage their risks; in particular they could manage them by co-managing their risks in their portfolios of sourcing contracts and sales contracts. Specifically, every supplier should seek to maximize their share of market-based retail contracts with price directly reflecting the spot price (IEA 2007). Stephen Littlechild expresses the same opinion:

> If the contract is really worth signing, the retail supplier could match any price reductions to customers and still come out ahead. A consequence of retail conception/competition is that suppliers who wish to sign long term contracts have to back their own judgment rather than pass the risks to consumers; this is likely to improve the quality of decision making. (Littlechild 2002, p. 13 of website source)

The third premise: on the top of forward contracts complete markets for financial instruments will offer all the means for hedging risks of generators, suppliers and consumers, besides physical contracting. Various alternatives for managing market risk for producers by specific long-term financial contracts – long-term options, contracts for differences, swaps – all play a role in securing investments in generation (Chao and Huntington 1998). Moreover long-term future markets would have an important informational function on the market fundamentals and the revenue advantage to invest in generation in the future. This hypothesis of complete market would give substance to Arrow–Debreu theoretical model of decision-making under risk in electricity markets for short-term and long-term decision coordination and efficient choices (Arrow and Hahn 1971).

The price volatility would normally be manageable by electricity producers, wholesale buyers and consumers if they could develop the contractual arrangements necessary to efficiently allocate the risks across generators, intermediaries and consumers. Using this logic of financial optimism, the producers would have no interest in securing generation investment by long-term forward contracts with suppliers or large consumers because they lose opportunities to make temporary high profits. The rewards will balance the higher risks (IEA 2007). So, in this perspective, hedging risks through long-term contracts could be seen as handing over these opportunities for greater benefits to other parties who arguably are not in such a good position to make the decisions as the power companies themselves.

The fourth premise: generators could obtain capital on comparable terms directly from financial markets; such as formerly regulated utilities could do with their assured fixed-cost recovery. Innovative structure finance offers new ways to finance new generation equipment in 'project finance', that is, without non-recourse debt and high leverage (for example, 60 to 80 per cent of debt and only 20 to 40 per cent of equity). The lender's collateral resides in the projected cash flow of the project and the resale value of the production asset (Esty 2004; Esty and Kane 2001). Because of the confidence in the market mechanisms, the lenders lobby for vertically de-integrated industrial structures and the greatest transparency for pricing by the market. They are so confident about the functioning of the new electricity markets that they do not require collateral in the form of fixed-price, long-term contracts guaranteeing the project's revenues. Merchant plants are supposed to gain revenues by spot sales (on energy and ancillary services markets) or short-term contracts. The investor will take his or her decision to finance a project after exploring returns that different technologies may deliver under a number of different assumptions on competitors' projects, fuel prices, influence of fuel price on electricity prices and their spread, hourly and seasonal demand pattern and capital cost. At the end the financial approach thinks out the generation firm as a series of separately financed projects in view of transparency in risk management – an approach which falls within both the province of the Arrow–Debreu theory of optimal investment under uncertainty and the theory of modern finance as developed by Etsy (2004).

3 MARKET FAILURES ON INVESTMENT IN THE DECENTRALIZED MARKET MODEL

In this section we show the limitations of the four premises on investment in the decentralized market model, and we insist on the disalignment of investors' and consumers' interests because it is the first factor of market failures in the technology mix development. For this analysis we combine the perspective of risk allocation and the transaction cost economics (TCE) perspective because the latter identifies opportunism of the parties in a contract linked to a specific technology investment as the source of internal risk, the so-called 'hold-up' risk.[4]

We underpin in the appendix our statement on the difficulty of sharing risks and establishing credible commitment between producers and wholesale buyers by empirical facts based on the record of investment in electricity generation in countries where the decentralized market model has been implemented. This record of investments between 1997 and 2007 in the USA, in Europe and in Australia shows that institutional conditions of successful capacity development in baseload and semi-baseload equipments are long-term contracts and vertically integrated companies. Indeed we observe three facts in the most liberalized markets in terms of vertical and horizontal de-integration: the failure of pure producers without long-term contracts, even with CCGT plants in the USA and the UK markets; a move to vertical integration in the UK, Australia and the USA, which is partly motivated by search of investment hedging; and exceptional decisions of coal plants and nuclear plants, which are always the lot of integrated firms, except for one case of a pure producer, but which is backed by contracts with a remaining regulated franchised supplier.

3.1 Limits on the Four Premises

3.1.1 Market failure in fixed-cost recovery

Fixed-cost recovery is not guaranteed at all in a stochastic perspective. Price spikes after the commissioning of the equipment are particularly difficult to anticipate in magnitude and duration whereas they are a significant part of the discounted net cash flow. Generators and investors are confronted not only with a problem of cost minimization, but with a problem of combining net present value maximization and risks minimization when choosing equipment in a stock of technologies in which to invest (gas turbine, CCGT, coal, nuclear or wind farms). Putting aside some specific risks under the control of the regulators and the policy makers,[5] there are, first, risks under the control of the company on construction cost and operation performance (see Table 3.1). Second, there are risks

Table 3.1 Cost structure and risks of different electricity generation technologies

Technology	Capital size per unit	Lead time	Fixed-cost share	Fuel cost share	CO_2 cost risk	Fuel price risk	Regulatory risk
CCGT	Low (€100–200 million)	Short	Low	High	Medium	High	Low
Coal	Large (€700–1000 million)	Long	High	Medium	High	Medium	High
Nuclear	Very large (€2–3 billion)	Long	Very high	Low	Nil	Low	High
Renewables (wind farm)	Medium (€300 million)	Medium	Very high	Nil	Nil	Nil	Medium

Source: Adapted from IEA (2005).

the management of the investor has to anticipate before deciding to invest and asking for loans to lenders, namely, the fuel price risk, the electricity price risk and the volume risk related to the demand variability and the non-dispatchability possibility.

The conclusions we stress from Table 3.1 are the following. First, cost of gas generation kWh (gas turbine and CCGT) has a relative low share of investment cost, which reduces financial exposure. Because of their high share of fuel cost, CCGT tends to become the marginal equipment on the hourly market and 'makes' the electricity marginal price during the major part of the year when the gas price is established at a high level. This has a positive effect: a good correlation between gas price and electricity price during the major part of the year, which means that they benefit from self-hedging effects. Conversely, if investment has been in supplying baseload, there is a risk of bankruptcy when the equipment is much less called on when gas price increases sharply because of higher price bid offer, what is called the 'dispatchability risk'.

Second, coal plants are very capital intensive but the fuel cost is relatively low and coal price has low volatility. They are therefore more exposed to the financial risks of whether they can repay the capital based on the volume and price of electricity off-taken from the project. It is the same for mostly up-front capital investment in nuclear or renewable. With high operating leveraging, that is, high net cash flows, small changes in revenues have large effects on profitability. So they have greater need of risk management than does the cost of CCGT with its low ratio of investment and capital costs.

Pure producers which invest in the more capital-intensive equipment, the less 'self-hedged' by input price and electricity price correlation and the less flexible (as nuclear plants and to a lesser extent coal plants) are obliged to develop a large range of transactions to sell their production and hedge their different risks, by comparison with the CCGT producers which benefit from the advantage of self-hedging. In the end, investments in the highly capital-intensive equipment (coal generation, nuclear plants, hydraulic plants, renewable) are hampered. As shown by approaches in terms of the mean variance theory of portfolio (Roques, Chapter 2 this book; Roques et al. 2006), producers are incentivized to invest only in the CCGT plants. And this is what is roughly observable on the generation investment record since the beginning of the reforms, in deeply reformed markets and even in 'imperfectly' reformed markets (see below).

The character of the uncertainty on electricity markets, rooted in its limited stochasticity – the non-storability of electricity results in an exceptional variability of hourly market price and a slackened consistency of price-making with the separation of hourly markets – adds to negative incentive for equipment presenting no advantage of correlation of its production costs with electricity price.

3.1.2 No possibility of long-term contracting to share investment risks without possible safeguards

The premise on the viability of consumers' and retailers' risk management combining different time-span contracts in a portfolio approach also has limitations. Investors and producers fail on the difficulty of establishing long-term contracts with creditworthy buyers, given retailers' risk aversion to commit long term if it is not possible for the latter to pass their risks on to their customers. Conversely a producer who might find a supplier inclined to sign up to long-term, fixed-price contracts could suspect it would ask for renegotiation or break the contract in case of price downturn on the wholesale market; this risk of the counterpart's opportunistic behaviour could be a disincentive to contract in order to secure an investment in capital-intensive equipment and so to develop a portfolio mix (De Vries and Neuhoff 2004). Given these difficulties a generator cannot rely on long-term contracting for hedging its new generation investment in the decentralized market model. More generally there is disalignment of interests of investors (or entrants) and large buyers, and it could be considered a market barrier because of the impossibility of securing long-term revenues for new generation equipment in the pure market model (De Vries and Hakvoort 2003). We elaborate on this market failure in the next sub-section, given that it determines limitation on the other premises.

3.1.3 The incompleteness of markets

The premise that a rapid and adequate development of markets for forward contracts and financial instruments will offer all the means for hedging risks of new generators, suppliers and consumers has been demolished by experience of the first decade of market reforms. First, observing the markets reveals that the duration of physical contracts and financial contracts, between generators and wholesale buyers (including large industrial consumers) is, at most, two years, but generally one year or less. They are too short to accompany the development of specific new capacities. Second, the use of derivatives to manage electricity price risk is difficult because the simple pricing model used to value derivatives in other energy industries does not work in the electricity sector, given the non-storability of electricity and the lack of stochasticity of price variations (Defeuilley and Meunier 2006; Geman 2005). The non-elasticity of real-time supply and demand does not allow the futures or the forward price to represent a correct anticipation of its price realization. This situation complicates investment decisions because financial investors do not attribute information quality to spot price and forward price, in the sense that they hardly reflect the situation of fundamentals. It dissuades banks and hedge funds from playing the role of counterparty on such markets for futures and over the counter (OTC), although they commonly speculate on other commodity markets and create liquidity. Long-term derivatives cannot develop in such a context of risk profile.

3.1.4 The failure of project finance arrangements

Consistent with the previous premise, lenders have adopted the method of project financing of merchant plants without securing vertical arrangements, but confident in the net cash flow of the equipment that they finance (Etsy 2004; Etsy and Kane 2001). But as it finances the project by raising as much debt finance as possible via non-recourse debt and project financing in the individual framework of 'special purpose vehicle', this imposes the self-financial sustainability of the project by its net cash flow without backing on cross-subsidy from the producer's other generation assets in periods of low price. This means that technological options are reduced to self-hedged CCGT. This means also that the profitability of each project will be critically dependent on the net revenues during the price spikes of the market after commissioning of the equipment. Conversely it will be altered dramatically by market change which alter revenues (price downturn, reduction of dispatchability period) as shown by the bankruptcies of all the CCGT merchant plants in the US liberalized market and in the UK in 2001 and 2002 (see, for instance, Joskow 2007; Michaels 2006).

Since then, even if CCGT remains the technology most inadequate for risk management as shown by some existing merchant plants in high-price electricity markets in Europe (see appendix), investors and producers are now convinced that pure merchant plant is not a viable business model. The approach of separated projects in a separated 'special vehicle' is also theoretically disputed, in particular because it misses the interaction effects among equipment (Williamson 1996). In the electricity industry both the technological and industrial realities of the industry are ignored, which gives advantages to having a portfolio of different assets related to different economic dispatchabilities on hourly markets, as well as vertical arrangements to hedge investment.

3.2 Disaligned Interests between Producers and Wholesale Buyers to Share Investment Risks

To go further on the limits of the premises of the decentralized market model concerning generation investment, even though the price-risk would be considerable, that does not, in and of itself, signify market failure. In other words, there is no theoretical reason why risks on the market price should impede investments in generation. And the fact is that there is investment in sufficient capacities when needed, but there is specialization of investment in CCGT technology. The problem results from the fact that the risk is not manageable for the investor, because it could not be adequately allocated to buyers. Projects in any technology should be better developed if an allocation of risks onto the consumers could be achieved in the decentralized market model.

In the following we focus on the limits of the second premise, that is, the difficulties of alignment of interests of producers who invest in new plants with the wholesale buyers' interests, because it is the key factor of the market failure. So institutional conditions should be identified which could remedy this de-alignment. As soon as such conditions could allow risk-sharing between investors and 'consumers', financial arrangements (premise 4) could be established for investing in capital-intensive technologies, and fixed-cost recovery (premise 1) will be guaranteed, allowing optimal technology mix to have more chances to be reached.

At first glance, interests of investors and large wholesale buyers are converging. Indeed, the basis of this is that the interests of producers and large purchasers who have to hedge their risks appear to converge for signing long-term, fixed-price fixed-quantity contracts. Ideally such a contract protects the producer against sustained low prices, while consents to get lower revenues during a period of high price to the benefits of the purchaser. And symmetrically the contract protects the purchaser against sustained high prices while forgoing higher revenues to the producer during periods of lower prices. Moreover with such a long contracting period, the generator can use the contract as security to obtain loans to finance construction. It could also use the contract as a guarantee to negotiate a long-term fuel supply contract in good conditions of risk allocation.[6]

Anyway, in reality there are no such long-term contracts in the decentralized electricity markets with effective competition in industrial and mass-market segments. A first glance interpretation of the difficulties in establishing a fixed-price, fixed-quantity contract would be consumers' passive opportunism because they avoid showing their need for hedging to these generators. Such wholesale purchasers which are well informed and wish to hedge such risks do not express their preference for technology mix and fuel diversity by contracting directly with entrants or specialized generators. But if we look into the details, the problem is basically elsewhere: there is no converging interest in fixed-price, fixed-quantity contracting when investment is at stake.

First, most consumers do not need fixed prices, because electricity is a small part of their cost and changing price is cheaper. The exception is electric-intensive industries which need long-term supply contracts with 10–20 years of predictable prices, in a particular situation: when firms have to invest in new industrial capacities. In this situation they want to be hedged against electricity price upraise (see Longva, Chapter 7 in this book). But their problems have two other dimensions: their international competitors are supplied in different markets with better conditions and their product price does not follow energy prices in the short term. A price indexation clause could link contractual electricity price to output price variation as well as to foreign currency exchange rates; but it is much less favourable to the new electricity producer than a stable price related to its cost price.

Second, for a supplier, a fixed-price, fixed-quantity contract protects him or her from the price risk during the episodes of price spike, but increases its volume risk and its price risk. Indeed, the suppliers sell their electricity under three types of retail contracts offered to industrial and commercial consumers as well as to households: (1) the fixed-price contract for one to two years (it could be tailored to the consumer load profiles, as the electro-intensive firms with a rather flat annual load curve to which flat price contracts can be offered); (2) the standard variable contract where the supplier may adjust the contract price either at regular intervals, or after some delays, when changes in supply costs occurs; and (3) the market-based contract where the price directly reflects the spot price plus a margin. In most countries, suppliers' contract portfolios are dominated by the first two types of contract, because there is a tradition of no direct pass-through of wholesale prices in retail price.

This raises two problems inherent to the supplier business. First, the supplier's quantity management is generally dependent upon the load variability in the short term and the uncertainty of his market share in the long term. The quantity clause, either with firmness or non-firmness, which contributes to protecting the generator investment, exerts restrictions on the need for flexibility for the suppliers which could not have only these types of contracts in their portfolio of sourcing. Indeed they prefer flexibility to meet their changing loads and to seek market shares in overall demand growth increment. Moreover in a non-firm contract, the buyer is quite exposed to moral hazard from the producer, an observation which is in line with Hart's observation (1995) about the disadvantages of not owning production equipment. Indeed, in the long-term contract, the power buyer is in an information asymmetry concerning the operating conditions of the equipment as well as the effects of environmental regulatory changes.

The second problem is that the supplier is locked in by his downstream portfolio of mid-term sales contracts with flat prices with few possibilities to adjust the price upward shortly after wholesale price increases. Their problem of price risk management is increased by the fact that, generally, regulators define favourable rules to consumers to switch in order to help retail competition. The latter have the legal opportunity to leave their contractors and switch to another one with a delay of a couple of weeks. So, in the case of price downward, they have to follow the move of the wholesale price, to limit the risk of important consumers switching before the end of running contracts.[7] Medium and large customers are always on the lookout for a lower price and, in the event of a drop in wholesale prices, they will switch to new entrants, which will capitalize on the new price if their original supplier does not pass on the wholesale price decrease in their sale price. If they are locked into the long-term contract by high penalties, the risk of bankruptcy is high.[8] Following a number of authors (Chao et al. 2008; Joskow 2007; Michaels 2006), this is the reason for which they do not wish to be bound by agreements with fixed prices on a long time span.

So, in such a situation, even if suppliers enter into a long-term contract related to new equipment with a generator, they will be expected by the latter to exit and break the contract when the wholesale market downturns (De Vries and Neuhoff 2004), because they are the party less committed in such a long-term contract related to new equipment. They would not provide credible guarantees for the producer investing in generating capacity. Before committing to investment, investors must anticipate the possibility of revenue losses if any of the long-term contracts they sign are challenged. Thus, they will be reluctant to engage in, and invest on the basis of, any long-term contracts on significant volumes.

The other ways to build long-term contracts do not solve the issue of sharing risks on equipment projects other than CCGT. Innovative contracting allows different modes of risk allocations which could help suppliers or large consumers to decide to commit. Call option contracts, indexed price contracting and tolling contracts, all these intermediate forms of contracting require at least one and usually both the parties to bear risks of one kind or another, but it is always at the expense of one of the parties. Financial call option contracts were a sort of insurance contract against volatile price. They are only favourable to the buyers' interest. Call option enables them to hedge against high price risk without exposure to the volume risk that it would have in the first types of contract if the contracted quantity exceeds the amount required to serve its market.[9]

The two other contracts are similar. Indexed-price contracts generally index the price of electricity to the cost of the fuel used to generate the electricity. The ability for an investor to pass through fuel price risks appears as a key issue to trigger investment. Indexing the contract price of electricity to the price of the fuel stabilizes net cash flow for fossil fuel generation plants. With such an indexation in a coal project, the fuel price risk is allocated to the buyer because the buyer receives a variable-priced product; this type of contract is considered as if the buyer committed in the long-term contract will be the owner-operator of the coal plant. In the case of a CCGT project, the fuel price risk is allocated to the buyer because the buyer receives a variable-priced product;[10] but the risk is limited in systems where CCGTs are the main marginal equipment during the year. In this case this type of contract converges in terms of risk-sharing with the so-called tolling agreement whereby the power purchaser delivers fuel to the generator and takes delivery of the resulting kWh, more clearly allocating the risk of fuel price variability to the buyer. This contract in fact leases the generation plant for converting natural gas to electricity. The seller is paid not only for the use of its facility, but also for simply being available to generate.[11] Note that these types of indexed-price contracts do not fit with the risk profile of investment in capital-intensive equipment with a low share of fuel cost or not all as nuclear, hydro or renewables plants. In their case a constant-price and fixed-quantity contract stabilizes the cash flow whatever the fluctuations in the spot price.

In any case in the set of contracting possibilities, there is no immediate solution to reconcile the interests of producers investing in new equipments and wholesale buyers in the decentralized electricity markets with effective retail competition. One solution includes conditions which allow credible commitment from wholesale buyers and equitable risk sharing.

4 INSTITUTIONAL CONDITIONS FOR RISK-SHARING VIA VERTICAL ARRANGEMENTS

The need of risk-sharing and control of hold up risk in vertical arrangement necessitates that suppliers are able to transfer their sourcing risks to a large number of their customers, and that electro-intensive industrial consumers will be involved in the generation investment.

4.1 Incentives for Suppliers to Search for Long-term Contracts with New Productions

Suppliers-retailers would commit to long-term purchase contracts at fixed price (or with indexed price) only if they could hedge their downstream risks. With the exception of very few countries (Norway in particular for cultural reasons), suppliers cannot be hedged by making both sides of their portfolios follow the market. On their side, pure producers who invest in high sunk cost technologies need creditworthy purchasers on the side of suppliers. Two ways get round these combined difficulties: an imperfect reform allowing dominant position for historic suppliers with a large core of sticky consumers (or a franchise on mass-market consumers) and vertical integration of production and supply.

4.1.1 The complementarities between long-term contracts and de facto retail monopoly

Suppliers' commitment to long-term power purchase agreements (PPAs) at a fixed price with new generation entities should be the major means to secure investment in high sunk cost equipment. But the competition is quite active in some Australian, American and European retail markets in which high cumulated rates of switching (that is, the total of switching since the opening of the markets) are observable when effective unbundling, historical supplier's brand changes and switching costs lowering have been realized by the regulator.[12] As the retail market is supposed to be completely open to competition with market rules that eliminate switching costs, suppliers bound by long-term fixed-price contracts with generators arc vulnerable to the previously mentioned price squeeze, because they risk losing their market share to entrants if they do not follow the price downturns on the wholesale price.

However in most of the US, European and Australian markets, in the households and commercial market segments, there remain a very large number of inactive customers who remain with the historical supplier ('sticky' customers), and in confidence prefer flat prices contracts or else the standard variable contract where the supplier may adjust the contract price at regular intervals. This is a matter of fact which is not simply linked to the dominant suppliers' strategies of branding and consumer loyalty building, but to the customers' deep aversion to price volatility and to continually monitor and control their consumption. There is a continuous role for suppliers in providing inter-temporal smoothing of retail prices, as did the cost-of-service regulated utility in the previous regime. This is an implicit premise of risk management on decentralized markets which is totally challenged by the facts. In concrete terms, given that this large number of consumers do not want to manage the price risk, the incumbent suppliers should assume this function for them, but in exchange should pass through a major part of their sourcing risks to them. This converges with investors' interest in meeting suppliers able to commit to long-term purchase contracts at fixed price (or equivalent).

To go further in this direction, it should be tolerated that historic suppliers retain de facto a very significant segment of its initial clientele that remains quasi-captive. After the complete opening of retail to competition, the retail market reform should leave the historic suppliers a significant base of 'sticky' customers. These conditions would enable them to pass the cost differential of the fixed price in purchase contracts over the wholesale market price in their retail prices in period of price downturn. It allows these suppliers to shift their risk on to some consumers and pass changes to the wholesale price on to their retail prices without risking the loss of too many clients. This situation appears to be the solution for curtailing opportunism risk of the suppliers, as Joskow (2007) suggests. It must be underlined that it essentially concerns the historic suppliers. Their position is generally comforted (or protected) by their role in default service supply which, in most of the cases they keep, because this gives them a real competitive advantage to retain their initial customers, or when it is allowed, to bring previously switching consumers back to default tariffs. In certain jurisdictions such as in Australia, these imperfect markets are conceived as contestable markets, in the sense that the regulators retain a regulated retail price cap. Note that this price cap is calculated by reference to the wholesale price, but aimed also to provide predictability for generation investment. In the NEM (Australian national electricity market), the wholesale energy component of the default tariff is derived from the so-called 'prudent retailer approach' hedging (definition of both a median spot price and combinations of base swap and peak swap, with financial allowances for load forecast errors, volatility, and so on) (Shimashauser 2010).

In such contexts of imperfect competition in the retail supply with large core consumers, experience shows that these suppliers sign long-term contracts with new production entities in Britain, Germany, New Zealand, the Netherlands and several jurisdictions in the USA and Australia (Shimshauser, 2009; Shioshansi 2007).

4.1.2 Backing the contractual credibility of suppliers to a consumer franchise

Another unconventional solution to be evoked is the preservation of partial franchise on the small consumers segment for historic suppliers. In US jurisdictions where reforms do not concern municipalities or organize some form of retail franchise, it is worth noting that after the bankruptcy of pure CCGT producers, several independent power producer (IPP) projects find financing solutions because they have a power purchase agreement with municipalities or a historic supplier which retains a form of franchised monopoly. This gives some grounds to the position of scholars such as Green (2004) and Newbery (2001, 2002) who stress the limitation of the advantages of retail competition extension to the household segment, regarding the long-term efficiency issue of adequate investment in capacity.

A limitation of this imperfect system lies in its difficulty to regulate partial monopoly, as stressed by Littlechild (2006). Regulation is complex and information costly. A disadvantage of retail monopoly is that utilities and regulators who do not have to test their judgement in the market, are typically not well placed to judge the costs and risks of long-term contracts or physical hedging by installing and producing own generation assets. The same applies to calculating default service tariffs of historic suppliers. The regulator must define a future path of evolution of spot prices and forward price and refer to a benchmark of purchase strategy by the historic suppliers, to assess the different risks and allocate them between producers, historic suppliers and consumers for each local or regional situation. The control problem could be solved by auctioning the long-term contracts of suppliers with a partial franchise or with default service obligations in order to benefit from the pressures of market mechanisms as suggested by Ropkoff (2007).[13] If it is considered that this approach does not guarantee a revenue stream for contracting in the long term with investors in high capital intensive technologies, retail tariff or default tariff regulation could be a blended weighting of this market-based approach and the theoretical cost of the long-run marginal cost of supplying the load, that is, given prevailing capital cost and investment costs of different technologies. Indeed, if forward prices used in the market component reflect conditions of transient oversupply, there would be a bias unfavourable to long lead-time investment in different technologies.

4.1.3 Vertical integration production-supply

From a general point of view, vertical integration is an entirely predictable outcome in decentralized electricity because of high wholesale price volatility and a discrepancy between wholesale market price and retail market price (Read 2004). It improves investment by improving risk management in different directions. Partial or complete vertical integration is another way for a supplier to hedge part of its sourcing, and conversely for a producer who develops a portfolio of different technologies. This leads to an analysis of the fitness of vertical industrial organization based upon both a successively grown portfolio of various generation technologies and a developed set of customer relations, with the purpose being to invest in a variety of generation technologies to lower on average its production costs.

On the supplier's side this evolution is observed in the exemplary case of Centrica's strategy of electricity sourcing which occurred at the end of the 1990s. Centrica was a pure electricity supplier on the UK retail market. In the first stage it entered into different long-term contracts. But the development of physical assets progressively became the most important element. Centrica bought a number of existing gas-fired power stations, with a total of 1650 MW, and in 2007–08 was developing a new one of 890 MW. Centrica will supply more than half of its power sales from its physical assets. More recently in 2009 it applied for a 25 per cent share in the stock of British Energy, the nuclear producer, to obtain direct access to existing nuclear plants' production at cost. The case of Centrica is not alone, because it could be observed in other former British pure suppliers (for example, EDF Energy), the four major Australian suppliers and different US suppliers. This suggests that for a pure electricity supplier, majority integration presents a necessary complement for risk management to long-term and short-term contracts. It is now a common practice that suppliers hedge at least 100 per cent of their sourcing for their mass-market customer segment by developing or acquiring physical assets.

On the side of the pure producer, entry to a market by investing in the equipment of different technologies could be secured by developing vertical integration by acquiring a local supplier: this enables the off-taken quantities and sales prices of the vertical entity's new productions to be guaranteed in one way or another and the fuel risk could be transferred to the supply unit, that is, the internal buyer.[14] This is Electrabel's strategy of combined entry in generation and supply business into the German, Dutch and Italian markets.

4.1.4 Comparison of long-term contracts and vertical integration for securing generation investment

Given the alternatives between long-term contracts related to a new equipment and vertical integration, the quest for vertical integration between generation and supply can be understood, from the two perspectives of the producer and the supplier, as a strategy for reducing endogenous risks of opportunistic behaviours of eventual contractors as well as external risks. There are also transaction cost savings, with regard both to negotiating the contract, monitoring contract performance (amending clauses, renegotiating, and so on) in a context of information asymmetry with the producer on operating conditions and impact of changing input costs and market regulation. In more mundane terms, the vertical entity controls the risks associated with asymmetrical changes in profit margins at each stage of the value chain under the effect of market price fluctuations. The case is clearer for a supplier than for a producer. Vertical integration stabilizes and secures the terms of its wholesale purchases, even if it does not completely control its volumetric and price risks in resale. (See Table 3.2.)

Considering a supplier who has the choice opened to vertical integration (by physical asset development or acquisition), long-term contract at fixed price (or indexed price) and short-term purchase, vertical integration makes risk management easier than in the pure supplier model with some long-term contracts. Incentives to adopt vertical integration rather than long-term contracts at fixed price (or price not indexed on spot price) are threefold. First as suppliers benefit from a segment of 'sticky' customers to limit their volume and price risk, they are inclined to develop a portfolio approach by segmenting both their outlets and their sourcing. They can efficiently manage their risk on the small-consumers segment by investing in capital intensive equipments with cost-price non-correlated to spot, while they could keep open their options for their sourcing on the industrial segment for which both sides of the portfolios follow the market.

Second, complexity in risk management is increased by their responsibility for load servicing. This gives partial physical hedging some advantages for a vertical integration over sourcing based only on short-term purchases on spot market and long-term contracts with new producers. Indeed, in a long-term arrangement between a supplier and any new producer, there is a clear opposition between its need for volume flexibility and the generator's need for off-take guarantee. Developing its own flexible equipment such as gas turbines or CCGTs, consolidates its hedging strategy.

Table 3.2 Comparison of risk-sharing between suppliers' long-term contracts and suppliers' vertical integration

	Contribution to investment	Technical and commercial shared risk	Governance issue	Margin over cost to be accepted by consumers
Fixed-price, long-term contract associated with new equipment	No	Yes for the price risk Yes for technical risk with non-firm contracts	Medium	Medium (depending on competition)
Suppliers' ownership of new equipment	Total	Total	Low	No

Consider now the pure producer who invests in a high upfront cost technology not propitious to self-hedging. While the long-term contract allows the sharing of investment risks (construction, fuel price, market price, volume risk) between different parties by a variety of provisions, under vertical integration all of them would be managed by a single entity. That means, in particular, that adaptation to uncertainty is more efficient inside the governance structure of the firm than in the framework of long-term contracts in which adaptation needs delays and transactions costs.

4.1.5 Combining generation portfolio and consumers portfolio: an ideal back-up for financing generation investment

Vertical reintegration is generally associated with a diversified portfolio of generation equipment, which gives an advantage in terms of hedging to investment projects of the vertically integrated company in comparison to a merchant plant project, even if backed by a long-term contract with a credible party. From the producer perspective, ownership of a diversified portfolio of generating equipments gives them a greater capacity to spread the operating risk attributable to the volatility of input prices (fuels, CO_2 permits), as well as market risk. This ability can be used in the trade strategy of portfolio bidding. From the vertically integrated supplier perspective, the generation portfolio approach presents the advantage of diversifying risks by owning and operating flexible CCGTs, some coal generation plants and non-fossil fuel plants, in particular wind power plants and nuclear plants. The supplier-producer could produce in an optimal way for the different hourly loads of its customers' portfolios. If it could commit both in investment in large capital-intensive units with low operational cost and in flexible, low capital-intensive generation units from the standard CCGT technology, it could have a chance not only to ideally manage market risks, but also to minimize its averaged generation costs.

The combination of production and consumers portfolios is perceived now as an ideal profile for risk diversification. For any non-integrated producers, a diversified portfolio gives them an advantage for accessing cheaper debt. Lenders are henceforth attracted by diversified portfolio of assets, and reluctant to lend to merchant plants (Lacy 2006). When asset portfolio diversification is extended to supply business by offering also the advantage of risk-sharing by vertical integration it gives another advantage; it could be extended from the production business on one market to several markets. Lenders and financial investors have understood that their risks are better controlled by corporate finance with a normal debt–equity ratio of 50–50 to an asset-diversified power producer than by project finance for each equipment to be developed.

Finally beyond a certain threshold, asset diversification and large size combine their advantage to help financing and reduce the capital cost of investment. Firms benefit from good ratings and do not bear risk premium on their capital costs. Large size allows large-scale and indivisible investment with normal financing arrangement. Corporate finance with large equity investment in several nuclear builds could stack up to reach the precautionary threshold of 15–20 per cent of market capitalization, for instance, €6 billion in equity for four plants for a market valuation of €40 billions, than one nuclear build for a small company.

To these advantages in risk management and cost of capital we shall add the possibility to negotiate long-term contracts for their fuel purchase with favourable conditions. So it is a means for the biggest among them to have bargaining power in their dealings with the manufacturer's oligopoly. These different advantages help them to invest not only in €200 million CCGT projects, but 10 to 20 times more in capital-intensive projects as a nuclear plant with corporate financing and a normal capital cost.

4.2 Establishing Vertical Arrangements between New Productions and Large Consumers

When energy costs are an important share of their costs of production, large consumers could search for access to physical resources of power

Table 3.3 Comparison of the implications of large consumers in different arrangements linked to a new production

	Contribution to investment	Technical and commercial shared risk	Governance issue	Margin over cost to be accepted by consumers
Fixed-price, long-term contracts	No	No	Low	Medium (depending on competition)
Consortium producer – industrial consumer	High	High	High	Low
Consumers cooperative of production	High	Medium (depending on the terms of PPAs)	Medium	Low to medium

plants the cost-price of which is independent or only loosely correlated to the wholesale price. As pointed out by Longva (see Chapter 7 in this book), motivation to search long-term contracting at a fixed price is the consolidation of its location on an industrial site, or more often in a country. Three options are of interest in this issue: first, the long-term contract solution at a fixed price between large consumers and new production; second, the development of own generation capacity and a variant of it, a cooperative of different industrial consumers owning and operating new equipment; and third, the capacity development in a producer-consumer joint venture. They could be compared in terms of risk-sharing but also of hold-up risk disincentives (see Table 3.3).

The first solution which has already been studied above is the long-term, fixed-price arrangement between generators and industrial consumers related to new equipment. It is the solution which is the least demanding for industrial consumers in terms of risk-sharing and guarantee for financing.

Rather than develop their own equipment to hedge electricity purchases in the face of random short-term price fluctuations because electricity generation activity is not in its core business, a large consumer can seek such long-term supply contracts. But, as said above, their interests are not completely converging with those of the producer who will invest. The producer is exposed to the risk of relocation or bankruptcy of its buyer. It is the same for the incentives to opportunism of the latter during periods of low prices on the wholesale market or when they are confronted with a downturn in the international market for their products with no relation to energy and electricity price cycles. On the side of producer, the arrangement will not give an opportunity to make more margins over cost when market prices are set at a high level. So to make this kind of contract interesting to invest in a new capacity for a producer, it must provide for sufficient volume and time to be associated with the construction cost recovery. So, large consumers interested by such contracts related to new production do not easily find investors to an *ex ante* contract in such a way. The reasons are both the need of the buyer's creditworthiness and the commitment on the buyer's part that the investor needs in financial and risk-sharing terms. Large upfront cost and risky investment need the buyer's participation.

The second type of arrangement is the producer-consumer joint venture which offers implicit protection against any risk of consumer's opportunism, by the common ownership and operation of new generation equipment. This common ownership constitutes 'hostages' in the relationship between the industrial consumer with the electricity company. As 10 European examples show, between 2000 and 2009, electricity companies and large industrial consumers (chemicals, metallurgy) can make joint ventures to develop large CCGT units with co-generation of heat and electricity.[15] The dominant product for the industrial consumer is the heat for the industrial process. They divide the power between the needs of the industrial partner and sales on the wholesale market. In order to let an important power surplus independent of the constraining process need for steam or heat, the electric power capacity is dimensioned above the industrial partner's need for power, with some flexibility in the production between heat and power. The supplementary power production is owned by the generator partner and can be sold on the market with high margin over cost during periods of high market price. This intertwined production reinforces the common interest of the parties.

The third way for large consumers to proceed is by horizontal arrangements in a consumers' cooperative of production as an alternative to vertical integration in self-production with capital-intensive equipment in hydro plants or nuclear production. The example of the Finnish TVO consortium which ordered a large nuclear plant in 2005 is illustrative of the way to share the risks of a new generator installation in order to control their electricity supply cost. Long before the 1996 market liberalization reform, an electric cooperative in generation owned by several very large consumers (pulp and paper) and local distributor was already established. Its purpose was to construct and operate large generating facilities yielding benefits from electricity sold at the cost-price in the framework of long-term contracts (40 years) signed ex ante and which gives off-take rights to each participant. After the reform, this type of long-term arrangements was reproduced to allow the order for a €3 billion nuclear reactor of 1700 MW in 2005. Large consumers do not want to be affected by the effects of random hydro inflow situation or future CO_2 price, and want to be protected against the market power risk. Fixed-price purchase agreements independent of the NordPool market price and harmonized with the levelized cost of around €30/MWh at low cost of capital of 5 per cent were signed for 'ribbon' deliveries, allowing the generator to obtain corporate financing with a high leverage ratio (75 per cent of debt) and to borrow at low rates (Tarjanne and Rissanen 2000).

Whatever it could be, contractual solutions that are designed to reduce price risk for large consumers help to collateralize and secure investments in generation. But as they represent at most a fifth of consumption in mature economies, they can be only one means of developing generation capacity in liberalized markets. However, these types of vertical arrangements could raise some problems with regard to competition principles which are defined in relation to the premises of the decentralized electricity market model and the issue of imperfect competition.

5 MARKET IMPERFECTIONS VERSUS LONG-TERM EFFICIENCY

This issue of long-term contracts and vertical integration in decentralized markets must be balanced with the issue of investment in generation. Discussion should be raised about the eventual drawbacks of these different arrangements on the effectiveness of competition and market efficiency with increased risk of foreclosure and market power exercise. Competition authorities are indeed sceptical of long-term contracts, extended vertical integration and oligopolistic concentration, for different reasons.[16]

Long-term contracts and vertical integration are seen first to prevent the development of transparent pricing mechanisms. Indeed, they reduce the amount of transactional trade on the organized market, which is supposed to reduce liquidity and increase volatility, itself propitious to exercise market power. Moreover contract flexibility on quantity prevents a bit more the development of the spot market (see Longva, Chapter 7 in this book). Such developments on spot markets would undermine entry and incentivize market players towards vertical integration and long-term contracting in a self-reinforcing effect. Second reason if they include exclusivity clauses, – for instance a buyer cannot resell its contractual electricity – they are seen to deny market access for new entrants (foreclosure).

Vertical integration typically hampers competition by reducing spot trade and limiting entries. For instance, entrants in production have to compete with newly integrated producers, and overcome the latter's competitive advantages, to combine investment in production with the acquisition of a supply business. Therefore, large vertical and horizontal companies, given their market share, have high horizontal concentration in their home market. (See, for instance, the European Commission's sector inquiry report – DG Comp 2007.)

Barriers to entry and risk of market power abuse could balance the social benefits from the greater ability to invest in capital-intensive generation equipments by controlling costs and risks. But this is not a clear conclusion. Long-term contracts redistribute market power. Following Allaz and Villa (2003) general results, theoretical arguments in electricity markets have been developed which tend to show that long-term contracting by dominant producers incentivize them not to exercise their market power on spot markets by capacity-withholding because increases in prices would only be profitable on the uncontracted part of their supplies (Green 2004; Willems and de Corte 2008). Another conclusion is that in the short term, long-term contracts or partial vertical integration tend to prevent double marginalization problems, which results in both higher profits and lower prices, and facilitates entry when sufficiently long (Onofri 2005).

We do not develop further the discussion on these issues. We consider that structured contracts and vertical integration combined with imperfect competition in retail are key for risk-sharing and investment development in generation. This is extensively developed here in different chapters (Meunier Chapter 6 and Hauteclocque and Glachant Chapter 9 in this book). Regulatory approach on contracts must be delimited to certain contracting clauses to stop foreclosing relationships. We must, however, underline that ensuring the stability of this amended electricity market model should force regulators and competition authorities to consolidate market monitoring.

From a competition policy perspective, imperfect competition structures are tolerable as long as there is no monopolization in the American sense, that is, creation and perpetuation of a dominant position by practices which limit competition and deter entries. The stabilization of the market structures must not be based on comforting incumbent positions. This completely justifies the European Commission's 'fight' to limit long-term contracts by historic suppliers (Hauteclocque 2009). But the focus of competition policy would be more appropriately oriented on market concentration than on vertical arrangements. From a 'contestable markets' perspective, the preservation of entry possibilities to maintain a credible threat should be sought to discipline the oligopolistic competition.

6 CONCLUSION

Even though the price-risk and volume risk is considerable in the decentralized market model, this does not, in and of itself, signify market failure. In another words, there is no theoretical reason why risks on the market price should impede investment in generation. And the fact is that there is investment in sufficient capacity when needed, with the exception of the missing money problem, for investment in peaking units. But none of the far-reaching experiments in electricity industry liberalization on the basis of the de-integrated market model proved able to develop capacity along the optimal technology mix. There is specialization of investment in CCGT technology. The problem results from the fact that the risk is not manageable for the investor in other technologies, because it could not be adequately allocated buyers. Moreover apparent consistency between the decentralized market model and project financing arrangements has proved to be ineffective even with the CCGT projects if we observe the number of bankruptcies of pure producers. The benchmark decentralized market model features market failures attributable to the specific volatility of market prices and the impossibility of transferring the various investment risks borne by the generator on to suppliers and consumers in order to allow development of capacity with various technologies. Projects in any technology would be better developed if an allocation of risks on to the consumers could be achieved, which means introducing market imperfections in the decentralized market model. Regulating competition by the quest for the maximum transparent market price for all stages of the electric industry, including the retail market, tend to hamper investments in generation by restricting possibilities of vertical integration and long-term contracting for an efficient allocation of investment risks between consumers and investors.

From the risk management and TCE perspectives we analysed different ways of securing large capital-intensive investment in generation equipment in a context of uncertainty, hold-up risk and transactional complexity. As for vertical arrangements with suppliers, analysis suggests that regulatory adjustments for allowing credible commitments by generators' counterparts may prove theoretically justified, in particular by helping historic suppliers to keep de facto or de jure a large share of core consumers. Alternatively, vertical integration between generation and supply business, as well as combination of generation assets portfolio and consumer's portfolio both present some advantages in terms of risk management and transaction cost minimization in this respect. Finally, combination of large size, vertical integration and horizontal diversification appears to be an economic advantage to manage large-scale investment risks at low capital cost, provided that it would be at the expense of too large a market concentration. This last statement invites us to be careful about barriers to entries and risk of market power abuse which could outweigh the social benefits coming from the larger capacity to invest in capital-intensive generation equipments by controlling costs and risks.

NOTES

1. A first version of this chapter, published in the LARSEN working paper, has benefited from the numerous comments of Yannick Perez, Assistant Professor in Economics, Technical University of Cergy-Pontoise to whom I address all my thanks for his useful initial contribution.
2. For an overview of reforms referring to this benchmark, see Joskow (2008).
3. We note that revenue on ancillary service markets (balancing mechanism, reserve market) complements revenue on the energy market.
4. The transaction cost economics (TCE) perspective (Williamson 1985) is first focused on the difficulties of contracting when the stake is the development of equipment specific to the transactions between investor and buyer and which will offer lower cost production and more benefits to all parties than standard technologies which perform less well for the same production, but are the sole technologies which could be developed in the framework of only spot market exchange. The TCE identifies the conditions determining the choice between different arrangements (spot transactions, contracts, vertical integration) in relation to the characters of the transaction. It takes into consideration the degree of equipment specificity, the frequency of transactions, the transactional complexity (here the complexity of risk management issued from the characteristics of electricity markets) and the environment uncertainty (here the price risk in the input markets, the regulatory environment). In this respect the long-term contract allows to share the risks of an investment in a relation-specific equipment (volumetric and price risks, technology risk), but the TCE introduces the dimension of the counterpart's opportunism which is a risk endogenous to the investor–buyer relationship, the so-called 'hold-up risk'. The TCE considers that, because firms do not behave cooperatively, safeguards are needed in long-term relationships, given this endogenous uncertainty in order to give credibility of the counterpart's long-term commitment. Contractual guarantees should limit opportunistic behaviour of the counterpart, as could be the so-called 'hostages' or common ownership of assets.
5. These risks concern changes of market rules on one side, environmental regulation (SO_2 norms, Carbon regulation) and uncertainty related to equipment siting procedure.
6. A contractual variant is the non-firm contract. It places the plant availability risks on the buyer in exchange for a lower price. It could be interesting for both parties when the equipment technology is mature and the constructor has good records.
7. Simulating situations in which retail companies with existing long-term contracts would incur losses, Green (2004) estimates the effects of such situations on the wholesale markets by combining models of electricity retail competition and of wholesale competition. He shows that retail competition might raise wholesale price by up to 20 per cent.
8. The example of TXU-Europe bankruptcy in 2002 made professionals discover the risk attached to the pure supplier model and the necessity to hedge the supply business by

more flexible contracts with indexed price and physical assets. (Cf. *Power in Europe*, December 2004.) TXU-Europe which had 17.8 per cent of the British market share sold 3.8 GW of its capacity of 6.5 GW that it owned in 2000 and which allowed it to hedge 80 per cent of its sales. This reduced its physical hedging to 20 per cent of its sales. When the wholesale price downturned in the British market in 2002 with the change of market rules to the NETA, TXU-Europe was locked in by long-term contracts negotiated at high prices during the former periods.

9. The 'contracts for difference' are in this category of option contract with symmetrical options 'call' and 'put'. Signing up to such a contract reflects the mutual incentives of producers and buyers for price guarantees. Note for the next developments in this chapter, that such contracts which have been used in the UK up to 2000 have been made possible with historic suppliers by the fact that they benefit from a remaining franchise on which regulated default tariffs could pass through the price cost of their contractual purchases to their captive customers.
10. A variant is the 'spark-spread contract' which enables the producer to hedge differences between fuel and power prices.
11. The experience in California of the long-term contracts which substitute to the power exchange after its crash in 2001 is illustrative of the diffusion of this innovative contracting. In their study of the long-term contracts signed by the California Department of Water Resources (DWR) in 2001 after the crisis, Wiser et al. (2004) find that 41 per cent of the electricity is supplied in 'tolling' agreements most of which give the DWR some flexibility to dispatch the facility. Fifty-nine per cent of the electricity is supplied at fixed prices fixed quantity (that is, non-dispatchable).
12. In 2005, the shares of switching customers were 11 per cent in Finland, 13 per cent in Spain, 25 per cent in Norway, 32 per cent in Sweden, and 45 per cent in Britain for the most important ones (Defeuilley 2009). In the US liberalized markets only the Texas retail market exhibited high switching rates, of 30 per cent.
13. Rothkopf (2007) recommends that auctions must be under the control of the regulator and new capacity should be procured by forbidding any entity with significant ties with the supplier from participating in the auction. It is only if no independent candidate can be selected that these entities could compete.
14. We put aside the issue of long-term contracts in the transition period where a deverticalization is organized by the regulators by blocking the retail price of the suppliers and their consequences on the competition. There is a vast literature about this choice of a stepped liberalization process in the USA, in particular after the Californian crisis and its consequences on bankruptcy for the historic distributor-suppliers which were restricted in their ability to obtain long-term contracts. (For a synthesis, see Michaels 2006.)
15. Partnerships include in some cases a valuing of a secondary fuel, as the blast furnace gas in the Dunkirk project developed by GDF and Arcelor.
16. See, for instance, extended discussion on the European jurisprudence on long-term contracts in electricity and gas industry by Hauteclocque (2009).

REFERENCES

Allaz, B. and J.-L. Vila (2003), 'Cournot competition, forward markets and efficiency', *Journal of Economic Theory*, **59** (1), 1–16.

Arrow, K. and F.H. Hahn (1971), *General Competitive Analysis*, San Francisco, CA: Holden Day.

Bohn, R.E., B.W. Golub, R.D. Tabors and F.C. Schweppe (1984), 'Deregulating the generation of electricity through the creation of spot markets for bulk power', *The Energy Journal*, **5** (2).

Chao, H.P. and H. Huntington (eds) (1998), *Designing Market Electricity Markets*, Boston, MA: Kluwer.
Chao, H.-P., S. Oren and R. Wilson (2008), 'Reevaluation of vertical integration and unbundling in restructured electricity markets', in F.P. Sioshansi (ed.), *Competitive Electricity Markets: Design, Implementation, and Performance*, London: Elsevier.
Cramton, P. and S. Stoft (2005), 'A capacity market that makes sense', *The Electricity Journal*, **18** (7), 43–54.
De Vries, L. (2007), 'Generation adequacy: helping the market do the job', *Utilities Policy*, **15** (1), 20–35.
De Vries, L. and R. Hakvoort (2003), 'The question of generation adequacy in liberalized electricity markets', in *Proceedings, 26th Annual IAEE Conference*, Prague.
De Vries, L. and K. Neuhoff (2004), 'Insufficient incentives for investment in electricity generation', *Utilities Policy*, **4**, 253–68.
Defeuilley, C. (2009), 'Retail competition in electricity markets. Theoretical background, current situation, prospects', *Energy Policy*, **37** (2), 377–86.
Defeuilley, C. and G. Meunier (2006), 'La gestion du risque d'une commodité non stockable: les limites d'une couverture financière', *Economies et Sociétés*, série Economie de l'énergie, 10–11, 1619–40.
DG Comp (2007), *DG Competition Report on Energy Sector Inquiry*, Brussels.
Esty, B. (2004), *Modern Project Finance*, Chichester, UK: John Wiley and Sons.
Esty, B. and M. Kane (2001), *Calpine Corporation: The Evolution from Project Corporate Finance*, Cambridge, MA: Harvard Business School Publishing.
Finon, D. (2006), 'Incentives to invest in liberalised electricity industries in the North and South. Differences in the need for suitable institutional arrangements', *Energy Policy*, **34** (5).
Finon, D. and V. Pignon (2008), 'Electricity and long-term capacity adequacy: the quest for regulatory mechanism compatible with electricity market', *Utilities Policy*, **16** (3), 141–2.
Geman, H. (2005), *Commodities and Commodity Derivatives – Modelling and Pricing For Agricultural, Metals and Energy*. London: John Wiley and Sons.
Green, R. (2004), 'Retail competition and electricity contracts', CMI Working Paper 33, Department of Economics, Cambridge.
Green, R. (2006), 'Investment and generation capacity', in Lévêque, F. (ed.), *Competitive Electricity Markets and Sustainability*, Cheltenham, UK and Northampton, MA, USA: Edward Elgar.
Hart, D. (1995), 'Firms, contracts and financial structures', *Clarendon Lectures on Economics*. Oxford: Oxford University Press.
Hauteclocque, A. de (2009), 'Legal uncertainty and competition policy in deregulated network industries: the case of long-term vertical contracts in the EU electricity markets', *World Competition*, **32** (1), 91–112.
Hunt, S. and G. Shuttleworth (1997), *Competition and Choice in Electricity*, Chichester, UK: John Wiley and Sons.
Hunt, S. (2002), *Making Competition Work in Electricity*, Chichester: John Wiley and Sons.
International Energy Agency (IEA) (2005), *Comparison of Electricity Generation Costs*, Paris: IEA.
International Energy Agency (IEA) (2007), *Tackling Investment Challenges in Power Generation*, Paris: OECD.

Joskow, P. (2007), 'Market electricity markets and investment in new generating capacity', in D. Helm (ed.), *The New Energy Paradigm*, Oxford: Oxford University Press, pp. 76–121.

Joskow, P. (2008), 'Lessons learned from electricity market liberalization', *The Energy Journal*, special issue: The Future of Electricity: Papers in Honor of David Newbery, 9–42.

Joskow, P. and R. Schmalensee (1983), *Markets for Power*, Cambridge, MA: MIT Press.

Joskow, P. and J. Tirole (2007), 'Reliability and competitive electricity markets', *Rand Journal of Economics*, **38** (1), 60–84.

Lacy, B. (2006), 'Nuclear investment: performance and opportunity', World Nuclear Association Annual Symposium, 7–8 September, London.

Littlechild, S. (2006), 'Competition and contracts in the Nordic residential electricity markets', *Utilities Policy*, **14** (3), 135–47.

Littlechild, S. (2002), 'Competition in retail electricity supply', *Journal des Economistes et des Etudes Humaines*, **12** (2/3), 379–402. Available at http://www.bepress.com/jeeh/vol12/iss2/art12 (accessed 17 January 2010).

Michaels, R. (2006), 'Vertical integration and the restructuring of the US electricity industry', Cato Institute Policy Analysis Series, No. 572.

Newbery, D. (2001), 'Issues and options for restructuring the electric supply industry', CMI Working Paper EP 01, Cambridge University.

Newbery, D. (2002), 'Regulatory challenges to European electricity liberalisation', CMI Working Paper EP 12, Cambridge University.

Newbery, D. (2005), 'Electricity liberalization in Britain: the quest for a satisfactory wholesale market design', *The Energy Journal*, special issue.

Onofri, R. (2005) 'Electricity market restructuring and energy contracts: a critical note on the EU Commission's NEA Decision', *European Journal of Law and Economics*, **20**, 71–85.

Oren, S. (2003), 'Ensuring generation adequacy in market electricity markets', working paper, UCEI, Berkeley.

Read, J. (2004), '*Re-verticalizing electricity*', Harvard Electricity Policy Group, working paper, Harvard.

Roques, F., D. Newbery, W. Nuttall, R. Neufville and S. Connors (2006), 'Valuing portfolio diversification for a utility: application to a nuclear power investment when fuel, electricity, and carbon prices are uncertain', *The Energy Journal*, **27** (4), 1–24.

Rothkopf, M.H. (2007), 'Dealing with failed deregulation: what would Price C. Watts do?', *The Electricity Journal*, **20** (7), 10–16.

Shimhauser, P. (2009), 'Resource adequacy, capital adequacy and investment uncertainty in the Australian power market', *The Electricity Journal*, **23** (1), 67–84.

Shimhauser, P. (2010), 'Vertical integration and retail price settings in energy-only markets: navigating the resource adequacy problem', working paper, Griffith University (Australia).

Shioshansi, F.P. (ed.) (2007), *Competitive Electricity Markets*, London: Elsevier.

Tarjanne, R. and Rissanen, S. (2000), 'Nuclear power: Least cost option for baseload electricity in Finland', The Uranium Institute 25th Annual Symposium, 30 August–1 September, London.

Vasquez, C. and I. Perez-Arriaga (2002), 'A market approach to long-term security of supply', *IEEE Transactions on Power Systems*, **17** (2), 349–57.

Willems, B. and E. De Corte, (2008), 'Market power mitigation by regulating contract portfolio risk', *Energy Policy*, **36** (10), 3787–96.
Williamson, O. (1985), *The Economic Institutions of Capitalism. Firms, Markets, Relational Contracting*, New York: Free Press.
Williamson, O. (1996), *The Mechanisms of Governance*, Oxford: Oxford University Press.

APPENDIX: RECORD OF INVESTMENTS IN GENERATION CAPACITY BETWEEN 1997 AND 2007 IN DIFFERENT LIBERALIZED MARKETS

The record of investments in generation capacity between 1997 and 2007 after market liberalization in the USA, Europe and Australia shows that institutional conditions of successful capacity development in baseload and semi-baseload equipment are long-term contracts and vertically integrated companies. We observe three facts in the most liberalized markets in terms of vertical de-integration: the failure of pure producers without long-term contracts, even with CCGT plants; the development of coal plants and nuclear plants by pure producers backed by contracts; and a move to vertical integration partly motivated by a search of hedging.

The US jurisdictions which liberalized their electricity industry along the decentralized model (mainly in the north-east, Texas and California) witnessed a boom of investment in the late 1990s, incited by a series of price spikes and anticipation of new capacity needs. Over 230 GW of new generating capacity was projected, with any coordination mainly in these states (90 per cent) and added between 1997 and 2005, among which were a lot of gas turbines for production during peak and two-thirds were CCGTs supposed to partly substitute for the old conventional gas and coal plants. This massive wave was exclusively made in merchant plants relying on project financing without long-term contracts. The problem is that most CCGT projects went bankrupt after 2001 when gas prices increased and limited their dispatchability, and average wholesale market prices collapsed at the same time.[1] As a consequence, the large pure producers (Dynergy, Mirant, Williams, and so on) were quite jeopardized by successive years of lower revenues and profitability. Today banks only lend money for generation investment in corporate financing, or they lend to vertically integrated incumbents and merchant plants as project finance only if the project is backed by long-term contracts with credible counterparts. These are exclusively the historic suppliers which retain a large segment of core consumers or a regulated business, or municipalities

(Chao et al. 2008; Joskow 2007). As a first example, in California over 90 per cent of the 8 GW of new capacity installed since the 2001 crisis has been financed by long-term, fixed-price and fixed-quantity contracts that a state agency purchases. As a second example, investment financing of the first two new nuclear reactors ordered in the US since 1979 (more precisely in Georgia) is backed by long-term contracts with municipalities.

In the Australian markets regrouped in the national electricity market (NEM) at the wholesale level (Shimshauser 2010), the initial greenfield investments (before 2000) in the NEM (for example, the 840 MW Millmerran coal plant launched in 1999) and privatized generators in Victoria and South Australian regional states were able to obtain project finance on a merchant basis. However, they experienced subsequent financial distress in the years following 2000. By that date, private sector merchant projects (that is, those reliant on spot and short-dated hedge contracts) represented just 9 per cent of investments. A large 73 per cent of all new plants between 1997 and 2007 (around 5000 MW) has either been originated by public power producers or underwritten by regional governments. Investments of 4050 MW, all of which have occurred since 2002, have been originated or underwritten by vertically integrated entities, all of which have investment-grade credit ratings.

In the British market, after the first reform of 1990, there has been a large stream of new investment in generation, despite initial spare capacity, under two types of arrangements: first, investment by the two dominant producers which modernized their portfolio of coal generation assets affected by new environmental regulation (5 GW of CCGTs) were backed by vested contracts with the regional distributors-suppliers; second, investment by new entrants after the signature of bilateral 15-year contracts with distributors-suppliers which retain a regulated captive market segment. Most of the new capacity (around 7.5 GW) was built by these new entrants to generation that were themselves minority subsidiary companies of the former distributors-suppliers. These look to have some hedging against the market power of the two dominant generating companies, diversifying their purchases and to earn some unregulated income[2] (Newbery 2001). After the suppression of retail monopoly in 1998, in confidence with market price prospects, a number of CCGT projects (5.8 GW in total) – among which some 'merchant plants' developed by subsidiary of oil and gas companies were programmed, backed by a long-term contract of 'tolling'[3] – before being suspended by the moratorium encouraged by the regulator to limit overcapacity.[4] Independent generators (Edison Mission, AEP) with no foot in supply and large supplier (such as the TXU-Europe) with no generating equipment to hedge their risks preferred to retire from this market or were eliminated by bankruptcies after the

Table 3A.1 Inventory of projects related to downstream supply business in the European continental market (effective realizations and current projects)

Country	Projects	Investors' relations with supply business
France	CCGT plant of 400 MW	Consortium between pure supplier Poweo and the Austrian Verbund
Germany	CCGT project of 400 MW	Electrabel investment in relation to the sourcing of two important own local distributors (in Saar in particular)
Germany	CCGT project of 800 MW in North Westfalia	Consortium between Norwegian Statkraft and the Dutch Essent which controls a local distributor. Signature of some 15-year PPAs with municipalities
Italy	Two CCGT projects	Partnership Electrabel-ACEA, the Roman distributor
Portugal	Several IPP projects	PPAs signed with the historic supplier EDP
Spain	Several CCGT developed by Gas Natural	Sales of electricity by dual fuels contracts to industry and households
The Netherlands	Sloe CCGT project of 870 MW	Partnership between EDF group and Delta a Dutch energy supplier

Source: 'New power plant tracker', *Power in Europe*, issue 508, 10 September 2007 and issue 534, 10 September 2008.

downturn in the market following the switch from the mandatory Pool to the National Electricity Trading Arrangement (NETA) and the resulting drop in wholesale prices in 2001–02 (Newbery 2005). Since that date, generation projects have been developed by newly integrated companies, and this concerns coal and nuclear projects.

In the other European liberalized markets,[5] investments in production were made mainly in South European countries (Italy, Spain, Portugal) where there was a need of new capacities for baseload and mid-load production in growing demand markets. They have been almost exclusively made by companies which have an important downstream business (ENEL, ACEA, AEM in Italy; Endesa, Iberdrola and Fenosa in Spain), generators which already have developed a supply business (ENIPower, Edison in Italy) and generators linked by long-term power purchase agreements to historical national suppliers (EDP in Portugal). The entries into generation by creating facilities are carried out either on the basis of long-term contracts with a historic supplier or by vertical integration, that is, by

Table 3A.2 Inventory of pure merchants projects in the European continental markets for the period 1998–2009

Country	Project	Companies	Remarks
Germany	CCGT 800 MW in Eisenhutt (Brandenburg)	Soteg (Lux.) and Gazprom	Postponement in 2009
Germany	Concord Power CCGT 800 MW in Lubmin (Mecklenburg)	Saalfel Group	No PPA relation
Italy	Two CCGT projects of 760 MW each (in Rizzinconi and Calenia)	Swiss company EGL	Tolling contract with the parent company No PPA relation
Italy	Two CCGT projects of 770 MW by Sogernia	Verbund in partnership with the Benedetti group	No PPA relation
Italy	CCGT projects of Tirreno Power	Joint company (Electrabel, ACEA, Verbund, and so on)	
Spain	CCGT 1200 MW	AES (71%) and GDF (now GDFSuez) (26%)	Project backed to a tolling contract of 24 years with GDF

Source: 'New power plant tracker', *Power in Europe*, issue 508, 10 September 2007 and issue 534, 10 September 2008.

alliances between suppliers and generators affiliated to foreign utilities. In the Nordic countries which were among the front-runners of the reforms of their industries with a low vertical integration, systems are mature. Very few investments in generation have been made. The EPR nuclear reactor ordered in Finland is the only project for the baseload supplies of power and it is realized and will be operated by a cooperative of large industrial users and municipal suppliers.

In the Netherlands, Germany, France and Belgium, which have mature markets, capacity developments were almost exclusively made from 1997 to 2005 in the development of very large CCGT projects on industrial sites in partnership with large industrial consumer, which let a large surplus of electricity be sold on the market (see below). Since the beginning of the new cycle of investment which began in 2005, most of the projects have been developed by vertical companies or assimilated. Almost all the capacity developments by independent producers are based on vertical arrangements (see Table 3A.1) but there exist some cases of real merchant plants (see Table 3A.2) set in markets where the average annual price (including revenues of opaque ancillary service markets) are high, namely the Italian and Spanish markets. There are also some cases in Germany and the Netherlands, but they have been postponed.

Some coal projects have been proposed and sometimes developed in Germany by the large energy groups E.ON and RWE, and in the Netherlands by vertical companies such as Electrabel which has a large supply business and by Essent. Nuclear projects in France and Italy are the lot of, respectively, EDF and ENEL.

Notes

1. When the gas price rose sharply, load factors of new gas plants were depressed and net cash flows did not allow debt payment. By 2004, 90 GW turned back to lenders, 23 GW had been bought by private investors and 10 GW had been repurchased by regulated utilities.
2. The Enron's 1875-MW CCGT 'Teesside project' which was developed as a merchant plant was the exception.
3. In a tolling contract the power purchaser delivers fuel to the generator and takes delivery of the resulting power produced. It is a way to allocate the fuel price risk to the buyer.
4. But only two of them were effectively realized after 2002 given the trend in Britain has been towards vertical integration
5. Projects and realization of new generation equipments are inventoried by the *Power in Europe* journal in its regular 'New power plant tracker' (*Power in Europe*, issue 508, 10 September 2007; issue 534, September 2008). Private reports such as the annual reports of the CERA-IHS *'European Power Watch'* entail precise information about developments of capacity (technology, size) and prognosis about realization of projects.

4. Comparison of long-term contracts and vertical integration in decentralized electricity markets

Richard Meade and Seini O'Connor

1 INTRODUCTION

A common view is that electricity sectors should be unbundled and opened to competition, and that in such decentralized (liberalized) markets long-term contracts are necessary to constrain generator market power, elicit competitive entry in retailing and support new generation investment and hence supply security (Boom and Buehler 2006; Vázquez et al. 2002). However, increasing levels of generation ownership by electricity retailers or large electricity customers (and vice versa) – that is, of vertical (re)integration – have been observed in several liberalized systems (Anderson et al. 2007; Gans and Wolak 2008; Hogan and Meade 2007; Thomas 2004). This has led to concerns about market performance, with policy-makers concerned that wholesale and retail competition might decrease, and generation investment and supply security may be under threat (European Commission 2007, Michaels 2006).[1]

However, problems have emerged with this 'conventional' view regarding sector unbundling and competition (Chao et al. 2005; Finon and Perez, 2008; Green 2006). In particular, *excessive* competitive entry in retailing may threaten the viability of short- and long-term contracts, and thus threaten – rather than promote – generation investment and supply security. Excessive competition can take the form of 'hit-and-run' retail entry, for example, under which retail entrants with low entry costs predate customers from existing retailers when the incumbents have signed long-term energy supply contracts at fixed prices but then wholesale energy prices fall. This creates critical 'hold-up' risks between retailers and consumers – that is, the risk that customers, facilitated by low switching costs and short contract durations, abandon their contracts with retailers, leaving them with contracts they then cannot honour. In turn this translates into *cascading* hold-up risks for parties having upstream contracts with those retailers, notably generators (and, ultimately, their fuel suppliers and financiers). Ironically, this leads to a conundrum – a liquid contracts market is seen as necessary to elicit retail entry, but risk of too much entry undermines the supply and viability of such contracts.

In this chapter, we examine problems arising in contract markets in electricity systems, identifying possible causes of hold-up as well as other contracting problems that can result in inadequate investment and supply security, and increased threat of market power. Specifically, hold-up risks arise not just from the threat of competitive retail entry, but also due to the competition faced by industrial customers, and other factors such as generator fuel mix and fuel supply security. Additionally, contracting in electricity systems is further complicated by factors such as mismatches in the preferred load profiles of generators and their customers, information asymmetries regarding generator outage rates and fuel security, generator market power, and strategic bargaining (in which more informed parties negotiate better contractual terms than their less informed counterparties). The resulting shortcomings in electricity contract markets suggest they are at best a partial and unsustainable solution to market power, retail competition, investment and supply security issues. Instead we argue they are largely a transitional form of institution, often arising artificially as an imposed element of electricity liberalizations reflecting initial reform priorities and concerns.

We argue that high levels of vertical integration should not be a cause for concern, but rather may represent a more 'natural' structure for the electricity sector. Where contracts have failed to emerge or operate as expected, and political priorities have shifted away from constraining generator market power in favour of ensuring supply security, the relative importance of contracts in the scheme of electricity system governance has diminished in favour of increased vertical integration (with contracting and spot energy markets providing complementary roles). Such vertical integration is, by contrast, argued to be a more self-sustaining institutional arrangement, and one which better addresses issues of wholesale market power, investment and supply security. Its endogenous rise – even in electricity systems with relatively liquid contract markets – further suggests it has a natural role to play in decentralized electricity systems. Arguments are presented that vertical integration may in fact become a necessary form of industry organization once a threshold level of integration has been reached.

We begin in section 2 by discussing the expectations and experience of contracting in decentralized electricity systems, noting rising levels of vertical (re)integration and discussing research on the impact of this trend. Section 3 then sets out our analytical framework, drawing on the transaction cost economics and property rights literatures, and empirical literatures on both contracting and vertical integration. We stress the importance of contracts in addressing hold-up problems, but also the circumstances in which ownership (specifically, vertical integration) is preferable. Section 4 examines in detail the particular problems confronting contracting in electricity systems, and the resulting shortcomings of contracting. Section 5 then sets out the ways in which vertical integration better addresses those problems than does contracting. While vertical integration is argued to be a more natural and self-sustaining principal approach to addressing electricity sector problems – such as risk management, securing investment, addressing generator market power, and supporting retail entry – it is argued that both spot and long-term market contracting remain natural complements to vertical integration. Alternative solutions to the problems of contracting in electricity are also discussed. Finally, section 6 discusses the resulting policy implications. We argue for a variation on proposals that have been made for the retention or reinstatement of retail franchise monopolies as a means to constrain hold-up risks between retailers and consumers, with some intermediate level of competition – between nil and absolute – being optimal. Hence, if policy responses are required to ensure supply security while also eliciting workable but not excessive retail competition, they should include less focus on generator market power, a greater tolerance of vertical integration, and a reduced emphasis on contracting.

2 THE EXPECTATIONS AND EXPERIENCE OF CONTRACTING, AND THE RE-EMERGENCE OF VERTICAL INTEGRATION

In this section we set out the expectations and experience of contracting in a variety of liberalized electricity systems, noting the shortcomings revealed in the 'conventional' liberalization model's assumptions about the role of contracting. We observe the increasing levels of vertical (re)integration emerging in many sectors in response to these shortcomings, and briefly refer to evidence on the implications of this trend for sector performance.

2.1 The Expectations of Contracting

The 'conventional' model of electricity sector liberalization holds that vertical and horizontal integration across all parts of the system is not a necessary form of organization. In particular, while transmission and distribution have 'natural monopoly' features that limit their contestability, it is possible to introduce welfare-enhancing competition across generation and retailing. This requires ensuring that existing and entrant generators and retailers have non-discriminatory access to network assets. Some form of wholesale market is also needed to facilitate transparent and competitive price discovery. Such markets include centralized pools, bilateral trading, energy-only spot markets, and a range of real-time and forward (including day-ahead) energy and capacity markets.

As noted by Chao et al. (2005), and Finon and Perez (2008), proponents of this model made two important assumptions about the efficacy of vertically separating generation from retailing, and of market-based competition: that contracts markets, complemented by spot markets, would naturally develop or could be sustainably imposed to replace the formerly integrated arrangements, and that generators would be able to raise capital to fund new investments without the security of cost recovery (whether via cost of service regulation of private utilities as in the USA, or through consumer franchises or taxpayer guarantees in state-owned systems such as in the UK, Australia and New Zealand).

As to the first assumption, of particular importance is contracting between generators and either large customers or energy retailers that aggregate portfolios of smaller customers. Assuming liquid physical and financial markets for such contracts are developed over a suitable range of contract horizons and contract types, then a number of benefits could be expected to flow:

- Large customers should be able to hedge their electricity price risks through direct purchases of wholesale contracts tailored to match their load profile, and rely on their scale to countervail against any market power held by oligopolistic generators (see discussion in Anderson et al. 2007; Chao et al. 2005; Finon and Perez, 2008). Risk management in turn is important for facilitating financing and investment, which has implications for supply security, and business survival.[2]
- Retailers should be able to reduce their exposure to demand uncertainty by pooling numerous smaller customer loads, and run a portfolio of supply contracts to match the risk characteristics and profile of that pooled load.
- A liquid contracts market, supported by institutional changes to ensure retail customer contestability (for example, switching rules), should enable the competitive entry of retailers, thereby ensuring competitive pressure is placed on retail margins.

- The ability of entrant generation to trade through a spot market or other contracts markets should introduce the prospect of increased competition in wholesale prices.
- Generators making new investments should be able to secure their investment returns by entering into suitable long-term contracts with one or more parties, which should go some way towards satisfying the second of the key assumptions underlying liberalization.

However, experience in many countries has not lived up to these predictions.

2.2 The Experience of Contracting

Most notably, liberalization has not led to as much competition in wholesale and retail markets, as many contractual forms to support long-term investment, or as favourable sector outcomes (in terms of generation adequacy and lower prices) as expected. In contrast, vertical integration has increasingly arisen, where it has been permitted, of its own accord.

2.2.1 Retail entry and generation investment

Despite entry by start-up independent electricity retailers, diversifying gas retailers, and incumbent electricity retailers from other regions, retail entry in unbundled sectors has been lower than expected (Defeuilley 2009). For example, even at their peak in 1999–2001, independent retailers were unable to secure more than a 2 per cent market share in the UK (which, along with Norway and Sweden, was one of the more vibrant retail markets) because they were unable to secure adequate physical and financial contracts to hedge their exposure to wholesale electricity price risks. The remaining independent firms have integrated upstream with generation to survive, with the exception of some horizontally integrated firms – for example, Centrica, the former gas utility, became the only major electricity retailer in the UK without generation interests.

Similarly, generation investment in these sectors has been lower than expected. Although significant investment arose in some markets when generation was first opened to competition (for example, in the USA, Joskow 2006a), investors appear to have become more wary, and long-term contracts did not develop or perform to the satisfaction of project financiers (see, for example, de Luze 2003). In the 1980s independent power producers were able to project finance new generation (typically gas-fired CCGT) using high debt levels on the strength of supply contracts written with utilities that retained some measure of customer franchise. In the 1990s such project financing of merchant generation continued, but without contracting. Instead, new entrants relied on high wholesale prices to finance investments – to the detriment of many when wholesale prices fell and gas prices rose. The resulting bankruptcies and withdrawal of merchant generation in the USA (notably California in 2001) has been reflected in similar experiences in the UK and elsewhere in Europe.

2.2.2 Contract markets

More in line with predictions, contract markets *have* developed to a significant degree in a number of electricity systems (Anderson et al. 2007; Chao et al. 2005; Finon and Perez 2008). Among these are the UK and Australia's east coast national electricity market (NEM). In both cases generation was unbundled or privatized (or both) with long-term vesting contracts in place to smooth the transition to competitive markets, providing both price certainty and constraints on remaining generator market power. The UK also radically restructured the centralized wholesale 'pool' in England and Wales and replaced it with the National Electricity Trading Arrangement (NETA) in 2002, which relies almost exclusively on bilateral contracting with only a limited centralized real-time balancing market. By contrast, contract markets developed organically in Scandinavia's NordPool and in Germany, driven by grid companies and utilities respectively.

Where contract markets have developed, however, they have typically not developed to the extent initially contemplated. Anderson et al. (2007) report that baseload generators in the NEM are 70–80 per cent hedged on average, which compares with 95 per cent in the UK, around 80 per cent in the USA's Pennsylvania–New Jersey–Maryland Interconnection LLC (PJM) and New Zealand's systems, and 73 per cent in New England. Moreover, trading volumes can be substantial – up to four to five times physical demand (HMDSG 2005). But Anderson et al. (2007) report that most NEM contracts are typically for less than four years' duration, mirroring the experience in the USA and New Zealand where contract duration is usually no more than three years (Chao et al. 2005; Hansen 2004). Similarly, low contract durations are reported for the UK, where most trades are for one year only (HMDSG 2005). Moreover, contract volumes can also be small, with trades in New Zealand representing around just 25 per cent of total demand (Electricity Commission 2006).

2.2.3 Varying degrees of vertical separation, and vertical re-integration

Even where contract markets have developed to a significant degree, and more so where they have not, vertical integration has increasingly arisen.

For example, in New Zealand, generation is dominated by five integrated companies ('gentailers'), accounting for around 91 per cent of generation capacity and 97 per cent of total demand (Hogan and Meade 2007). Similarly, in Spain, four integrated firms account for 93 per cent of generation and 97 per cent of retail sales (Kuhn and Machado 2004). And in the PJM system in the USA, the six largest retailers account for roughly 70 per cent of the retail market and 90 per cent of generation capacity (Bushnell et al. 2008).

Although such a high degree of vertical integration has been characteristic of, for example, the PJM and New Zealand markets since restructuring in the 1990s, other markets began with a fully disaggregated sector (post-restructuring) that has subsequently moved towards greater integration. For instance, the UK market had three major generation companies and 22 retailers in 1990, but now features substantial vertical integration. In 2005, six major retailers, collectively owning approximately 50 per cent of the country's generation assets, supplied 99 per cent of electricity customers (International Energy Agency, 2005). Similarly, in Australia, the state of Victoria began with complete separation of generation and retailing in the mid-1990s, but now vertical integration appears to be becoming a 'dominant strategy' not only within that state, but throughout the NEM (Simshauser 2008). As of 2007, four major retail businesses, with a combined 75 per cent of market share, had ownership stakes in approximately 73 per cent of generation assets (NERA 2007).

In both the UK and Australia, mergers and acquisitions between retailers and generators were not explicitly prohibited by new regulations, and have generally been approved by competition authorities (although initially the Loy Yang merger in Australia was opposed on competition grounds – Gans and Wolak 2008). In contrast, in markets such as California, regulation brought in during reforms required complete separation, excluding the possibility of any vertical integration (or long-term contracts).

In New Zealand, vertical integration quickly arose as an unintended consequence of simultaneous reforms in 1999 (Evans and Meade 2005; Hansen 2004). At a time when the existing contracts market was limited due to the nature of contract requirements imposed on the then dominant generator, the government horizontally unbundled that generator, lifted former restrictions on integration between generation and retailing, and required the ownership separation of retailing and distribution. The newly created generators rapidly integrated into retailing. The dominance of this model was cemented in 2001, when a winter supply crisis resulted in soaring wholesale electricity prices, placing the largest non-integrated retailer under such a severe price squeeze that it urgently sold its retail base to generators.

Thus, the endurance of vertical integration, where it has been permitted, suggests it is an *ex ante* efficient institutional form. Furthermore, its re-emergence against a backdrop of imposed vertical separation suggests it can be a natural remedy for poor structural reforms.

2.3 Implications

The incidence of low or decreasing levels of contracting, and high or increasing levels of vertical integration, has led to concerns about market performance. In particular, one fear is that vertical integration enables firms to exercise market power, resulting in higher retail prices (Gans 2007; Micola-Ruperez et al. 2008). Similarly, the European Commission (2007) observed that vertical integration appears to reduce liquidity in European electricity markets, and may constrain entry.

However, empirical investigations of market performance have not borne out these concerns. For example, Bushnell et al. (2008) proposed that foreclosure is seldom a problem in practice due to open access and non-discriminatory pricing requirements for distribution and transmission networks. By running simulations based on the performance in the three largest and oldest US electricity markets – California, PJM and New England – they found that vertical integration resulted in the exercise of less market power and contribute to *lower* retail prices than in an unbundled sector, controlling for horizontal market structure. In contrast, Mansur (2007) found that restructuring in the PJM market *did* lead to an increase in anti-competitive behaviour by vertically integrated firms that were large net-sellers, but that vertical integration overall had a mitigating effect on market power.

Conversely, de-integration (unbundling) may be harmful in sectors with existing vertical integration: if the PJM and New England markets had been forced to fully unbundle (as happened in California) retail prices in those areas would have been significantly higher, as would have production inefficiencies (Bushnell et al. 2008). In a similar vein, Michaels (2006), and Sioshansi and Oren (2007), note that forced divestitures may increase incentives for firms to exercise market power. In a review of empirical studies of gasoline refining and sales, Lafontaine and Slade (2007) find that 'divorcement' can lead to cost and price increases and a reduction in service quality. This does not imply that vertical integration is necessarily better for consumers, though this conclusion is reached by Cooper et al. (2005) in their review of empirical evidence from a range of industries.

Finally, vertical integration may also have a positive impact on investment. As Newbery (2002) explains, competing retailers in a vertically separated market tend to prefer short-term over long-term contracts to mitigate their risk of falling wholesale prices. This increases the wholesale price risks to generators, leading to a decrease in investment. In such a situation, generators will have incentives to vertically integrate with retailers (and horizontally integrate with other generators) in a bid to increase prices to more profitable levels. Thus, vertical integration allows both retailers and generators to manage risks (Chao et al. 2005; Meade 2001), and in doing so also enables increased investment.[3]

Against this background we now turn to the analytical framework used in later sections to assess the relative merits of contracting and vertical integration in liberalized electricity systems.

3 ANALYTICAL FRAMEWORK

In this section we present a framework for reviewing the roles of long-term contracts and vertical integration. We largely draw from the transaction costs theory of governance structure, under which a firm's choice of governance mechanism (such as contracting or vertically integrating) is based on the costs that firm faces in attempting to transact in the market (Coase 1937; Wlliamson 1985). We also discuss the importance of ownership costs (following Hansmann 1996) which interact with transaction costs to influence governance choice. This leads in to our more detailed exploration of electricity contracts and vertical integration in sections 4 and 5.

3.1 A Spectrum of Governance Choices

Sector transactions may be governed under a spectrum of different – explicit or implicit – contracting mechanisms, ranging from markets to firms to bureaucracies (Williamson 1985). Because each mechanism provides a different level of incentives and involves different costs, each will be 'ideal' under a different set of conditions (related to transaction costs, organizational costs, incentives and ownership) and under different sets of institutional endowments and paths of institutional change (Glachant and Perez 2009; Williamson 1999). However, experience and theory suggest that a given sector will seldom favour a single ideal governance mechanism; rather, different sector needs and characteristics give rise to complementary combinations of governance mechanisms. Indeed, in the context of electricity sector reforms, Glachant and Perez (2009) stress that identifying the ideal combination of governance mechanisms is complicated by the sheer difficulty of delineating which activities naturally belong together.

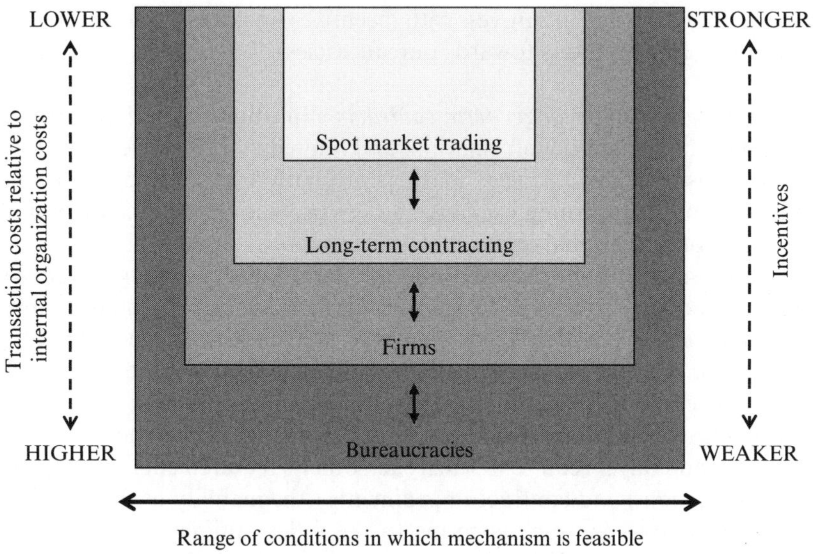

Figure 4.1 Different governance mechanisms are feasible in different ranges of conditions

3.2 Moving Along the Governance Spectrum – From Markets to Bureaucracies

Williamson (1985, p. 87) starts from the premise that 'in the beginning there were markets' and hence that 'Only as market-mediated contracts break down are the transactions in question removed from markets and organized internally'. This suggests a hierarchy among the alternative governance forms (see Figure 4.1), with markets being presumed the most desirable form in situations in which they are feasible, then private internal organization (firms), then bureaucracies (i.e. "political markets").

However, as Figure 4.1 indicates, markets are feasible under a narrower range of conditions than are firms and bureaucracies. As the nature of the transaction changes, so too does the ideal form of governance, leading to a shift 'down' the hierarchy (for example, from spot markets to long-term contracts) or re-balancing of the mix of governance mechanisms used (for example, some spot contracts may remain, but the majority of trading may be through long-term contracts). Which governance mechanism is ideal for a given set of transactions depends on two key factors: (1) the size of transaction costs relative to internal organization costs, and (2) the desirability of strong incentives, with incentives weakening as transactions shift away from markets towards bureaucracies.

From spot markets to longer-term contracts In situations with low transaction costs, symmetric information, and limited market power or risk of opportunistic behaviour, spot markets are both a feasible and desirable mechanism for governing exchange – they provide strong incentives and have low organizational costs.

As transaction costs increase, and the desirability of strong incentives decreases, other forms of governance become more feasible and desirable. This may involve a shift from spot-type contracts to longer-term contracts. For example, Adler et al. (1998) note different contract types (such as fixed-fee or cost-plus) are preferred in different transaction cost conditions. These conditions include contract knowledge ('the contact hours the seller and buyer require to learn each other's requirements to complete the transaction') and contract impediments ('the inability of the buyer to adequately state contractual terms to the seller, ultimately lengthening contract duration, and changing the technical design'). Fixed-price, spot-type contracts are only feasible when contract impediments are low; as it becomes more difficult to state performance requirements in full, longer-term and more incentivized contracts play a greater role.

From contracts to firms As transaction costs increase further, the shift may be from contracts to firms. For example, in repeated market-based transactions either repeated contracting (such as through the repeated use of spot markets) or long-term contracts are required (Coase 1937). Such contracts need to be specific about the rights and obligations of the contracting parties in all relevant states of nature. Achieving such specificity – or contractual completeness – becomes increasingly difficult as asymmetric information, uncertainty, bounded rationality and transaction costs increase. In such situations, internalizing transactions with a firm may be a more desirable form of governance. When contracts are internalized they can be less prescriptive and comprehensive. Furthermore, instead of relying on external contract monitoring and enforcement mechanisms, the firm can devise internal mechanisms and tailor these to the particular nature of the transactions.

Authors such as Williamson (1985) extend Coase's theory further by highlighting the importance of asset specificity in motivating internal organization (through firms or vertical integration) over market-based transacting. When parties to a contract make long-lived relationship-specific investments, they are then exposed to the risk of *ex post* opportunistic behaviour in which either or both of them seek to extract rents from the other by renegotiating or reneging on (that is, 'holding-up') the contract once the relationship-specific investments have been made (that is, sunk). This exposure arises because these investments cannot be costlessly redeployed in the event of hold-up. Such behaviour, if anticipated by the contracting parties, results in less contracting and investment than the parties might otherwise jointly prefer, unless they can otherwise credibly commit to each other not to act opportunistically. Where such commitment mechanisms are too costly to institute, ownership of one party by the other can be a viable alternative – whence the rationale for either backwards or upstream vertical integration (one party owning its supplier) or forwards or downstream integration (one party owning its customers).

From firms to bureaucracies Finally, at the far end of the spectrum from markets, where transaction costs are particularly high, and high-powered incentives would exacerbate problems such as market power, asymmetric information and opportunism, bureaucracy can be the optimal governance form – it provides weaker incentives and, although it has higher internal organization costs, these would be offset by the benefits of avoided transaction costs. Despite often being criticized as an institutional form, Williamson (1999, p. 316) observes that there are transactions and functions – such as sovereign transactions – for which bureaucracies remain efficient under his 'remediableness' criterion (that is, because 'no superior feasible alternative can be described and implemented with expected net gains').

Multiple forms of governance Importantly, firms may not choose a single 'optimal' governance form based on their overall transaction costs, but rather use multiple forms to address different market needs. For example, Wolak (1996) notes that electric utilities in the USA use both spot and long-term contracts, simultaneously, to purchase the same product (coal, although the situation is similar for gas and oil purchases, and also occurs in the water sector with bulk water purchases). Wolak concludes that, although long-term contracts are good for ensuring supply stability for the majority of demand, 'for the most part, plants use spot market transactions to satisfy residual demands due to unforeseen events and are willing to pay even higher prices for and purchase from even more distant suppliers the larger is this residual demand' (p. 164). Thus, spot contracts play an important role in *complementing* long-term contracts; a role that may also be played in relation to vertical integration, which shares many structural similarities with long-term contracts.

Choosing between contracts and ownership/integration The particular governance 'boundary' that we are interested in for this chapter is that between market-based contracting and vertical integration of otherwise contracting partners within a firm. Hansmann (1996) provides a model for considering how market participants decide on which side of the boundary to fall. He acknowledges that long-term contracts have their virtues – in particular, they can be an effective remedy to many of the problems related to reliance on spot transactions. Long-term contracts may be designed to avoid hold-up problems (such as when an investor wants to avoid sinking costs in a long-lived asset only to be held up by its counter-party upon the renewal of a short-term supply contract). Long-term contracts can also be used to allocate specific risks – for example, determining to what extent a supplier is liable for interruptions to supply. Finally, long-term contracts may be used to mitigate adverse selection risks – for example, requiring performance warranties where product or service quality becomes apparent over time.

However, Hansmann (1996) also notes that long-term contracts have costs which, if high enough, will favour vertical integration. He points out that severe problems of contractual imperfection or incompleteness can arise from a combination of asset specificity (that is, physical and human capital with large sunk costs), temporal specificity (that is, the requirement that certain products and services be provided at specific times) and high contracting costs. These combined factors explain, for example, why farmer-ownership of dairy processors (that is, downstream vertical integration) often dominates over investor-owned processors. Milk's perishability exposes farmers to daily hold-up problems, and homogeneity of interest lowers costs of collective decision-making. Similarly, customer-owned rural electricity distribution cooperatives, and upstream generation and transmission cooperatives in the USA – both examples of upstream vertical integration – can be explained in terms of low collective decision-making costs (homogeneity of interests) as well as risk of market power abuse by investor-owned firms, or the absence of such firms where investment is not profitable.

Findings in other sectors confirm this preference for vertical integration when contracting costs are high and contracts are necessarily incomplete. For example, from a review of over 100 empirical studies across a diverse range of sectors, Lafontaine and Slade (2007) find substantial evidence that the following factors significantly increase the presence of backwards vertical integration (that is, influence firms to 'make' rather than to 'buy'):

- greater specificity of physical capital and of human capital;
- more dedicated and more complex assets;

- greater site specificity (in other words, when co-location is more important);
- greater temporal specificity; and
- greater uncertainty about demand.

Similarly, Lajili et al. (2007) conclude from their review of over 50 studies that 'empirical findings generally corroborate the importance of various forms of relationship-specific investments for explaining and predicting vertical integration' (p. 15). In particular, their review confirms the significance of transaction frequency, numbers of trading partners, asset specificity, certainty of asset life span, and demand uncertainty in the decision to vertically integrate. They note that several of these factors are interrelated: for example, higher levels of asset specificity limit the number of trading partners, making it more likely that the firm will be inclined to vertically integrate.

Interestingly, Klein and Murphy (1997) propose that vertical integration is more likely in conditions of uncertainty not because of asset specificity related transaction costs, but because uncertainty makes it more likely that an explicitly specified performance contract 'will move outside the self-enforcing range' (p. 420). Similarly, Arrow (1975) develops a model which supports the endogenous evolution of imperfectly competitive vertical integration, even starting with competitive initial conditions. In his model it is uncertainty in the supply of an upstream good – that is, the risk of a quantity squeeze – that induces downstream firms to integrate upstream.

Ownership costs combine with transaction costs to affect governance choices The relative costs of contracting and market transacting, however, are only part of the story. Hansmann (1996) extends the discussion of transaction costs in vertical integration decisions to also include a discussion of property rights or ownership costs.[4] Under his scheme, ownership optimally falls to the class of firm patrons (that is, suppliers, customers, workers, capital providers) enjoying the lowest *combined* costs of market contracting and ownership (that is, internal organization). For example, if market contracting costs should happen to be highest for a patron class that also has the lowest costs of ownership, then clearly they are the best patrons to own the organization.

Market contracting costs include the costs of hold-up risks, market power, asymmetric information and strategic bargaining (where a better informed party to the contract negotiates better terms at the other's expense), problems in credibly signalling patron preferences and the costs of long-term contracting. To this can be added regulatory risk (Helm

1994; Meade 2005b). Ownership costs, by contrast, include the costs of internal governance mechanisms (that is, the classic agency costs of Jensen and Meckling 1976 and Fama and Jensen 1983), the costs of collective decision-making, and the costs of risk bearing (which relates to patrons' diversification and access to capital).

Under Hansmann's scheme, vertical integration is a mechanism for internalizing a range of risks and costs to the firm. By dispensing with the contracting requirements of market-based transactions there are savings in terms of both direct contracting costs and the costs arising from imperfect contracting. Incentives for opportunism are mitigated (though replaced to some extent by agency costs of internal governance), since the costs of that opportunism are borne within the same organization. Exposure to volatile market prices is removed or reduced, since price changes that disadvantage one part of the firm advantage another part. Information asymmetries give rise to agency costs of internal governance, but once again the costs of asymmetric information and strategic bargaining are internalized to the firm and hence should be lower overall than when they are borne by only one party to a contract. Although opportunities for double marginalization may remain with integration, exercise of market power may now become moot, since monopoly pricing in one part of the firm directly increases costs in another part, leaving total firm profit unchanged (Hogan and Meade 2007). By removing market variables from the firm's objective function (or simply from view), vertical integration also reduces the risk of (and scope for) adverse regulatory interventions such as price regulation. Integration can also remove the need for otherwise beneficial regulation, since the integrated firm potentially internalizes the costs that such regulation would seek to mitigate. It is only when the costs of ownership exceed these combined cost savings that market contracting should remain preferred to vertical integration.

4 CONTRACTS IN DECENTRALIZED ELECTRICITY SYSTEMS

In this section we explain and elaborate on the problems that occur in contracts-based electricity markets, identifying why the 'conventional' view of appropriate sector structure may fail to produce desired sector outcomes in practice.[5] Reasons for this failure include hold-up risks, adverse selection risks due to market power and asymmetric information, contract market illiquidity (due to features inherent in both electricity systems and electricity markets), and mismatches between generators and retailers in terms of preferred load profiles and relative risk aversion.

4.1 The Need for Risk Management in Electricity Markets

Generators face both price and quantity risks in their output and input markets. While risks regarding the price or quantity of capital inputs are amenable to risk management in most developed capital markets (financial crises aside), the same is not always true for other inputs. Supply or price insecurity for gas, such as that in the UK with declining North Sea reserves or other European countries reliant on gas from Russia, create one set of risks. Similar risks arise for hydro generators exposed to variable inflows, storage constraints and possible environmental regulation affecting off-take (as is the case in New Zealand – Evans and Meade 2005). Uncertainty about plant availability creates additional input risk. On the output side generators face highly variable real time demand, as well as daily and seasonal load variations that may not align well with capacity. Real-time demand variability can be especially costly where plant is expensive or slow to 'ramp up', such as for coal generation (Wolak 1996). Moreover, given highly price-inelastic demand in the short term, small changes in plant availability or demand shifts (for example, due to weather changes) can result in highly volatile prices. These features can be exacerbated in systems with transmission constraints and locational pricing (such as PJM and New Zealand), since transmission system operators can 'constrain off' or 'constrain on' generation to maintain system stability, with significant spatial price separation as a result.

Similarly, retailers face price and quantity risks in wholesale and retail markets. They too face input quantity risk, especially where generators are input constrained (for example, in hydro systems such as New Zealand's with limited reserves) or have plant prone to outages (for example, thermal). Such risks also correlate with price risks – often demand is highest in electricity systems precisely when prices are also highest (Chao et al. 2005; Meade 2001), resulting in highly convex costs. Such convexity is shown to be an important rationale for hedging (Mackay and Moeller 2007). On their output side retailers face relatively less price risk, in that smaller customers often tend to prefer fixed price contracts. While this exposes retailers to price squeezes if they do not have hedged supplies, in principle they can reduce this risk with appropriate contracts. Like generators, however, retailers remain exposed to real-time demand variability, and hence can be exposed to uncertain wholesale spot prices if their contract positions are inadequate.

Large customers, by contrast, face price and quantity risk in their output markets that is less correlated with that of retailers. Moreover, except for aluminium smelters, steel mills and other firms for which electricity costs are a significant part of their overall cost structure, large customers are

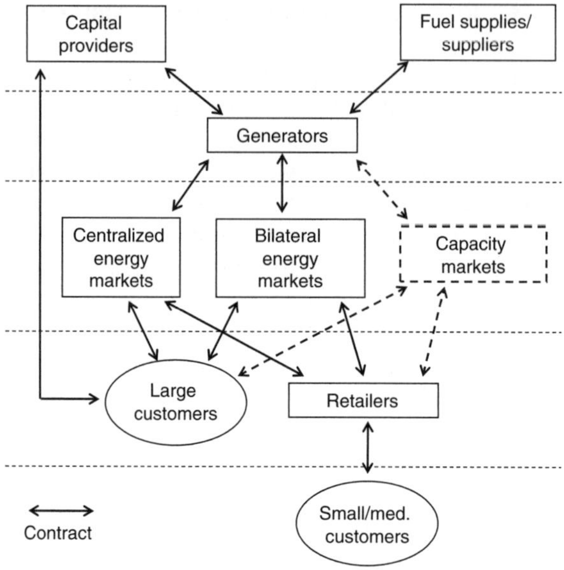

Figure 4.2 Contracting in stylized decentralized electricity systems

not exposed to input price risks to the same degree as retailers (for whom energy costs are by far the biggest cost). They remain exposed to some degree, however, to price and quantity volatility in wholesale electricity markets, which affects their need and preference for hedging arrangements. Even when electricity costs are a small part of their overall costs, a secure electricity supply can be essential for their business viability, and hence hedging quantity risks (that is, securing supply) may matter more to them than hedging price risks.

Contracting can help to manage these risks (see Figure 4.2). In terms of hedging short-term exposure to price or quantity risks, generators and retailers (and to a lesser extent, large customers) are in principle natural counter-parties. By entering into hedge contracts they can lock in some part of their desired demand or assured supply, and at prices that need not be tied to volatile wholesale market prices. Retailers with spiking demand and fixed price customers will not wish to be exposed to spot market prices for top-ups; whereas generators will not wish to over-commit supply and be forced to purchase at spot prices to make up supply shortfalls. Consequently generators cannot afford to be over-contracted, whereas retailers cannot afford to be under-contracted, possibly creating an overlapping set of contracting preferences. Furthermore there is a natural role for generators that have uncorrelated input or output risks to contract among themselves rather than to bear the risk of having to trade in spot markets to make up supply shortfalls when over-committed, or sell surplus when under-committed. In that way they can hedge themselves against unforeseen plant outages, input shortages or input price hikes. This in turn enables them to issue contracts to retailers and generators over a larger share of their capacity without risking an unhedged exposure.

Large customers and retailers also share some ability to use contracting as a device to constrain generator market power. Requiring generators to commit some part of their capacity via fixed price contracts can reduce their incentive to exercise market power (though see Bonacina et al. 2008, for the range of views), which is one reason why generation privatizations have sometimes involved vesting contracts. Contracting can be used by large customers or organized customer groups, however, as a more proactive tool to address market power concerns, sometimes in lieu of explicit regulation.[6]

In terms of supply security it might be thought that generators and retailers (or large customers) will share incentives to contract. Where common security obligations are imposed on all parties this might be so, but common pool resource (that is, non-excludable but rivalrous) attributes of supply security do not ensure this if free-rider problems are severe.[7]

4.2 Factors Undermining the Effectiveness of Contracting

Despite the rationale for contracting set out above, contract markets have failed to develop to the extent expected (see the discussion in section 1). This is largely because several factors undermine the effectiveness of contracting as a risk-management tool, leading to a reduction in the supply of contracts, an increase in wholesale prices and a reduction in investment and supply security. In addition to these factors, as a general principle risk should be attributed to the parties with the best incentives and ability to bear them, further favouring vertical integration over contracting.

4.2.1 Hold-up risks for generators

The generation investments required for supply security are usually large, sunk and long-lived, creating a preference for generators, their funders and possibly fuel suppliers to secure investment returns for commensurately long periods. By contrast, entry costs in retailing (for example, to set up energy contracting, billing systems and call centres) are low, as are the costs of smaller customers changing their supplier. This means that retail firms risk losing market share to new entrants, if they fix their input costs by hedge contracts for any sustained period in which spot or contract prices then fall, inducing entry (particularly by 'hit and run' retailers). The problem is similar for large customers that contract with generators – if they have competitive output markets (meaning output prices are difficult to increase, despite potentially large increases in input prices), these customers may face hold-up risks that in turn induce them to potentially renege on their contracts with generators.

In such circumstances generators may be unwilling to offer as many long-term contracts as they would otherwise prefer, for fear of hold-up. This reduces the level of investment they can secure against supply contracts, and creates the additional risk of reduced supply security. If such hold-up is sufficiently severe then generators too might find themselves financially at risk, and hence possibly renege on their own upstream contracts (for example, with fuel suppliers). This is less an issue for generators that are already integrated upstream with fuel supplies (such as coal-fired or hydro stations), but may give rise to cascading hold-up risks with gas or uranium suppliers that have their own large, long-lived and sunk investments. The result may be suboptimal upstream investments in exploration, extraction or transmission, which would serve to exacerbate the fuel and quantity squeeze risks faced by generators, resulting in reduced investment and supply security, and reduced contracting.

Overall, hold-up risks are most pronounced where the generator has undiversified positions. For example, a generator with geographically dispersed plant and a mixture of fuel types is less exposed to quantity squeezes than a merchant generator with a single plant. Moreover, a generator with a portfolio of supply contracts combining a mixture of loads can smooth out demand volatility that both reduces quantity squeezes and also its exposure to hold-up by any one customer. Facing a smoother load profile means it is also able to write contracts over a greater share of its capacity, all fuel and other supply risks being equal. A merchant generator with a single off-take agreement is clearly in a more vulnerable position.

4.2.2 Hold-up risks for retailers and large customers

Retailers and large customers also face hold-up risks from generators – for example when replacing expiring hedge contracts. Retailers and customers with undiversified positions (for example, a single supply contract) face greater hold-up risks. Retailers with a portfolio of supply contracts for different maturities and/or from different generators diversify their exposure to hold-up by any one generator.

For large industrial customers the hold-up risk posed *by* generators may be greater than that they pose *for* generators, particularly if the customer operates in a competitive output market. This is because any given industrial customer may account for a fraction of a generator's output, whereas any given generator may account for a large share of their supply. However, if a secure electricity supply at a competitive price is important for the ongoing competitiveness of industrial customers (for example, aluminium smelters) then the location of the customer's plant would presumably have been decided on the strength of the long-term electricity supply contracts they could negotiate at the outset, which reduces their exposure to generator hold-up.

For incumbent retailers, other sources of hold-up risk may be significant – including the sector reform (liberalization) process. In particular, reforms may involve an unanticipated shift from regulated and smooth pricing (amenable to political lobbying) to volatile or increased prices set by market processes (less amenable to political control). Indeed, Anderson et al. (2007) report that participants in the NEM regard regulatory risk and ongoing reforms as their single greatest risk. In contrast, entrant generators have the benefit of determining whether reformed market conditions enable economic entry.

4.2.3 Adverse selection risks

Generator market power (which is greater when contract markets are thin – Green, 2006) and information asymmetries can conspire to create adverse selection problems for retailing firms and large customers. As a result, retailers/customers are less willing to lock into long-term contracts, particularly if contract prices are temporarily high (for example, as in the lead-up to peak demand periods in New Zealand when hydro storage is low). Aside from the general difficulty in predicting supply and demand conditions more than a few years out (Anderson et al. 2007) – an example of bounded rationality that hinders effective contracting – these parties can be reluctant to contract with generators whom they believe to possess market power, as well as better knowledge than they about impending outages or fuel insecurity. Where contract prices are perceived to be neither competitive nor reliable then this only increases the risk that they enter into a contract price and then face being outcompeted in fixed-price retail markets by competing retailers (or in product markets by competing industrials) who can secure more favourable prices through either superior information or greater negotiating leverage.

4.2.4 Market illiquidity

The adverse selection problem, leading to generator hold-up risks, is only made worse by the general problem of illiquid forward markets for which standard arbitrage pricing conditions do not hold. Since electricity is not economically storable, contracts for forward delivery of different maturities are effectively contracts for distinct commodities – energy at defined future times. This thins the relevant markets – potentially exacerbating market power issues – and means temporal hedge markets do not satisfy arbitrage relations based on storage costs. Arbitrage is made even more difficult in systems with transmission capacity auctions (such as system residue auctions for interconnector congestion rents in the NEM, interconnector capacity auctions in the EU, or financial transmission rights [FTR] auctions), due to asynchronous energy and transmission auctions (Anderson et al. 2007). Additionally, the delivery of electricity has a spatial dimension in systems with transmission constraints and either zonal or nodal pricing, which further thins the relevant forward markets.

4.2.5 Mismatch of supply and load

Generator supply and retailer/customer demand may be aligned, enabling straightforward contracting (for example, aluminium smelters may contract with baseload generators, or retailers may hedge peak demands by contracting with peak generators). However, any divergence of preferences limits the standardization of hedge contracts and thus reduces the liquidity of hedge markets. For instance, generators exposed to significant input risk will prefer *force majeure* or other availability clauses that do not commit them to supply during outages or fuel shortages. Writing contracts that do not align with their supply profiles leaves generators with uncommitted supply that may be harder to contract; thus, generators will seek a premium to write contracts that badly fit their supply profile. In contrast, retailers or industrial customers will generally prefer contracts that follow their own load profile and demand swings, rather than generator supply availabilities. They will also prefer asymmetric instruments, such as options, which limit both their quantity and price risks.

Both sides to a contract will therefore need to weigh whether their interests are better served by contracting at a price, or to only contract to a more limited extent so that residual contracting options are preserved (especially when demand or supply conditions are particularly volatile). In all cases the market cost of each option must be weighed against its benefits.

4.2.6 Relative risk aversion

Misalignment of contracting preferences is exacerbated by differences in relative risk aversion between the parties. For example, Anderson et al. (2007) report that state-owned generators in the NEM are more risk averse than private generators. This may bias them in favour of greater contracting relative to private generators, but also increases their preference for contracts that do not commit them to supply during outages or fuel shortages. Private generators by contrast may be less inclined to issue contracts (all other things being equal), but be more prepared to offer terms favouring customers who do not wish to bear outage risk. Depending on the fuel type and variety of private and state-owned generators, such differences in risk preferences could create distinct sub-markets for contracts.

Contracting problems become more severe if generators have market power and are also less risk averse than retailers and large customers (because of soft budget constraints for state-owned generators, or because their input and output risks are better offset than those faced by their customers). In this case generators have less incentive to write contracts for two reasons: they do not wish to reduce their ability to increase prices, and they have less need to hedge in the first place. This does not mean that they will offer no contracts, but rather that contract prices will be higher, contract volumes will be lower and contract terms will be less favourable than if generators did not enjoy market power or have relatively low risk aversion.

4.3 Effects of Initial Conditions on Contract Market Evolution

In addition to the factors described above, the success of contracting as a governance device for managing risks in liberalizing electricity systems may also be limited by the initial conditions at the commencement of reforms. Where decentralized systems emerge against a backdrop of significant excess capacity, for example, generators will be more likely to offer contracts for sale and to do so on more favourable terms (for example, with less protective *force majeure* clauses or better demand load matching) than if this were not the case. In the same circumstances, however, retailers or large customers face less imperative to sign such contracts, and indeed may prefer not to do so given that prices will already be relatively low. As demand grows and excess capacity diminishes, the supply of contracts may shrink at the same time that customers increasingly prefer to hedge against future price rises, unless large customers (for example) are prepared to contract forward to secure investments offering them greater security of supply. Such forward contracting is facilitated where those customers enjoy some degree of market power in their output markets, or their competitors are also locked into the contracts (for example, via joint venture).

The extent of pre-existing vertical integration or long-term contracts also plays a role. While vesting contracts are often imposed on dominant generators as a means to constrain their market power as liberalization unfolds, even in horizontally de-integrated systems pre-existing contracts or vertical integration affect the supply of and demand for contracts. Systems with large industrial customers on long-term contracts signed pre-liberalization often inherit those contracts as states seek to mirror their commitments in a way that does not crystallize or reveal liabilities to taxpayers. A consequence of this, however, is that the evolution of contracts markets will necessarily be constrained by the scope and terms of such contracts. Similarly, vertical integration, with large customers or otherwise, will also affect contract market evolution since the supply of and demand for contracts will be lower, and hence contract markets less liquid, if significant vertical integration already exists.

With these particular electricity sector contracting issues in mind, we now turn to how vertical integration might be a preferable form of organization, and discuss other possible solutions to the shortcomings of contracting.

5 VERTICAL INTEGRATION IN DECENTRALIZED SYSTEMS

In this section we argue that vertical integration, compared to contracting alone, is a more natural and self-sustaining approach to risk-management in decentralized electricity systems. As a consequence it offers additional benefits over contracting in areas such as investment and security of supply, but also for retail entry and competition.

Importantly, this does not mean that all forms of contracting should be eschewed: both spot and long-term markets have a role to play in supporting vertical integration. For example, generators with uncertain fuel supplies will be willing to integrate only if they expect their native generation to mostly be sufficient to meet their embedded load. If their generation capacity is insufficient, they must supplement it with purchases from other generators (at least under some fuel supply scenarios), either on spot or longer-term contract markets. Conversely, if generators under-integrate they will seek to offload some of their excess capacity via spot markets or contracts, the returns from which will have different risk characteristics. Hence, even integrated generators will seek to access spot and longer-term contracts markets to some degree.

5.1 Lower Comparative Ownership and Contracting Costs

As outlined in section 3, when the costs of internal organization or ownership are outweighed by the costs of market transactions and of lower investment (resulting from inadequate contracting markets), integration should be preferred over contracting. Importantly, in vertically integrated firms both sets of costs are likely to be lower than for separated firms.

First, vertically integrated firms are likely to have lower costs of internal organization and ownership, including lower agency costs (which arise

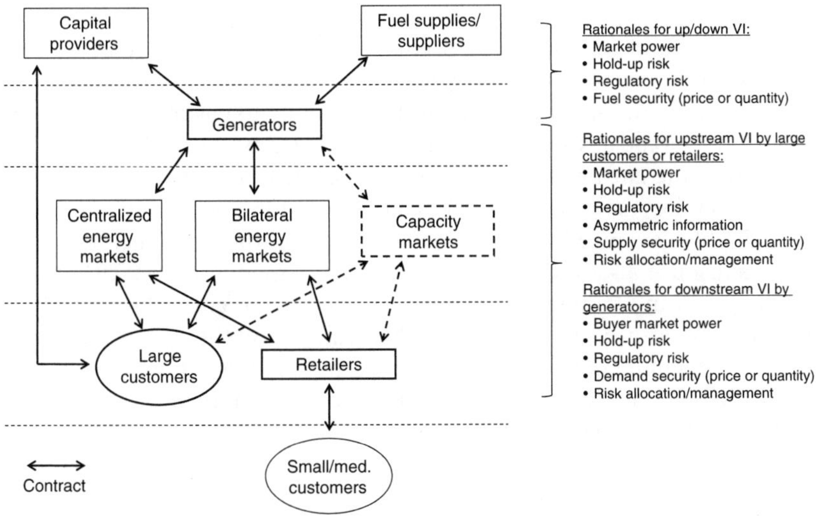

Figure 4.3 Rationales for vertical integration in decentralized electricity systems

when ownership and control are separated), costs of collective decision-making, and costs of risk-bearing. In particular, costs of risk-bearing are lower for vertically integrated firms because of their often greater diversification relative to stand-alone retailers and generators, and their larger scale and balance sheets (particularly relative to retailers), which enables integrated firms to access greater capital.[8]

Secondly, vertically integrated firms face lower costs of market contracting. As summarized in Figure 4.3, the potential to avoid high contracting costs provides the rationale for both upstream and downstream vertical integration. We discuss these avoided costs further below.

5.2 Reduced Hold-up Risk While Sustaining Retail Competition

In addition to its direct cost benefits over contracting, vertical integration has another clear advantage: it fundamentally reduces the risk of hold-up that can plague non-integrated electricity systems reliant on contracting. By thinning contract markets, vertical integration immediately reduces the scope for the type of retail entry that creates hold-up risks: entry by low-cost, undiversified retailers that are highly reliant on liquid contract markets for supply.[9] Even if such retailers did enter a market dominated by vertical integration, they would only be able to access a small amount of contract capacity, placing them at a disadvantage in negotiating with large (integrated) generators. Because of the limited capacity available to purchase and on-sell, the non-integrated retailer will only be able to vie for some portion of the customer base of an integrated generator. Furthermore, an integrated generator needs only to ensure it can recover long-run average costs to ensure its survival against entry. Hence even if it matches the entrant's prices for its at-risk customer classes it may still remain viable, particularly if it relies on more modest debt financing rather than highly leveraged project financing. Moreover, in principle it can cross-subsidize at-risk customer classes using any non-at-risk customers, further ensuring its financial viability in the face of entry. Overall, these imbalances of size, cost-bearing ability and negotiating power work in favour of incumbent generators, ensuring they are less exposed to hold-up and failure should the entrant retailer succeed, and ultimately supporting higher levels of generation investment.

At the same time, thin contract markets encourage a more sustainable type of retail entry: entry by firms that jointly invest in both retailing and generation, or by incumbent generators that expand into retailing. Of these possibilities, downstream integration by generators seems the most probable. Generators have scale and balance sheet advantages that favour their integration into multiple retailers (as opposed to, for example, integration by multiple retailers into generation, which would raise additional internal organization costs). Furthermore, new entrants attempting to jointly invest in both retailing and generation (or retailers attempting to integrate upstream) are likely to face barriers to generation ownership.[10]

Capital market constraints are one possible barrier, particularly where capital market development or depth are insufficient for new firms or existing retailers to raise the large sums required for upstream investments into diversified (rather than single plant) generators.[11] Another important barrier is human capital requirements – running generation plants requires engineering (designing, building and operating) and project management expertise, and fuel supply contracts, commonly possessed by generators but which may be difficult for new firms to obtain. Conversely, it is relatively simple for incumbent generators to procure the non-scarce marketing, billing and other operational resources required for retail entry. Interestingly, these arguments suggest that one common concern about integration – that it raises retail entry barriers by thinning contract markets and therefore requires entrants to also have generation capacity – may be misplaced. The concern is natural if it is presumed that non-integrated 'bottom-up' retail entry supported by contracts is necessary, but the natural ability of integrated generators to incrementally expand generation capacity and then enter into downstream retailing 'top-down' must also be considered.

These entry and risk-management advantages apply not only for generators integrating downstream into retail, but also for those integrating upstream into fuel supply. Such integration reduces the threat of hold-up in, for example, third party gas exploration, since generators have large sunk investments in thermal generation that could be stranded if contracted gas supplies do not materialize. It also reduces the potential hold-up risk faced by an independent gas explorer, particularly given uncertainties regarding future (for example, climate change) policies for thermal generation investments. Furthermore, this form of vertical integration may provide the funding security for such upstream investments. Without embedded customers both generators and fuel suppliers would face downstream hold-up risks that potentially impede such investments.

5.3 Internalization of Contracting Costs

In addition to reducing hold-up risks, vertical integration can internalize a range of price, quantity, and strategic bargaining costs and risks within the firm that otherwise must be managed – less well – through contracting.

With any form of vertical integration (upstream or downstream), wholesale price risks become largely moot: if prices are too high then one part of the firm gains while the other loses (Hogan and Meade 2007). Since contracting is reduced to cover only any remaining uncommitted (or over-committed) capacity (as illustrated in Figure 4.4), wholesale prices play a much reduced role, and hence any volatility in wholesale prices is of less consequence in the firm's objective function.

Indeed, while spot market prices typically allow recovery of only short-run marginal production costs, integrated firms are concerned more with the recovery of long-run average costs. This goes some way towards addressing the 'missing money' problem identified in Joskow (2006a), and therefore supporting investment and supply security.

Thus, generators integrate into retailing not to avoid spiking wholesale prices (which they would otherwise prefer to face in contract markets), but rather to provide a natural hedge against low prices in the context of long-lived investments. The same rationale applies for upstream integration by generators into fuel supplies, which can remove exposure to volatile input prices or quantities. This risk is becoming evident in European gas supplies, given the increasing market power exerted by Russia. Upstream integration enables generators to improve fuel supply security or to better manage price risks, reducing their risk of price or quantity squeezes and therefore supporting their generation investments. While the internal organization costs of upstream investments by generators may be large,

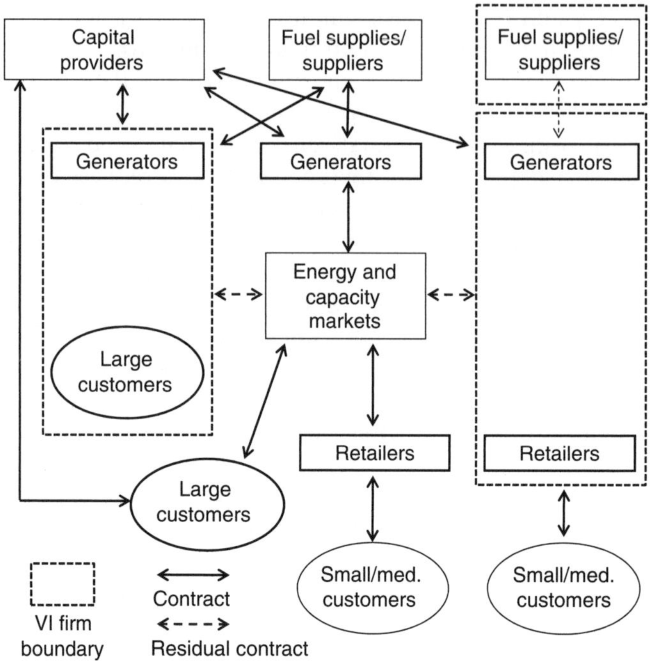

Figure 4.4 Internalizing wholesale prices via vertical integration

hold-up risks in fuel supply mean that contracting may be particularly costly, justifying the costs of integration.

Additionally, while vertical integration thins the markets for contracts, it has the positive externality that it potentially reduces – if not eliminates – the problems of generator market power and strategic bargaining that otherwise would be commonplace in contract markets.[12] Generators face less incentive to exploit any short-term informational or bargaining advantages they may hold when the bulk of their output is already committed to their (downstream) integrated customers. Integration also protects retailers against generator informational advantages regarding capacity availability, and reduces their adverse selection risk otherwise faced in negotiating hedge contracts. By internalizing the costs of retail-level hold-up, retailer investments in peaking capacity are made more viable, which in turn provides credible commitments to funders of and fuel suppliers to such generators.

Looking at market power from another angle, generators may conceivably acquire customers to limit their exposure to *buyer* market power. While this exposure may not naturally arise in respect of retailers, it may do so in respect of industrial customers. In Australia, for example, aluminium smelters can exert buyer power over stranded generation investments by threatening to relocate when renewing long-term contracts.

5.4 Better Matching of Supply and Load

Vertical integration can also provide a long-term match between generator and customer preferences in terms of supply-security and load matching. For any given level of retail entry risk (or output market competition for large customers), diversified and integrated firms are less exposed to the hold-up risk arising with non-integrated customers. For instance, retailers fearful of short-term wholesale price spikes or supply insecurity for which durable contracting arrangements are not available can invest in peaking plant. Large customers with unusual or seasonal load profiles (for example, dairy processors or pulp and paper processors) can invest in co-generation plant with output that correlates with their production patterns and that also affords them greater control over their achieved level of supply security.

The combined effect of marginalizing the integrated firm's exposure to wholesale price risk, and enabling a better matching of capacity and demand characteristics, means that vertical integration more effectively manages wholesale price risks than does contracting. Moreover, it does this on a secure long-term basis, whereas contracting achieves effective risk management – to the extent it does – only for the contract horizon, which in practice is for only a limited period. Beyond that horizon contracting parties are exposed to renegotiation risks not shared by integrated firms. Internalizing the limited wholesale price risks to the firm thus provides a more durable hedge.

5.5 Reduced Regulation Risks

Recognizing that regulation brings both benefits and costs and risks, integration can beneficially reduce the need for and risk of regulatory intervention. Because wholesale prices are internalized to integrated firms, they become a less reliable signal to regulators and policy makers regarding firm conduct and reform success. As noted above, integrated generators with balanced portfolios have less incentive to exercise wholesale market power; and if customers are on fixed price contracts offered by integrated generators then they are insulated from wholesale price movements anyway. Furthermore, the impact of any price regulation that is imposed is weaker (relative to the impact on non-integrated firms), because wholesale prices are relevant to integrated firms only at the margin – so it is only at the margin that any regulatory costs or benefits would accrue. An integrated firm's more important decision variables – such as fuel stocks and average production costs – are not known to regulators, further complicating any attempt to regulate it. As a result, integrated generators are naturally less exposed to regulatory or system operation interventions that serve to depress wholesale electricity prices.[13]

Existing regulations may also affect incentives for incumbent retailers to integrate upstream. The incentive for upstream investment will be affected by regulatory or system operation decisions such as price caps or reserves management which affect wholesale price peaks. Stand-alone peaking investment relies on transitory scarcity rents in wholesale prices, and hence can be made non-viable by constraints on price spikes. Similarly the rationale for and viability of upstream integration by retailers is also reliant on such (avoided) rents. Thus upstream integration by retailers may not be as sustainable as downstream integration by generators.

5.6 Favourability in Systems with Transmission Constraints

The advantage of vertical integration over contracting in terms of reduced hold-up risk can also arise from an unexpected quarter – transmission constraints. In systems such as the UK's where there are relatively few transmission constraints, national energy prices and 'postage stamp' transmission charges are supported. In turn this facilitates retail-only entry – and hence hold-up risk – at a national level. By contrast, in systems with significant transmission constraints and locational energy pricing significant and often unpredictable price separation can arise between pricing nodes. In the absence of tools to mitigate the risks to generators and customers of such price separation – such as financial transmission rights or the NEM's system residual auctions – such price separation can expose either generators or customers to the risk of significant under-hedging via contracts. Accordingly, in such systems vertical integration by generators with plant geographically dispersed above and below, constraints can be a more effective option for managing risks and sustaining investment incentives.

5.7 Possible Threshold Level of Vertical Integration[14]

It is possible that there is a threshold level of vertical integration – specific to the characteristics of each system – above which vertical integration becomes a necessary form of organization. If contracting is not widespread in a non-integrated system, then as higher levels of vertical integration emerge in response to contracting shortcomings, this 'fixes' prices for the integrated firms' share of wholesale market trades. In turn this means that any inherent volatility in generation (that is, in fuel supplies or plant availability) finds its expression in a diminishing pool of wholesale trades at spot prices. As a result those spot prices become more volatile, further increasing the rationale for integration (as a tool for managing price risks, absent effective contract-based solutions).[15] While it can be argued this simply gives rise to a coordination problem that might be resolved in favour of contracting by mandating contracting or prohibiting integration, the arguments in this chapter suggest this tendency towards integration is in fact the efficient solution.[16]

5.8 Solutions to Contracting Problems other than Vertical Integration

With these advantages of vertical integration relative to contracting in mind, we now briefly consider possible non-integration based fixes to the problems of contracting in decentralized electricity systems.

5.8.1 Regulating for contracts

Regulating for contracts is often a principal driver of contracting in decentralized electricity systems. Vesting contracts are commonly employed to limit market power and provide wholesale price certainty in liberalizing systems, particularly while generator market power is seen as an important risk. Virtual power plant agreements are sometimes imposed on dominant generators as a means to reduce their market share while deferring horizontal de-integration or privatization. Similarly, regulations can require non-dominant generators to sell a minimum share of their capacity via contracts. Long-term contracts can be imposed on generators so that liberalizing states can offload legacy long-term supply contracts previously entered into with industrial customers. Also, contracts have been imposed in states where liberalization processes have not performed in a politically sustainable way, giving rise to reactive interventions (for example, California, Ontario – see Chao et al. 2005 and Tetrault 2006, respectively).

The fact that regulation may be required in order to sustain contracts markets begs the question as to the market failure such regulation is intended to remedy (see Willems and De Corte 2008 for one such rationale). This is especially so if vertical integration has been dismantled or prohibited as part of a liberalization process. If either is the case then a potentially endogenous approach to risk management has been artificially precluded, and so the basis for regulating for contracts is potentially faulty. Where vertical integration is permitted, however, but does not arise, a more natural question is why such integration might be impeded, rather than why contracts need to be encouraged. If there should happen to be natural impediments to vertical integration then there is a clearer rationale for contracting, and hence regulating for contracting might have a more sound rationale.

5.8.2 Reducing retail competitiveness

It is curious that hold-up problems have arisen in electricity sectors as a consequence of retail competition, given that competitive entry into retailing has been less than comprehensive (Defeuilley 2009). Indeed, aside from barriers to retail entry such as transmission constraints and vertical integration, there are a range of reasons why customers have proved reluctant to switch to new suppliers. Among these are bounded rationality (for example, customers' inability to understand new retail contracts) and a lack of customer motivation (for example, because power bills are often only a fraction of overall household expenditures, so any switching savings are relatively modest). Retail customers can also be reluctant to switch suppliers if only short-term contracts are on offer in case they face price increases after switching (although Defeuilley, 2009, reports that the gains from switching tend to be sustained, with incumbent prices typically exceeding entrant prices over time). Other explanations include the risk of disconnection from changing suppliers, loss of loyalty benefits or relative unfamiliarity with, and hence possible distrust of, new suppliers. While some 'active' customers are highly price-sensitive and inclined to switch (Amundsen and Bergman 2006), most customers are 'inactive' and remain loyal to their incumbent supplier.

Additionally, states experiencing the highest levels of customer switching are often also those implementing measures favoring entry. For example, Defeuilley (2009) reports that Texas, Victoria and South Australia all implemented price regulations designed to encourage entry, with incumbent Texas suppliers required to offer a regulated 'price to beat' until their franchise market share fell below 40 per cent. Hence, to the extent that retail entry in such jurisdictions has resulted in hold-up problems, this may be a consequence as much of pro-competitive regulation as it is of flaws in contracting or vertical integration.

Such considerations aside, some authors have proposed the retention or reinstatement of retail franchise areas as a solution to hold-up problems created by retail entry (Chao et al. 2005; Newbery 2002, 2005; Roques 2008).[17] Doing so means retailers have locked-in customer bases that are insulated from competitive predation. This in turn reduces their incentive to renege on contractual commitments to generators, and affords them greater protection against predation when entering into longer-term supply contracts. Such reduced hold-up risk induces generators to commit a larger share of their output via contracts, which can also reduce their incentive to exercise wholesale market power, thereby further supporting the use of contracts as a risk management device. Furthermore, reduced hold-up risks and greater use of long-term contracts with retail counterparties that are less likely to face financial distress means generators are better able to manage their investment risks, lowering their cost of capital and increasing their access to investment capital. By locking in customers, retailers should also be able to enter into less diversified contracts with generators whose capacity better matches their load requirements (for example, merchant peaking plant), enabling more tailored contracting.

Such measures may be necessary in electricity systems otherwise lacking natural constraints on retail competition (such as transmission constraints), other causes of customer 'stickiness', or sources of scarcity rents supporting investment (for example, as in hydro-exposed systems). However, they appear to be a blunt instrument to achieve the desired end. For example, similar hold-up risks can also arise in respect of large customers operating in competitive output markets (for example, aluminium smelters), but prescribing entry barriers in such markets would seem an unnecessary and unnatural response to support generation investment. Additionally, the same considerations discussed in relation to regulating for contracting apply, since retaining or reinstating retail franchise areas are examples of such regulation. This approach shifts the problems of risk management into the regulatory domain, which raises its own hold-up risks and hence threats to investment and supply security. If it succeeds, then the risk is that it does so at the undue expense of consumers.

5.8.3 Other demand-side fixes

At least some of the problems presented by contracting can be mitigated by demand-side fixes not requiring constraints on retail competition. In particular, there are long-standing reform areas such as increasing real-time demand-side responsiveness that help to smooth load profiles, reduce demand peaks and uncertainty, mitigate the impacts of generator market power, reduce generation investment needs and enhance supply security.

If retail customer demand can be better managed so as to avoid peak demands, this reduces the need for often idle peaking generation capacity (and, therefore, the possible adverse effects of wholesale price regulation and system operating rules on investment). By inducing greater demand-side responsiveness, such as by affording retail customers with options to profit by voluntarily curtailing load during times of peak demand, the transitory exercise of generator market power during times of tight system conditions results in lower welfare loss (Evans and Meade 2005). Such responsiveness could be achieved either *ex ante* via load-limiting devices (Doorman 2003), or in real time via retail power exchanges.

By reducing the possible welfare losses from generator market power this also reduces the need for regulatory interventions such as wholesale price caps, and hence supports the lower required levels of capacity investment. In unintegrated systems this should also be reflected in lower retail prices, all other things being equal, thus reducing the need for further retail competition (which would worsen any hold-up risks). Hence a suite of such measures should both reduce contracting costs and improve supply security and investment incentives for any given level of retail competition. Where they are combined with vertical integration this should be more so, and they also should ameliorate concerns that vertical integration creates barriers to retail entry.

Given these considerations we conclude that unless the costs of internal organization are severe, some form of vertical integration is likely to more naturally dominate in decentralized electricity systems over contracting as a mechanism to manage wholesale price, market power, information asymmetry and investment risks. This leaves complementary roles for spot market and long-term contracting, and de-emphasizes hold-up risks from retail entry.

6 POLICY IMPLICATIONS

Decentralized electricity systems have been premised on the efficiency and welfare benefits of competition, and have intentionally shifted investment risks from taxpayers and consumers to investors. Where this coincided with excess capacity in generation, this has supported the evolution of contracts markets and retail entry. However, as capacity margins shrink post-liberalization, the shortcomings of reliance on contracting – hold-up risks, risk-management mismatches between generators and customers, and market power, asymmetric information and strategic bargaining risks – have become apparent. These shortcomings hinder new investment and threaten the perpetuation of suboptimal capacity margins. Absent complementary or alternative devices (such as vertical integration, forced contracting or capacity obligations) to compensate for such shortcomings, this threatens supply security and hence the political sustainability of liberalization, and risks the introduction of destabilizing interventions that worsen those shortcomings, or outright re-centralization.

Contract markets have often arisen more by design than evolution, for example reflecting long-term contracts entered into pre-liberalization by states with industrial customers. Often they are imposed to facilitate a transition to generator competition while generator dominance is still a concern. Moreover, vertical de-integration has often been a concomitant of horizontal de-integration, artificially (if unintentionally) limiting the role of vertical integration as a risk management device. These have all served to give contracting a prominence that it may not naturally deserve, and eventually highlighted the difficulties in sustaining contracting. This raises the question of whether contracting is simply a stepping stone to greater use of vertical integration (or other mechanisms not sharing the shortcomings of contracting). Indeed, if contracting is such a stepping stone, then beyond a certain threshold level of vertical integration it is possible that integration will naturally become the dominant mode of organization in any given electricity sector.

As such limitations are revealed the liberalization pendulum appears to be swinging away from pure reliance on contracting in favour of mixed approaches involving either endogenous vertical integration or impositions such as capacity mechanisms. Such a swing coincides with an evolution in the political imperatives surrounding liberalization. While safeguarding consumers against generator market power was commonly a political necessity accompanying decentralization, ensuring supply security – especially in the face of notable reform failures – is increasingly the political priority. Where reformers have retained confidence in decentralized solutions this has involved a tolerance of greater vertical integration. Otherwise it has involved imposed solutions such as capacity obligations, which contain their own inherent shortcomings (Meade 2005b).

Importantly, this evolution requires re-evaluation of the optimal degree of competition in electricity systems, particularly in retailing. This chapter stresses that the pursuit of unfettered retail competition – as well as the elimination of other aspects of electricity systems limiting competition (for example, transmission constraints) – exacerbates hold-up risks, impedes generation investment and threatens supply security. Hence textbook pure competition should not be the policy aim. The reinstatement of retail franchise monopolies is an extreme alternative, however, and may only be justified in the absence of other inherent barriers to retail competition, or by a lack of other system characteristics supporting generation investment. Where such barriers (for example, 'regionalization' due to grid constraints) arise, or system characteristics (such as prolonged rather than only transitory price rises as in hydro-exposed systems) otherwise support investment, less extreme levels of retail market power may be sufficient to resolve investment and supply security issues. This is particularly so where systems involve significant degrees of vertical integration to complement or substitute for contracting, in which the hold-up and other risks inherent in contracting are less prominent. Notably, the trade-offs in electricity systems based around contracting suggest a lower optimum level of retail competition than in those allowing integration.

A key challenge for policy-makers wishing to stop short of outright reinstatement of retail franchises is to identify the degree of retail market power striking the optimal balance between protecting consumers while maintaining efficient investment incentives. Where those incentives are distorted by interventions such as price caps – particularly in vertically integrated systems where such caps are most likely redundant – the removal of such distortions is an obvious starting point. If there is to be a bias in policy-makers' approach, it is likely to best be in favour of supporting investment incentives at the possible risk of short-term retail market power. Policy parameters can then be incrementally refined if it proves that investment incentives are overly generous. The difficulty with the alternative approach is that undue emphasis on controlling retail market power can result in inadequate investment in many systems. The objective should be to encourage desirable long-term decision-making even if this involves short-term biases, since the alternative is to avoid those biases while forestalling or otherwise distorting those long-term decisions. Where other solutions to market power can be implemented without raising retail entry risks – such as measures to improve demand side responsiveness – these are worthy of exploration in their own right. They also de-emphasize the importance of retail market competitiveness, and further complement the benefits of vertical integration over contracting in electricity systems.

Abandoning the relentless pursuit of retail market competition involves breaking from one of the important premises of reform – that retail prices will be necessarily reduced or constrained by greater competition over time. Politicians are required to facilitate or allow the emergence of an acceptable level of retail competition, and trust that the decentralized investment signals this produces are sufficient to elicit acceptable generation capacity and supply security. Alternatively, they can substitute for those signals by imposing investment requirements through capacity obligations or otherwise, and in doing so possibly create the need for greater interventions should the signals prove inadequate, particularly given the greater regulatory risks they create. The merit of greater use of vertical integration instead of contracting is that it better insulates electricity systems from their inherent imperfections, as well as from imposed imperfections (for example, price caps) introduced to address the inherent ones.

Contracting, just like spot markets, continues to play an important role even in vertically integrated systems. Uncertainties in both supply and demand mean integrated generators cannot continuously maintain perfect balance between capacity and embedded load, and hence can integrate only to some degree. Relying simply on spot trading to compensate for any real-time imbalances exposes integrated generators to more short-term price volatility than is likely to best enable risk-management over their long-lived generation portfolio. Combining such spot trading with a portfolio of longer-term contracts enables better management of investment and risks for that part of the generator's portfolio that cannot be perfectly balanced through integration. Integration is naturally the dominant risk-management approach where the costs of contracting are large, or simply greater than the costs of internal organization. Just as competition through market mechanisms is expected to enable lowest-cost generation to displace higher-cost generation, policy-makers should anticipate that market mechanisms will also enable the efficient mix of contracting and integration to emerge where each is permitted.

There is currently a lack of formal theoretical work identifying the optimal degree of retail competition supporting efficient investment levels and endogenously determined optimal supply security. This chapter presents a natural framework for modelling the optimal use of contracting and integration as a question of mechanism design, given different degrees of retail competition. Such formal modelling presents rich possibilities for future work.

NOTES

1. In this chapter we set aside questions of whether 'natural monopoly' network activities such as high voltage transmission or low voltage distribution should or should not be integrated with potentially competitive activities such as generation and energy retailing. We assume throughout that network activities are not combined with generation or retailing, but see Littlechild (2008) and Meade (2005b) for discussions of examples where they might be efficiently combined.
2. Risk management by electricity operators is also important at a political level, in terms of supply security and price stability, since failures to achieve any of these increases the risk of large customer or voter backlash.
3. Though in deciding whether or not to increase investment, generators will be mindful of its impact on their ability to exercise market power.
4. Hart (1995) and Whinston (2003) go further, suggesting that a property rights model may be a better explanatory approach than transaction costs. The property rights model argues that asset ownership changes investment incentives because the property rights confer the right to make decisions on asset use if contingencies arise that were not provided for in a contract, and the likely outcomes of *ex post* bargaining will affect *ex ante* investment. Despite the potential for property rights theory as an explanatory tool, Lafontaine and Slade (2007) observe that there has been little testing of property rights theories of integration. From what testing has been, they conclude that property rights theory appears best able to predict manufacturer–retailer or franchisor–franchisee relationships, whereas it has less support from studies of supplier–manufacturer relationships (which strongly support a transaction costs theory of integration).
5. A more in-depth discussion of these issues can be found in Meade and O'Connor (2009).
6. See Glachant et al. (2008) for a discussion of the German electricity sector model, and Littlechild (2008).
7. See Meade (2005a) for a discussion.

8. These arguments are explored further in section 5.2.
9. This type of entry has other disadvantages, in addition to increasing hold-up risk – for example, Joskow and Tirole (2006) show that 'too much' retail competition (among non-integrated firms) may lead to inefficiencies such as overinvestment in smart metering.
10. Though this is perhaps less so if the entrant is an incumbent generator of another country.
11. In New Zealand, an additional barrier is state ownership of most of the competing generators (Evans and Meade, 2005). Even if retailers had the capital to acquire generation, they would be reliant on contracting or generator break-up to offload any surplus capacity acquired, but more importantly the bulk of that generation has simply not been for sale due to political opposition to privatization. In contrast, retail companies were available for purchase as a consequence of legislation unbundling distribution and retailing, meaning generators were able to buy into such retailers.
12. The benefits of integration for wholesale prices are tied to the degree of balance between generation and retailing activities, not the degree of generator market power per se (Hogan and Meade 2007).
13. On the other hand it should be acknowledged that the greater opacity and irrelevance of wholesale prices under vertical integration may induce regulators to pay greater attention to retail prices. Any attempts to regulate such prices, however, would have to be tailored to the inherent volatility in wholesale prices and fuel supplies, and to institutional arrangements for firms to either manage wholesale price volatility (in contract-based systems) or the margin between retail prices and generation costs (in integrated systems). Any failure to do so could result in a California-like crisis and widespread firm failures.
14. We thank Seamus Hogan of the University of Canterbury for suggesting this line of argument.
15. This argument is analogous to the idea in finance that increased financial leverage increases the riskiness of returns to shareholders for any given underlying level of business risk.
16. Gaudet and Van Long (1995) similarly identify a coordination problem affecting firms' integration decisions. Using a theoretical model in a more abstract setting (including the absence of price risk) they predict that the number of firms is a key determinant of integration. If there is an equal number of upstream and downstream firms, then under their model integration is a dominant strategy in industries comprising less than a threshold number of firms, but is merely one possible equilibrium configuration beyond that level.
17. In a related vein, Joskow (2006b) questions whether attempting to extend competition to retail or small commercial customers justifies the costs (see Littlechild 2006 for a contrary view). Instead he favours local distribution companies acting as energy buyers on behalf of such smaller consumers.

REFERENCES

Adler, T., R. Scherer, S. Barton and R. Katerberg (1998), 'An empirical test of transaction cost theory: validating contract typology', *Journal of Applied Management Studies*, **7**, 185–200.

Amundsen, E. and L. Bergman (2006), 'Why has the Nordic electricity market worked so well?', *Utilities Policy*, **14**, 148–57.

Anderson, E., X. Hu, and D. Winchester (2007), 'Forward contracts in electricity markets: the Australian experience', *Energy Policy*, **35** (5), 3089–103.

Arrow, K. (1975), 'Vertical integration and communication', *The Bell Journal of Economics*, **6** (1), 173–83.

Bonancina, M., A. Creti and F. Manca (2008), 'Imperfectly competitive contract markets for electricity', Istituto di Economia e Politica dell'Energia e dell'Ambiente (IEFE) Working Paper no. 8.

Boom, A. and S. Buehler (2006), 'Restructuring electricity markets when demand is uncertain: effects on capacity investments, prices and welfare', discussion paper, Centre for Industrial Economics.

Bushnell, J. (2007), 'Oligopoly equilibria in electricity contract markets', *Journal of Regulatory Economics*, **32**, 225–45.

Bushnell, J., E. Mansur and C. Saravia (2008), 'Vertical arrangements, market structure, and competition: an analysis of restructured U.S. electricity markets', *American Economic Review*, **98**, 237–66.

Chao, H., S. Oren and R. Wilson (2005), 'Restructured electricity markets: reevaluation of vertical integration and unbundling', EPRI Technical Paper.

Coase, R. (1937), 'The nature of the firm', *Economica*, **4**, 386–405.

Cooper, J., L. Froeb, D. O'Brien and M. Vita (2005), 'Vertical antitrust policy as a problem of inference', *International Journal of Industrial Organization*, **23**, 639–64.

De Luze, G. (2003), 'Investment in power generation: a banker's perspective', IEA/NEA Workshop on Power Generation Investment in Liberalised Electricity Markets, Paris.

Defeuilley, C. (2009), 'Retail competition in electricity markets', *Energy Policy*, **37**, 377–86.

Doorman G. (2003), 'Capacity subscription and security of supply in deregulated electricity markets', SINTEF Energy Research Paper prepared for Research Symposium: European Electricity Markets, The Hague.

Electricity Commission (2006), 'Hedge market development – issues and options', Hedge Market Development Overview Paper, 18 July.

European Commission (2007), 'Inquiry pursuant to Article 17 of Regulation (EC) No 1/2003 into the European gas and electricity sectors – Final Report', COM(2006) 851 final.

Evans, L. and R. Meade (2005), *Alternating Currents or Counter-Revolution? Contemporary Electricity Reform in New Zealand*, Wellington: Victoria University Press.

Fama, E. and M. Jensen (1983), 'Agency problems and residual claims', *Journal of Law and Economics*, **26**, 327–50.

Finon, D. and Y. Perez (2008), 'Investment risk allocation in restructured electricity markets: the need of vertical arrangements', LARSEN Working Paper 17.

Gans, J. (2007), 'Vertical contracting when competition for orders precedes procurement', *Journal of Industrial Economics*, **55**, 325–46.

Gans, J. and F. Wolak (2008), 'A comparison of ex ante versus ex post vertical market supply: evidence from the electricity supply industry', working paper draft, 8 October.

Gaudet, G. and N. Van Long (1995), *Vertical Integration, Foreclosure and Profits in the Presence of Double Marginalisation*, CIRANO Scientific Series, 95s–40, September.

Glachant, J. and Y. Perez (2009), 'The achievement of electricity competitive reforms: a governance structure problem?' in C. Menard and M. Ghertman (eds), *Regulation, Deregulation, Reregulation: Institutional Perspectives*, Cheltenham UK and Northampton, MA, USA: Edward Elgar, pp. 196–215.

Glachant, J., U. Dubois and Y. Perez (2008), 'Deregulating with no regulator:

Is the German electricity transmission regime institutionally correct?', *Energy Policy*, **36**, 1600–1610.
Green, R. (2006), 'Market power mitigation in the UK power market', *Utilities Policy*, **14**, 76–89.
Hansen, C. (2004), 'Improving hedge market arrangements in New Zealand', paper for the 6th Annual National Power New Zealand Conference.
Hansmann, H. (1996), *The Ownership of Enterprise*, Cambridge, MA: Harvard University Press.
Hart, O. (1995), *Firms, Contracts and Financial Structure*. Clarendon Lectures in Economics. Oxford and New York: Oxford University Press, Clarendon Press.
Hedge Market Development Steering Group (HMDSG) (2005), 'International electricity market survey', report for New Zealand Electricity Commission, 19 July.
Helm, D. (1994), 'British utility regulation: theory, practice and reform', *Oxford Review of Economic Policy*, **10**, 17–39.
Hogan, S. and R. Meade (2007), 'Vertical integration and market power in electricity markets', New Zealand Institution for the Study of Competition and Regulation (ISCR) working paper.
International Energy Agency (IEA) (2005), *Australia 2005 Review*, Paris: International Energy Agency.
Jensen, M. and W. Meckling (1976), 'Theory of the firm: managerial behavior, agency costs and ownership structure', *Journal of Financial Economics*, **3** (4), 305–60.
Joskow, P. (2006a), 'Markets for power in the United States: an interim assessment', AEI-Brookings Joint Center Working Paper No. 05-20.
Joskow, P. (2006b), 'Introduction to electricity sector liberalization: lessons learned from cross-country studies', in F. Sioshansi and W. Pfaffenberger (eds), *Electricity Market Reforms: An Institutional Perspective*, London and Amsterdam: Elsevier, pp. 1–32.
Joskow, P. and J. Tirole (2006), 'Retail electricity competition', *The RAND Journal of Economics*, **37**, 799–815.
Klein, B. and K.M. Murphy (1997), 'Vertical integration as a self-enforcing contractual arrangement', *American Economic Review*, **87** (2), 415–20.
Kuhn, K. and M. Machado (2004), 'Bilateral market power and vertical integration in the Spanish electricity spot market', CEPR Discussion Paper No. 4590.
Lafontaine, F. and M. Slade (2007), 'Vertical integration and firm boundaries: the evidence', *Journal of Economic Literature*, **45**, 629–85.
Lajili, K., M. Madunic and J. Mahoney (2007), 'Testing organizational economics theories of vertical integration', *Research Methodology in Strategy and Management*, **4**, 343–68.
Littlechild, S. (2006), 'Foreword: the market versus regulation', in F. Sioshansi and W. Pfaffenberger (eds), *Electricity Market Reform: An Institutional Perspective*, London and Amsterdam: Elsevier, pp. xvii–xxix.
Littlechild, S. (2008), 'Some alternative approaches to utility regulation', *Economic Affairs*, **28** (3), 32–7.
Mackay, P. and S. Moeller (2007), 'The value of corporate risk management', *Journal of Finance*, **6**, 1379–419.
Mansur, E. (2007), 'Upstream competition and vertical integration in electricity markets', *Journal of Law and Economics*, **50**, 125–56.
Meade, R. (2001), 'Options, hedges and gamma in the electricity business', *Competition and Regulation Times*, **6**, 11–12.
Meade, R. (2005a), 'Electricity investment and security of supply in liberalised

electricity systems', in W. Mielczarski (ed.), *Development of Electricity Markets*, Series: The European Power Supply Industry, Elecktroenergetyki Politechniki Lodzkiej.
Meade, R. (2005b), 'Ownership vs. regulation in electricity reform: the role of governance', New Zealand Institute for the Study of Competition and Regulation (ISCR) working paper.
Meade, R. and S. O'Connor (2009), 'Comparison of long-term contracts and vertical integration in decentralised electricity markets', EUI Working Paper, RSCAS 2009/16.
Michaels, R. (2006), *Vertical Integration and the Restructuring of the US Electricity Industry*, CATO Institute Policy Analysis Series, no. 572.
Micola, A., A. Banal-Estanol and D. Bunn (2008), 'Incentives and coordination in vertically related energy markets', *Journal of Economic Behavior & Organization*, **67**, 381–93.
National Economic Research Associates (NERA) (2007), 'The wholesale electricity market in Australia', report to the Australian Energy Market Commission.
Newbery, D. (2002), 'Mitigating market power in electricity networks', paper prepared for the conference 'Towards a European Market of Electricity', SSPA Italian Advanced School of Public Administration.
Newbery, D. (2005), 'Refining market design', paper presented at the 'Implementing the Internal Market of Electricity: Proposals and Time-Tables' conference, 9 September, Brussels.
Roques, F. (2008), 'Market design for generation adequacy: healing causes rather than symptoms', *Utilities Policy*, **16**, 171–83.
Simshauser, P. (2008), 'The dynamic efficiency gains from introducing capacity payments in the NEM Gross Pool', *Australian Economic Review*, **41**, 349–70.
Sioshansi, R. and S. Oren (2007), 'How good are supply function equilibrium models: an empirical analysis of the ERCOT balancing market', *Journal of Regulatory Economics*, **31**, 1–35.
Tetrault, M. (2006), 'Restructuring Canadian electricity markets', available at: http://library.findlaw.com/2006/Jan/1/245132.html (accessed 26 February 2010).
Thomas, S. (2004), 'Evaluating the British model of electricity deregulation', *Annals of Public and Cooperative Economics*, **75**, 367–98.
Vázquez, C., M. Rivier and I. Pérez-Arriaga (2002), 'A market approach to long-term security of supply', *IEEE Transactions on Power Systems*, **17**, 349–57.
Whinston, M.D. (2003), 'On the transaction cost determinants of vertical integration', *Journal of Law, Economics, and Organization*, **19** (1), 1–23.
Willems, B. and E. De Corte (2008), 'Market power mitigation by regulating contract portfolio risk', *Energy Policy*, **36**, 3787–96.
Williamson, O. (1985), *The Economic Institutions of Capitalism: Firms, Market, Relational Contracting*, New York: Free Press.
Williamson, O. (1999), 'Public and private bureaucracies: a transaction cost economics perspective', *Journal of Law, Economics, and Organization*, **15** (1), 306–42.
Wolak, F. (1996), 'Why do firms simultaneously purchase in spot and contract markets? Evidence from the United States steam coal market', *Contributions to Economic Analysis*, **234**, 109–68.

5. Vertical relations and energy networks: selected issues

Gert Brunekreeft[1]

1 INTRODUCTION

The focus of this volume is on vertical relations and contracts between commercial, potentially competitive, stages in the value chain such as generation and retail in electricity markets or commodity contracts in gas markets. This contribution takes a small side-step and focuses on the vertical relation between the commercial stages and the (monopoly) network. The European Union (EU) third energy package is in the process of being implemented (see EU 2009a, 2009b) and should be finalized by 1 March 2011. While the main aim of ownership unbundling was not politically feasible, it is possible that this issue may be further addressed in a future fourth energy package. The main focus of this contribution will be on the effects of ownership unbundling on infrastructure investment and usage. Above all, this concerns interconnector capacity.

In 2007, the EU Commission presented the so-called sector inquiry,[2] in which it assessed the developments of competition and liberalization of the European energy markets. The developments were deemed to be disappointing. The developments in electricity markets were slow but nevertheless encouraging, while in the gas markets the developments were simply too slow. This raises two questions which are addressed in this contribution. First, how much can (network) unbundling contribute to an improvement of lagging competition? Second, the situation raises the obvious question: why is there a difference between the two markets? Several explanations may contribute to the second issue. First, the liberalization of gas markets started later (1998) than in electricity markets (1996). Second, whereas the structure and thereby the stakeholders' interests are more or less comparable throughout the European electricity markets, the interests of the gas markets are diverse, which make political consensus more difficult. Third, at least in terms of Europe, much of the gas is imported from Russia, with Gazprom being the primary supplier. This implies that even if the European gas market were fully competitive the market would still face uncompetitive supply at its border. Furthermore, faced with Gazprom as an economically dominant supplier,[3] the EU Commission seems to have a preference for large, non-fragmented buyers on the European side, reflecting the argument of countervailing power (cf. Galbraith 1952, 1954). In both cases, the argument can be made that the EU Commission has less incentive to press on the gas market than on the electricity market.[4] Fourth, and this is the main argument driving this contribution, in contrast to the electricity network access to the gas network relies strongly on (long-term) transportation contracts. This reliance is a problem for developing gas markets. This contribution argues that the gas markets may be subject to *multiple equilibria*, meaning that there might be a low-liquidity equilibrium, where spot markets have difficulty to develop, and a high-liquidity equilibrium, where long-term contracts go along with liquid spot or capacity markets. The problem with multiple equilibria is that self-enforcing effects make it difficult for liquid markets to develop gradually and naturally. Instead, active policy measures may be required and transition costs and jumps should be expected.

In section 2 we first characterize the unbundling debate and discuss a selection of arguments and issues in this debate. Section 3 then focuses on the issues around interconnector capacity in electricity markets. The argument here is that vertically integrated firms would have insufficient incentives to expand congested interconnector capacity in order to protect the home market. We discuss this argument of 'strategic investment withholding' in more detail. Section 4 discusses the role of infrastructure transportation contracts in gas markets. As mentioned above, this seems to be a critical difference between gas and electricity and can, at least theoretically, be argued to cause multiple equilibria. Section 5 summarizes and gives concluding remarks.

2 VERTICAL RELATIONS, UNBUNDLING AND INVESTMENT

This section first very briefly characterizes the debate on network unbundling in energy markets, while focusing on the effects on infrastructure investment.

The current state of European legislation is that the third legislative energy package was approved and is now in the process of being implemented. The package followed a sector inquiry and was accompanied by an impact assessment (EU 2007). The package contains a gas and an electricity directive and three regulations. In terms of unbundling the gas and electricity directives are very similar. In both cases, article 9 of the directive states that a transmission system operator (TSO) should be established. This implies ownership unbundling, unless a member state decided otherwise (article 9.8), in which case an independent system operator (ISO) should be installed, or (a strong form of) legal unbundling following a set of rules set out in the directives is to be implemented (the so-called independent transmission operator –ITO – approach). Given the options, this basically implies that if member states wish, nothing much will change. It is thus unlikely that this political compromise is an institutional equilibrium and thus further developments can be expected.

Changes can already be observed. Major political opposition against mandatory ownership unbundling came from Germany. Enforced ownership unbundling would have involved enforced divestiture of private assets which it was feared would violate the constitution, as it might be determined to be an expropriation of private assets (cf. Ehlers 2010). Furthermore, sector watchdogs, like the regulator (BNetzA), the competition commission (Bundeskartellamt) and the monopoly commission (which is a high-level advisory board to the government) all claim that the rules and regulations are actually adequate (if imperfect) and ownership unbundling would not greatly improve competition. Nevertheless, of the four electricity transmission networks two have meanwhile been sold 'voluntarily'. First, Transpower, which was the Eon transmission network, was sold to the Dutch TSO, TenneT; together with a plan to sell 5 GW generation capacity, this divestiture was offered by Eon in exchange for the dropping of a cartel investigation by the European Commission. Second, 50Hertz Transmission, which is the Vattenfall transmission network, was sold to Belgium-based Elia and a group of investors. The sale seems to be genuinely voluntary. The status of the two remaining integrated TSOs is currently uncertain, but further changes are likely.

Below, we discuss arguments in the unbundling discussion related to investment. This does not aim to be comprehensive, nor does it intend to come to an overall assessment of ownership unbundling.

2.1 Competition

An often mentioned an important positive effect of unbundling is the reduction of cross-subsidies. The cross-subsidies argument is that (under imperfect regulation), an integrated firm has an incentive to shift costs administratively from the competitive business to the regulated network. In doing so, the firm can inflate the regulatory cost base of the network and thereby try to raise the level of allowed network charges. Vertical ownership unbundling would remove this incentive and thereby improve the level playing field on the competitive market and decrease network charges to the benefit of the consumer. The line of argument is strong, but contains three critical points. First, it relies on some medium level of regulatory imperfection, such that the regulator cannot perfectly observe the cost shift. Second, the effectiveness of cross-subsidies depends on the type of regulation. In a system with benchmarking-based, price-cap regulation, inflating the cost base only means that the efficiency catch-up factor (the 'X' factor in RPI-X) will be higher. Third, cross-subsidizing is actually difficult to do in practice. The case of distribution network operators in the Netherlands illustrates this point. After repeated informal complaints the competition agency in the Netherlands, Nederlandse Mededingings Autoriteit (NMa), started an inquiry into cross-subsidies in the Dutch electricity sector (NMa 2007). At the time of the inquiry the distribution network operators were subject to legal and administrative unbundling following the rules of the EU directives of 2003. Somewhat surprisingly, following in-depth inquiries at the four distribution network operators, the NMa concluded that there was no convincing case of cross-subsidies. The NMa examined four questions:

- Does the vertically integrated firm have an adequate system for internal transfer pricing?
- Is it certain that the holding does not and cannot influence internal negotiations?
- Are internal transfers controlled by a certified accountant?
- Are the internal transfer prices uniform and the same for all internal departments?

Since the answer to all four questions was affirmative, the NMa concluded that cross-subsidizing did not take place. Assuming that the incentives were present, apparently thus the rules and regulations under administrative legal unbundling were sufficiently strong to control these incentives. Yet, NMa remarks that apart from cross-subsidies there might be other forms of discrimination against third parties, but these were not part of the inquiry.

2.2 Synergies

One of the more prominent issues concerns the cost of unbundling. Here we discuss briefly the loss of synergies (also known as vertical economies of scope). Sometimes the debate over the loss of synergies and economies of scope is merely stated without specifying what exactly they are, let alone trying to quantify these. To delve into this issue this section studies the case of the Netherlands, where we distinguish between one-off cost of reorganization and permanent (or, recurring) loss of synergies. The cost items specified in the case of the Netherlands carry over to other countries as well, but utmost care should be taken while translating the numbers, which are specific for the Dutch case.

The unbundling of distribution network owners (DNO) was heavily debated in the Netherlands around 2005. We should note that ownership unbundling of the distribution networks is rather exceptional and we only know of New Zealand as another example. The arguments for ownership unbundling of the distribution networks include:

- the improved competition of retail and generation activities;
- improved network connection conditions (which gets an additional dimension with the developments towards distributed generation);
- improved efficiency due to more focused management; and
- improved regulation due to higher transparency.

The main driver, however, is a bit special for the debate in the Netherlands. The owners of the distributors, being local and regional governmental bodies, wanted to sell the distributors. The central government in The Hague, however, follows a policy to retain critical networks in state ownership. The compromise approach is to sell the commercial parts to the market but to retain the networks in state hands, which inevitably leads to ownership unbundling.

On the downside of DNO ownership unbundling, we find in particular the loss of vertical economies of scope. The debate in the Netherlands provides useful insights. To prepare for the discussion, the Ministry of Economics commissioned Deloitte (2005) to make an in-depth management study of the costs of DNO unbundling (cf. De Nooij and Baarsma 2007). Deloitte distinguishes between a high-cost and low-cost case. We note that even the conservative low-cost case gives a prohibitively high cost of unbundling. We stress though that this study is for DNO unbundling and not TSO unbundling. We will discuss the study by Deloitte (2005) in some detail. Importantly, Deloitte basically takes two steps: first, the step from no unbundling (or weak unbundling) to administrative unbundling ('fat DNO') and, secondly, the step from a fat DNO to full ownership unbundling. The key conclusion is that the first step causes very substantial costs, while the costs of the last step are relatively small. We think that this generally holds true and carries over to other countries as well.

Deloitte makes a lower and a higher estimate and distinguished for each estimate the one-off costs of reorganization and the structural or permanent costs. We discuss the low-cost case here. The first thing to note is that the permanent costs are up to €350 million *each* year. In contrast, the one-off costs are only €70 million, which is not very high, especially considering that it is a one-time occurrence. Secondly, we note that the vast majority of the costs are incurred by the step to the fat DNO (that is, far-reaching legal and administrative unbundling, but one step short of ownership unbundling), whereas the last step towards full ownership unbundling causes only modest additional cost. Deloitte notes that for the last step basically only the cost of relocation would be added, since we would expect different firms to be located in different locations. All else would already be required and therefore the cost would already be incurred by the fat DNO. Upon reflection, Deloitte misses the point of negative effects of poor coordination of investment decisions. If generation and network investments are not properly coordinated the overall system costs will not be optimized. For distribution networks this aspects gains importance with the wave of distributed generation. The decisive difference here is the step to ownership unbundling, as coordination is still allowed under administrative unbundling. Deloitte's method studies firm-internal costs and therefore does not pick up this argument.

For the one-off costs, the Deloitte study suggests that the information and communication technology (ICT) and personnel costs are especially important. However, more relevant by far are the permanent cost of restructuring, as these are genuine losses of synergy and reflect duplicating tasks. Deloitte distinguishes five broad functional groups. Within these five groups, Deloitte identifies several major candidates for synergies for a total of 26 cost items. The most important cost items showing significant synergies are:

- ICT products and services in the group ICT;
- customer-care and billing in the group support;
- reporting and analysis in the group finance;
- strategy in the group management; and
- facilities in the group support.

Notwithstanding the advantages of promoting a level playing field and thus competition, the Deloitte study suggests that unbundling may come at a cost. Although the literature is ambiguous, there is empirical support for the claim that economies of scope may be lost with vertical separation (cf. the survey by Meyer 2010).

2.3 Coordination of Investment Decisions

A problem with vertical separation which received only scant attention concerns the coordination of decisions.[5] Where decisions used to be coordinated internally by the firm the separation prohibits this and coordination now must be determined by the market, either by (long-term) contracts or by price signals. The decisive difference between firm-internal and firm-external is that the incentives between parties may not be aligned.

2.3.1 Governance and moral hazard in teams

Separation of two interrelated steps in the production chain may create governance problems. Joskow and Tirole (2005) formalize the notion of 'moral hazard in teams', concentrating on the separation of system operators (SO, or ISO) from the transmission owner (TO). Assume that securing a certain reliability standard requires both good system operation and maintenance of the assets. If the accountability of a system breakdown is not perfectly clear, the parties will have an incentive to reduce their efforts (*moral hazard*): the asset owner will have an incentive to reduce maintenance and the system operator will have an incentive to reduce its efforts towards a good system operation. The key point in these cases is that the accountability problem is unambiguous for integrated firms: the integrated firm would be responsible and the accountability problem would have to be resolved within the firm, which is an internal governance problem.

2.3.2 Coordination and investments

Any required network upgrade critically depends on generation expansion, which creates a coordination problem. To illustrate this problem, we follow Baldick and Kahn (1993). Consider Figure 5.1. K and H are generation nodes and V is a load node. The line between K and V already exists, but should possibly be upgraded, whereas the other lines still need to be constructed. If the generation capacity of K or H or both is expanded, the network needs to be upgraded. Baldick and Kahn distinguish two options. First, the 'radial connections', which is a direct connection between generator and load (K–V and H–V), and second, 'network connection', which implies building the line H–K, such that the connection between H and V is in fact the combination H–K–V. Network expansion takes a longer route (than H–V) but can be cheaper, for instance, due to economies of scale in the K–V expansion, as Baldick and Kahn (1993, p. 374) assume.

Baldick and Kahn illustrate how the optimal transmission investment depends on how the generation capacity expansion is divided over the two generators (at K and H). Radial expansion tends to be optimal if either of the generators takes over most of the additional generator capacity. If, on the other hand, the additional capacity were divided more or less evenly over the two generators, network expansion would be optimal. The coordination problem arises when a new investment at H occurs while it is

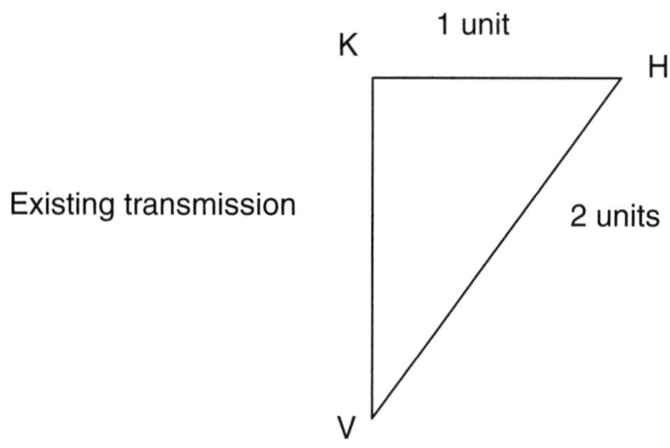

Source: Baldick and Kahn (1993, p. 373).

Figure 5.1 Coordination problem in network upgrading

unknown what will happen at K. The rather important implication is that the lack of information about investment plans of third party investors complicates network planning and possibly leads to inefficiencies.

One is tempted to argue that the coordination problem is a 'mere' informational problem, which can be solved by simply asking the generators. Two problems arise. First, as argued in Brunekreeft and McDaniel (2007), in a liberalized world, information about investment plans is increasingly seen as commercially sensitive information and seems to be withheld as long as reasonably possible. Therefore, the network operator gets the information rather late. Second, the investors may have an incentive to lie about their investment plans. Using a formal framework relying on the cheap-talk incentive-compatibility criterion of 'self-signalling',[6] Brunekreeft and Friedrichsen (2010) find that although in many cases information exchange could effectively achieve investment coordination (that is, the information is credible), a positive external effect of network size benefits the generators asymmetrically and creates situations where cheap talk is not incentive compatible. Unfortunately, the result of this situation is that cheap talk becomes ineffective. In other words, simple exchange of information alone cannot resolve the investment coordination problem.

The coordination of investment decisions is a non-trivial problem, which finds inspiration in practice. In Germany, for example (but quite similar trends take place in other countries), a relatively large part of new generation capacity is planned in the north of the country for two reasons. First, offshore wind capacity must necessarily be built in the north.

Second, private investors plan coal plants along the coast partly to save on the cost of transporting the coal. Since most of the load is the mid-west or south, the power must be transported through the transmission network, which does not have adequate capacity and should be reinforced. The point made here is not that the transmission network should be expanded, nor that the coal plants are built in the north, but rather that the effects of the location decisions on the network are not internalized by the generator investors. The decisions are neither firm-internally coordinated, nor is there a locational pricing system to reflect these effects. The implication of the coordination is not to return to the old, fully closed vertically integrated industry but, rather, to find adequate market mechanisms (for example, locational network pricing) to handle the coordination.

2.4 Strategic Investment Withholding

An important aim of the vertical unbundling of the transmission networks is the improvement of the incentives to expand (cross-border) interconnector capacity (cf. especially EU 2007). This in turn is comprised of three goals. First, more interconnector capacity should improve competition because it relieves cross-border congestion and thereby expands access to other markets. Second, more interconnector capacity should improve supply security, or more precisely, increase network reliability. Higher network capacity will usually mean a lower probability of a network overload. Third, more cross-border interconnector capacity improves the European internal energy market.

The underlying rationale for the interconnector effect is the incentive for a vertically integrated utility (VIU) to show what we call, 'strategic investment withholding'. The argument is straightforward. Assume areas A and B. Assume that A is a high price area and B a low price area and assume furthermore that there is a network constraint from B to A. Assume further a local vertically integrated utility with (local) monopoly power in A. Building a larger line to B increases import capacity into A and would allow third parties from B to supply demand in A, and would thus intensify competition for the local supplier in A. Therefore, in order to protect its position in generation, the integrated TSO in A will have insufficient incentives to expand the interconnector capacity. Therefore we call this 'strategic investment withholding'. In contrast, an unbundled TSO does not have an incentive to protect a local generation monopoly (as it does not gain directly from generation profits) and will therefore have stronger incentives to invest in interconnector capacity.

The argument is convincing, but it has its limits. First, vertically integrated utilities may be long or short in generation as compared to their retail activities. If own production is short compared to retail, then on aggregate the firm may have an interest to increase interconnector capacity to broaden the options to purchase power. Second, integrated utilities with excess capacity and low variable costs will want to export their power and therefore need interconnector capacity. Third, even if the strategic investment withholding argument may hold in principle, in practice there are of course other investment limitations. In particular, permission to build new lines is a legal hurdle; the procedures are long and public opposition is strong. Fourth, interconnector capacity can lead to more imports or to more exports; if the interconnector capacity is used predominantly for more exports, we find that competition actually decreases locally. Globally, competition is likely to increase, but in an area considered in isolation competition may actually decrease, which would thus give a stronger rather than a weaker incentive to build the interconnector. We consider this argument in more depth in section 5.

The argument of strategic investment withholding would at first seem to apply to the electricity market; for the gas industry the predominant problem seems to be that although there may be adequate network capacity it is not made adequately available. As we will discuss in more detail in section 4, among other reasons, one reason may be 'strategic capacity withholding'. It would be in the interest of vertically integrated gas suppliers to hoard capacity rights, in other words, to not release transportation contracts. In the electricity industry transport contracts hardly play a role (with the exceptions of some congested interconnectors and merchant lines), whereas they are vital in the gas industry. Therefore, to allow contracts for capacity, it seems that network unbundling might adequately address the issue of strategic capacity withholding. To facilitate a level playing field, transportation capacity release programmes seem to be necessary. Exactly this method is suggested by the US experience with the gas market, in which the unbundling of pipelines was introduced in 1992 with Federal Energy Regulatory Commission (FERC) Order 636 and at the same time the use and hoarding of transportation contracts was restricted.

2.5 ISOs, the Investment Issue and Tendered Transmission Investment

As an alternative model to the full ownership unbundling of the transmission system operator we find the approach of the independent system operator, where the transmission network ownership remains in the hands of the formerly vertically integrated utility, while the system operation is split off and transferred into an independent entity (the ISO).[7] The primary argument for an ISO approach as compared to ownership unbundling is that it does not involve the expropriation of private ownership.

Yet, a major flaw of the approach is that it does not adequately address the 'strategic investment withholding' argument. As explained in section 2.4, this argument basically states that the vertically integrated firm will have inadequate incentives to expand transmission capacity because hesitating to do so would hold off competition from other areas. However, under an ISO, an integrated network investor would still take the effects of the generator's profitability into account. The so-called 'deep-ISO' repairs this problem by shifting the network investment decision-making competence to the ISO, which can subsequently order the responsible TO to invest. As a result the deep-ISO model creates an uncomfortable governance split between decision-maker and risk-bearer.

Stronger involvement of decentralized network investment decisions by third parties could address the resulting governance problem (cf. Balmert and Brunekreeft 2010). One option is *tendered transmission investment*. The ISO would identify investment projects and then organize a tender for the construction and operation of the project. The eligible transmission owner could, but would not need to participate. This addresses both the problem of strategic investment withholding and the problem of the investment governance split between decision-maker and risk-bearer.

Tendered transmission investment still is a centralized model as the ISO makes the investment decision. The scope for genuinely decentralized decisions in the electricity network business is limited, and useful applications seem to be restricted to peripheral investments. The scope for decentralized investment decisions is larger in the gas industry. In fact, in the gas industry we observe that independent third parties build pipelines parallel to the incumbents' ('pipe-to-pipe' competition) and we sometimes find multiple ownership of a single pipeline ('pipe-in-pipe' competition). This is not to say that the gas pipelines industry would be competitive, but it does mean that there is room for third-party participation. The pressure alone can trigger a race for investment: if an incumbent strategically withholds investment, he may be too late.

3 INTERCONNECTOR INVESTMENT IN ELECTRICITY MARKETS

Brunekreeft (2008) presents a social cost–benefit analysis (SCBA) of ownership unbundling of the electricity transmission system operators in Germany. Within a set of effects that are examined, one is the effect of interconnector expansion on social welfare where the effects are channelled through the effects on competition on the one hand and investment costs on the other hand. Brunekreeft (2008) and Özdemir et al. (2009)

examine the effects of additional interconnector capacity for the case of Germany with the help of a zonal differentiated electricity market model. These approaches reach similar conclusions. This section will briefly summarize the findings. We should remark that the need for and consequences of additional interconnector capacity depends critically on the actual situation; therefore care should be taken in transferring these insights to other markets.

The crucial step in the SCBA in Brunekreeft (2008) is to define the competitive concept. The study relies on the so-called Residual Supply Index (RSI), linked to a variation of the Lerner Index (LI), which serves as a measure for the price-cost mark-up. This results in the RSI–LI equation which is the core of the analysis. Parameter values are taken from London Economics (2007). The key notion of this concept is to relate competitive conduct to the relation between available generation capacity and market demand. If generation capacity relative to demand is abundant, then competition is strong. If generation capacity relative to demand is scarce, we find that competitive intensity gets weaker and prices start to go up. Therefore, any changes of available generation capacity will affect competitiveness of the market. In industrial economics terms, the conjectures on competitive behaviour change endogenously with scarcity. Since additional interconnector capacity affects available capacity, it also affects market competitiveness. The analysis then makes assumptions on the effects of unbundling, which affect the parameters of the RSI–LI equation and thereby provide an idea of the magnitude of the competition effect. Notably, the magnitude of the competition effect depends on the current situation of both available capacity and current competition. Contrasted to the cost of achieving these effects (in particular additional investment cost) it then gives an overall idea of the balance of cost and benefits. Overall, the SCBA in Brunekreeft (2008) suggests that the weighted net effect on social welfare of TSO ownership unbundling in Germany is likely to be positive, but small. In a way this is unsurprising as the analysis explicitly focuses on the marginal step from administrative unbundling to ownership unbundling; this step is small, and therefore it is no surprise that any quantitative effects are small.

Özdemir et al. (2009) examine the effects of additional interconnector capacity for the case of Germany with the help of a locationally differentiated electricity market model.[8] Following the logic of the RSI approach, it clearly matters whether additional interconnector capacity is used for imports or exports. If additional interconnector capacity leads to more imports, then available generation capacity increases (*ceteris paribus*) and thus competition improves. In contrast, if additional interconnector capacity implies more exports, in effect, available generation capacity decreases (or analytically equivalent, demand goes up) and thus competition on the exporting market weakens. If we take into account both sides of the line, overall we expect an improvement of global competition. What the above argument means is that the incentives to invest in additional transmission capacity depend, among other things, on whether the firm will use it for imports or exports.

Running the calculations for Germany, we find that the net effect depends on whether Germany will run into a situation where generation capacity is scarce or abundant (cf. Özdemir et al. 2009). If generation capacity is scarce, wholesale prices in Germany are likely to be relatively high, and therefore more interconnector capacity would lead to increased imports, which in turn would increase competitiveness of the market. The reverse argument also holds. If available generation capacity turns out to be adequate, low prices on the German market would imply that Germany would increase its exports, meaning that additional interconnector capacity would decrease the competitiveness of the German market. The uncertain future of the nuclear phase-out will determine the outcome. The current state of this debate is that the planned nuclear phase-out (of approximately 20 GW) will be abandoned.

4 PIPELINES AND TRANSPORTATION CONTRACTS IN GAS MARKETS

Whereas competition and dynamics in electricity markets seems to steadily develop, developments in gas markets are slow. A prominent difference between electricity and gas markets is the extensive use of contracts for the use of transport capacity in the gas markets.[9] This is not (or less) so in electricity markets. It can be argued that the use of transportation contracts causes a situation of 'multiple equilibria'. We examine the developments in Germany in more detail and compare these developments with those in the USA to come to this conjecture.

The first steps of reform in the German gas market were the first EU gas directive of 1998 and the subsequent opening of the market. A major step was taken with the further development of the Energy Act in 2005 which established regulated third-party access and authorized the newly founded regulator Bundesnetzagentur (BNetzA) to enforce the Energy Act and set up a system for network access and network regulation. Since then several milestones in market design were achieved.

First, network access has been settled on an entry–exit approach per market area. The market area is defined (cf. BNetzA 2008, p. 134) as a collection of networks within which the transport capacity can be used flexibly, meaning that there is no congestion within the market areas by mechanisms and thus path-specific contracts are not required. Instead, network congestion is resolved at the entry and exit points and thus at the borders of the market areas. For the entry and exit points the network users do need transportation contracts. As one transaction requires one entry contract and one exit contract, the mechanism is also called the two-contract model. The entry and exit points demarcate the borders of the market area. The identified congestion should be permanent in order to justify a market-area border. The number of market areas has decreased rapidly; since October 2009 there are just six market areas. The 'two contract' model applies only within one market area. A transaction which includes two market areas actually requires four transportation contracts and requires dealing in two different balancing zones. This proves to be cumbersome. Experiences so far suggest that inter-market area trade does not develop easily (BNetzA 2008, p. 136; Monopolkommission 2009, p. 87).

Second, the structure of the German market is strongly vertically interrelated. The degree of vertical integration between importers, producers and shippers on the one hand and transport network owners on the other hand is relatively high. The pipeline owners tend to be importers and shippers as well. Furthermore, as is often the case elsewhere, the vertical relations are firmly embedded in a web of long-term commodity contracts, many of which are take-or-pay contracts. The details of these contracts are commercially sensitive and therefore only limited information is available, but a data-set presented by Neumann and von Hirschhausen (2006) suggests a European average of about 20 years and a maximum duration of 40 years.

Whereas long-term contracts may have good justification as risk-sharing devices, at the same time they set a high hurdle in a developing market. We stress 'developing' market as long-term contracts do not pose a problem in a 'developed' market with adequate competition and a large number of players. Customers cannot switch (or more accurately they do not have an incentive to switch) and therefore it is difficult for third parties to enter the market and for competition to develop. There is a more subtle self-enforcing mechanism. For a competitive market sufficiently liquid markets (both for commodity and transportation) are crucial. If much of the trading is by long-term contracts, spot markets do not develop and as a result traders will be forced to use long-term contracts, which implies that the process is self-enforcing.

In 2006, the competition agency (Bundeskartellamt) addressed the issue and ruled that existing long-term contracts were anticompetitive and put restrictions on contract durations in place. Contract durations may now not be longer than two years where a customer (these are usually the distributors) purchases more than 80 per cent from one supplier and no longer than four years if it buys more than 50 per cent from one supplier.

There are several market places in the German gas market. Trading takes place at two hubs (NetConnect and Gaspool) and the EEX in Leipzig. Until recently, liquidity was still considered to be too low (cf. Monopolkommission 2009, p. 82 ff.), but recently liquidity is developing quite well. Furthermore, there are two secondary capacity markets. Trac-x exists for transportation capacity and store-x exists for storage capacity. Especially in the trac-x the trading and liquidity is very low (Monopolkommission 2009, p. 141), which conforms to poor experiences in other European countries.

4.1 Access to Transportation Capacity

Access to transportation capacity and, more specifically, to the entry points is difficult. It is common to distinguish between physical congestion and contractual congestion (cf. for example, ERGEG 2007; EU 2009c). Physical congestion reflects that there is no more capacity, while contractual congestion means that there are no transportation contracts available. If there is no physical capacity, then obviously we would also expect contractual congestion. However, we do observe contractual congestion without physical congestion. Following the detailed reports of the European Regulators' Group for Electricity and Gas (ERGEG) (2007), the BNetzA (2008), the Monopolkommission (2009) and the EC (2009c), we note that the relevant problem is contractual congestion, whereas the problem of physical congestion is low or at least unclear. While making the caveat that the exact numbers change rapidly, numbers provided by the BNetzA (2008, p. 145) suggest that availability of free capacity within Germany is only 7 per cent, while at the borders about 90–97 per cent of capacity is booked as long-term transportation contracts of one year or longer. At the same time, the actual capacity usage factors are about 35 per cent within the system and 65 per cent at cross-border locations (BNetzA 2008, p. 146). This 'capacity-usage gap' cannot be interpreted unambiguously; due to fluctuating load, capacity usage cannot actually be 100 per cent. What can be concluded though is that it is hard to obtain transportation contracts. The Monopolkommission (2009, p. 144) suspects that there might be at least some 'strategic capacity withholding'. Finally, the limited transparency on congestion and capacity availability is sometimes criticized (for example, Monopolkommission 2009, p. 89).

Looking at the total picture the following pattern emerges. The vertically integrated structure means there are inadequate incentives (1) to invest in transportation capacity, (2) to make existing capacity available, and (3) to reveal sufficient and transparent information on transportation capacity. The second point seems to be the key problem and is a crucial difference compared with an electricity market. Transportation contracts do not play a decisive role in an electricity market, whereas they are required in the gas market. Even the authorities do not accurately know whether there actually is sufficient physical pipeline capacity, but they do know that there is strong contractual congestion. This may be market power on the side of the vertically integrated firms or it may be a genuine problem within the market.

First, theoretically, vertically integrated firms have incentives to withhold transportation capacity to foreclose the market to potential competition. There is no easier way to hold off competition than to deny access to the network. This may thus well be part of an explanation of the capacity-usage gap.

Second, the market may be locked into a vicious circle of self-enforcing effects leading to multiple equilibria. If transportation contracts are scarce, shippers require firm transportation contracts, because they cannot rely on short-term availability. If transportation contracts are not adequately available, shippers will have a strong incentive to hoard transportation contracts to secure capacity rights if needed. The trade-off is the following: if a transportation contract is hoarded but not needed, the shipper forgoes additional revenues of not having sold the capacity right. If, however, the capacity right is needed but the shipper does not have a contract, the shipper forgoes the margin of the transaction (or pays a penalty). If the shipper sells now, he will have to buy back transportation contracts at a later stage and will thus have to face the uncertainty of price fluctuations and possible unavailability. This is a mechanism of self-enforcing or self-fulfilling expectations: if the expectation is that contracts will not be available, then hoarding of contracts will happen, and thus contracts will not be sufficiently available and thus expectations are fulfilled. This holds true the other way around as well.

Transportation contracts are important for network investment. Yet, they can cause a lock in and thereby a situation of 'multiple equilibria' owing to the self-enforcing effects explained above. In a case of insufficient liquidity in the market (in this case for transportation contracts) shippers will not sell to the market, but rather hoard their rights and thus prevent the development of the market. This implies a lock-in in the low-liquidity equilibrium. If the market is sufficiently liquid, shippers will want to sell to the market (if this is profitable) precisely because they will be confident that they can buy the rights if needed and at market prices. The latter case reflects a high-liquidity equilibrium.

4.2 Comparison with the US Gas Market

The comparison with the gas market in the USA is illustrative and experience in the US suggests that a move from a low-liquidity equilibrium to a high-liquidity equilibrium can be made but that this needs to be enforced (especially by the events of 1992 – see below). Legislation in the gas market in the USA has a long tradition, with the following major occurrences (cf. Juris 1998; Makholm 2006, 2007):

- 1906: as a side-effect of the antitrust case against Standard Oil, gas transportation was exempted from third-party access.
- 1935: divorce of pipelines from distribution, which split long-distance transport from local distribution. Note, however, that this is not a split of infrastructure from shipping and thus is not the same as network ownership unbundling in the European sense.
- 1985: FERC's Order 436 introduced open access and restricted the use of long-term contracts.
- 1992: FERC's Order 636 enforced a split of pipelines from shipping and production and thereby established what Europeans would call network ownership unbundling. In particular, the so-called 'commodities clause' secured that pipeline owners were no longer allowed to own the gas in their pipeline. Furthermore, Order 636 enforced a stronger resale of transportation contracts, which can be called a capacity release programme.
- 2000: FERC's Order 637, which created a better defined parallel market for transport rights and established 'incremental pricing' for capacity expansion, promoted competition in pipeline capacity expansion.

Whereas authors like Makholm (2006, 2007) and Juris (1998) point to the successes of the market, others like Teece (1990) are critical and point to the cost of the reforms. Makholm and Juris point out that prices went down (both well-head and end-user gas prices, as well as transportation prices) and that liquid markets developed very quickly. There is a now a wide variety of markets (spot, balancing, financials, storage and transportation contracts). The most prominent example is Henry Hub which was established in 1988 in Erath, Louisiana and is owned by Sabine Pipe Line LLC. Markets are liquid, non-dominated and activities in the markets are dynamic. Contract duration, at least for the commodity, has become short. A long-term contract is defined as longer than 18 months and, following Teece (1990, p. 15), by 1990 most gas was traded on a 30-day basis or less.

Teece (1990) criticizes the open-access regime implemented stepwise in the late 1980s and stresses the loss of vertical economies and the high transition costs after setting the limitation of the use of long-term, take-or-pay contracts. Juris (1998, p. 12) describes the transition costs of stranded take-or-pay contracts that were calculated in 1990 at about US$20 billion which is high compared to a total book value of the pipeline companies of about US$24 billion (in 1984). The burden was shared between producers, distributors and pipeline owners.

The US experience suggests that a system with liquid (spot) markets and *contractualization*, which is in effect a combination of long-term pipeline transportation contracts and short-term gas commodity contracts, can work (cf. in particular Makholm 2006, 2007) and it may well be that the US gas market is now in high-liquidity equilibrium.

5 SUMMARY AND CONCLUDING REMARKS

Without an attempt to be comprehensive this contribution studies a selection of issues on vertical relations in energy markets. The focus is on the vertical relation between the network infrastructure and competitive stages (such as production and trade) and thus this contribution also covers the debate on unbundling. We should stress that this volume tends to cover the vertical relation between the non-network businesses in the gas business; therefore, this chapter takes somewhat of a side-step within this volume.

In section 2 we first characterize the unbundling debate and discuss a selection of arguments and issues in this debate. Section 3 then focuses on the issues around interconnector capacity in electricity markets. The argument here is that vertically integrated firms would have insufficient incentives to expand congested interconnector capacity in order to protect the home market. We discuss this argument of 'strategic investment withholding' in more detail. Section 4 Discusses the role of infrastructure transportation contracts in gas markets. As mentioned above, this seems to be a critical difference between gas and electricity and can, at least theoretically, be argued to cause multiple equilibria. This section summarizes and gives concluding remarks.

Section 2 summarizes key arguments in the unbundling debate. First, one of the main aims of unbundling is the direct promotion of competition. One vehicle to achieve this is the removal of cross-subsidies. Whereas the arguments are theoretically sound and receive wide support among economists, empirical investigation of the Dutch distributors by the Dutch competition agency suggests, somewhat surprisingly, that administrative unbundling might actually be adequate. Second, the advantages of unbundling may come at a cost. Empirical evidence, although there is only a small amount, suggests that lost synergies might be substantial. We note that the major effects are to be found in the step from full integration to administrative unbundling, whereas the step from administrative unbundling to full ownership unbundling is not very costly. Third, we examine the coordination of investment. In a fully integrated setting, investment decisions between network users and network infrastructure are firm-internally coordinated; in an unbundled setting, the market should take over the coordination. The design of locational price signals or contracting is required to this end. Fourth, we explore the issue of strategic investment withholding, which claims that vertically integrated firms may have inadequate incentives to invest in interconnector capacity. This argument is a main driver of the unbundling discussion. Fifth, the contribution notes practical developments in the decentralization of network investment and in particular, what is called tendered transmission investment, which is also an option under the ISO model in the third EU energy package.

Section 3 focuses on electricity markets and picks up the discussion on the incentives to invest in interconnector capacity. As mentioned, the underlying rationale is the argument of strategic investment withholding. The argument is theoretically sound but does have its limits. Interconnector capacity can lead to more imports or to more exports; if the interconnector capacity is used predominantly for more exports, we find that competition actually decreases locally. Globally, competition is likely to increase, but in an area considered in isolation competition may actually decrease, which would thus give an incentive to build the interconnector. Practically, the more substantial problems are the legal hurdles raised in the process of building permissions. Even if all incentives would be correct, it would still be legal challenge to build new (overland) lines.

Section 4 focuses on gas markets and concentrates on the use of transportation contracts. Transportation contracts are heavily used in gas transportation, which is thereby a difference compared to the electricity transmission system. A major obstacle in the European gas markets is that although there does not seem to be substantial physical congestion on the transportation network, it is difficult to get access to the network because transportation contracts are not readily available. This is called contractual congestion. One claim put forward in this contribution is that the transportation contracts, important as they are for network investment, may cause a situation of multiple equilibria. In a case of insufficient liquidity in the market for transport capacity rights, shippers will not sell to the market, but rather they will hoard their rights and thus prevent the development of the market. If the market is sufficiently liquid, shippers will want to sell to the market (if this is profitable) precisely because they will be confident that they can buy the rights if needed and at market prices. It is striking to observe how strongly the gas market in the US differs from the European gas market. This may hint at a situation with multiple equilibria and it suggests that lessons can be learned from the US case.

NOTES

1. The author gratefully acknowledges useful comments by two reviewers and support from NGInfra. Parts of this contribution rely on results from the research project UNECOM (www.unecom.de) funded by the Netherlands-based research council Next Generation Infrastructures (NGInfra).
2. DG Competition report on energy sector inquiry (SEC(2006)1724, 10 January 2007) and somewhat later the Impact Assessment for the third energy package (EU 2007).
3. To avoid confusion, 'dominance' is a settled and well-defined term in economics and competition policy, basically meaning a very high market share for one firm only, with a fringe of small competitors; we do not mean 'political dominance'.
4. See for a critical assessment of the bargaining situation Finon and Locatelli (2008) and Brunekreeft and Guliyev (2009).
5. The issues are touched upon in Joskow and Schmalensee (1983) and Brousseau and Glachant (2002), and in detail but slightly different setting in Finon and Roques (2008) and Finon and Perez (2008). The latter two focus on risk allocation between different commercial parts of the value chain and not so much on the relation between network and commercial parts.
6. The credibility criterion of self-signalling in the context of cheap talk was developed by Aumann (1990) and Baliga and Morris (2002).
7. See Rious et al. (2008) for a good characterization of different organizational models.
8. In this case, the ECN model COMPETES which was updated to a 10-node representation of the German electricity market. See for details, Hers and Özdemir (2009).
9. We refer to Brousseau and Glachant (2002) for an excellent and extensive treatment of contract theory including applications. It is remarkable that gas markets are not covered in the quoted volume.

REFERENCES

Aumann, R. (1990), 'Nash equilibria are not self-enforcing', in J.J. Habszewicz, J.-F. Richard and L. Wolsey (eds), *Economic Decision making. Games, Econometrics and optimisation*, Amsterdam: Elsevier, pp. 201–6.

Baldick, R. and E. Kahn (1993), 'Network cost and the regulation of wholesale competition in electric power', *Journal of Regulatory Economics*, **5**, 367–84.

Baliga, S. and S. Morris (2002), 'Co-ordination, spillovers, and cheap talk', *Journal of Economic Theory*, **105** (2), 450–68.

Balmert, D and G. Brunekreeft (2010), 'Deep ISOs and network investment', *Competition and Regulation in Network Industries*, **11** (1), 27–49.

BNetzA (2008), *Monitoringbericht 2008*, Bonn: BNetzA.

Brousseau, E. and J.-M. Glachant (2002), *The Economics of Contracts*, Cambridge: Cambridge University Press.

Brunekreeft, G. (2008), 'Ownership unbundling in electricity markets – a social cost benefit analysis of the German TSOs', Working Paper EPRG 08-16, University of Cambridge.

Brunekreeft, G. and N. Friedrichsen (2010), 'Vertical unbundling and the coordination of investment and network pricing', *Bremen Energy Working Papers*, No. 3, September, Jacobs University Bremen/Bremen Energie Institut.

Brunekreeft, G. and J. Guliyev (2009), 'Gas supply security and the competitiveness on the European gas market', in C.J. Jepma (ed.), *Gas Market Trading*, Groningen: Energy Delta Institute, University of Groningen, pp. 68–122.

Brunekreeft, G. and T.M. McDaniel (2007), 'Policy uncertainty and supply adequacy in electric power markets', in D. Helm (ed.), *The New Energy Paradigm*, Oxford: Oxford University Press, pp. 320–47. (There is an updated version of article with same title in *Oxford Review of Economic Policy*, **21** (1), 111–27).

De Nooij, M. and B. Baarsma (2007), 'An ex ante welfare analysis of the unbundling of the distribution and supply companies in the Dutch electricity sector', SEO Discussion Paper 52 and UNECOM Discussion Paper P 2008-02.

Deloitte (2005), *Reorganisatiekosten Splitsing Energiebedrijven*, April, Deloitte Amstelveen.

Ehlers, E. (2010), *Electricity and Gas Supply Network Unbundling in Germany, Great Britain and the Netherlands and the Law of the European Union: A Comparison*, Antwerp, Oxford and Portland, OR: Intersentia.

European Regulators' Group for Electricity and Gas (ERGEG) (2007), *Secondary Markets: The Way to Deal with Contractual Congestion on Interconnection Points?*, ERGEG, February.

European Union (EU) (2007), 'Impact assessment', Commission staff working document accompanying the legislative package on the internal market for electricity and gas, European Commission, Brussels.

European Union (EU) (2009a), *Directive 2009/72/EC of 13 July 2009 Concerning Common Rules for the Internal Market in Electricity and Repealing Directive 2003/54/EC*, OJ L211/55.

European Union (EU) (2009b), *Directive 2009/73/EC of 13 July 2009 Concerning Common Rules for the Internal Market in Natural Gas and Repealing Directive 2003/55/EC*, OJ L211/94.

European Union (EU) (2009c), *Regulation (EC) No 715/2009 of 13 July 2009, on Conditions for Access to the Natural Gas Transmission Networks and Repealing Regulation (EC) No 1775/2005*, OJ L211/36.

Finon D. and C. Locatelli (2008), 'Russian and European gas interdependence: could contractual trade channel geopolitics?', *Energy Policy*, **36**, 423–42.

Finon, D. and Y. Perez (2008), 'Investment risk allocation in restructured electricity markets', Larsen working paper, April.

Finon, D. and F. Roques (2008), 'Contractual and financing arrangements for new nuclear build', *Journal of Competition and Regulation in Network Industries*, **9** (3), 147–81.

Galbraith, J.K. (1952), *American Capitalism: The Concept of Countervailing Power*, Boston, MA: Houghton Mifflin.

Galbraith, J.K. (1954), 'Countervailing power', *American Economic Review*, **44** (2), 1–6.

Hers, J.S. and O. Özdemir (2009), *A Nodal Pricing Analysis of the Future German Electricity Market*, ECN-E--09-013, Petten, in cooperation with the Bremer Energie Institut.

Joskow, P.L. and R. Schmalensee (1983), *Markets for Power*, Cambridge MA: MIT Press.

Joskow, P.L. and J. Tirole (2005), 'Merchant transmission investment', *Journal of Industrial Economics*, **53** (2), 233–64

Juris, A. (1998), 'Development of natural gas and pipeline capacity markets in the United States', World Bank, Policy Research Working Paper 1897, March.

London Economics (2007), 'Structure and performance of six European wholesale electricity markets in 2003, 2004 and 2005', *Study for the European Commission*, DGCOMP, February.

Makholm, J. (2006), 'The theory of relationship-specific investments, long-term contracts and gas pipeline development in the United States', NERA working paper, April.

Makholm, J. (2007), 'Seeking competition and supply security in natural gas: the US experience and European challenge', paper prepared for the first CESSA Conference, Berlin University of Technology, Berlin, Germany, 31 May.

Meyer, R. (2010), 'Vertical economies and the costs of separating electricity supply – a review of theoretical and empirical literature', mimeo, Jacobs University, Bremen.

Monopolkommission (2009), 'Strom und Gas 2009: Energiemärkte im Spannungsfeld von Politik und Wettbewerb', *Sondergutachten 2009*, Baden-Baden: Nomos.

Nederlandse Mededingings Autoriteit (NMa) (2007), *Onderzoeksrapport inzake de interne verrekeningsprijzen van energiebedrijven*, May, The Hague: NMa.

Neumann, A. and C. von Hirschhausen (2006), 'Long-term contracts and asset specificity revisited – an empirical analysis of producer–importer relations in the natural gas industry', Working Paper 06-010, Center for Energy and Environmental Policy Research, MIT.

Özdemir, Ö., S. Hers, E.B. Fischer, G. Brunekreeft and B.F. Hobbs (2009), 'A nodal pricing analysis of the future German electricity market', *EEM 2009 Conference Proceedings*, Amsterdam: ECN.

Rious R., J.-M. Glachant, Y. Perez and P. Dessante (2008), 'The diversity of design of TSOs', *Energy Policy*, **36** (9), 3323–32.

Teece, D. (1990), 'Structure and organization of the natural gas industry: differences between the United States and the Federal Republic of Germany and implications for the carrier status of pipelines', *The Energy Journal*, **11** (3), 1–35.

PART II

Long-term Contracts and Imperfect Competition

6. Imperfect competition and long-term contracts in electricity markets: some lessons from theoretical models

Guy Meunier

1 INTRODUCTION

The textbook model of an efficient electricity market is comprised of many producers and consumers, decisions of which are decentralized through an efficient and liquid spot market. A complete set of future markets complete this setting to enable agents to hedge their medium and long-term decisions. Horizontal and vertical relationships can be seen as brakes to the development of such a market.

The high concentrations observed on both wholesale and retail electricity markets together with the vertical integration of many major firms, naturally raise concerns about the exercise of market power. This concern is particularly acute because short-term supply and demand are quasi-inelastic in situations of tight conditions.

Competition authorities are suspicious with regard to long-term contracts (LTCs), particularly when one of the parties is a dominant player on its market. Whereas there is a relatively standard framework to analyse horizontal mergers[1] there still lacks such a standard framework to deal with the efficiency of LTCs. Long-term contracts are suspected of draining short-term markets, limiting entry and consequently raising short-term market power. However, contracts have meaningful economics purposes and offer tools to exploit gains from trade. Furthermore, vertical relations are recognized as a cure to market power exercise on the wholesale market, and the development of forward trade has been recommended to limit excessive market power exercise in the very short term.

Some aspects of the debate are not new and echo a vivid debate in the US emerging in the 1970s both on academic and regulatory fronts which was more precisely on the efficiency of exclusive contracts and their use by incumbent firms to deter efficient entry.

Several strands of the literature in industrial organization highlight these issues by analysing the *strategic* use of forward or long-term contracts and their normative consequences. Given the absence of clear consensus among academics, it is understandable that competition authorities prudently analyse LTCs (Hauteclocque and Glachant 2009). However, the absence of consensus does not signify that there is a lack of analyses, and this survey aims at identifying the results obtained so far that could be relevant for the electricity sector. Some analyses explicitly consider electricity markets, but others are more general and should be carefully applied to the electricity sectors.

This survey is organized as follow. First, the analyses of the positive roles of LTCs in a fixed industry structure are presented. Then, we turn to the debate and analyses of exclusive dealing and demand foreclosure and, finally, the issue of investment is considered.

2 FORWARD CONTRACTS AND COMPETITION WITHOUT ENTRY

The most important consequence of a forward contract in a strategic framework is to influence the physical equilibrium of production and consumption. A forward contract, even a purely financial one, does not only modify the allocation of revenue between agents but also their incentives and consequently their decisions to produce and consume. Most of the literature in industrial organization, and particularly the literature on electricity markets, naturally focus on the supply side.

2.1 Forward Contracts and Short-term Efficiency

Because of the low elasticity of demand and supply in the short term and the high degree of concentration observed in electricity markets, market power – the ability of firms to influence market outcome – has been a major subject of concern and analysis since the beginning of the liberalization process. Given the predominance of forward contracts in electricity trades their interrelation with market power has been much theoretically and empirically studied.

In a static framework, the fundamental consequence of a forward contract is to reduce the incentive of producers to raise spot prices. In the short term, the commitment to sell a quantity of electricity at a pre-specified price reduces the revenue of a producer associated with a high spot price and consequently its incentive to raise this price. It is even possible that a producer has an incentive to decrease the spot price if it is a net buyer on the spot market, that is, it produces less than its contractual obligation. Forward contracts can therefore mitigate market power, in a way quite close to vertical integration. A vertically integrated firm has a lower incentive than a pure supplier to raise the price of an intermediary input because it is on the two sides of the market (Spengler 1950) and forward contracts can be interpreted as an intermediary form of vertical integration.[2]

Several empirical studies have confirmed these results. Bushnell et al. (2008) analyse vertical relationships in US electricity markets and according to them the poor performance of California's market is related to the lack of vertical relation (forward contracting or vertical integration). Wolfram (1999) shows that electricity producers in England and Wales do not raise prices to the level their market power could have allowed, and this can be explained by the high degree of contract cover. Gray et al. (1996) link increases in Pool prices in England and Wales between 1991 and 1999 to the reduction of producers' contracts. Wolak (2000) stresses the positive role of forward contracts in the Australian electricity market.

However, vertical integration and forward contracts can interact in counterintuitive ways because they are substitutes. In a recent analysis of the Australian electricity market, Gans and Wolak (2007) shows that passive vertical integration (that is, that does not modify the behaviour of the partially acquired firm) could raise wholesale prices because it reduces the demand for forward contracts. The acquisition by a retailer of a share of a producer reduces the exposure to the wholesale price risk of the retailer. Therefore, a risk-averse retailer has a lower demand for forward contracts after the acquisition. The acquired producer can still not internalize the effect of the wholesale price on the profit of the acquiring retailer (because the acquisition is passive), thus the reduction of the quantity of forward contracts sold by the producer increases the wholesale price. Even if vertical integration leads to higher wholesale price, this analysis is still favourable to forward contracting.

2.2 The Equilibrium of the Forward Market

The question that naturally arises is the incentive for producers to spontaneously sell forward contracts that constrain their market power. In their seminal contribution, Allaz and Villa (1993) consider an oligopoly[3] of strategic producers and established that this incentive is positive; in a quantity game, each firm wants to sell forward contracts because of their strategic dimension. The strategic aspect of a forward contract refers to the effect of the contract on the competitors' short-term strategies. By selling forward, a firm increases its production and reduces the production of its rivals and, as a firm benefits from a reduction of the others' production, it has a *strategic* incentive to sell forward. Each firm has a positive incentive to sell forward, but the overall effect of a forward market can be negative for producers. Allaz and Villa (1993) show that when there is a forward market, all firms strategically sell forward contracts and the overall effect is an increase of the total production of the oligopoly and a decrease of producers' profit. There is a kind of prisoner's dilemma where every firm has an incentive to contract forward but all firms are worse off once they are all contracted. But, what is negative for producers is positive for consumers as the price of electricity is lower with forward contracting than without. However, Neuhoff and Hirschhausen (2005) show that if the price-elasticity of demand is lower in the long term than in the short term, a forward market could increase both consumer's surplus and firms' profits. Furthermore, if producers are asymmetric a forward market enhances efficiency by increasing the production of the most efficient firm (Gans et al. 1998).

The analysis of Allaz and Villa (1993) applies in a particular setting: Cournot competition in the spot market and Cournot conjecture in the forward market. Furthermore, they assume that the forward price is equal to the expected spot price which can be justified by risk-neutrality and perfect anticipation of some traders. With Cournot competition the strategic variable of a firm is the quantity it produces and quantities are *strategic substitutes* (Bulow et al. 1985). With price competition the strategic effect is reversed, prices are *strategic complements* – if a firm increases its price other firms increase theirs – and, consequently, a firm has an incentive to *buy* forward in order to increase its price as well as that of its rivals. Thus with price competition a forward market softens competition (Mahenc and Salanié 2004). However, it is worth emphasizing that the short-term effect of forward contracts is robust to the level of competition assumption: a firm with a forward commitment to sell has a lower incentive to raise prices, and the analysis of Mahenc and Salanié (2004) predicts that producers *buy* forward.[4]

Several authors (Green 1999; Green and Newbery 1992; Newbery 1998) use 'supply functions' to model short-term competition on electricity markets, arguing that it better represents the auctions implemented on these markets. In this framework, originally developed by Klemperer and Meyer (1989), firms' strategies are functions and not single quantities or prices. Newbery (1998) and Green (1999) show that the short-term strategy of a firm – its supply function – is not affected by the contract cover of its rival and, thus, the strategic incentive to contract forward vanishes and producers do not sell or buy forward. In such case, the introduction of a forward market has no effect.

However, Newbery (1998) and Green (1999) show that, with supply functions, the incentive to contract can be restored by relaxing the assumption of Cournot conjecture on the forward market. With Cournot conjecture each firm considers its rivals' contract quantities fixed when choosing its own; if the other firms' contracted quantities decrease when a firm increases its own, there is a positive incentive to contract. Green (1999) even shows that at the extreme, with Bertrand Conjecture (that is, a reduction of one for one), producers sell all their production forward and have no incentive to raise the wholesale price above their marginal cost.

A last line of research on forward contracts analyses collusive agreement. Following the tradition of infinitely repeated games and collusion, several authors have analysed how forward contracting influences the ability of firms to sustain a profitable agreement. In such framework, there is a tacit agreement on a price and a deviation from this agreement by a firm leads to a price war (a punishment). Le Coq (2004) shows that forward contracting can help to sustain collusion by limiting the profit of a deviator. A deviator that undercuts the collusive price can only shift the uncontracted demand.[5] However, forward contracts also limit the severity of punishment, and Green and Le Coq (2009) shows that when the duration of contracting increases collusion is harder to sustain.

The mentioned analyses concern forward contracts without explicitly considering their term. Whether these analyses can be applied to consider long-term contracting is not evident. In particular, the formation of the forward price in the framework of Allaz and Villa (1993) can be challenged when analysing long-term contracts that are bilaterally bargained.

The determination of the forward price in the model of Allaz and Villa (1993) is based on the assumption that there are competitive, risk-neutral traders with rational expectations; it ensures that the forward price is the expected spot price. The influence of producers' forward decisions on the forward price is indirect: an increase in forward selling reduces the forward price because it reduces the expected spot price. This setting is relevant when dealing with short-term or mid-term forward contracts with relatively liquid markets, but it seems rather unrealistic when considering long-term contracts. This issue, the determination of the contract price, is related to the way the contract conditions are bargained for between producers and consumers. In a recent work Anderson and Hu (2008) consider that retailers propose pairs of prices and quantities to producers. They show that the forward price can differ from the expected spot price, and, more importantly, that welfare is maximized. In their framework the forward market creates an opportunity for consumers to bypass producers' market power on the spot market and offer a Pareto improving trade on the forward market. This result illustrates the general point that efficient bargaining between producers and consumers leads to a Pareto optimal situation, and if the spot market is inefficient the forward market could be the place for such a bargaining. This kind of argument plays an important part in the debate on exclusionary clauses that is presented in the next section.

3 EXCLUSIVE DEALINGS AND ENTRY

Most analyses of contracts in the electricity industry are built on a framework similar to that of Allaz and Villa (1993), which concerned financial futures markets and short-term forward contracting. However, these analyses can still be interpreted in a long-term perspective, where quantities are interpreted as capacities, though there are several difficulties with such interpretation. Despite the issue of price formation, there is also the rigidity of the market structure and the absence of entry that is problematic. It is a fundamental reason why these results do not influence regulatory authorities which are suspicious of LTCs because of their potential use by incumbent producers to prevent entry and foreclose demand.

There are at least two benefits awaited from entry: (1) the development of more efficient production technologies and (2) the reduction of market power exercise because the more firms there are, the less they are able to raise the price. Incumbent firms have an interest in limiting or preventing entry, and to do so they need a commitment device and LTCs can be such a device. The strategic use by incumbents of LTCs to limit entry is an important issue that has been extensively analysed. In particular, the consequences of exclusionary clauses were at the heart of an important debate among US antitrust authorities and scholars. Even if the debate focuses on exclusivity there are numerous insights that are relevant for LTCs in general, all the more so if any LTCs require some exclusivity – at least the exclusivity for the specified quantity. The debate about these clauses also raises the issue of the contractual environment and the possibility that some forms of LTC can be good while others can be bad.

In several antitrust cases, US antitrust authorities have condemned exclusive dealings on the ground of their anticompetitive effect.[6] But, several antitrust experts have criticized these decisions. The 'Chicago school' (Bork 1978; Posner 1976) argues that if exclusion were socially inefficient there would be less surplus to share with exclusion than without it, and therefore the payment required to compensate consumers would exceed the incumbent firm's benefit from entry exclusion. An incumbent is able to offer an interesting exclusive deal to a buyer, one that he will accept, if there are some efficiency gains from exclusion. Thus, some benefits should justify observed exclusive dealing and authorities should not condemn them. The Chicago critique has been formally stated and discussed by Bernheim and Whinston (1998).

This view has been challenged by several authors. One challenge is based on uncertainty and contract incompleteness. Aghion and Bolton (1987) shows that exclusive dealing and breach penalty can be used by an incumbent producer to prevent some efficient entry when there is uncertainty regarding the entrant's costs. In their analysis, the incumbent producer can offer the buyer a contract composed of a price and a breach penalty. If the buyer decides to trade with the entrant he has to pay the incumbent the breach penalty. Once the cost of the entrant is known, the entrant can set a price and the buyer decides whether to breach the contract and accept the entrant's offer. At the first stage, the buyer accepts to sign a contract with the incumbent because it forces the entrant to lower its price. The drawback of the contract is that the entrant has to be highly competitive to compensate for the breach penalty and some efficient entry is prevented. The incumbent and the buyer use the LTC to extract surplus from the entrant but they do so inefficiently because of uncertainty and contract incompleteness. If the breach penalty could be made conditional on the entrant cost, efficient entry would not be deterred.

Spier and Whinston (1995) and Masten and Snyder (1989) argue that the result of Aghion and Bolton (1987) no longer holds if renegotiation is feasible, and renegotiation is likely given that the incumbent and the buyer still have to trade. If an entrant is able to produce the good more efficiently than the incumbent, it is in the interest of all parties, including the incumbent, that he does so. Thus, renegotiation prevents inefficient entry deterrence. However, Spier and Whinston (1995) show that inefficient entry deterrence is still possible if investment is considered, which is further discussed in section 4.

A second strand of literature that supports the argument of inefficient entry deterrence was initiated by Rasmusen et al. (1991) and complemented by Segal and Winston (2000a). They consider that incumbents can pay consumers for exclusivity; LTCs are only composed of an exclusivity clause, hence the title 'Naked exclusion' of the article of Rasmusen et al. (1991). They show that if a minimum quantity of buyers is necessary for a profitable entry to take place, the incumbent is able to prevent entry if buyers cannot coordinate. The incumbent can thin the spot market by paying some consumers to accept exclusive dealing. Even if buyers as a whole lose from entry deterrence, the monopoly can exploit their lack of coordination; the profits gained on non-signatory buyers are used to 'bribe' signatory buyers. In that case the Chicago critique does not hold, because some adversely affected buyers should not be compensated by the excluding producer.[7]

This approach has been developed along several lines. The analysis by Fumagalli and Motta (2006) is of particular interest for the electricity industry. They introduce competition among buyers in the framework of Rasmusen et al. (1991). In the initial framework, buyers are assumed to be final consumers whose demands are unrelated, but instead it is likely that buyers are competing firms. For instance, buyers can be retailers operating on the same final market; in such a case, it is more difficult for the incumbent to thin the spot market because a unique retailer is able to serve the whole final market. Fumagalli and Motta (2006) assume that buyers have to pay a fixed cost to be active in the final market; this fixed cost represents the cost that a retailer must pay to be in the market independently of the quantity it buys and sells; it implies that with tough (Bertrand) competition only one retailer is active. Thus, the entrant producer has only to serve one retailer at a low price in order to secure the whole market. It is consequently more difficult for the incumbent to foreclose entry when buyers compete.

Simpson and Wickelgren (2007) and Abito and Wright (2008) challenge this result; they establish that it is driven by the combination of the fixed cost paid by retailers and the perfect substitutability of retailers' products. Without the fixed cost, competition between retailers drives their profit to zero and thus passes gains from any efficient entry to final consumers. A high wholesale price implies a high retail price and possibly more profit for the vertical structure composed of producers and retailers.[8] Thus, entry deterrence can increase the profit of the pair of incumbent-retailers by indirectly maintaining a high retail price. Therefore, entry deterrence is more likely, the more intense the competition between retailers.[9] In such case, entry deterrence is good for the vertical structure but not for final consumers, but these cannot participate to the contractual stage and have not to be compensated. To apply these results to the electricity industry would require determining the precise form of the competition between retailers and the level of the fixed cost. In particular, the existence of switching costs for final consumers can imply that even though electricity retailers sell a perfectly homogeneous good, competition works *as if* these products were imperfectly substitutable. This means that entry deterrence is feasible because it is difficult for an entrant producer to make a retailer gain a large share of the retail market.

Another development relevant for the electricity industry has been made by Gans and King (2002). Motivated by the observation of contractual practice by US electricity producers (Shepherd 1997), they analyse how producers can offer exclusive contracts to large consumers to the detriment of 'small' consumers. In their approach there is no asymmetry between producers at the contracting stage, and the contractual environment is relatively rich: producers can propose exclusive contracts composed of a lump-sum transfer and a quantity to a coalition of large buyers. The asymmetry is on the consumers' side as small consumers are not present at the contracting stage because transaction costs are too high. Furthermore, there is an efficient scale and the small-consumers segment is not large enough to reach this size; thus, a firm that only serves this segment is less efficient that a firm that serves both. The authors do not analyse entry deterrence but analyse how firms compete to offer contracts to large consumers. A producer tries to sign contracts with large consumers so that the other producer only serves the small-consumer segment and does not reach the efficient scale. Therefore, a producer has an incentive to offer low prices to large consumers to get more profit on sales to small consumers. Production is efficient on the segment of large consumers but LTCs are detrimental because of the loss endured by small consumers. Long-term contracts worsen welfare because otherwise price competition would ensure that production is efficient for both consumer types.

From a theoretical point of view, Spector (2007) points out that in most analysis of exclusivity and demand foreclosure, (1) contracts have rather simple forms, and (2) some adversely affected parties – some consumers or an entrant – are absent at the contracting stage. He analyses in a highly stylized framework whether inefficient exclusion is mostly driven by one of these conditions. It is clear that if both are lifted, only Pareto optimal LTCs would be signed among all parties. He shows that with a sufficiently rich contractual environment inefficient exclusion does not occur even if the incumbent has a first-mover advantage that allows him or her to propose contracts before the entrant does. For this result to hold, contracts should comprise breach penalties and can be made conditional on the acceptance by other consumers of contracts offered to them. Within this contractual environment the entrant is able to implement all necessary monetary transfers to counter any exclusive dealings proposed by the incumbent. The Chicago critique is therefore restored. And concerning condition (2), the absence of some affected parties, he shows that exclusion can occur even if both firms are present at the contracting stage if simple exclusive contracts without breach penalties can be proposed. These results question the implementation of constraints on the contractual environment by antitrust authorities. Furthermore, Bernheim and Whinston (1998) show that even if exclusive dealings are prohibited, LTCs can be used to prevent entry, but less efficiently.

As illustrated by this brief review, there is no academic consensus on the welfare implication of exclusionary clauses and LTCs. It is therefore difficult for competition authorities to assess these LTCs. However, these analyses provide important insights on the possible use of LTCs to prevent entry; in particular, they stress that adversely affected parties should be looked for and that the contractual environment matters and should be carefully modified. Furthermore, the application to electricity markets is not straightforward. It should be noticed that in most analyses there is a kind of scale economies that is assumed – either a fixed cost[10] or a minimum scale – that explains why entry deterrence or exclusion is feasible and profitable. Whether or not there is some form of scale economies in the production of electricity is decisive when applying these frameworks to analyse electricity LTCs. Concentrations observed in European electricity markets strongly support the view that there are some forms of scale economies. Some technologies are likely to be characterized by scale economies and others not, so LTCs might be used to prevent entry with some technologies but not others.

4 INVESTMENT

An important question when evaluating LTCs is their influence on investment. The literature on electricity markets has mainly addressed the influence of forward contracts on investment in frameworks similar to Allaz and Villa's (1993), that is, with a fixed market structure. Another strand of relevant literature considers entry of producers and analyses how exclusive agreement might facilitate some kind of investment by securing customers.

4.1 Forward Contracts

The consequences of forward contracting on investment are the subject of controversy. First, there is a possible direct interpretation of quantities in a Cournot game as being production capacities. With this interpretation, forward commitment should increase capacity by reducing the incentive for firms to under-invest to raise spot prices. This interpretation neglects many features of electricity markets, but stresses a potential positive role of LTCs on investment that could still hold in more complex representations. For instance, Arellano and Serra (2009) consider an electricity market subject to peak-load pricing – that is, without short-term market power – and show that the more retail demand is contracted, the more generators invest.

The above result requires that forward contracts are signed before investment decisions are made. If the timing is reversed, that is, if investment takes place before forward contracting, the effect of the introduction of the contracting intermediary stage on capacity decisions and efficiency is ambiguous. It should be noticed that with strong capacity constraints, the strategic role of forward contracting vanishes if the rival firms produce at capacity. A firm does not have any incentive to sell forward because its forward sells do not influence the production of its rival which is capacity constrained. If demand does not vary, forward contracting has no effect on investment and production because firms always produce at full capacity with or without forward contracting.

With demand variation, several assumptions regarding the forward market can be made. Adilov (2006) considers that forward contracting occurs before uncertainty is resolved, and shows that the evaluation of the forward market depends upon uncertainty. With a small degree of uncertainty or demand variation, the forward market has no influence; with greater uncertainty the forward market increases competition thus reducing price when capacity is not fully used, but also reducing investment incentives. The comparison of the positive effects (on baseload prices and production) and negative effects (on capacity and peak prices) of the forward market is ambiguous.

Grimm and Zoetl (2006) make the alternative assumption that forward contracts can be signed for each demand realization, a representation that better suits short-term forward markets. Their results, however, are similar to Adilov's. They show that the introduction of forward markets increases production in baseload demand states but reduces investment incentives and raises peak prices; they do not compare those two effects to determine the overall welfare consequences. Finally, Murphy and Smeers (2009) consider heterogeneous firms (a peak and a baseload player) and a similar timing to that of Grimm and Zoetl (2006), and show that forward markets can increase or decrease total investment depending on the load curve and technology characteristics.

Even though these analyses provide important insights on the influence of forward contracts on investment, they can hardly be applied to analyse the effect of long-term contracts for similar reasons to those mentioned above: the price formation requires the existence of risk-neutral traders and a liquid market, and the market structure is fixed. Furthermore, buyers are not active players that bargain and sign contracts, but are solely represented in an aggregate and anonymous way, in these models forward contracts are not bilateral but centralized. Thus, these analyses cannot be used to consider the interrelation between LTCs, entry-deterrence and investment. This issue has been addressed in the incomplete contracts literature.

4.2 Incomplete Contracts

A recurrent argument about long-term exclusive agreements is that they protect relation-specific investment. The Chicago critique argues that inefficient strategic entry deterrence cannot explain exclusive agreement but that some positive, efficiency enhancing, effects should. Whereas most of the subsequent formal analyses focus on the first part of the argument and establish that strategic and socially inefficient uses of exclusive agreement are theoretically possible, few have considered the potential positive role and compared both effects.

If an incumbent producer can invest in order to decrease its cost or improve the quality of the good sold, its investment depends on the expected surplus obtained from trade with the buyer and this surplus is related to the trade opportunities of the buyer. If investment is non-contractible[11] an exclusive agreement could foster this investment by protecting the producer from opportunistic behaviour by the buyer. Spier and Whinston (1995) reconsider the analysis of strategic use of breach penalties by Aghion and Bolton (1987); they introduce renegotiation and relation-specific investment. As we have seen before, they show that, without investment opportunity, renegotiation prevents inefficient entry deterrence, but this strategic inefficiency might be resurrected when investment is considered. More precisely, they consider an incumbent and a buyer that sign an exclusive contract with a breach penalty, then the incumbent can invest to reduce its cost before entry occurs. The entrant observes the contract and makes a price offer before the incumbent and the buyer renegotiate the term of the contract. *Ex post* renegotiation between the buyer and the incumbent ensures that the most efficient firm produces. Investment influences the efficiency of the incumbent producer, and consequently the price offered by the entrant. Thus, the incumbent and the buyer have a joint incentive to encourage investment not only to increase the value of trade between them but also to lower the price offered by the entrant, and they can do so by specifying excessive breach penalties.

Investment by a producer can have many consequences; it can not only decrease the cost of production, but it can also influence other agents' valuations of the good: in particular it can enhance the value of trade between a buyer and an alternative producer.[12] Segal and Whinston (2000b) analyse how these 'internal' and 'external' effects influence the investment-promoting role of an exclusive agreement between an incumbent and a buyer before entry takes place. In a framework with renegotiation, and a non-strategic entrant, they show that exclusive dealing does not promote investment if there are no external effects. This is because exclusive dealing, even if it increases the share of the total surplus that passes to the incumbent, does not modify the total surplus available (which determines the investment of the incumbent). However, exclusive dealing has a socially positive effect if the investment increases the value of trade between the buyer and the entrant thus confirming the view that producers should be protected from opportunistic behaviour. The analysis can be generalized to consider investment by any of the parties, particularly, Segal and Whinston (2000b) show that if the entrant is the one investing – for instance, incurring an entry cost – the social evaluation of exclusive agreement is ambiguous because the producer and the buyer have an excessive incentive to use it.

Recently Fumagalli et al. (2009) revisited the analyses of exclusive dealing and specific investment. Compared with Segal and Whinston (2000b) they consider that the exclusive agreement cannot be renegotiated and modify the bargaining structure. They show that the interrelation between entry deterrence and investment promotion can complicate the evaluation of an exclusive agreement. Without any investment purposes, an exclusive agreement would not be signed by a consumer, the Chicago critique holds, but when investment is considered, socially inefficient exclusive dealing might be agreed to. These contracts are signed precisely because they prevent entry and thus foster investment; they are not always socially detrimental but can be because of the incomplete nature of the contract signed. Investment with the incomplete contract is less efficient than would be implemented with a complete contract, and thus the evaluation of these contracts is based on the comparison of two suboptimal situations (incomplete contracts versus no contracts), and contract incompleteness explains that contracts do not always enhance welfare. These conclusions are close to those of Spier and Whinston (1995); it is the promotion by exclusive agreements of relation-specific investments that explains a *potential* inefficient strategic use of these agreements to deter entry. However, whether exclusionary clauses enhance or reduce welfare depends upon parameter values.

Whether these analyses can be used to evaluate LTCs in electricity markets is difficult because of their high degree of stylization. They provide a formal analysis and justification for the intuitive argument that exclusive dealing protects investors from the opportunistic behaviour of buyers, but the kind of investment considered can hardly be compared with investment in an electricity power-producing plant. Furthermore, they do not explicitly model the existence of a wholesale market: the quantity produced is fixed, there is an incumbent, a buyer and an entrant, and the price is bargained for. These models analyse relation-specific investment that reduces the production costs of the incumbent, and investment in power-producing plants are not relation-specific because they can be used for trade with other parties. It is thus unclear that electricity producers need to be protected from opportunistic behaviour. It should be investigated whether some parts of the investment can be considered relation-specific, some characteristics of the plant or of the portfolio of plants of the producer, such as localizations and cost characteristics, might be tailored to the relation and the characteristics of a consumer, its load profile and its localization. The same kind of analyses should be done on the buyer side, to determine whether he has to make some relation-specific investment such as investment in transmission lines to connect production facilities to the grid. Concerning the representation of the wholesale market, given the strategic behaviour of producers and large consumers it is unclear whether it is better represented as a competitive market or a Nash bargaining process. These analyses can therefore provide some insights even if their specifications hardly suit an electricity market, and some research still remains to be done to determine how exclusive LTCs can enhance welfare by securing investment. These points are further discussed by Meade and O'Connor in Chapter 4 in this book. Furthermore, Meade and O'Connor present several other arguments that could be made in favour of contracting to support investment.

5 CONCLUSION

Several subfields of the literature in industrial organization provide insights for the analysis of LTCs in electricity markets. Most analyses directly related to electricity markets have considered forward contracts and reach an overall consensus on the positive effect of forward markets on the short-term efficiency of electricity wholesale markets. These analyses are built on frameworks close to the seminal one of Allaz and Villa (1993) which is more suited to the analysis of short-term forward contracts because of the assumption of no arbitrage, the simplicity of the contract structure and the absence of bargaining between signatories.

The complexity of LTCs observed and, particularly the existence of exclusionary clauses, calls for another type of analysis. Exclusive dealings are subject to controversy and are at the root of an important literature. It appears that the precise structure of the market considered, the contractual environment and the bargaining process all influence the possibility of inefficient strategic use by an incumbent of exclusive agreements to prevent efficient entry. Long-term contracts can be detrimental if an adversely affected party (such as final consumers or entrant) is absent at the contracting stage, or if the contractual environment is too limited. Whereas this analysis supports the view that inefficient entry deterrence can be the purpose of an exclusive agreement, it also suggests a need for caution over the limitation of the contractual environment by prohibiting some practices.

Finally, concerning the major question of investment and its interrelation with LTCs, the conclusions are also ambiguous. With a fixed market structure, the introduction of a forward market can limit the incentive of firms to invest by reducing their short-term revenue; this negative effect should be balanced with short-term efficiency gains. However, if forward contracts are signed before production capacities are built, they could increase investment. When entry is considered, LTCs and exclusive agreements can be used to protect contractual parties from opportunistic behaviour of the other and consequently foster investment. The promotion of investment is therefore intrinsically linked to the entry deterrence role of exclusive dealings. The conclusions regarding exclusive agreements are therefore ambiguous and call for a careful analysis of the kind of investment considered; all the more so, given that it is questionable whether the existing frameworks are relevant to considering investment in the electricity industry.

NOTES

1. The standard approach to analyse a merger is to compare loss related to the increase of market power and gain due to cost synergies. See Farrel and Shapiro (1990) for an analytical analysis of this issue in a Cournot game with production capacities.
2. In this book, Meade and O'Connor analyse how vertical integration and LTCs differ. They explain why vertical integration between producer and retailer could be preferred to forward contracting.
3. The case of a monopoly has been analysed previously by Anderson (1985), Anderson and Sundareson (1984), and the case of a dominant producer and a competitive fringe by Newbery (1984).
4. That large producers manipulate futures market by buying forward has been observed, for instance, in the coffee market (Greenstone 1981) and in the copper market (Gilbert 1997).
5. Similar results have been obtained in a different setting: Ferreira (2003) considers an infinite number of forward contracting rounds before a unique spot market, and Liski and Montero (2006) model alternating rounds of forward contracting and spot interactions.
6. See Gilbert (2000) for a description of several cases and a discussion.
7. This is a particular kind of contract externality: the contract between the incumbent and a consumer has an external effect on other consumers. Contract externalities have been further analysed by Segal (1999, 2003) and Segal and Whinston (2003).
8. Bernheim and Whinston (1998) shows that exclusive dealing is a choice to avoid a setting of 'common agency', that is, a situation of several competing principals.
9. A second contribution of Simpson and Wickelgren (2007) is to consider that a buyer can breach contracts by paying expectation damages to the incumbent; such breach penalty being determined by a court – they are not set by the incumbent as in Aghion and Bolton (1987). They show that the introduction of breach penalty is sufficient to prevent inefficient foreclosure with independent buyers but not with competing buyers.
10. Here, the term 'fixed cost' is used for a cost that is independent of the quantity produced – in particular it should be distinguished from an investment cost proportional to capacity.
11. Evidently if investment is contractible the buyer and the incumbent can agree on the optimal investment. Several arguments are advanced in the literature to justify that an investment can be non-contractible. It might be too costly to describe, or impossible to verify *ex post* by a court.

12. For instance, in the case of United Shoe Machinery Corporation (see Aghion and Bolton 1987; Masten and Snyder 1993) the education of shoe manufacturers increases the value of trade of manufacturers with other machine producers. Masten and Snyder (1993) suggest that the exclusive agreement was used to protect United Shoe Machinery Corporation from opportunistic behaviour by the manufacturers, who, once educated, could trade with another machine producer.

REFERENCES

Abito, J.M. and J. Wright (2008), 'Exclusive dealing with imperfect downstream competition', *International Journal of Industrial Organization*, **26** (1), 227–46.

Adilov, N. (2006), 'Strategic use of forward contracts and capacity constraints', Cornell University working paper.

Aghion, P. and P. Bolton (1987), 'Contracts as a barrier to entry', *American Economic Review*, **77** (3), 388–401.

Allaz, B. and J.-L. Vila (1993), 'Cournot competition, forward markets and efficiency', *Journal of Economic Theory*, **59** (1), 1–16.

Anderson, E.J. and X. Hu (2008), 'Forward contracts and market power in an electricity market', *International Journal of Industrial Organization*, **26** (3), 679–94.

Anderson, R. (1985), 'Market power and futures trading for durable goods', mimeo, Graduate Center, City University of New York.

Anderson, R. and M. Sundaresan (1984), 'Futures markets and monopoly', in R. Anderson (ed.), *The Industrial Organization of Futures Markets*, Lexington, MA: Lexington Books.

Arellano, M.S. and P. Serra (2009), 'Contracts and market power in price-regulated power industries', working paper, Centro de Economia, Aplicada, Universidad de Chile.

Bernheim, B.D. and M.D. Whinston (1998), 'Exclusive dealing', *Journal of Political Economy*, **106** (1), 64–103.

Bork, R. (1978), *The Antitrust Paradox: A Policy at War with Itself*, New York: Basic Books.

Bulow, J.I., J.D. Geanakoplos and P.D. Kemplerer (1985), 'Multimarket oligopoly: strategic substitute and complements', *Journal of Political Economy*, **93**, 488–511.

Bushnell, J.B., E.T. Mansur and C. Saravia (2008), 'Vertical arrangements, market structure, and competition: an analysis of restructured US electricity markets', *American Economic Review*, **98** (1), 237–66

Farrel, J. and C. Shapiro (1990), 'Horizontal mergers: an equilibrium analysis', *American Economic Review*, **80** (1), 107–26.

Ferreira, J.L. (2003), 'Strategic interaction between futures and spot markets', *Journal of Economic Theory*, **108** (1), 141–51.

Fumagalli, C. and M. Motta (2006), 'Exclusive dealing and entry, when buyers compete', *American Economic Review*, **96** (3), 785–95.

Fumagalli, C., M. Motta and T. Rønde (2009), 'Exclusive dealing: the interaction between foreclosure and investment promotion', CEPR Discussion Paper No. 7240.

Gans, J.S. and S. King (2002), 'Exclusionary contracts and competition for large buyers', *International Journal of Industrial Organization*, **20** (9), 1363–81.

Gans, J.S. and F.A Wolak (2007), 'A comparison of ex ante versus ex post vertical market power: evidence from the electricity supply industry', mimeo, University of Melbourne.

Gans, J.S., D. Price and K. Woods (1998), 'Contracts and electricity pool prices', *Australian Journal of Management*, **23** (1), 83–96.

Gilbert, C.L. (1997), 'Manipulation of metals futures: lessons from Sumitomo', CEPR Discussion Paper.

Gilbert, R.J. (2000), 'Exclusive dealing, preferential dealing and dynamic efficiency', *Review of Industrial Organization*, **16** (2), 167–84.

Gray, P., D.R. Helm and A. Powell (1996), 'Competition versus regulation in British electricity generation', in G. McKerron and P. Pearson (eds), *The British Energy Experience: A Lesson or a Warning*, London: Imperial College Press.

Green, R.J. (1999), 'The electricity contract market in England and Wales', *The Journal of Industrial Economics*, **47** (1), 107–24.

Green, R.J. and C. Le Coq (2009), 'The length of contracts and collusion', *International Journal of Industrial Organization*, **28** (1), 21–9.

Green, R.J. and D.M. Newbery (1992), 'Competition in the British electricity spot market', *The Journal of Political Economy*, **100** (5), 929–53.

Greenstone, W.D. (1981), 'The coffee cartel: manipulation in the public interest', *Journal of Futures Markets*, **1** (1), 3–16.

Grimm, V. and G. Zoetll (2006), 'Access to commitment devices reduces investment incentives in oligopoly', University of Cologne Working Paper 25.

Hauteclocque, A. and J.-M. Glachant (2009), 'Long-term energy supply contracts in European competition policy: fuzzy not crazy', *Energy Policy*, **37** (12), 5399–407.

Klemperer, P.D. and M.A. Meyer (1989), 'Supply function equilibria in oligopoly under uncertainty', *Econometrica*, **99**, 1243–77.

Le Coq, C. (2004), 'Long-term supply contracts and collusion in the electricity market', SSE/EFI Working Paper Series in Economics and Finance 552.

Liski, M. and J.-P. Montero (2006), 'Forward trading and collusion in oligopoly', *Journal of Economic Theory*, **131** (1), 212–30.

Mahenc, P. and F. Salanié (2004), 'Softening competition through forward trading', *Journal of Economic Theory*, **116** (2), 282–93.

Masten, S.E. and E.A. Snyder (1989), 'The design and duration of contracts: strategic and efficiency considerations', *Law and Contemporary Problems*, **52** (1), 63–85.

Masten, S.E. and E.A. Snyder (1993), 'United States versus United Shoe Machinery Corporation: on the merits', *Journal of Law and Economics*, **36** (1), 33–70.

Murphy, F. and Y. Smeers (2009), 'The ambiguous effect of contracts on competition and prices in restructured electricity markets', paper presented at 'The Economics of Energy Markets' conference, 28–29 January, Toulouse.

Neuhoff, K. and C. Hirschhausen (2005), 'Long-term vs. short-term contracts: a European perspective on natural gas', *Cambridge Working Papers in Economics*.

Newbery, D.M. (1984), 'The manipulation of futures markets by a dominant producer', in R. Anderson (ed.), *The Industrial Organization of Futures Markets*, Lexington, MA: Lexington Books, pp. 35–62.

Newbery, D.M. (1998), 'Competition, contracts, and entry in the electricity spot market', *RAND Journal of Economics*, **29** (4), 726–49.

Posner, R.A. (1976), *Antitrust Law: An Economic Perspective*, Chicago, IL: University of Chicago Press.

Rasmusen, E.B., J.M. Ramseyer and J.S. Wiley (1991), 'Naked exclusion', *American Economic Review*, **81** (4), 1137–45.

Segal, I. (1999), 'Contracting with externalities', *Quarterly Journal of Economics*, **114** (2), 337–88.

Segal, I. (2003), 'Coordination and discrimination in contracting with externalities: divide and conquer?', *Journal of Economic Theory*, **113** (2), 147–81.

Segal, I. and M.D. Whinston (2000a), 'Naked exclusion: a comment', *American Economic Review*, **90** (1), 296–309.

Segal, I. and M.D. Whinston (2000b), 'Exclusive contracts and the protection of investments', *RAND Journal of Economics*, **31** (4), 603–33.

Segal, I. and M.D. Whinston (2003), 'Robust predictions for bilateral contracting with externalities', *Econometrica*, **71** (3), 757–91.

Shepherd, W. (1997), 'Anti-competitive impacts of secret strategic pricing in the electricity industry', *Public Utilities Fortnightly*, **135**, 24.

Simpson, J. and A.L. Wickelgren (2007), 'Naked exclusion, efficient breach, and downstream competition', *American Economic Review*, **97** (4), 1305–20.

Spector, D. (2007), 'Exclusive contracts and demand foreclosure', Paris School of Economics Working Paper No. 2007-07.

Spengler, J.J. (1950), 'Vertical integration and antitrust policy', *The Journal of Political Economy*, **58** (4), 347–52.

Spier, K.E. and M.D. Whinston (1995), 'On the efficiency of privately stipulated damages for breach of contract: entry barriers, reliance, and renegotiation', *RAND Journal of Economics*, **26** (2), 180–202.

Wolak, F.A. (2000), 'An empirical analysis of the impact of hedge contracts on bidding behavior in a competitive electricity market', *International Economic Journal*, **14** (2), 1–39.

Wolfram, C.D. (1999), 'Measuring duopoly power in the British electricity spot market', *The American Economic Review*, **89** (4), 805–26.

7. Long-term contracts in electricity markets: long-term contracting and risk management from the point of view of a large consumer

Petter Longva

1 INTRODUCTION

The environmental policy of the European Union is particularly challenging for the power-intensive industry. The goals and targets are necessary for the climate, but increased costs on top of an already high European energy cost level may lead to capacity closure. Price increases due to trading in emission allowances are already a reality, increases in renewable support are being introduced, and increases in grid cost will be a direct consequence of enabling more renewable power generation.

Power-intensive industries compete globally, and cannot retrieve cost increases through the prices of their products. Failure to implement consistent, long-term measures to protect European industries from such cost elements will lead to a phase-out of the industry. Without investment in new production lines with new technology, it will stagnate and face a gradual erosion of competitive strength and environmental credibility.

Electricity market liberalization has turned out to be a mixed blessing for power-intensive industries. Ultimately, as the third package takes effect, competition in the electricity market will hopefully reduce the cost of power supply to the benefit of power consumers. In the short term, however, the Commission's efforts to weaken the position of dominant generators by restricting long-term contracting has instead hurt the interests of power-intensive industries. Furthermore, real or artificial fear of intervention regarding the duration of long-term contracts has weakened the consumer interests in negotiations to renew existing supply contracts.

This chapter argues that:

- Foreclosure is not the main problem for the development of a competitive European electricity market.
- In those cases where foreclosure is a problem, the focus should be on contract clauses such as exclusivity or destination, not on duration.
- Long-term, fixed-price supply contracts will in general increase the margin risk for generators and distributors.
- Industries that compete in a world market have a particular need for price predictability through long-term power supply contracts.
- The present anti-foreclosure policy, limiting the duration of supply contracts, is detrimental to these industries, and should be changed.

2 MARKET DESIGN AND LONG-TERM CONTRACTS

In an early phase of market development, creation of a day-ahead spot exchange should have top priority. Any contract may have clauses that are negative for the development of market liquidity, but such features are more related to volume flexibility than to contract duration. Most long-term contracts with a fixed volume will improve market liquidity, since they transfer volumes from a flexible player (generator) to a less flexible player (consumer) who has to use the market to balance his or her portfolio.

In later phases of electricity market development, lack of trust in market pricing due to real or potential spot price manipulation should be the main issue. In electricity markets, foreclosure is in most cases less critical and, moreover, the main 'cure' used to combat foreclosure does not serve its purpose. Limiting the duration of long-term contracts does not weaken the dominant players, price transparency is not improved and volumes for potential market entrants are available from the spot market, anyway.

Market transition has already lasted more than a decade, and continues to pose challenges to power intensive industries. The problems related to high energy cost levels and added environmental costs are exacerbated by the particular focus given to long-term contracts by the Commission. If a single supplier with a large market share provides more than 80 per cent of a customer's consumption, it is seen as de facto exclusivity, which is particularly serious if the buyer is big enough to motivate a new entry or the contract has a duration of more than four or five years. Directorate General of Competition has opened and settled a number of cases with the companies in question, among others Distrigaz and EdF, restricting contract duration and the allowed share of supply to each customer.

To secure investments, power-intensive industries need to secure long-term power prices at an affordable level, and entering into long-term contracts is in most cases the only option. Long-term contracts, per se, would not solve the fundamental problem of competitive disadvantage in Europe, however. Concerns related to high and increasing electricity supply cost levels also need to be addressed.

3 SOME FEATURES OF LIQUID MARKETS

In European-style electricity market liberalization the main basis of the market is a day-ahead exchange, an auction where buyers and sellers give a bid curve for each hour of the next day, indicating how much they would buy or sell as a function of price. The exchange aggregates those bids and sets the market price and the resulting volume for each bidder. Price takers, that is, players that are relatively small,[1] will bid according to their marginal cost of generation and marginal value of consumption, respectively. The spot price forms the basis for optimal physical balancing of the portfolios of the players and of the total power system.[2] It also forms the basis for the management of unplanned imbalances.

Most market participants need a planning horizon that is longer than one day ahead. Small consumers are usually supplied through tariffs or contracts at prices that are set for up to a year ahead. Distributors therefore want to secure their power supply costs for a corresponding period, generally through bilateral contracts. Such transactions are the starting point of trading in standardized forward contracts. Initially, such contracts are physical, that is, volumes are delivered outside the day-ahead auction and the agreed price is paid in full between the buyer and the seller at the time of delivery.[3] In the further development of the market, spot market prices are the reference for financial contracts.[4]

The maturity of a market is judged by the liquidity of trading contracts and the duration of a stable forward curve,[5] gradually stretching further into the future. In a liquid market, prices in supply contracts are set by the forward curve, with a small margin on top reflecting the special conditions and service features of the supply. Supply contracts are not as standardized as trading contracts, and the market in such contracts is not liquid enough to provide independent price discovery.

4 CONTRACT FORMULATION

Contracts clauses that keep volumes or customers out of the market will hurt market liquidity, and the effect of such clauses will be more serious if they are part of long-term contracts. This might have been a valid concern in the early phases of market reform, and particularly in the gas market. However, Directorate General of Competition seems to overemphasize the importance of contracts in general and of contract duration in particular. Contracts with fixed total volumes will in general not prevent development of the market or reduce the size of it. On the contrary, such contracts will tend to increase trading volumes, since the buyers (consumers and traders) have less flexibility than generators and will have to use the market to balance their portfolios. Moreover, regulators sometimes make use of flexible contracts ('virtual power plants') to create a spot market where market dominance would otherwise prevent the transparency of marginal costs and prices ('capacity release programs').[6] The beneficial effect of such contract features is stronger with long contract duration.

Contracts with a fixed price and flexible volumes are often challenging to interpret in a market context. A typical example would be a supply contract where the buyer has to take what he or she needs from one seller and then pay a given (fixed or indexed) price for what he or she has taken. In order to prevent reselling in those periods where contract prices are lower than the market price, such contracts may prevent full market access for the customers, and are then clearly detrimental to market development. Similar supply contracts to distributors are often accompanied by geographical constraints to prevent competition further downstream. Contract clauses restricting market participation are probably no longer enforceable independently of contract duration.

5 INDUSTRIAL POWER SUPPLY

End-users of power do not need fixed prices unless electricity constitutes a large part of their overall costs. Experience shows that contract prices in general are higher than floating prices, that is, you have to pay for price security. Industries with high power costs that have low capital intensity or are close to the end of their economic lives may also choose to operate with short power contracts or floating power prices.[7]

Power-intensive industries are highly capital intensive, and investing in a plant links production to a certain site for decades. Since there is a common, globalized product market for most of these industries and competitors are exposed to different, regional electricity markets, no major investments are made without security of electricity cost at an affordable level for at least 10–20 years. There are only two long-term supply options: developing own generation capacity or concluding a long-term supply contract. In some cases, there will be a common interest for buyers and sellers to enter into long-term contracts. In isolated, small markets, generators may wish to secure off-take by entering into a contract. In a mature energy market, investors in new, capital-intensive generation like hydropower and nuclear, may have their capital cost reduced through long-term fixed price contracts.

In most other circumstances, however, it is less obvious that a counterpart for simple long-term contracts will be found. Suppliers with a variable fuel cost in their generation may find that their total risk is increased by selling at fixed prices, since fuel costs and electricity market prices correlate positively in the first place, and will consequently charge a risk premium. Furthermore, companies with a strong financial position frequently want their profit to correlate positively with the price of their main product, and do not want to enter into fixed-price contracts even if it should reduce their financial volatility.

6 POWER SUPPLY IN MARKET TRANSITION

In most of Europe, reform of cross-border trading has largely failed, and wholesale markets are still national in scope, dominated by the incumbent power generator. Only a few national markets in north-west Europe are reasonably well functioning, and the Nordic market is the only example of a transnational wholesale market. In order to make markets in 'grid-bound' energies function effectively, strong regulation and standardization is required. The European Union (EU) will have no effective regulatory powers to enforce a standardized pan-European market design until the implementation of the third energy legislation package and the establishment of the new regulatory agency, the Agency for the Cooperation of Energy Regulators (ACER). A real market integration ending the domination of the national champions is therefore still at least a decade away.

Shortening of contracts' duration will increase frequency of renewal and might in principle improve market liquidity and price transparency in such contracts. In any reasonably well-functioning electricity market, however, the wholesale market will provide the required price transparency independently of liquidity in supply contracts.

Restrictions on long-term contracts are frequently based on the implicit contention that the incumbents foreclose the market by offering long-term contracts below the market price. The reality as seen from the customer, however, is that the restrictions reduce competition. They are used as negotiation tools by the suppliers; restrictions are referred to as a political risk, and are used to shorten contract duration and/or prevent contract renewal that would otherwise be made as a matter of routine. This reduces the possibility for power-intensive industries to get electricity supply at prices reflecting the real price expectations and to get a contract duration that could open up for investment.

The main improvement focus for most European electricity markets should be on lack of trust in market pricing due to real or potential manipulation of the spot price and the forward curve by dominant generators. Foreclosure is less critical and the main 'cure' for foreclosure, limiting the duration of long-term contracts, does not serve its purpose. Volumes for potential market entrants are already available from the spot market, and price transparency is not improved by more frequent renewals.

A policy aimed at opening the market by reducing overall supply costs for the benefit of power users may thus end up hurting a particularly vulnerable customer group. Supply conditions that the industry depends on are outlawed without good reason in a situation where the market conditions are such that no real alternative is available.

NOTES

1. Dominant players will be able to influence prices in a way that increases their profit. Withholding generation capacity from the market, that is, bidding prices above their marginal cost, is the most common strategy in such cases. Creating uncertainty for other players by bidding unpredictably is another.
2. In this case, the market price equals system marginal cost, and the total value of generation and consumption cannot be increased by moving generation or consumption between market players.
3. Physical bilateral contracts reduce market volumes, but do not influence spot market pricing and liquidity, since the same volume is taken from both supply and demand.
4. A financial contract is an agreement to fix the price for a nominal volume by paying the difference between the reference price and the agreed price. Volumes on the day-ahead exchange are not affected by such contracts. Physical and financial contracts are in most ways equivalent; the main difference is the extent of counterpart risk.
5. Forward curves are set by the pricing of trading contracts and thus indirectly by expectations of the spot market price and the risk profiles of those offering and demanding such contracts.
6. The buyers of such contracts pay a fixed (or indexed) sum per time unit and a fixed (or indexed) price per unit of electricity taken, corresponding to fixed (capital) cost and variable (fuel) cost in fossil-fuelled generation, respectively.
7. Staying flexible has a financial value. Entering into a fixed-price contract may reduce operational flexibility by increasing the cost of ceasing operation temporarily or permanently.

8. Competition and long-term contracts in the Dutch electricity market

Machiel Mulder[1]

1 INTRODUCTION

About a decade ago competition was introduced in the electricity industry in the Netherlands which significantly influenced both the structure of the market and the way market players operate. Central coordination of supply decisions was replaced by decentralized decision-making while markets were created to take care of coordination. In addition vertical relationships within the industry became increasingly commercial owing to the implementation of ownership unbundling between network activities on the one hand and production and supply activities on the other. Moreover reducing bottlenecks in transport and trade between countries enlarged the size of the markets in geographical sense, making producers and traders more vulnerable to foreign competition.

Although these structural measures undoubtedly have significantly improved the functioning of the electricity market, a number of factors remain which potentially hinder competition. One of those factors might be the presence of long-term contracts and other kinds of vertical relationships between producers and retailers. Such relationships might result in foreclosure if it hinders other (new) firms in production or retail to enter the market or to increase market share (see EC 2007). After all, long-term contracts between a dominant supplier, on the one hand, and customers, on the other, might prevent other suppliers from gaining access to uncommitted generation or to customers. As a result competition is seriously hindered.

In this chapter we analyse from an empirical perspective the significance of long-term contracts in the Dutch electricity market and its impact on competition in this market. How essential are long-term contracts in terms of numbers and, more importantly, what is the impact of these contracts on competition in the electricity market? What is the relative importance of long-term contracts compared with other factors affecting competition in this market, like concentration in generation, transparency and switching costs? A related matter is to what extent long-term contracts are needed to facilitate investments in new power plants.

In order to answer these questions we first describe the structural changes which have been implemented in the Dutch electricity market over the past decade and the consequences for the relationships between the different players in the industry (section 2). Next, we focus on the role of long-term contracts in investment, dispatch and trading behavior of electricity producers (section 3). Afterwards we go into the relationship between players in the wholesale market and the infrastructure owners (section 4). Finally we analyse the retail market,[2] discussing the role of long-term contracts between suppliers[3] and consumers and analysing other factors which influence competition in this market (section 5). In section 6 we formulate some conclusions about the impact of long-term contracts on competition in the Dutch electricity market.

The analysis is mainly based on the annual monitoring activities conducted by the Dutch energy regulator (see NMa 2008a, 2008b, 2010), but also some references are made to economic literature and reports of the European Commission.

2 STRUCTURAL CHANGES AND CONTRACTS

Since the introduction of competition in the electricity market at about the turn of the twenty-first century, several structural changes have been implemented. Vertically integrated firms have been replaced by fully separated network operators, on the one hand, and commercial firms active in wholesale and retail, on the other.[4] As a result, different types of commercial and contractual relations have replaced internal relations within the firms. In the past, investment, production and maintenance decisions in both transport and generation were centrally coordinated at national level. All Dutch generation firms were united in the Sep[5] which took care of the coordination. Now all firms are assumed to take, independently, their strategic and operational management decisions, while the coordination at industry level is achieved through exchanges, over-the-counter (OTC) markets and bilateral contracts.

The structural changes in the industry have resulted in different types of contracts between the different players in the market. Electricity producers and traders book both medium-term and short-term capacity on interconnections in order to import or export. They also conclude different type of contracts to buy their inputs (for example, natural gas) and to sell and buy electricity. The production of electricity is mainly concentrated in the hands of five firms, while a large number of fairly small producers (such as horticulture growers and wind farms) act as a kind of fringe suppliers. In the retail market, which was liberalized in 2004, electricity is also sold and bought on both a short-term and a long-term basis. The contracts can be distinguished in undefined-period contracts as well defined-period contracts. The retail market is also still relatively concentrated: the share of the three largest suppliers in the sale of electricity is approximately 80 per cent (NMa 2010).

The structural changes have also affected the relationships between network firms and commercial firms. The network operators include one operator of the national high-tension transmission network (TenneT) and approximately 10 regional electricity distribution operators. All network operators are owned by public authorities: the state owns 100 per cent of the shares of TenneT, while local and regional authorities have the shares of the distribution network operators. All network operators are subject to incentive regulation which determine the annual revenues and, hence, the tariffs for using the networks. As a consequence users of the networks do not need to conclude financial contracts with network operators for access to the domestic network. For using cross-border transport capacity, however, these contracts exist.

3 WHOLESALE MARKETS

In the Dutch wholesale electricity market supply originates from a small number of large producers, a large number of small producers and, finally, import. The large producers have a significant share in the market, both regarding generation capacity and actual production. The Herfindal–Hirschman Index (HHI) varies from about 1700 to 2000. These firms mainly have both coal-fired and gas-fired power plants and no longer have stakes in the (domestic) distribution sector since the (forced) separation of networks from commercial activities. Some of these firms belong to vertically integrated companies also active in the distribution industry, while others are fully directed at the wholesale market. Some vertically integrated companies are also active players in the gas market, as shippers, operators of gas storages and/or producers.

The small electricity producers mainly include industries and horticultural farmers using combined heat and power (CHP) installations in order to meet their own need for heat. The power produced by these installations is both used for own consumption and sold on the power market, depending on the actual electricity price. Besides domestic production, import is

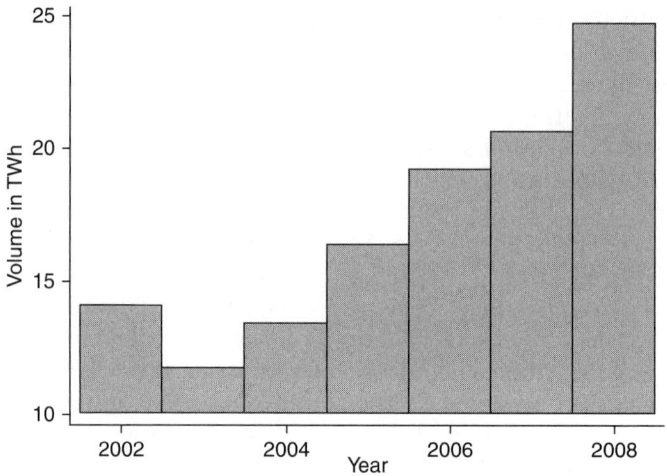

Source: NMa (2010).

Figure 8.1 Traded volume on the day-ahead exchange (APX), 2002–08

relatively important in the Dutch market: annual import is about 20 per cent of total supply. The import capacity is allocated by auctioning (see section 4). In order to improve the market structure, domestic producers face a restriction in booking import capacity. Each of the large firms can only book 400 MW in total, while the total import capacity is about 10 times as high.

On the demand side of the wholesale market several groups of buyers are active: suppliers on the retail market, large companies in energy-intensive industries and traders. The sale of electricity occurs on various market places, both exchanges (Amsterdam Power Exchange [APX] and European Energy Derivations Exchange [ENDEX]) and OTC markets, and via bilateral trading. In all cases different types of products are traded, from the very short term (intraday) to the long term (year ahead). These markets can be viewed as highly liquid. The (traded) volume on the day-ahead exchange (APX) has grown sharply. Since 2003 the volume has doubled (see Figure 8.1). Also the traded volume in forwards has increased significantly (see Figure 8.2).

Long-term contracts are broadly used by electricity producers as an important instrument to reduce their risks related to the baseload production. By concluding long-term contracts (yearly and longer) for both inputs (gas, coal) and output (electricity), the return on investment in baseload production can be fairly well assured *ex ante*. Contracts for

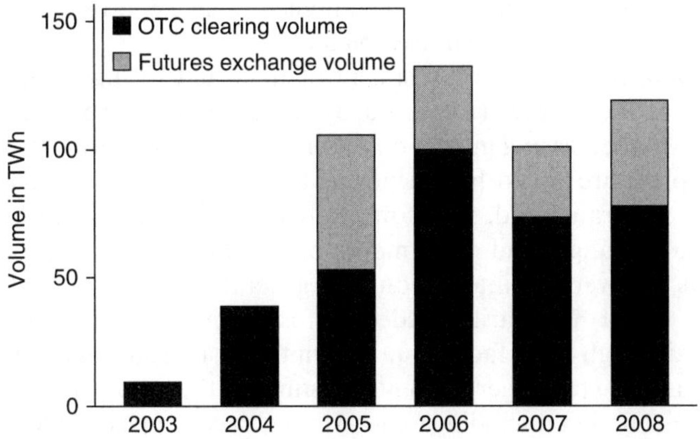

Source: NMa (2010).

Figure 8.2 Volume on the forward markets on the exchange (ENDEX) and the OTC, 2004–08

shorter terms (quarterly ahead up to intraday) are used for matching the level of production to actual market circumstances. The relative importance of long-term and shorter-term contracts depends on the portfolio of a company. Companies having mainly baseload generation capacity use more long-term contracts than companies more directed at producing peak load. In general one can conclude that long-term contracts have a high share of the total portfolio of producers. This can also be seen from the differences between Figures 8.1 and 8.2: the traded volume in forwards is about four times as high as the traded volume in day-ahead products while the churn factor[6] on both marketplaces has a comparable size. In other words, the share of the day-ahead exchange in the total Dutch electricity market is about 25 per cent.[7]

From this it follows that long-term contracts form a key instrument in risk management for both electricity producers and their customers. These contracts are also needed to solve a hold-up problem related to irreversible investments. As several marketplaces for long-term contracts exist which are highly liquid, investors can be sure they will be able to recoup the costs of investments, provided of course those investments are efficient. The experience of the Dutch market shows that investments in power plants can be triggered by liquid commodity markets where electricity can be sold through different type of contracts.[8] If all recently published investment plans were realized, the total size of generation capacity in the Dutch market would double (TenneT 2009). Note that these plans not only include peak-load plants (such as combined cycle gas turbines), but also baseload plants (such as coal-fired plants).[9]

The realization of these investment plans would strongly improve the structure of the market (measured by the Residual Supply Index) and would have a decreasing impact on the electricity price (NMa 2010). Some of these plans are issued by independent power producers which are not vertically integrated and, therefore, fully depend on the sale of electricity on the exchanges and other marketplaces. From these empirical facts it follows that vertical integration of a generating company and a retail company is not necessarily needed to foster investments in new power plans.[10] Although these facts do not form the final proof that energy-only markets are able to trigger efficient investments, they show that the Dutch energy-only market (including long-term contracts) appears able to trigger many investment projects. As a result there is no ongoing debate on a looming shortage of generation capacity as was the case a number of years ago. Instead, the policy debate now focuses on the question of whether the existing capacity of the networks is able to facilitate the investment in generation capacity which the power producers are planning to make.[11]

The key issue now is whether long-term contracts have adverse effects on competition. Regarding the Dutch market, one can conclude that the wholesale market is characterized by imperfect competition, but this is not due to the importance of long-term contracts. A relatively large part of electricity is sold on the day-ahead basis, partly on the power exchange (APX) and partly on the OTC market.[12] These marketplaces offer new players, among others, the possibility to get access to energy users. In addition a significant part of the long-term contracts is concluded through the OTC which also offer better options for new players than bilateral contracts do. Moreover, from the annual survey among traders in the electricity markets, gaining access to the markets is not mentioned as one of the issues which should be improved (NMa 2010).

The imperfections in competition in Dutch markets follow mainly from the high degree of concentration in supply and the inefficiencies in the utilization of the interconnections (see section 4). In particular during peak hours, at least one producer is pivotal, meaning that its capacity is needed for producing the load which is needed at that moment (NMa 2010). The presence of (one or more) pivotal producers happens to be related to the price of electricity (on the day-ahead market, APX) and, hence, the profitability of producers.

Figure 8.3 shows the relationship between the Residual Supply Index (RSI)[13] and the profit at the margin. Estimating the relationship econometrically (and correcting for the impact of other factors like the scarcity in the market), it appears to be statistically significant. The more players are

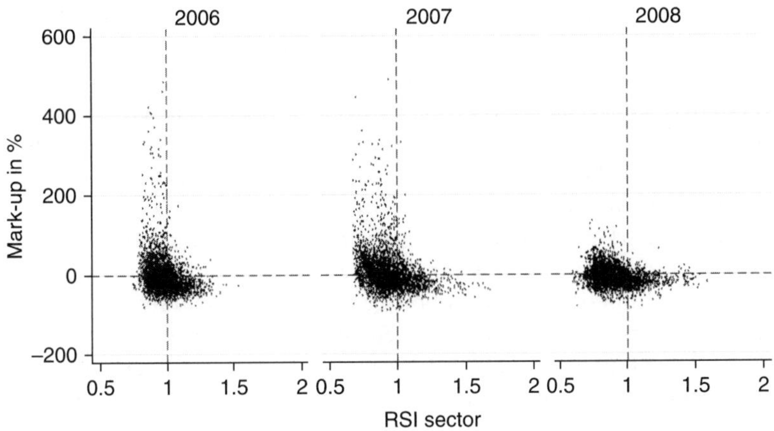

Note: RSI sector < 1: at least 1 player is pivotal; mark-up > 0: marginal plant makes a profit.

Source: NMa (2010).

Figure 8.3 *Relationship between pivotality and market results in the Dutch electricity market, 2006, 2007 and 2008*

pivotal, the higher the profit at the margin (see also London Economics 2007 where the same conclusions were found).

Hence longer-term contracts (on monthly, quarterly and yearly bases) play a key role in enabling electricity producers to reduce their risks, but they do not necessarily obstruct competition. In the Dutch market, the lack of competition during many peak hours, however, is one of the driving factors behind market results. Policies to improve competition should therefore be directed at enlarging the relevant geographical market and removing any inefficient barrier for new investments.[14]

4 ACCESS TO INFRASTRUCTURE

Long-term contracts play a limited role in the utilization of the infrastructure in the electricity industry. The capacity of the interconnection capacity on the Dutch borders with Germany and Belgium is allocated on annual, monthly, daily and intra-day bases. For all these periods capacity is allocated by means of auctions. The auctioning of day-ahead capacity on the Dutch–German border is done explicitly, but on the Dutch–Belgium (and France) border implicitly, which means that the auction of transport capacity is integrated with the trade on the day-ahead market of the commodity in these countries (APX, Belpex and Powernext, respectively). Capacity that is obtained for year-ahead or month-ahead has to be used (nominated shortly ahead) by the owners otherwise the TSO will apply Use it or lose it (UIOLI) and make that capacity available to other market players. On the Dutch–Norwegian border the capacity (of NorNed) is fully allocated on day-ahead basis by means of explicit auctioning.

In using market-based mechanisms in allocating cross-border capacity, the electricity industry is far ahead of the gas industry (see also EC 2007). In that industry, cross-border capacity is mainly allocated on long-term basis by non-market-based methods, in particular first come first served (FCFS). As a result long-term contracts between incumbents and the network operator hinder access of new players and traders to the gas market (NMa 2008a). This problem does not occur in the electricity market: cross-border capacity is not allocated for the long term, while market-based mechanisms are used to allocate capacity in the short (intra-day, day-ahead) and medium term (month-ahead, year-ahead) and UIOLI is applied to make unused booked capacity available to the market.

Although long-term contracts do not obstruct efficient utilization of the infrastructure in the electricity industry, the current interconnections are not optimally used. This holds in particular for the capacity on the Dutch–German border. Because of the explicit auctioning of day-ahead capacity, the allocation of transport capacity is not fully coordinated with the need for transport following from transactions on the day-ahead market. By replacing the current explicit auction mechanism by an implicit form, as planned for 2010, the utilization will become more efficient as can be seen by the experience on the Dutch–Belgium (and France) border. Figure 8.4 shows the degree of utilization of this interconnection in relation to the prices on the Dutch (APX) and Belgium day-ahead market (Belpex), while Figure 8.5 shows the comparable data for the Dutch-German border. On the Dutch-Belgium border the capacity is mostly fully utilized when differences in prices between the two day-ahead markets exists. In other words if prices differ between these countries, the interconnection is often fully used. Hence remaining price differences between these countries are fully due to physical restrictions of the interconnections.[15]

The Dutch–German border tells a completely different story: here, price differences go together with utilization of the interconnection below 100 per cent. It happens frequently that prices differ significantly (50 or 100 euros/MWh) while the interconnection is not completely utilized. This inefficiency is almost fully due to the inefficiency of the explicit auctioning. Firms have bought capacity on the interconnection before they know how much capacity they actually need.

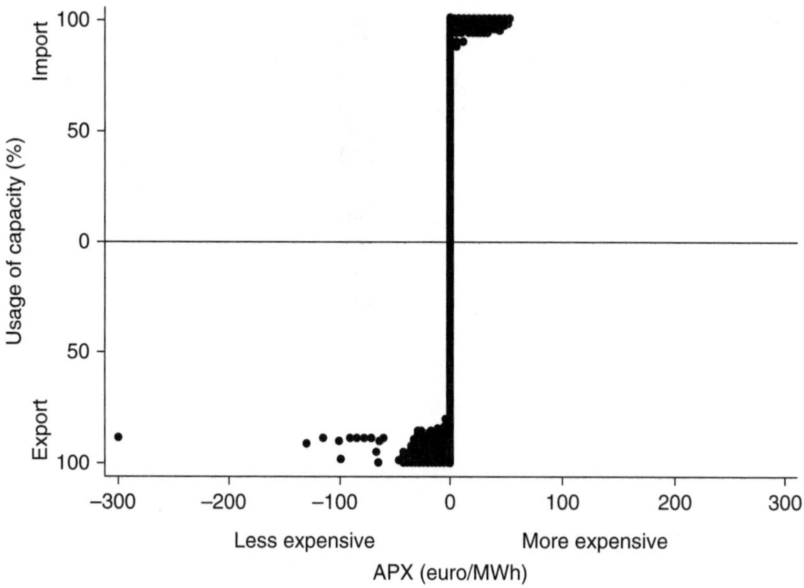

Source: NMa (2010).

Figure 8.4 Utilization of Dutch–Belgium interconnection (percentage) in relation to differences in prices between APX and Belpex, 2008 (daily averages)

The figure also shows inefficiency: in a number of hours firms import electricity from Germany when the price at the APX is below the price at the German day-ahead exchange. It would of course be more efficient to leave the electricity in Germany and sell it on the German market and buy cheaper electricity on the Dutch market. The same inefficiency occurs in export: the Netherlands is exporting to Germany during hours when the APX price is above the European Electricity Exchange (EEX) price. These inefficiencies are caused by the transaction costs related to changing current contracts.

Regarding the access to the national grid, long-term contracts do not play a role at all. Network operators (both the national and the distribution) are legally obliged to connect all producers. Producers pay connection charges, but do not pay for transport. In the Dutch system, all transport costs are passed on to the final energy users. The tariffs, both for connection as for transport, are determined by the regulator (NMa). Because of the regulation (and the legal framework behind it), the network operators can be sure they will be reimbursed for all (efficient) investments

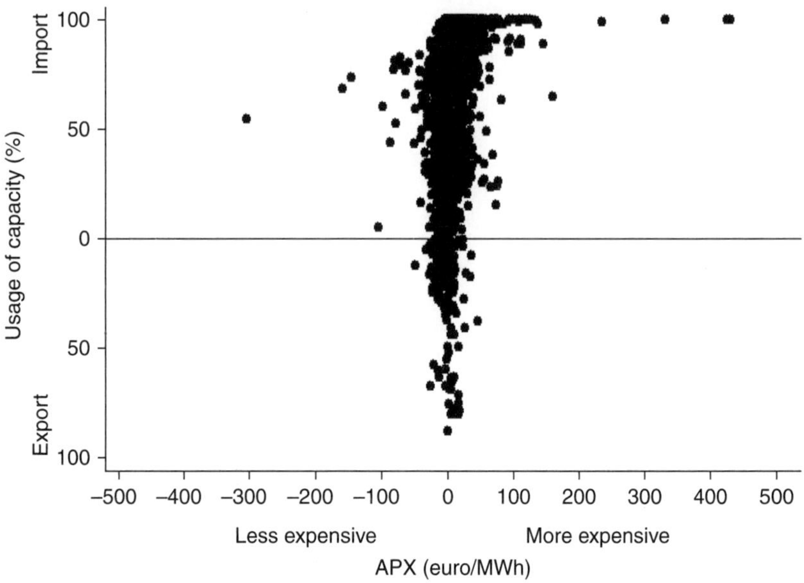

Source: NMa (2010).

Figure 8.5 Utilization of Dutch–German interconnection (percentage) in relation to differences in prices between APX and EEX, 2008 (daily averages)

costs. Hence in the domestic network there is no need for long-term contracts with users of the infrastructure when network operators have to decide about investments in network extension.

5 RETAIL MARKET

The Dutch retail market for electricity is liberalized since July 2004. Although a significant number of new retailers have entered the market since market opening, the market is still fairly concentrated. More than 20 retailers are active in this market, but the market share of the three largest suppliers is approximately 80 per cent. The aggregated market share of these players declined strongly immediately after market opening in 2004, but it has been rather constant over the past four years. Apparently, entering the market as a new player is less difficult than acquiring larger stakes in the supply to consumers. One of the factors hindering growth of new players is the rather passive attitude of a large number of consumers (see

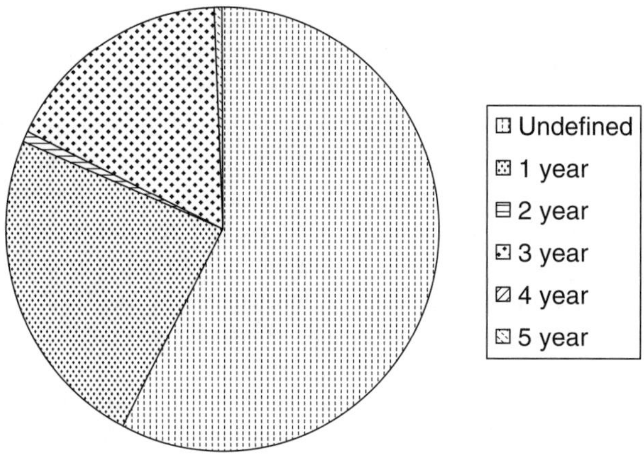

Source: NMa (2010).

Figure 8.6 Contract durations in the Dutch retail market for electricity, per ultimo 2008 (percentage)

also Waddams 2005 for the UK market). The majority of all consumers have never switched to another supplier. Assuming consumers being rational economic agents, they likely expect that the potential benefits do not clearly outweigh the costs and risks of switching (NMa 2008b).

A significant number of consumers have switched, however, to another type of contract offered by the same supplier. At 31 December 2008 approximately 40 per cent of all consumers had concluded fixed-term contracts (one, two, three and four years), which imply that they have changed the default contract characterized by an undefined time period to a defined-period contract (see Figure 8.6). The largest group of consumers (about 60 per cent) still had an undefined-period contract, while about 25 per cent had a one-year contract. Compared to earlier years the number of consumers choosing for defined-period contracts is growing slightly, albeit at a relatively low level.

Consumers choose long-term contracts to mitigate the risk of price changes during these periods. For many consumers, however, it seems to be difficult to fully assess future developments in the retail price. As a result they easily might conclude inefficient (and expensive) contracts, for instance by choosing long-term contracts when the current electricity price is high while the future price can be expected to decline significantly. These suboptimal decisions were taken by many consumers recently, as they concluded defined-period contracts at relatively high price levels, while choosing undefined contracts would have been more efficient as spot-market prices declined shortly afterwards. It appears that consumers were not aware that the electricity price in the Dutch retail market lags a number of months behind the wholesale price.

Although consumers are fully free to choose the contract they like, there should be some kind of protection because of the lack of transparency as well as knowledge about future prices. In the Netherlands, therefore, consumer prices are assessed by the regulator before suppliers can make new price offers to customers. In addition, rules are in place regarding cancellation fees for defined-period contracts in order to enable consumers to change contracts relatively easy when they would like to do so.

Given the existence of these consumer protection measures, the emergence of long-term contracts in the retail market can be seen as an improvement of the market as consumers have more options to choose while they are protected from choosing (very) inefficient (that is, expensive) contracts. For suppliers in the retail market long-term contracts can also be seen as beneficial as these contracts enable them to mitigate their price risks. This depends of course on the contracts they have concluded on the wholesale market. If the long-term retail price is directly related to the long-term price in the wholesale contract, the price risk is fully shifted to the seller on the wholesale market. In this case both supplier on the retail market and end-user together have to pay the risk premium for this shifting of risk. How this risk premium is allocated among these two depends on the degree of competition in the retail market. Anyway, as long as consumers can easily change contracts and have the option to choose another supplier, the occurrence of long-term contracts can only be seen as an improvement in the functioning in the retail energy market. If these conditions are met, there is no need to implement any other measures to improve competition and to protect the customers.

The measures to improve the retail market should primarily focus on increasing transparency. Consumers will become more active players in the retail market when the (perceived) costs and risks of switching to another supplier are reduced and the consumers can have more confidence in the quality of the information about the different contracts offered by suppliers.

6 CONCLUSION

In this chapter we have explored empirical evidence on the significance of long-term contracts in the Dutch electricity market and its impact on competition. To what extent do the presence of long-term contracts affect competition, what other factors are affecting competition and by which measures could competition effectively be enhanced?

It appears that long-term contracts are a key element in the functioning of the wholesale market, while also becoming more important in the retail market. In the wholesale market long-term contracts are concluded on liquid marketplaces (both exchanges and OTC markets) where rights can be transferred freely to other interested parties. Although specific parties might conclude bilateral long-term contracts (between a generation company and a large industrial user, for instance), these contracts do not limit other parties from buying or selling electricity. As about 25 per cent of all electricity is traded on the day-ahead exchange, one can expect that new players (traders) are able to enter the market and gain access to uncommitted generation capacity or to existing energy users.

Regarding the utilization of the infrastructure, long-term contracts do not play a role, except from one-year bookings of cross-border capacity. Looking at the available empirical data one cannot conclude that the current long-term contracts in the electricity market negatively affect competition. Contrary to the gas industry where incumbents have longstanding access rights to the infrastructure (pipelines and storages), newcomers are able to get access to the essential infrastructure. Moreover the cross-border infrastructure is allocated on a market-based basis (auctions) giving all players an equal chance to obtain capacity.

In the retail market long-term contracts might hinder competition if consumers could not easily cancel the contract. In the Dutch retail market, however, regulation has been implemented to protect consumers against inefficiently high prices and to enable consumers to easily change contracts if needed. Also here there seems to be no real evidence that the current long-term contracts have a foreclosure effect on the market.

Although there is no empirical evidence that long-term contracts currently form a key problem in the functioning of the Dutch electricity market, other factors do seriously have a negative effect on market outcomes. These factors are the lack of competition between producers, the suboptimal use of the interconnections and the rather passive attitude of consumers in the retail market (see also EC 2007). In order to solve these problems in the functioning of the electricity market, different kind of measures are needed.

In order to reduce the pivotality of existing producers, inefficient barriers for investments in new plants should be removed, like the long lead time of permit procedures as well as scarcity in the national grid. The competition in the wholesale market will also be improved by introducing more efficient allocation procedures regarding cross-border capacity, like implicit auctioning. In order to foster competition in the retail market, transparency has to be improved. In particular, consumers should get more adequate information about prices and conditions in the different type of contracts as well as information about the real costs and risk of switching supplier.

So, several measures have to be taken to improve the functioning of the electricity market further. Measures regarding long-term contracts seem not to be needed, except from the existing one which is directed at the retail market. Nevertheless, careful attention to effects of these contracts is needed as they are a possible threat to competition.

NOTES

1. The author thanks his colleagues and the anonymous reviewers for valuable comments on the draft version. The views expressed in this chapter are those of the author and do not necessarily reflect those of the Netherlands Competition Authority.
2. By 'retail market', we refer to the energy market for residential users as well as small business users.
3. Note that we use the term 'suppliers' for both producers on the wholesale market and those players supplying electricity to end consumers. The term 'traders' is used for those players, not being producers, which are active on the wholesale market. The term 'distribution' is only used in relation to the (regional and local) networks. Because of the full unbundling, distribution operators may not have any linkage with traders, producers or suppliers.
4. See Mulder et al. (2007) for an overview of the debate on costs and benefits of introducing ownership unbundling in the Dutch distribution industry.
5. Sep stands for Samenwerkende Elektriciteitsproductiebedrijven, which means cooperation of electricity producing firms.
6. The churn factor is the ratio between the traded volume and the volume actually delivered.
7. This is a fairly high percentage given the fact that traders do not have a (legal) obligation to trade via the exchange as exists in some other countries (see EC 2007).
8. See Hogan (2005) for similar conclusions.
9. About 50 per cent of all investments plans refer to coal-fired or coal-gas fired power plants (NMa 2008a).
10. As EC (2007) concludes, the existence of liquid market places reduces the need for vertical integration and bilateral long-term contracts.
11. One of the topics in this debate is congestion management, that is, how to implement market-based measures in order to give incentives to producers whether or not to produce in certain (congested) areas at certain moments.
12. Note that the day-ahead prices on the APX are closely related to the day-ahead prices on the OTC. The correlation coefficient between those prices is about 85 per cent. As a matter of fact, the relationship between the short-term prices and the long-term prices is much less stronger as these prices refer to quite different products. After all, electricity to be supplied the next day differs largely from electricity to be supplied all days in the coming year.
13. The Residual Supply Index measures per producer the relationship between the generation capacity of other producers and the total demand. If the ratio is below 1, the other producers are not able to fully supply what is needed. Hence, the producer is pivotal. The RSI in the graph refers to the RSI of the most pivotal player at that moment.
14. Even if the investments in new plants are made by the players currently active in the

market, the market structure would improve. After all, each extension of generation capacity of each player makes the other players less pivotal (*ceteris paribus*).

15. By the wording 'physical restrictions of the interconnections' is meant the restriction of the capacity which is made available by the TSOs for market transactions. After all, TSOs reserve a (significant) part of the really physical capacity for system balance purposes (like handling loop flows).

REFERENCES

European Commission (EC) (2007), *DG Competition Report on Energy Sector Inquiry*, Brussels: EC.

Hogan, W.W. (2005), 'On an "energy only" electricity market design for resource adequacy', Harvard Electricity Policy Group Working Paper.

London Economics (2007), *Structure and Performance of Six European Wholesale Electricity Markets in 2003, 2004 and 2005*, London: London Economics.

Mulder, M., V. Shestalova and G.J.T. Zwart (2007), 'Vertical separation of the Dutch energy distribution industry: an economic assessment of the political debate', *Intereconomics: Review of European Economic Policy*, **42** (6), 305–10.

Netherlands Competition Authority (NMa) (2008a), *Monitor Energy Markets 2007; Analysis of Developments on the Dutch Wholesale Markets for Gas and Electricity*, The Hague: NMa.

Netherlands Competition Authority (NMa) (2008b), *Monitor kleinverbruikers-markt gas en elektriciteit*, The Hague: NMa.

Netherlands Competition Authority (NMa) (2010), *Monitor Energy Markets 2009*, The Hague: NMa.

TenneT (2009), *Monitor leveringszekerheid 2009*, Arnhem: TenneT.

Waddams-Price, C. (2005), *The Effect of Liberalising UK Retail Energy Markets on Consumers*, Oxford: Oxford University Press.

PART III

Competition Policy and Long-term Contracts

9. Long-term contracts and competition policy in European energy markets

Adrien de Hauteclocque and Jean-Michel Glachant

1 INTRODUCTION

Today the allocation of regulatory powers in the European Union (EU) is increasingly biased in favour of the *ex post* enforcement of EU competition law (Hauteclocque 2009). The institutional structure of the European Union does not give the European Commission the power to *ex ante* alter property rights in the different member states and thus to carry an aggressive policy of horizontal de-integration which would probably deliver better and faster results (Green and Newbery 1997; Newbery et al. 2003). In addition, the lack of an EU-wide energy regulator with the effective power to monitor and regulate market developments, especially cross-border trade issues, is particularly detrimental to the integration and the good functioning of European energy markets (Glachant and Lévêque 2009). The third liberalization package is nonetheless initiating the creation of an Agency for the Cooperation of Energy Regulators (ACER). In order to optimize the development of the transmission grid at the European level and facilitate a consensual approach to the regulation of interconnection, the ACER is to create an institutionalized forum where decisions will be made more easily. However, the ACER is likely to be vested with limited discretionary powers in practice. We last note that whatever the scope of the ACER regulatory powers, it does not constrain in any way the use of EU competition law by the European Commission as Articles 101 and 102 Treaty on the Functioning of the European Union (TFEU) are superior to secondary EU law in the hierarchy of European legal norms.

While sector-specific regulation shows obvious signs of weakness, the European Commission has announced it would use its competition powers with even more strength in the coming years (DG COMP 2007;

Monti 2003). We note that in the period leading to the first liberalization directive, the use of the internal market rules to fight import and export monopolies was systematically favoured and, subsequently, merger control took a more prominent role with the merger wave of the late 1990s and early 2000s (Lévêque and Montorus 2008; Thomas 2007) despite the relatively small number of prohibitions (Cameron 2007). The increased use of the rules on cartel and abuse of dominance (and in another field, state aid) is an important change in the dynamics of European regulatory practice.

The case of long-term contracts is particularly interesting as they have become one of the main priorities for competition enforcement at the EU level (DG COMP 2007). Long-term contracts are indeed a topical example of the difficulties faced by competition authorities with the liberalization of network industries. While energy supply and transport relationships often keep on being structured on a long-term basis for the sake of hedging or financing, they also carry risks of foreclosure and abuses of dominance. Hence, the short- and long-term effects of long-term contracts on the competitive structure, consumer welfare and investment are ambiguous. The objective of this chapter is thus to investigate and characterize how the European Commission manages these trade-offs in the context of competition cases.

The chapter is divided as follows. Section 2 reviews the different arguments for and against long-term contracts discussed in the economic literature. Sections 3 and 4 analyse the new methodology which has emerged in the European Commission to analyse foreclosure of access to customers in the new liberalized context since the early 2000s. The chapter particularly focuses on the analysis of the following cases: *Gas Natural/Endesa* (2000), *Synergen* (2001), *Repsol* (2005), *E.ON Ruhrgas* (2006) and most importantly *Distrigaz* (2007) and the pending *EDF* case (2009).

2 LESSONS FROM THE COMPETITION ECONOMICS OF LONG-TERM CONTRACTS IN THE CONTEXT OF LIBERALIZED ENERGY MARKETS: A SYNTHESIS

Competition policy is about maximizing long term social welfare, with sometimes a bias in favour of consumer welfare in the European Union (for example, Eilmansberger 2005). This often implies constraining the freedom of some economic agents in the short term to reach a greater social value over several periods of times. The balance between the efficiency gains of long-term contracting for a few individual market players and the potential negative effects on social welfare are at the heart of the dilemma with long-term contracts in decentralized energy markets. This section undertakes an assessment of the competition economics of long-term contracts in the context of fully or partially decentralized markets, with a focus on the electricity sector,[1] and shows that economic analysis, though yielding interesting insights, does not bring any easy solution.

2.1 Long-term Contracts Not Only Have Advantages for Contracting Parties . . .

The main advantage of long-term contracting for individual firms is to hedge price and quantity risks in their input and output markets and therefore facilitate investment, operation and entry. In the 'textbook' reform model, sufficiently deep and stable spot markets were to coordinate behaviour. Longer-term contracts traded on financial forward markets or over-the-counter were to replace vertical integration of utilities regulated in cost of service and complement spot market contracting (Joskow and Schmalensee 1983). The fast development of innovative financial instruments such as call/put options, contracts for differences, or swaps was thus intended to support physical contracting by providing insurance devices (Chao and Hutington 1998).

Yet, spot markets and financial instruments most often remain underdeveloped, hence viable entry and investment tend to depend on the possibility to organize more durable vertical arrangements. Where they have developed to a substantial extent (for example, in the UK following the National Electricity Trading Arrangement [NETA], Pennsylvania–New Jersey–Maryland regional market [PJM] in New England, and Australia), financial forward contracts have not developed to the extent predicted, especially on duration (Anderson et al. 2007; Finon and Perez 2008; Meade and O'Connor 2009). In electricity for instance, the underdevelopment of spot markets and financial instruments has several causes. First, the pricing models for derivatives used in other energy industries do not work well (Defeuilley and Meunier 2006). The non-storability of the commodity and the lack of supply and demand elasticity do not allow forward prices to correctly represent anticipation of their price realization (Finon and Perez 2008).

In addition, as price spikes are particularly hard to anticipate, the usual financial counterparties are not incentivized to bring liquidity to the market. Consequently, spot and forward markets are highly volatile and remain limited to two to four years, with a drastic drop in liquidity levels over one year in most markets (Parsons 2008). This does not facilitate investment and does not provide any reliable guidance for the pricing of longer-term bilateral contracts. In practice, this resulted in the wide failure of the pure merchant producer model, as has been shown by the USA and the UK experiences (Michaels 2006). When market structures are highly concentrated, spot and forward markets generally remain underdeveloped as well because vertically integrated incumbents generally tend to rely on inside dealing (DG COMP 2007).

However, it is not clear whether short-term cash management rationale should extend to pure long-term hedging strategies not linked to any new investments in capacity. Indeed, long-term hedging in this case would severely limit profit opportunities (Parsons 2008).

As concerns investment in electricity generation capacity, future cash flows are uncertain when forward markets are underdeveloped. The uncertainty on the returns will lead risk-averse investors to under-invest.

Long-term contracts may mitigate this by providing an insurance device which will also help secure funds with investment banks under project financing structures (Finon and Roques 2008). In the early stages of liberalization, lenders trusted market mechanisms and agreed to finance highly leveraged special purpose vehicles without any other collateral than the project's physical and financial assets. There was a belief that merchant generators could obtain financing on comparable terms with the former utilities, without needing to rely on rigid vertical arrangements with retailers holding a reliable customer base to transfer risks further downstream (Chao et al. 2008). As a result, highly leveraged project financing schemes coupled with hybrid financing structures and asset-backed securities were to ensure capital for investment at sufficiently low cost. This then put pressure on project profitability as no risk diversification was possible and the lenders soon started to look for projects backed by credible long-term contracts.[2] When organized wholesale markets are underdeveloped, the inherent asset specificity of electricity generation tends to increase and well-tailored long-term contracts may help economize on the resulting transaction costs (Adler et al. 1998; Williamson 1975, 1985). Long-term contracts may indeed help solve the problem of counterparty credibility and thus increase the total surplus to be shared (Klein et al. 1978; Williamson 1983). The different players face different price and quantity risks depending on their position on the supply chain and the technology used. Long-term supply contracts might then enable them to allocate that risk to the party best able to manage it (Finon and Roques 2008; Wiser et al. 2004). The pricing scheme should thus mirror the risk aversion profiles of the parties and risk premiums will depend not only on the counterparty's characteristics and risk aversion but also on diverse political, regulatory and macroeconomic risks (Glachant and Hallack 2009).

It is important to note that long-term contracts are not monolithic and display different results in terms of surplus and risk management depending not only on the contracting party but also on contract characteristics and on the technology involved (Wiser et al. 2004). This will have consequences for competition analysis. The inclusion of tacit renewal clauses for instance decreases the transaction costs of renegotiation (EDF-IDEI Report 2007). Reduction clauses may allow the buyer to reduce off-take in case the supplier starts reselling in its commercial area, which protects the buyer's market and his sunk investments. Volume clauses may include rebate mechanisms which may reduce the price for the buyer. Exclusivity clauses also enable the buyer to decrease transaction costs. Indeed, the take-or-pay clauses[3] may provide enough flexibility to avoid breach and thus expensive renegotiation of contracts (Crocker and Masten 1988; Masten and Crocker 1985). Long-term contracts will thus be the most efficient governance structure for contracting parties only when it ensures flexibility for renegotiation and solves the counterparty credibility problem (Borison and Hamm 2005).

The problem of the alignment of contracting incentives between trading partners has been widely underestimated in the early phases of liberalization as it was thought that incentives to contract between producers and consumers would naturally align (Chao et al. 2008). In particular, resellers with different retail commitment downstream in terms of duration, price and quantity would be able to translate short-term downstream commitments into longer-term upstream contracts. Overall, the 'textbook' competition model assumed that large industrial customers, and especially retailers, would be able to both predict the evolution of generation production costs and match these predictions with their resale commitments. However, experience has shown that if most market players are interested in long-term contracts, at least as a complement to spot market contracting and vertical integration, their expectations do not necessarily align (Meade and O'Connor 2009). Pure retailers in particular face the risk of switching of final consumers who are tied for much shorter periods (Neuhoff and De Vries 2004). When spot prices become lower than the price of the contract previously concluded, alternative retailers will be able to propose lower retail prices, which will incentivize consumers to switch. The retailer who contracted for the long term on the wholesale market in the previous period then cannot but align with its rivals and be squeezed. From the generator point of view, the risk of retail entry thus amounts to a problem of hold-up which undermines the counterparty's credibility of any retailer. This risk of hold-up also impacts in cascade fuel suppliers upstream of generators (Meade and O'Connor 2009). Additional factors such as mismatches on preferred load profiles, information asymmetries on generator outage rates and fuel security, generator market power and strategic bargaining all concur to the misalignment of contracting incentives (Meade and O'Connor 2009).

Energy-intensive industries, however, appear more suitable counterparties for long-term contracting with producers. Their needs to access baseload electricity at the lowest cost possible through long-term contracts open new opportunities (Finon and Perez 2008). Competing on a global scale, energy-intensive users may indeed face competitors with largely lower and less volatile fuel prices, which is detrimental to their competitiveness. Similarly to retailers, fixed price contracts may also create margin risks for energy-intensive users but the current state of organized wholesale markets and the need to mitigate CO_2 price risks seem to make them willing to share a limited amount of risk with producers for investments in new hydropower and nuclear plants (Finon and Perez 2008).

As a consequence, long-term contracts will not be efficient for individual market players in all cases. This complicates competition analysis as efficiency gains from long-term contracting will depend on the interplay between the market position of the contracting parties and the market structure itself. In fully de-integrated markets, all market players have a clear interest in contracting forward, at least as a complement to spot contracting, but they cannot find reliable counterparties or they cannot manage the risk of price squeeze. In more concentrated market structures however, the dominant incumbents being vertically integrated, securing dispatch for investment purposes might not be required or simply be an efficient solution. It might be preferable to rely on inside dealing and benefit at the margin from the profit opportunities opened by immature contract markets. Pure new entrant and industrial customers then face input or output foreclosure on spot and forward markets and find themselves in a position of dependency on the incumbent with whom they cannot help but contract with to secure supply or dispatch.

In the face of these constraints, some innovative contract structures involving long-term contracts such as consortium, joint ventures and collective buying schemes are increasingly thought about and implemented. The treatment of these hybrid structures will be one of the biggest challenges for regulators and competition authorities in the coming years.

2.2 . . . They Also Have Positive Effects on the Emergence of Truly Competitive and Sustainable Energy Markets

Some positive effects of long-term contracts may also clearly be depicted from an antitrust point of view. In the short term, long-term supply contracts tend to limit double marginalization (Onofri 2005) and may prevent abuse of dominance on spot markets, although this is still debated.

The strategic behaviour of firms on spot and forward markets has been the main stream of research in the economics of long-term contracts since the early 1990s following the seminal work of Allaz and Vila (1993). The policy recommendations are not unanimous though. Owing to the high concentration levels of supply and demand and the low-demand elasticity, at least in the short term, abuses of market power on spot markets are likely. The different strategies used to exercise market power are complex and 'the researcher rarely knows the strategic variables that firms use to influence market prices or often even the details of how market prices are set' (McRae and Wolak 2009, n.p.). Limiting the potential exercise of market power on organized wholesale markets thus remains a difficult task for competition policy and the potential mitigating properties of long-term contracts on market abuse must be considered with even more care.

Long-term contracts may indeed limit the incentives of dominant operators to abuse their market power on the spot as increases in prices would only be profitable on the uncontracted part of their supplies, hence long-term contracts tend to increase traded volumes as suppliers have fewer incentives to limit supply to drive up prices for the remaining quantities sold, especially when supplier concentration is low (Bushnell 2007; Green 1999; Willem and de Corte 2008).

From a theoretical point of view, Bonasina et al. (2007) argues that the set of assumptions used in the diverse models are too uncertain to firmly ground policy actions. Smeers (2009) shares this view and argues that the insights derived from these models on how market power is (or will be) exercised is too rough to order contract or asset divestiture and might even be counterproductive in terms of efficiency compared to other possible solutions such as promoting single market integration. From a practical point of view, it will indeed be difficult for competition authorities to differentiate between the exercise of market power and legitimate scarcity rents (Fraser 2003). It is also likely that the standard of proof used in courts would in any case be too high to use that argument.

Positive effects of long-term contracts on social welfare are much more obvious in the medium to long term. First, long-term contracts available to new entrants facilitate entry and thus contribute to market building when spot prices are volatile, when contracts (available to new entrants) are sufficiently long and when they can cover sufficiently high volumes (Boom and Buehler 2006; Green and Newbery 1997; Newbery, 1998). For electricity the second positive effect is not only that it facilitates investment and thus contribute to long-term generation adequacy (Vasquez et al. 2002), but it also helps achieve optimal fuel mix diversity by facilitating investments in baseload technologies such as nuclear or coal (Finon and Perez 2008). Indeed, the greater the fixed costs are, the greater are price and quantity risks (Finon and Roques 2008; Roques et al. 2005). In the 'textbook' model, liquid and stable spot and forward markets were deemed to provide reliable signals for timely investment decisions and technology choices (Hunt 2002). From the point of view of producers, investment costs would indeed be recouped when the variable costs of the new plant are below the variable costs of the marginal unit (Chao et al. 2008; Finon and Perez 2008). More precisely, as the marginal unit changes, investments are undertaken when the discounted sum of all positive marginal revenues is expected to be bigger than the initial investment. From the point of view of fuel-mix diversity, transparent information on current profit margins for each technology would ensure more investment in baseload capacities owing to the infra-marginal rent of low variable cost equipment (Hunt and Shuttleworth 1996).

Buyers were also thought to be able to express their preferences in terms of technology mix and fuel diversity in the wholesale market, which would contribute to achieving an optimal fuel mix for society as a whole and limit wholesale price volatility (Finon and Perez 2008). Competitive markets would thus ensure both adequate investments in quantity and an optimal fuel mix. However, the belief in the ability of competitive markets to combine both optimal investment choices and the long-term benefits of competition on the rationalization of operations has been somehow overstated.

Interestingly, generation investment did not come up as a problem in the early to mid-1990s as substantial amount of capital was mobilized to finance new merchant power plants, especially in efficient combined-cycle gas turbine (CCGT), for instance in the USA, the UK, Argentina, Chile or Australia (Jamasb 2002). Indeed, there has been in de-integrated markets a general bias towards investment in the least capital-intensive technologies (Joskow 2008). This bias does not involve a threat to long-term generation adequacy but shifts the system away from the optimal fuel mix and increases market prices as well as volatility (Green 2006). Investment in this sector is not only about cost minimization, it is also about managing risks and these risks widely diverge across technologies (Finon and Perez 2008). Table 9.1 gives the characteristics of costs and risks of different electricity generation technologies. Investments in gas tend to be less capital intensive, with shorter lead times, and benefit from a greater operational flexibility (Roques 2007). Gas equipment has tended to become the marginal technology in most markets which results in a strong correlation between fuel and market prices for this technology, thereby reducing risks for peak units but increasing risks when (more rarely) intended as a baseload equipment. On the contrary, investments in high-fixed costs technologies such as nuclear or coal, mostly conceived for baseload supply,

Table 9.1 Characteristics of costs and risks of different electricity generation technologies

Technology	Capital size per unit	Lead time	Capital cost share	Regulatory risk on construction cost	Fuel cost share	CO_2 cost	Fuel price risk	Market price risk
Gas turbine (100 MW)	Very low (€20 million)	Very short	Low	Low	Very high	Medium	High	High (Volatily in peak)
CCGT (400–600 MW)	Low (€100–200 millions)	Short	Low	Low	High	Medium	High	Low (correlated to fuel price)
Coal (2×700 MW)	Large (€700–1000 millions)	Long	High	High	Medium	High	Medium	Medium
Nuclear (1600 MW)	Very large (€2–3 billions)	Long	Very high	High	Low	Nil	Low	High if trend of low gas price)
Renewables (Wind farm 200 MW)	Medium (€300 millions)	Medium	Very high	Medium	Nil	Nil	Nil	High

Source: Finon and Perez (2008).

face lower input price volatility but risks of margin squeeze are strong if wholesale prices drop. The problem is different for renewables as their revenues are regulated in general through administered tariffs.

Whereas large, diversified and vertically integrated incumbents can implement portfolio strategies and obtain a relatively greater value from baseload technologies (Roques et al. 2007), unstable spot markets constitute an especially high barrier to entry for new players in these technologies. It has indeed been shown that without long-term contracts, CCGT is the preferred technology for new entrants as it is self-hedged given the correlation between electricity and gas prices observed in most markets (Roques 2007). This makes CCGT particularly attractive to new entrants (Watson 2004). Long-term contracts might thus enable new entrants to invest directly in high fixed-cost technologies.

Overall, long-term supply contracts also have advantages from a social welfare perspective. They may limit abuses of dominance on the spot market and induce more investment in high fixed-cost technologies in electricity, though the latter argument does not apply to the same extent according to the size, market positioning and portfolio of technologies of the firm. We will see in the next section that it is also true with anti-competitive effects.

2.3 Long-term Contracts in Highly Concentrated European Energy Markets: The Anti-competitive Effects to Mitigate

Long-term contracts have both positive and negative effects from the point of view of long-term social welfare, especially in a context of transition. The main problem with long-term contracts is the risk of foreclosure of more efficient players. If a significant part of demand is tied in the long run, a lack of retail outlets may lead to significant output foreclosure at the generation level and tied consumers will not be able to benefit subsequently from future and potentially more profitable offers by new entrants. Long-term contracts may thus constitute a barrier to entry and have a negative effect on third parties. Conversely, if the market structure at the producer level is very concentrated, input foreclosure may occur and prevent entry in retail.

For the Chicago School,[4] an inefficient attempt to monopolize the market is impossible as it would require the acceptance by the buyer of the loss of not dealing with a more efficient entrant (Bork 1993; Posner 1976). This holds only under perfect information and if all possible parties are able to negotiate at the contracting stage. Under perfect information about the likelihood of entry of a more efficient supplier, economic theory shows that the current supplier is able to propose a contract with both a price and a penalty for the default clause that is strictly advantageous for the supplier but neutral or positive for the buyer. Rent would thus jointly be extracted by the incumbent and the buyer from the potential entrant but this would not impact social welfare. Therefore, under complete information, long-term contracts could not be motivated by anti-competitive motives and would never be detrimental to welfare. An alternative explanation introduces buyer-to-buyer externalities while keeping the rationality hypothesis of the Chicago School. A buyer might agree to sign an inefficient long-term contract in order to reduce the size of a potential entrant's market, thereby reducing the probability of entry. As a result, other buyers will have to accept a higher price in the next period (Aghion and Bolton 1987), which will give a competitive advantage to the first buyer. While it is rational to sign a long-term contract for a buyer in that case, buyer-to-buyer externalities render it negative for social welfare. Rasmusen et al. (1991) and Segal and Whinston (2000) introduce scale economies in production and multiple buyers to show that if an incumbent is able to secure a profit superior to the amount required to compensate the buyer from being tied, he or she will use long-term supply contracts to fully foreclose the market. In case of competition between retailers, the risk of exclusion increases when the intensity of downstream competition increases (Fumagalli and Motta 2006). However, some argue that the opposite is true when buyers are allowed to breach exclusive contracts and pay damages (Simpson and Wickelgren 2007).

Long-term contracts also indirectly have exclusionary effects by drying out spot markets. Spot markets deliver better results than bilateral contracting only if sufficiently liquid. A competitive spot market allows more transparency than bilateral contracting on the evolution of supply and demand and current production costs of the firms in place. The ability to contract efficiently on the spot also limits the opportunity of dominant agents to abuse their market power when they contract bilaterally with smaller players. It mitigates as well the risk that, in the long term, contracts will lead to tacit collusion on spot markets by stabilizing the market shares of an oligopoly of collectively dominant suppliers (Le Coq 2004; Liski and Montero 2006; Neuman and Hirschhausen 2006). However, it has been suggested that the longer contracts are, the lesser the risk is that these long-term contracts will lead to tacit collusion (Green and Le Coq 2006).

Finally, some contract clauses other than duration and exclusivity might also result in anti-competitive effects or express an attempt at monopolizing the market. Similar exclusionary effects may arise both from the fidelity rebates granted by dominant firms and from unclear termination rights, which provokes foreclosure effects and higher switching costs, thereby contradicting the current market building efforts of the European Union. Destination clauses and use restrictions also limit the size of markets and facilitate collusion between sellers, thereby artificially creating multiple dominated markets, and thus decreasing competition intensity in the downstream market (Neuman and Hirschhausen 2006). Reduction clauses, clauses of 'right of first refusal'[5] and 'most favoured customer',[6] or similar adjustment mechanisms, all have similar market partitioning effects.[7] Clauses of tacit renewal (that is, that the contract is automatically renewed at the end of the contract period) which typically decreases transaction costs for individual contracting parties may easily have lock-in and thus foreclosure effects when the producer is overwhelmingly dominant. Finally, we note that, although not linked directly to the duration or exclusivity clauses, long-term contracts might also entail severe price restraints such as excessive pricing or price discrimination. The price negotiated in a long-term contract depends on contracting parties' information about market conditions as well as on their respective bargaining power.[8] As a result, an incumbent might well abuse the position of dependency of a new entrant or unfairly discriminate in favour of another incumbent. Indeed, price discount linked to a long duration or a significant volume may distort competition in the downstream market if this rebate gives a competitive hedge to the downstream dominant firm.

2.4 Synthesis

An economic analysis of long-term contracts in decentralized market settings shows that anti- and pro-competitive effects are highly context specific. While they (generally) create substantial efficiency gains for individual contracting parties, their effects from a social welfare point of view are ambiguous. Tables 9.2 and 9.3 sum up the above findings.

It is thus impossible in theory to conclude that the 'net competition effect' (the sum of efficiency gains for contracting parties plus the sum of the positive effects on the opening of markets and long-term efficiency criteria, minus the sum of negative effects on the opening of markets and long-term efficiency criteria[9]) will be positive or negative in general. We know, however, what the relevant factors to take into account are. Positive and negative effects of long-term contracts are primarily linked with the market position of contractors, the structuring of the contract itself (namely, contract clauses), the technology involved in case of investment in electricity, the intensity of retail competition and the general level of horizontal and vertical integration.

However, a multitude of elements have to be looked at when one tries to determine the net competition effect of long-term contracts. Table 9.4

Table 9.2 Efficiency gains and losses of long-term contracts for individual market players

Efficiency gains	Efficiency losses
Hedge price and quantity risks	The mark-up paid for contracting forward may be too high given the potential gains from hedging
Mitigate counterparty credibility risks	By limiting their ability to exercise market powers on the spot market, long-term contracts may be negative for individual contracting parties
Facilitate bank financing	If they do not allow for efficient renegotiation/adaptation, long-term contracts may yield efficiency losses for individual contracting parties in the long term
Duration, volume, use and destination clauses might increase the surplus to be shared	

Table 9.3 Effects of long-term contracts on the opening of markets and long-term efficiency criteria

Positive effects	Negative effects
Enable entry if sufficiently long and cover sufficiently high volumes	Customer foreclosure is created by the exclusivity, tacit renewal and penalty clauses, and by rebate mechanisms
Facilitate investment and thus have a positive effect on long-term generation adequacy	The illiquidity of spot markets does not create transparency on the evolution of supply and demand, and on the production costs of the incumbents, which limits entry
Facilitate investment in high fixed-cost technologies and thus have a positive effect on fuel mix diversity	Excessive pricing and price discrimination are possible
Mitigate risks of market power abuse on the spot market	Certain contract clauses (for example, use restriction) create market partitioning

Table 9.4 Relevant factors to analyse the 'net competition effect' of long-term contracts

Market characteristics	Development of spot and forward markets Horizontal and vertical market concentration Intensity of retail competition Political, regulatory and macroeconomic risks
Contract and contracting parties characteristics	Contract clauses (duration, exclusivity, termination rights, debate, destination, use restriction, pricing scheme . . .) Market shares Technology (when the contract is linked to an investment) Technology portfolio Contracting party's position in the supply chain Extent of vertical integration Sensitivity to CO_2 price risk Conditions for project financing

recalls the most important elements. Economic analysis thus points out where to look when assessing long-term contracts but is poor on practical insights. It does not provide guidance on what is the optimal mix of contract durations and vertical integration, and even less on how to get there from a given mix. It provides guidance neither on how to quantify efficiencies and anti-competitive effects nor on how to balance them from a dynamic, long-term efficiency perspective.

In the context of decentralized markets, two basic strategies are thus possible for a competition authority. The first strategy is to let market players contract forward as long as spot and forward markets do not mature. The second strategy is more radical and consists of forbidding all long-term contracts. In this case, liquidity would mechanically increase on spot and forward markets, asset specificity would decrease and the value of long-term contracting for market players would fall. However, there is no estimate of how long it would take for this effect to play in full and thus of how long this policy would be detrimental for investment, entry and all the benefits of long-term supply contracts depicted above. Overall, long-term supply contracts thus appear both as a barrier to liberalization and as a cure from the shortcomings of restructuring in electricity markets.

2.5 Conclusion

In the aftermath of the California crisis, the Enron scandal and the ending of the liberalization process in the USA, it appeared with more clarity that the new competition model had not delivered all its promises and in particular had not solved the problem of vertical relationships in a decentralized market setting. This has resulted from several causes. First are the diverse risk profiles of the different technologies and the inability of investors to secure sufficient cash flow to recoup investments. Contrary to most expectations, reliable spot and forward markets have not developed and financial instruments for hedging are missing.

In particular, the time horizon of available forward contracts on organized wholesale markets, usually less than a year, does not facilitate investment in high-fixed costs technologies. The nature of the commodity, the lack of suitable risk management techniques and the misalignment of contracting incentives among wholesale market players have led to the wide failure of the pure merchant plant and supplier models where full decentralization has been applied. The extreme of fully de-integrated competitive retail models thus does not seem to deliver long-term efficiency, especially in view of the forthcoming investment cycles. Even if the theoretical economic model of competitive reform was fully implemented, it seems that some misunderstood factors such as the dynamics of retail competition and the problem of high fixed-cost investments would still hamper its overall efficiency. The model thus appears inherently incomplete.

A natural response from market players to the misalignment of contracting incentives between producers and retailers has indeed been vertical reintegration in several markets (for example, in the UK or New Zealand), when it was allowed (Anderson et al. 2007; Gans and Wolak 2008; Thomas 2004). Vertical reintegration occurs when the costs and risks of contracting (transaction costs, contractual incompleteness and bounded rationality, hold-up costs, regulatory risks, market power costs) exceed those of ownership (agency costs, costs of collective decision-making, costs of risk-bearing). As for long-term contracts, the virtues of vertical integration are widespread for individual market players. It improves not only investment and risk management but also provides a natural and self-sustaining hedge against wholesale price and quantity risks, as well as market power and asymmetric information costs, as it internalizes these risks and costs to the firm (Hansmann 1996). It enables better matching of load profiles and supply security preferences. It also enhances scale differences between integrated firms and retail entrants, thereby reducing integrated firms' exposure to predation (Meade and O'Connor 2009).

However, an oligopoly of fully reintegrated market players does not appear as a more satisfactory solution for decentralized electricity markets. In particular, if it tends to limit wholesale market power and support retail competition among incumbent players, it not only limits retail entry (by permitting negative retail margin and thus cross-subsidization between generation and retail segments in vertically integrated entities) but also the need to trade on wholesale markets.[10] It also limits the regulators' ability to monitor wholesale prices as such prices are marginalized and other relevant variables such as generation costs are less easily observable (Meade and O'Connor 2009). Regulators and competition authorities should thus aim to reach a middle path where spot contracting would combine with a satisfactory share of longer-term supply contracts and vertical integration.

In decentralized electricity markets, long-term contracts overall appear both as a barrier to liberalization and as a cure for its shortcomings. It thus seems reasonable to allow and even encourage long-term contracts in fully de-integrated market settings whereas the policy prescription is more ambiguous for less de-integrated markets. In the latter situation, which as we will see is the case of the European Union, a case-by-case analysis seems necessary as strong anti-competitive effects may arise, for instance from the exclusivity clause. However, the right mix of long-term contracting, vertical integration and spot trading, which would support both investment and entry, remains an unsettled question in theory.

3 HOW DOES THE EUROPEAN COMMISSION ANALYSE THE POTENTIAL ANTI-COMPETITIVE EFFECTS OF LONG-TERM CONTRACTS IN THE NEW MARKET CONTEXT?

There is a multiplicity of long-term contracts all along the electricity supply chain in the European Union. They include fuel supply contracts to power producers, tolling agreements and diverse power purchase agreements with energy-intensive users,[11] commercial and household customers, or resellers and traders. As we saw, if all these long-term contracts lead to varying degrees of foreclosure, they also have different effects on consumer surplus, investment, risk management, entry and wholesale spot prices. From an antitrust perspective, contract clauses regarding duration, exclusive dealing and use restrictions are particularly relevant in electricity, whereas exclusive distribution and destination clauses are more relevant in gas. Restraints relating to prices such as discrimination, predation or resale price maintenance might also be found but have so far rarely been addressed at the European Community level in cases relating to long-term contracts.

Despite their importance for the success or failure of liberalization, long-term contracts are almost absent in gas and electricity secondary EU law[12] so guidance must be sought in the case law. Prior to the first liberalization directive, enforcement of competition law did not occur on a very regular basis in energy and there were only a few cases involving long-term contracts. Most of these concerned independent power producers supplying the national incumbent on an exclusive basis. In the early to mid-1990s, the European Commission started to look at these contracts to limit their duration so that they would not hamper the future opening of markets to competition. The durations were in general limited to 15 years as in *Electricidade de Portugal/Pego*, *Isab Energy/Enel*, *Sarlux*, *Rosen*, *REN/Turbogas, Scottish Nuclear* or *Api Energia.* Owing to the monopolistic context, these decisions did not display any methodology for the analysis of foreclosure effects, leading to decisions unlikely to be replicated today, at least on the same terms. For instance, the formation of selling and purchasing consortia contracting on a long-term basis was accepted in *Jahrhundertvertrag* to allow the development of local energy sources (coal in this case) for the sake of 'national security', despite the risks of foreclosure and collusion. However, we can note that the 'security of supply' argument as a justification for the long duration was already accepted with some reluctance by the European Commission in *Jahrhundertvertrag* and *Ijsselcentrale.*

Market players anticipate today that the 15-year duration will probably not be accepted but legal uncertainty remains strong as no methodology has ever been spelled out on how to assess foreclosure effects in the new context. Since liberalization, and apart from *Synergen* and *Gas Natural/Endesa* which relate as much to gas as to electricity, relevant cases in this sector have essentially concerned the long-term reservation rights of cross-border interconnectors signed before liberalization, the so-called 'grandfathering' rights. In addition, since the early 2000s, the European Commission has repeatedly voiced strong concerns over the risks of anti-competitive effects inherent in long-term electricity supply contracts. Since then, no clear methodology to analyse foreclosure effects in the context of deregulated energy markets has been clearly communicated by competition authorities and this is why legal uncertainty is so strong currently in the marketplace (Hauteclocque 2009). However, since the early 2000s and especially for the past two years, a series of decisions has been taken concerning the portfolio of long-term contracts of several incumbents (*Repsol*, *E.ON Ruhrgas*, *RWE* and, most importantly, *Distrigaz* and *EDF* – still pending) and new proceedings are regularly opened (*Electrabel*, *GDF*). This section shows that the European Commission has developed a two-step strategy to analyse the anti-competitive effects of long-term contracts in the new market context and that this methodology is clearly inspired by sound economic principles (the appendix presents a table of cases (Table 9A.1) showing the progression towards a more economic approach in enforcement).

3.1 Step 1: Limiting Regulatory Costs by Concentrating on the Potentially Most Harmful Infringements

The enforcement of competition laws is constrained by the rules contained in the EU Treaty as firms may appeal against the decisions of the European Commission before Community Courts. Article 101 TFEU, which deals with anti-competitive practices, and Article 102 TFEU, which tackles abuses of dominance, together with relevant guidelines, notices and regulation, do not a priori allow or ban long-term contracts.

They provide instead a framework of analysis based on market share thresholds which define which situations must be fully investigated. This system is designed to provide predictability to the firms and allow competition authorities to focus their enforcement resources on the most serious infringements. It is based on the insight that vertical restrictions of competition are more likely to be harmful to competition when horizontal competition is distorted (Motta 2003). This means that the European Commission will act only when the long-term contract is implemented by a company with market power, market shares being used to approximate the level of dominance. This is an imperfect proxy for market power in many cases in energy but, as concerns customer foreclosure, market shares seem a good and easy tool to use.

In practice, long-term contracts between small and medium-sized companies are normally not considered by the European Commission as being capable of affecting appreciably trade between member states, except when they engage in cross-border trade. In fact, as long as the market shares of each contracting party does not exceed 15 per cent, long-term contracts do not fall under the jurisdiction of the European Commission. Beyond 15 per cent of market shares, long-term contracts are presumed to be legal as long as the market share threshold of 30 per cent is not exceeded and duration is not indefinite or over five years. In case of collective dominance by several suppliers below the 30 per cent threshold, the European Commission or a national competition authority retains the right to conduct a full competition analysis. Long-term contracts for companies with larger market shares will require a full competition analysis in all cases.

To the system of market share thresholds has been added a list of blacklisted clauses, called 'hard-core' restraints. These contract clauses are thought to contravene the fundamental treaty objective of market integration and hence will almost never be accepted, which amounts to a quasi per se prohibition. Blacklisted clauses relevant for energy are essentially market partitioning clauses, use restrictions and contractual provisions having similar effects. Forbidding market partitioning clauses and use restrictions makes sense for a homogenous product and in an industry that has traditionally been organized along national borders. During the course of recent decisions in energy (for example, *Gas Natural/Endesa*, *KalibaXe/EDF*), the European Commission has also made clear that clauses other than duration and exclusivity leading to significant switching costs would almost never be accepted when implemented by dominant firms. Among them, unclear termination rights, fidelity rebates and tacit renewal clauses have been considered illegal in several decisions. In these instances, the European Commission has clearly favoured the fight against foreclosure over the saving of transaction costs for individual contracting parties, even to the detriment of the non-dominant firms contracting with a dominant incumbent.

The EU law framework to analyse anti-competitive effects of long-term contracts is thus primarily based on market share thresholds and a series of blacklisted clauses. Even if these thresholds are set somewhat arbitrarily and have not been designed specifically for energy markets, they nevertheless contribute to ensuring more predictability in enforcement. In addition, they rely on the fact that a firm with low market shares will not be able to distort competition sufficiently to justify a full competition analysis, which is justified from an economic point of view. As concerns the blacklisted clauses, it is obvious that the market integration objective played a big part in their definition. They, however, fit well in energy where the low level of market integration remains hard to overcome. When over 30 per cent, and provided that certain clauses are not included in the contract, competition authorities see a 'grey' area where the assessment of anti-competitive effects becomes more complicated and where in theory a multiplicity of elements should be taken into account.

3.2 Step 2: Is the Contract or Portfolio of Contracts Likely to Create Substantial Anti-competitive Effects?

In case the long-term contract does not include any hard-core restraints and the market shares of at least one of the contracting parties exceed the 30 per cent threshold, the European Commission will conduct a full competition analysis of the anti-competitive effects of the agreement to decide if it infringes EU competition law. This de facto limits enforcement in energy to the cases involving dominant incumbents. We will see in the next section that this occurs only when there is a strong presumption that the long-term contracts will result in substantial anti-competitive effects that the analysis of potential efficiency gains attached will be carried out and that a balancing exercise will be conducted. Long-term contracting by dominant firms is therefore far from being illegal per se.

Competition authorities will consider a lot of different elements to analyse anti-competitive effects. Some are purely intrinsic to the vertical relationship as the duration or the volume specified, while others help analyse the market context, such as the level of vertical integration in the industry. This is reasonable in so far as the potential anti-competitive effects of a long-term contract, or a portfolio of long-term contracts, cannot be understood without taking into account the specificities of the market context. We will thus first analyse how the European Commission assesses market characteristics before going on to its analyses of the contract itself.

3.2.1 Elements external to the supply relationship

Market characteristics are usually what competition authorities analyse first. Economic theory is poor on insights regarding the patterns of entry in energy markets and the specific market features which favour it. In the recent line of decisions, elements taken into account included the maturity of demand, the level of vertical integration in the market, the real opportunity to set up a new resale network and the existence of buyer power. The last is important as contracting parties frequently have diverging interests and thus incentives to contain each other's exercise of market power. In general, the European Commission considered that the presence of numerous buyers de facto limits the possibilities of abuse of a dominant position by the supplier. When assessing market characteristics, the European Commission also looks at potential entry in supply and demand, and its potential impact on future competition. This largely depends on the existence of potential competitors, usually foreign incumbents present in neighbouring markets. A potential competitor is usually a firm able to undertake the required investment to enter the market within one year following a small but significant increase in prices as well as having a certain brand image and financial strength. For entry in electricity, readily available gas capacities have been considered an important factor.

The most important element will be the assessment of the cumulative effect of all the long-term contracts signed by the different producers on market foreclosure. Indeed, long-term contracts can foreclose markets to new entrants only to the extent that a substantial part of market demand is tied for the long term. The doctrine of cumulative effect had been devised in a famous series of cases in the beer and ice-cream sectors and had been one of the cornerstones of the 'more-economic' approach in EU competition policy. As a general rule, the European Commission considers that a significant cumulative foreclosure effect is unlikely to arise if the total market demand tied in the long term does not exceed 30 per cent of global demand. In the case of a 'super-dominant' incumbent like in the *Distrigaz* case, the European Commission considered that no competition concerns would arise if its portfolio of long-term contracts covered less than 20 per cent of the market. In *E.ON Ruhrgas*, the Bundeskartellamt estimated that the firm contributed significantly to cumulative foreclosure with 75 per cent market shares in its supply area, within a national market where 80 per cent of total demand was supplied in the long term. This demonstrates that when a firm is largely dominant, the anti-competitive effects of its demand tied in the long term arise sooner. In the case of a group of leading suppliers, the European Commission will look similarly at the cumulative effects of their long-term contracts but there will be no need to prove that they lead to tacit collusion to show that significant foreclosure effects occur (Kjolbye 2007).

3.2.2 Elements internal to the supply relationship

Having analysed market conditions and their likely evolutions, the focus will be on the characteristics of both the long-term contract itself and the contracting parties. Most prominently, the European Commission will conduct a combined analysis of duration, exclusivity and whether buyers who represent a substantial part of total market demand alone are tied for the long term with the dominant supplier, or the collectively dominant suppliers.

The European Commission will first look at the percentage of the consumer demand tied under the long-term contract, namely, the exclusivity clause, as it is one of the main sources of foreclosure effect. Indeed, if a customer must meet all or a big part of its needs with a particular supplier for a long period of time, he does not constitute any longer an available outlet for a potential entrant. In *Gas Natural/Endesa* in 2000, the Commission reduced the size of the contract from nearly 100 per cent to 75 per cent of Endesa global purchases as Endesa was one of the leading electricity producers in Spain and thus could motivate entry in gas supply in its own right. More generally, the European Commission is looking here at the degree of economic dependency of the buyer vis-à-vis the dominant supplier. The share of the customer's demand tied is in the European Commission's view, the best way to demonstrate dependency and it repeatedly used that proxy. Most importantly, the analysis of the European Commission is based on quantities actually received and not on quantities contracted. Indeed, take-or-pay or flexibility clauses are one of the main reasons why long-term contracts dry out spot markets. Quantities effectively used are generally not the same as quantities previously forecast. Without flexibility mechanisms, buyers would be obliged to trade their surplus or source their missing quantities from spot markets. Long-term contracts could therefore contribute to the deepening of these markets while providing a fair level of supply security (Longva 2009). However, flexibility mechanisms are not forbidden per se and the European Commission conducts its analysis on a case-by-case basis.

European competition authorities recognize when they analyse the share of the customer's tied demand that transaction costs may become too high when negotiating for a small quantity and that it may become uneconomic for an alternative supplier to provide less than a certain amount. Recent decisions seem to indicate that it is considered that 20 per cent of a customer's demand is the threshold for having incentives to enter into a relationship with a second supplier (*E.ON Ruhrgas* and *RWE*). Competition authorities are thus more reluctant to accept long-term contracts accounting for more than 80 per cent of a customer demand. Some commentators close to the European Commission think that foreclosure effects could be found for contracts amounting as low as 50 per cent of a customer's demand in case these contract terms are widely spread in the market (Schnichels and Nyssens 2007).

The share of the customer's tied demand has to be analysed along with the duration of the contract. Even if 100 per cent of a customer's demand is tied to a particular supplier, foreclosure will not occur if this customer can return to the market on a regular basis. As a general rule, the European Commission is very suspicious of contracts longer than five years and considers that efficiencies generally do not offset foreclosure effects beyond that limit. We also note that the Commission considers contracts with tacit renewal clauses or no last delivery date as contracts of indefinite duration (*E.ON Ruhrgas*).

Recent decisions show that the duration of contracts accepted by the European Commission will mainly depend on the competition position of the counterparty. If the counterparty is an established reseller, accepted duration will probably not exceed two years as in *Distrigaz*. The Bundeskartellamt in *E.ON Ruhrgas* restricted duration to four years for contracts with resellers who have more than 50 per cent of their demand tied under the contract, but only two years above 80 per cent. European competition authorities will thus play with the two factors. Interestingly, where requirements are satisfied by several suppliers, the Bundeskartellamt specified that contracts should distribute the risk of demand fluctuations among suppliers according to the actual supply share provided by each of them so as not to disadvantage the second supplier. In *Repsol*, five years' duration was accepted for exclusive contracts with established resellers but the market share of the dominant firm reached only 30 to 50 per cent, which shows that the European Commission adjusts duration according to the level of market dominance of the supplier. For a new entrant in retail, a duration of five years is most likely to be accepted. One also notices a more lenient approach by the European Commission towards fuel supply contracts than to electricity producer/reseller contracts. This shows that even dominant firms need and can claim for some degree of long-term security in fuel supply.

4 BALANCING ANTI-COMPETITIVE EFFECTS WITH EFFICIENCY GAINS AND NEGOTIATING REMEDIES

Once the European Commission has considered that a long-term contract, or a portfolio of long-term contracts, is likely to create significant anti-competitive effects, it will analyse the potential efficiency gains and proceed to a balancing exercise. When efficiency gains do not seem to clearly offset anti-competitive effects, the contract might still be accepted if satisfactory remedies can be imposed or negotiated.

4.1 Balancing Anti-competitive Effects and Efficiency Gains: An Uncertain Exercise

The balancing exercise follows a methodology based on four criteria directly derived from the wording of the EU Treaty. In theory, for long-term contracts with substantial anti-competitive effects to be cleared by competition authorities, they should (1) substantially improve economic efficiency, (2) give a fair share of benefits to final consumers, (3) be indispensable or at least proportional to the achievement of the efficiency gains and (4) not afford contracting parties the possibility of eliminating competition in respect of a substantial part of the products in question. Objective factors out of the control of the company, such as public service obligations, may also be taken into account. In practice, we note that it is often difficult to trace back elements of competition authorities' decisions precisely to the four criteria.

The first criterion indicates that the long-term contract must create significant efficiency gains to be accepted. Recent decisions are, however, less clear on how to analyse efficiency gains than on how to assess anti-competitive effects, which is a general problem in competition policy (Lugard and Hancher 2004). The outcome of the balancing will thus be even harder to predict. The two main efficiency gains recognized by the European Commission have been when long-term contracts effectively allowed investment to be sunk and/or entry by a new competitor.

In *Synergen* for instance, the Commission accepted both a 15-year gas supply contract with Statoil for 100 per cent of the needs of the new CCGT plant and a 15-year power purchase agreement for 50 per cent of its output with the electricity incumbent, the Electricity Supply Board (ESB). It thus recognized the need of secure output levels and long-term upstream fuel commitments to facilitate investments and project financing. However, the mere objective of securing loans might not be sufficient to have a long-term contract accepted as the European Commission in other sectors did not always consider it indispensable. In case the loan comes from a dominant supplier, it is likely to be considered an efficiency gain only if it cannot be obtained on the same terms with commercial or investment banks. It is also noticeable that the European Commission has once acknowledged that even dominant firms could claim for a certain level of security in fuel supply (*Gas Natural/Endesa*). The second criterion does not seem to have led to very substantial developments and in general was analysed along with the first criterion on efficiency gains. As a general rule, the European Commission considered that long-term contracts helping investment and entry contributed to the success of the liberalization process, which was in itself thought to be good for final consumers.

The third (proportionality) and fourth (exclusion) criteria are obviously very difficult to implement and this is where the discretion as well as the difficulties of competition authorities really lie. European competition authorities are still struggling with them today. For instance, an open question concerns the duration that an incumbent electricity producer really needs to sink a very high fixed-cost investment (criterion 3) and how to make sure that this duration will not result in excessive exclusionary effects (criterion 4). A first indication was given by the European Commission in the *Exeltium* case in September 2008. Exeltium was a consortium of energy intensive users to whom Electricité de France (EDF) was to supply base load electricity for over more than 20 years. Alleged efficiency gains mainly included security of fuel supply and hedging for the buyers. The European Commission finally cleared this contract, after almost three years of analysis, provided that resale restrictions were cancelled and an opt-out clause introduced to mitigate anti-competitive effects. In addition, the European Commission explicitly stated that the Exeltium agreement would be included in the analysis of the cumulative foreclosure effect of the contract portfolio of EDF currently being conducted.

Interestingly, one of the main advantages attached to long-term contracts recently discussed in economic literature, the potential mitigation effect of long-term contracts on spot market abuses, has never been used by the European Commission. This probably reflects the fact that such economic analysis based on oligopoly modelling would not reach the legal standard of proof required before the court.

4.2 Remedies: The New Treatment of Incumbents in *Distrigaz* (2007) and *EDF* (2009) – Methodology Settled Once and for All?

In case efficiency gains do not seem to clearly offset anti-competitive effects during the balancing exercise, long-term contracts might still be accepted if satisfactory remedies can be imposed pursuant to Article 7 of Regulation 1/2003, or negotiated (Article 9).

A first group of remedies has consisted of modifying the drafting of contracts, for instance by deleting certain clauses such as use restrictions or limiting duration. In this case, the whole agreement is not cancelled and it is the responsibility of the parties to decide whether the contract is still valid. Other more behavioural remedies have been imposed, such as forbidding any vertical mergers or acquisitions for a certain number of years (*Repsol*). These are classical remedies in EU competition policy and are not specific to the energy sector. One notes here that if long-term generation adequacy is clearly a core policy goal of the European Commission, the vague concept of 'security of supply' is itself approached with increasing scepticism in competition cases. Today, even long-term gas import contracts are not certain to be accepted on the basis of a 'security of supply' argument.

The second group of remedies has been specifically devised for the energy sector and coincided with the decision of the European Commission to use its power against abuses of dominance (Article 102 TFEU) to directly attack the portfolio of long-term contracts of the incumbents. This was thought to be the only way to bring about rapidly substantial improvement in the competitive structure. The European Commission recognized that some of these long-term contracts created real efficiency gains (criterion 1) but that the criterion on exclusion and proportionality could only be fulfilled if foreclosure effects were severely mitigated. This led the Commission to impose remedies better able to accommodate market players' needs while limiting foreclosure.

The *Distrigaz* decision constitutes, according to the European Commission, the landmark case for future competition enforcement on long-term contracts in energy. The European Commission opened proceedings against the Belgian electricity incumbent for possible breaches of the EU Treaty rules on abuse of a dominant position owing to its long-term contracts with industrial customers. The European Commission started by excluding from the analysis of cumulative foreclosure effects all the long-term contracts linked to a new investment in gas-fired power plants, in line with its analysis of efficiency gains. A strict limitation of five years was then imposed on remaining contracts to avoid customers who would be particularly likely to switch suppliers being tied for a

Table 9.5 The Distrigaz *and* EDF *commitments compared*

	Distrigaz (2007)	*EDF* (2009)
Max contract duration	5 years	5 years
Percentage of sales to come back on the market every year	70	65 (large consumers buying directly *or through a consortia*)
Contract clauses	No use restraint, no tacit renewal clauses	No use restraint
Duration of commitments	4 years or Distrigaz under 40 per cent market shares	10 years or EDF under 40 per cent market shares
Monitoring of commitments	Annual report	Annual report + third-party auditor
Other	Contract with new power plant not included	Effective right to contract with alternative supplier

Commitments may be reopened if there are material changes in national law or the market context

very long period of time, and unilateral termination rights were granted to buyers with contracts longer than five years. The innovation here is in the flexibility parameters granted to the dominant firm. Distrigaz was allowed to adjust its portfolio of contracts to its own needs as long as it complied with a duration of a maximum of five years and if 70 per cent of its customers came back to the market every year. As a result, Distrigaz could for instance have 37.5 per cent of customers supplied under five-year contracts and 62.5 per cent supplied under one-year contracts or 40 per cent supplied under four-year contracts and 60 per cent supplied under one-year contracts. These commitments were due to last for a minimum of four years and until Distrigaz's market shares decreased below 40 per cent (or another supplier reaches the level of Distrigaz market shares minus 20 per cent).

In late 2009, the European Commission released the market test[13] for the *EDF* case opened in 2008. The case is thus still pending but it nonetheless gives us the position of the European Commission and an opportunity to see whether the *Distrigaz* jurisprudence has effectively been followed. Table 9.5 presents a comparison between the *Distrigaz* and *EDF* commitments. We see that the commitments negotiated are extremely similar, in particular that the flexibility granted to Distrigaz has been retained, that the maximum contract duration remains five years and that the percentage of sales to come back to the market every year is roughly equal. The new rules of the games on long-term contracts have thus been clarified (through cases) over time and we can now consider that the *Distrigaz* jurisprudence is sufficiently established to provide reliable guidance to market players.

5 CONCLUSION

The analysis of the recent series of decisions shows that the European Commission is using an economic approach to analyse foreclosure effects of long-term contracts and imposing (or negotiating) remedies in energy. Its combined analysis of duration, exclusivity and the pattern of consumption are particularly interesting. Even if the two-step methodology has not been devised for the specificities of newly deregulated energy markets, we have to conclude that this methodology balances favourably between the need for predictability and the need for a full competition analysis in complicated cases. However, the hierarchy among elements to be taken into account during the balancing exercise still lacks clarity and hence predictability. Furthermore, the maximum duration imposed, for instance three to five years in the most recent cases, seems to closely follow what has become the current practice in other sectors such as beer and ice-cream, which appears problematic given, for example, the capital-intensive nature of the energy industry. We can nonetheless already have a first picture of the emerging doctrine of European competition authorities.

NOTES

1. We do not treat long-term import gas contracts.
2. However, this analysis holds only for Organisation for Economic Co-operation and Development (OECD) countries as project lenders always required a form of sovereign (or at least sub-sovereign) guarantee to back the project cash flows in emerging economies.
3. Take-or-pay clauses give flexibility to the buyer by granting him or her the possibility of nominating the quantity of energy it wishes to purchase within a minimum and a maximum contractual threshold. If the minimum quantity threshold is not reached, the buyer will have to pay for the shortfall at the full contractual price. For a lengthy description of the different take-or-pay clauses, see Coop (2006).
4. The Chicago School is a group of scholars, largely associated with the University of Chicago, which started in the early 1970s to argue that some business conducts such as vertical restraints that were originally considered anti-competitive could actually be explained by efficiency reasons and thus promote competition. The Chicago School generally advocated a light and case-specific approach to antitrust policy. See, for example, on this Kovacic and Shapiro (2000).
5. A 'right of first refusal' grants to the buyer, before any others, the right to buy the goods of the supplier due for its sales area.
6. A 'most favoured customer' clause entails the buyer to obtain the same commercial terms as any other buyers.
7. For an in-depth analysis of these clauses, see Kjolbye (2007).

8. We note here as a side remark that in gas the 'net back' clause which indexes the contract price on the price of oil products tends to mitigate the market power of the dominant exporter.
9. A competition authority will not take into account the potential efficiency losses for an individual contracting party arising from its own business conduct.
10. Vertical integration not only reduces the overall volumes to be traded but may also have an impact on the number of players and the size of the positions to be cleared of the remaining participants. See on this DG COMP (2007).
11. Energy intensive users typically include electricity resellers and some industries where electricity represents an important part of variable costs (for example, steel, chemistry). The latter have sometimes used complex contractual and financial arrangements to pool their electricity purchases. These contracting schemes for instance include risk-sharing in generation between industrial consumers and electricity operators (EPR, Zandvliet, Roselectra, TVO), partnership between consumers and generators valuing a secondary fuel (DK6) or consumers' cooperatives purchasing electricity (Exeltium).
12. Except concerning long-term import gas contracts in Directive 2003/55/EC. Recital 25 reads: 'Long-term contracts will continue to be an important part of the gas supply of Member States and should be maintained as an option for gas supply undertakings in so far as they do not undermine the objective of this Directive and are compatible with the Treaty, including competition rules. It is therefore necessary to take them into account in the planning of supply and transportation capacity of gas undertakings.'
13. In a market test, the European Commission officially publishes the commitments negotiated with the firm and gives the opportunity to interested third parties to give observations before they are made legally binding.

REFERENCES

Adler, T.R., R.F. Scherer, S.L. Barton and R. Katerberg (1998), 'An empirical test of transaction cost theory: validating contract typology', *Journal of Applied Management Studies*, **7** (2), 185–200.

Aghion, P. and P. Bolton (1987), 'Contracts as a barrier to entry', *American Economic Review*, **77** (1987), 388–401.

Allaz, B. and J.-L. Vila (1993), 'Cournot competition, forward markets and efficiency', *Journal of Economic Theory*, **59** (1), 1–16.

Anderson, E.J., X. Hu and D. Winchester (2007), 'Forward contracts in electricity markets: the Australian experience', *Energy Policy*, **35** (5), 3089–103

Bonasina, M., A. Creti and F. Manca (2007), 'Im-perfectly competitive contract markets for electricity', working paper, Bocconi University.

Boom, S. and A. Buehler (2006), 'Restructuring electricity markets when demand is uncertain: effects on capacity investments, prices and welfare', discussion paper, Center for Industrial Economics.

Borison, A. and G. Hamm (2005), 'Better power contracts: using flexibility to increase value', *The Electricity Journal*, **18** (10), 64–9.

Bork, R.H. (1993), *The Antitrust Paradox: A Policy at War with Itself*, New York: Free Press.

Bushnell, J. (2007), 'Oligopoly equilibria in electricity contract markets', *Journal of Regulatory Economics*, **32** (3), 225–45.

Cameron, P. (2007), *Competition in Energy Markets*, Oxford: Oxford University Press.

Chao, H. and H.G. Hutington (1998), *Designing Competitive Electricity Markets*, Dordrecht: Kluwer Academic.

Chao, H., S. Oren and R. Wilson (2008), 'Reevaluation of vertical integration and unbundling in restructured electricity markets', in F. Sioshansi (ed.), *Competitive Electricity Markets: Design, Implementation, and Performance*, Amsterdam: Elsevier, pp. 27–65.

Coop, G. (2006) 'Long-term energy sale contracts and market liberalization in new EU member states – are they compatible?', *International Energy Law and Taxation Review*, **2**, 64–71.

Crocker, K.J. and S.E. Masten (1988), 'Mitigating contractual hazards: unilateral options and contract length', *RAND Journal of Economics*, **19** (3), 327–43.

Defeuilley, C. and G. Meunier (2006), 'La gestion du risque d'une commodité non stockable: les limites d'une couverture financière', *Economies et Sociétés*, Série Economie de l'Energie, **10–11**, 1619.

Directorate General of Competition (DG COMP) (2007), *Report on Energy Sector Inquiry*, SEC(2006) 1724.

EDF-IDEI (2007), 'Contrat de Long Terme, Concurrence et Efficacité'. report to EDF R&D.

Eilmansberger, T. (2005), 'How to distinguish good from bad competition under article 82 EC: in search of clearer and more coherent standards for anti-competitive abuses', *Common Market Law Review*, **42** (1), 129–77.

Finon, D. and Y. Perez (2008), 'Investment risk allocation in restructured electricity markets: the need of vertical arrangements', LARSEN Working Paper.

Finon, D. and F. Roques (2008), 'Financing arrangements and industrial organization for new nuclear build in electricity markets', *Competition and Regulation in Network Industries*, **9** (3), 3247–82.

Fraser, P. (2003), *Power Generation Investment in Electricity Markets*, Paris: OECD/IEA Publication.

Fumagalli, C. and M. Motta (2006), 'Exclusive dealing and entry, when buyers compete', *American Economic Review*, **96**, 785–95.

Gans, J.S. and F. Wolak (2008), 'A comparison of ex ante versus ex post vertical market supply: evidence from the electricity supply industry', working paper, Stanford University.

Glachant, J.-M. and M. Hallack (2009), 'Take or pay contract robustness: a three step story told by the Brazil-Bolivia gas case?', *Energy Policy*, **37** (2), 651–7.

Glachant, J.-M. and F. Lévêque (2009), 'Electricity internal market in the European Union: what to do next?', in J.-M. Glachant and F. Lévêque (eds), *Electricity Reform in Europe. Towards a Single Energy Market*, Cheltenham, UK and Northampton, MA, USA: Edward Edgar. pp. 3–32.

Green, R. (1999), 'The electricity contract market in England and Wales', *Journal of Industrial Economics*, **47** (1), 107–24.

Green, R. (2006), 'Investment and generation capacity', in F. Lévêque (ed.), *Competitive Electricity Markets and Sustainability*, Cheltenham, UK and Northampton, MA, USA: Edward Elgar, pp. 21–53.

Green, R. and C. Le Coq (2006), 'The length of contracts and collusion', CSEM Working Paper 154, University of California Energy Institute.

Green, R. and D. Newbery (1997), 'Competition in the electricity industry in England and Wales', *Oxford Review of Economic Policy*, **13** (1), 27–46.

Hansmann, H. (1996), *The Ownership of Enterprise*, Cambridge, MA: Harvard University Press.

Hauteclocque, A. (2009), 'Legal uncertainty and competition policy in European deregulated electricity markets: the case of long-term exclusive supply contracts', *World Competition*, **32** (1), 91–112.
Hunt, S. (2002), *Making Competition Work in Electricity*, New York: John Wiley & Sons.
Hunt, S. and G. Shuttleworth (1996), *Competition and Choice in Electricity*, New York: John Wiley and Sons.
Jamasb, T. (2002), 'Reform and regulation of the electricity sectors in developing countries', CMI Working Paper 08, University of Cambridge.
Joskow, P. (2008), 'Lessons learned from electricity market liberalization', *The Energy Journal*, special issue, The Future of Electricity: Papers in Honour of David Newbery, 9–42.
Joskow, P. and R. Schmalensee (1983), *Markets for Power*, Cambridge, MA: MIT Press.
Kjolbye, L. (2007), 'Vertical Agreements', in C. Jones (ed.), *EU Energy Law Volume II: EU Competition Law and Energy Markets*, 2nd edn, Brussels: Claeys and Casteels.
Klein, B., R. Crawford and A. Alchian (1978), 'Vertical integration, appropriate rents, and the competitive contracting process', *Journal of Law and Economics*, **28** (2), 297–326.
Kovacic, W. and C. Shapiro (2000), 'Antitrust policy: a century of economic and legal thinking', *Journal of Economic Perspectives*, **14** (1), 43–60.
Le Coq, C. (2004), 'Long-term supply contracts and collusion in the electricity market', SSE/EFI Working Paper Series in Economics and Finance No. 552.
Lévêque, F. and R. Monturus (2008), 'Mergers and acquisitions within the European power and gas sectors: cases and patterns', CERNA Ecole des Mines.
Liski, M. and J.P. Montero (2006), 'Forward trading and collusion in oligopoly', *Journal of Economic Theory*, **131** (1), 212–30.
Longva, P. (2009), 'Long-term contracting from the point of view of a big industrial energy consumer', communication to CESSA Conference, Florence.
Masten, S.E. and K.J. Crocker (1985), 'Efficient adaptation in long-term contracts: take-or-pay provisions for natural gas', *American Economic Review*, **75** (5), 1083–93.
McRae, S. and F. Wolak (2009), 'How do firms exercise unilateral market power?', working paper prepared for the workshop 'Manufacturing Markets: Legal, Political and Economic Dynamics', Florence.
Meade, R. and S. O'Connor (2009), 'Comparison of long-term contracts and vertical integration in decentralized electricity markets', working paper prepared for the workshop 'Efficiency, Competition and Long-term Contracts in Decentralized Electricity Markets', Florence.
Michaels, R.J. (2006), 'Vertical integration and the restructuring of the US electricity industry', Cato Institute Policy Analysis Series, No. 572.
Monti, M. (2003) 'Applying EU competition law to the newly liberalized energy markets', communication to the World Forum on energy regulation, Rome.
Motta, M. (2003), *Competition Policy: Theory and Practice*, Cambridge: Cambridge University Press.
Neuhoff, K. and L. de Vries (2004), 'Insufficient incentives for investment in electricity generation', *Utilities Policy*, **12**, 253–67.
Neumann, A. and C. Hirschhausen (2006), 'Long-term contracts and asset

specificity revisited – an empirical analysis of producer-importer relations in the natural gas industry', EPRG Working Paper 0610, University of Cambridge.

Newbery, D. (1998), 'Competition, contracts and entry in the electricity spot market', *RAND Journal of Economics*, **29**, 726–49.

Newbery, D., E. van Damme and N. von der Fehr (2003), 'Benelux market integration: market power concerns', report of the Market Surveillance Committee, Dutch Competition Authorities.

Onofri, L. (2005), 'Electricity market restructuring and energy contracts: a critical note on the EU Commission's NEA decision', *European Journal of Law and Economics*, **20**, 71–85.

Parsons, J. (2008), 'Fact & fantasy: risk management in electricity markets', communication to EEM Conference, Lisbon.

Posner, R. (1976), *Antitrust law: An Economic Perspective*, Chicago, IL: University of Chicago Press.

Rasmusen, E.B., J.M. Ramseyer and J.S. Wiley (1991), 'Naked exclusion', *American Economic Review*, **81**, 1137–45.

Roques, F. (2007), 'Technology choices for new entrants in liberalized markets: the value of operating flexibility and contractual arrangements', EPRG0726 & CWPE 0759, University of Cambridge.

Roques, F., D. Newbery and W. Nuttal (2005), 'Investment incentives and electricity market design: the British experience', *Review of Network Economics*, **4** (2), 93–128.

Roques, F., D. Newbery and W. Nuttall (2007), 'Fuel mix diversification incentives in liberalized electricity markets: a mean–variance portfolio theory approach', *Energy Economics*, **30** (4), 1831–49.

Schnichels, H. and D. Nyssens (2007), 'Energy', in J. Faull and A. Nikpay (eds), *The EC Law of Competition*, 2nd edn, Oxford: Oxford University Press.

Segal, I.R. and M.D. Whinston (2000), 'Naked exclusion: comment', *American Economic Review*, **90**, 296–309.

Simpson, J. and A.L. Wickelgren (2007), 'Naked exclusion, efficient breach, and downstream competition', *American Economic Review*, **97** (4), 1305–20.

Smeers, Y. (2009), 'How well can one measure market power in restructured electricity systems?', in J.-M. Glachant and F. Lévêque (eds), *Electricity Reform in Europe. Towards a Single Energy* Market, Cheltenham, UK and Northampton, MA, USA: Edward Edgar. pp. 207–68

Thomas, S. (2004), 'Evaluating the British model of electricity deregulation', *Annals of Public and Cooperative Economics*, **75** (3), 367–98.

Thomas, S. (2007), 'Corporate concentration in the EU energy sector', report commissioned by the European Federation of Public Service Unions.

Vasquez, C., M. Rivier and I.J. Perez-Arriaga (2002), 'A market approach to long-term security of supply', *IEEE Transactions on Power Systems*, **17** (2), 349–57.

Watson, J. (2004), 'Selection environments, flexibility and the success of the gas turbine', *Research Policy*, **33** (8), 1065–80.

Willems, B. and E. de Corte (2008), 'Market power mitigation by regulating contract portfolio risk', *Energy Policy*, **36**, 3787–96.

Williamson, O. (1975), *Markets and Hierarchies*, New York: Free Press.

Williamson, O. (1983), 'Credible commitments: using hostages to support exchange', *American Economic Review*, **73** (4), 519–40.

Williamson, O. (1985), *The Economic Institutions of Capitalism – Firms, Market, Relational Contracting*, New York: Free Press.
Wiser, D., R. Bachrach, M. Bolinger and W. Golove (2004), 'Comparing the risk profiles of renewable and natural gas-fired electricity contracts', *Renewable and Sustainable Energy Reviews*, **8**, 335–63.

APPENDIX

Table 9A.1 Evolution of economic analysis in competition cases

Period	Key cases	Use of economic analysis
Pre-liberalization	*Electricidade de Portugal/Pego, Isab Energy/Enel, Jahrhundertvertrag*	No structured analysis of foreclosure, exclusive focus on duration, political considerations strongly influence competition analysis
Early post-liberalization	*Synergen, Gas Natural/Endesa*	Analysis of potential entry is refined, new remedies (such as VPP) are devised, interactions gas/elec are taken into account, duration may remain rather long, threshold-based analysis is introduced
Recent Art 82 EC cases (2004–)	*Distrigaz, Repsol, E.ON Ruhrgas*	Full analysis of cumulative foreclosure effects is conducted; combined analysis of exclusivity, patterns of consumption and duration; flexibility introduced in remedies

10. Long-term contracts and state aid: a new application of the EU state aid regime or a special case?

Leigh Hancher

1 INTRODUCTION

This chapter examines two recent decisions adopted by the European Commission (EC) against Poland and Hungary, condemning power purchase agreements (PPAs) as state aid within the meaning of Article 107(1) Treaty on the Functioning of the European Union (TFEU) (ex Article 87(1) EC).

The energy sector has yielded abundant case law on the definition of state aid within the meaning of Article 107(1) TFEU in the past decades. Given the long history of state intervention in and through the energy sector, this is perhaps not so remarkable. The two decisions discussed in this chapter may, however, signal a significantly new direction in the application of the European state aid rules to deal with what is essentially a competition-related problem, that is, market foreclosure caused by long-term vertical contracts. But it is crucial to point out that a state-aid analysis pursues a different line of investigation from that followed in a typical Article 81 EC (now Article 101 TFEU case). Under the latter article the standard 'test' is whether the contracts in question would have prevented efficient alternative suppliers from accessing customers, hence reducing consumer welfare. The application of this test requires complex market-based analysis. The two state-aid decisions discussed here, in effect investigated where it was most efficient to allocate risk in energy markets and to some extent attempted to analyse how different forms of vertical arrangements could deliver this allocation of risk. However, as is explained below, the decisions did not put forward any real market analysis to support the conclusion that the PPAs were inefficient. Rather, it would appear that the Commission considered that the risk should have been allocated differently, and based its conclusion on the assumption that if it had not been for these contracts, liquid wholesale markets would have developed more rapidly. This type of market structure should have delivered a better outcome.

This chapter begins with a short overview of the competition concerns raised by long-term vertical contracts. The application of the EC state-aid rules to the contracts in the two recent decisions are then analysed in greater detail.

1.1 Recent Developments in Competition Law and Long-term Contracts and Past Precedent under the EC State-aid Rules

The European electricity and gas sector is usually considered to be characterized by two main features – extensive vertical integration and a penchant for long-term contracts at all stages of the supply chain. If this had not already been evident to any informed observer, then the evidence gathered in the course of the Commission's Sector Inquiry Report of 2007 merely confirmed the obvious.[1] That report signalled follow-up action would be pursued to deal with market foreclosure and other anti-competitive effects of long-term contracts. A flurry of dawn raids followed and virtually every major European energy company has been the subject of an antitrust investigation in the course of the past two years.[2]

To supplement this concerted *ex post* attack, the Commission's third package of legislative measures on the internal energy market, originally launched in September 2007, and adopted in August 2009, envisages a combination of *ex ante* structural and behavioural approaches to remove those barriers to competition attributed to vertical integration.[3] The third package – like its two predecessors – does not directly deal with long-term contracts. Indeed the existing as well as the new directives and regulations for the internal gas and electricity markets take a rather equivocal approach to long-term supply contracts. They merit a brief mention in the annex to the Regulation 1228/03 on cross-border electricity trade[4] but are deemed worthy of a more central place in the machinery erected by the EC Gas Directive of 2003.[5]

It was perhaps with a view to filling the gap – or giving clearer guidance on the role of long-term contracts in liberalized – and by implication – more competitive gas and electricity markets that the Commission announced that it would come up with some sort of guidelines on long-term energy contracts.[6] This was not the first time the Commission had declared its intention to throw some light on this murky subject. Yet the Commission still appears reluctant to commit itself to a clear policy on long-term contracts in the energy sector – whether upstream or downstream. Instead it continues to opt for a pragmatic, case-by-case approach. The content of its decisions tend to vary – as do their legal form. In particular the Commission has opted for an informal settlement agreement, together with mutually agreed 'commitments', in numerous cases, and has resorted only to formal decisions as an exception.[7]

Certain individual decisions can and often are supplemented with policy guidance, albeit in the form of frequently asked questions (FAQs). Perhaps the most comprehensive decision to date is its decision relating to the *Distrigaz* settlement, in October 2007.[8] The *Distrigaz* settlement is significant for several reasons. First, it was intended to give clear guidance to other dominant gas and electricity supply companies in relation to their existing (and proposed) long-term contracts with customers. Indeed the Commission indicated that these companies would be much less likely to be subject to an antitrust investigation if they use the *Distrigaz* decision as a basis when concluding their own contracts. Second, *Distrigaz* could also be interpreted as introducing a 'bright-line approach' in relation to the application of Article 82 EC (now Art 102 TFEU).[9]

The Commission's Sector Inquiry of 2007 also announced that it would apply Articles 87 and 88 EC (now Articles 107 and 108 TFEU) to long-term contracts in the energy sector.[10] That report did not offer any further explanation of the tests to be applied, however, or any other hint as to how Article 107(1) TFEU would be applied in the contractual context. Obviously, the application of this Article is not subject to the same refined economic analysis as Article 81 and 82 EC (now Articles 101 and 102 TFEU). The so-called State Aid Action Plan (SAAP) of 2005[11] has introduced a more economic approach, not to defining the concept of aid itself in Article 107(1) TFEU, but rather as a way of assessing the compatibility of a proposed state-aid measure with the objectives of the internal market. The Commission subsequently released in April 2009, a staff paper on applying economic analysis to ascertain the compatibility of state financial support.[12] In contrast to the application of Article 101 and 102 TFEU, in respect of Article 107 TFEU the Commission is not required to define relevant markets with any precision, nor need it analyse market shares. Providing that all the cumulative conditions are met, Article 107(1) TFEU will apply to any state-aid measure which confers an economic benefit and, as such, distorts competition.[13]

For the application of Article 107(1) TFEU, the crux of the matter is that the state measure in question must confer an economic advantage on the recipient, in the sense that the company in question enjoys a selective benefit that it would not have enjoyed under normal market conditions, and in this respect the recipient can be deemed to have been given an advantage over its competitors.[14] The European courts have always emphasized that the decisive factor is not the form, but the *effect* of the state-aid measure in question. Is the effect of the measure to place the recipient at an advantage vis-à-vis its competitors?

Given that the resources of publicly owned or controlled firms can also be deemed 'state resources' for the purposes of Article 107(1) TFEU, then contracts for the sale or purchase of energy could also fall within the scope of the state-aid rules. The courts however require that the Commission demonstrates that the decision to use such resources must be 'attributable' to the state – that is, it must be demonstrated that state has somehow been involved and has pursued public policy goals, overriding the company's otherwise commercial objectives. Where a state owner follows the same course of action as any other private market investor, the courts and the Commission consider that the so-called market investor test (MEIT) should be applied and, if met, then no state aid will be involved. No 'abnormal' advantage or benefit is conferred in this scenario. In the energy sector, this has been confirmed once again in the recent case *EDF* v. *Commission* on 15 December 2009.[15] In that case the Commission had held that various measures put in place by the French government in relation to the restructuring of its high-tension network were aid within the meaning of the state-aid provisions. The French government as the sole shareholder in EDF at the relevant time had been prepared to recognize that EDF was badly under-capitalized and in order to finance the necessary restructuring, the French state had made various fiscal concessions to EDF, cancelling accumulated debt. EDF argued that the French state had therefore acted as a normal market investor would have done in similar circumstances. The Court of First Instance (CFI) – now the General Court – upheld this argument.

Prior to the two decisions under review here, the application of the European Union (EU) state-aid regime to long-term vertical contracts had arisen in several cases, all of which were closed without opening a formal investigation under Article 88(2) EC (now Article 108(2) TFEU). In particular, in a state-aid decision concerning the compulsory annulment by Portugal of existing long-term contracts between power generators and the Portuguese electricity company, Electricidad de Portugal (EDP), and the awarding of compensation for that annulment, the Commission noted that the contracts constituted an advantage for the power generators.[16] In its 2004 decision, the Commission allowed the planned compensation for future termination, subject to compliance with the guidelines espoused in its 'Stranded Cost Methodology' of 2001.[17] In effect then the Commission confirmed that compensation could and should be paid if long-term contracts were prematurely terminated to make way for new wholesale market arrangements. Portugal had, as was permitted under the First Electricity Directive 96/92/EC of

1996, opted for a so-called single buyer arrangement.[18] The phasing out of the latter arrangement involved the phasing out of the so-called PPAs. The Commission had also examined the contract between Électricité de France (EDF) and Péchiney in France,[19] but considered that this contract covered only Électricité de France's variable nuclear plant costs. Many other contracts of that type were concluded in France in the 1990s. They were all based on the principle that the generator undertakes to deliver electricity to the buyer over a long period at a price which only covers its marginal costs.

At around the same time it began its deliberations on the Portuguese case, the Commission began to turn its attention to long-term PPAs in several new member states. Just prior to their accession to the EU in May 2004, both Hungary[20] and Poland had notified their plans to deal with the restructuring of their electricity markets, including a gradual amendment to their respective single-buyer systems and the provision of stranded costs compensation. The Polish government notified draft legislation designed to terminate the various PPAs which its single buyer, Polski/Sieci Elektroenergetyczne (PSE), had concluded in the mid-1990s and, at the same time, to provide compensation for the stranded investments of both domestic and foreign generators. The Hungarian government, however, only notified a plan to compensate its single buyer, Magyar Villamos Müvek Zrt (MVM), for the losses incurred selling PPA-purchased electricity on to distributors at tightly regulated prices.

The Commission expressed its concern in both cases that the PPAs themselves could involve aid to the generators and, because it expressed its doubts as to the compatibility of the alleged aid, it opened a full investigation into both countries under Article 88(2) of the EC Treaty (now Article 108(2) TFEU). A complicating procedural factor – that the schemes had been notified of prior to accession – was also effectively bypassed in order to allow the Commission to proceed to a full inquiry. The governments withdrew their original pre-accession notifications so that the Commission could mount a new investigation after accession. In both cases the Commission classified the PPAs as 'new' aid, to be treated as post-accession support which was potentially subject to repayment or recovery from the alleged beneficiary as from 1 May 2004.

1.2 Background to the PPAs – The Privatization Process

In the mid-1990s the Polish government decided to launch a programme designed to modernize the Polish electricity sector and bring it into line with the technical and environmental standards of Western Europe. In order to implement this programme, Poland launched a tender procedure with a view to selecting projects for new or modernized electricity generation plants. These projects would be awarded long-term PPAs for their generation capacity. The decision to launch the tendering procedure was taken by the Ministry of Trade and Industry. The procedure was organized by Polskie Sieci Elektroenergetyczne S.A., the publicly owned Polish electricity operator, in August and September 1994. The tender documents indicated three objectives to be met by the projects: procurement of cheap electricity, maintenance of a reasonable level of security of supply and improvement of environmental standards/prevention of environmental deterioration, taking into account the requirements of integration between Poland and Western Europe. Various criteria were used to evaluate the bids, including: the project's efficiency, the volume of capital expenditure, pro-environmental action and the use of proven technologies and stable and secure sources of fuel.

A similar procedure was followed in Hungary. As part of the restructuring of the sector, the Hungarian government partially privatized its electricity generation sector in the mid-1990s. The previously vertically integrated monopoly, MVM, was split into separate generation and supply functions and the generator companies were sold by way of tender, primarily to international energy companies. In this respect Hungary followed international practice. The Polish PPAs were signed between 1996 and 1998, and their durations ranged from seven to 20 years. The last PPA expires in 2027.

At the same time, Hungary also overhauled the regulatory regime for the electricity sector. From 31 December 1991 to 31 December 2002, the Hungarian electricity market was structured around the 'single buyer' model. MVM, a 99 per cent state-owned entity, was designated as the single buyer and, in accordance with this legislation, it was entrusted with the obligation to ensure security of supply in Hungary at least cost to the consumer. On 1 January 2004 price regulation was abolished. The dual-market model, however, was not abolished until 1 January 2008, following the adoption and entry into force of the Energy Act 2007. As a result of these legislative amendments, from 1 January 2004, the price of electricity purchased by MVM was determined on the basis of the price formulae specified in the PPAs (except for the period between December 2006 and December 2007, when wholesale price regulation was reintroduced). The generators remained under a statutory obligation to supply MVM, however, *inter alia*, in order for MVM to meet its own legal obligations on the public utility (or 'regulated') segment of the market. The Energy Act had also provided for certain transitional arrangements, in particular for compensation of payment of stranded costs incurred by MVM.

1.3 Grounds for Initiating the Procedure

In its decision to initiate a formal investigation into the contracts (the so-called Article 88(2) EC (now Article 108(2) TFEU) procedure), in both cases the Commission expressed the view that PPAs did not constitute existing aid as – on the basis of the Accession Act[21] – none of the PPAs was eligible for one of the three categories of aid that were regarded, as of accession, as existing aid within the meaning of Article 108(1) TFEU. Second, the Commission had not been given notice of the PPAs under the so-called 'interim procedure' and, third, none of the PPAs had been indicated on the existing aid list annexed to the Accession Treaty. Since the PPAs had not been notified to it under Article 88(3) of the EC Treaty (now Article 108(3) TFEU), they constituted unlawful aid within the meaning of Article 1(f) of Council Regulation (EC) No 659/1999 of 22 March 1999 – the Procedural Regulation.[22]

The Commission also noted that the electricity markets had been opened to competition and that electricity had been traded between member states at least since the entry into force of Directive 96/92/EC. Measures that favour companies in the energy sector in one member state were therefore regarded as potentially impeding the scope for companies from other member states to export electricity to that member state, or favouring exports of electricity to the second group of member states.

As the Commission considered that all PPAs are underpinned by the same basic principles: power generators undertake to create new capacity, to modernize equipment and to supply the respective single buyer with a fixed minimum volume of electricity from the plant in question, a generic approach was followed in the analysis of the various PPAs concluded by MVM in Hungary and PSE in Poland respectively. The single buyer (that is, PSE in Poland and MVM in Hungary) was held to have agreed to purchase at least a minimum volume of electricity while the power generators charged the single buyer an amount equivalent to all their fixed and variable costs, plus a profit margin. The Commission therefore had to consider whether the buyer would have entered into these types of arrangements if operating under normal market conditions.

1.4 The Decisions

The Commission assessed the legality of the Polish long-term contracts in some detail in its final decision of September 2007.[23] It confirmed its initial suspicions that the contracts as such gave rise to aid as defined by Article 107(1) TFEU – that is, they conferred an economic advantage on the generators that they would not have enjoyed under normal market circumstances. As is analysed in detail below, it is actually very difficult to pinpoint the exact nature or scope or even economic value of this advantage. It is also worth noting that the terms and effects of the various contracts between PSE and the generators are not examined separately. Obviously such an approach precludes any real appraisal of market conditions or market shares. Although it is evident from the decision that, as with 'classic competition cases', the Commission is concerned about foreclosure effects caused by long-term vertical contracts, it does not indicate at any point in its analysis whether it is primarily concerned about contract duration, or about certain contractual terms or about prices being above a 'market' price. Although the Commission found that the contracts contained aid, it did not go on to calculate the value of this aid to the generators, but instead turned to a detailed analysis of the proposed legislation to compensate the generators for the early termination of the PPAs.

Following the Polish decision in September 2007, the Commission reached a final decision in the Hungarian case in June 2008 establishing that a number of electricity producers had received state aid in the period from May 2004 onwards. Unlike the Polish decision, which was not challenged, the Hungarian decision is now subject to four separate appeals. This is explained by the fact that whereas the Polish decision also positively assessed the compatibility of an Act providing stranded cost compensation for the terminated PPAs, the Hungarian government had not made any such provision. Hungary has subsequently adopted legislation declaring all those contracts listed by the Commission decision to be null and void. Unlike its Polish counterpart, the Hungarian scheme did not involve any compensation. Recent national legislation makes provision for future stranded cost compensation, on the assumption that the sums payable to each company are approved by the Commission, following separate notification and assessment.[24] The Hungarian law provides, however, that the compensation will not exceed the amount of alleged aid already received by the generators under their respective PPAs.

Article 1 of the Hungarian Decision[25] provides that: 'The purchase obligations as defined in the Power Purchase Agreements between MVM and the named generators contain State aids within the meaning of Article 87(1) EC [now Article 107(1) TFEU] to the electricity generators.'

Article 2 of the decision provides for recovery of the aid referred to in Article 1 from the beneficiaries. Article 3 provides that the Commission should be kept informed about various steps taken to implement the decision, until the recovery of the aid referred to in Article 1 has been completed. Article 4(1) provides that the exact amount to be recovered from the beneficiaries should be calculated by Hungary on the basis of an appropriate simulation of the wholesale electricity market 'as it would have stood if none of the PPAs referred to in Article 1(1) had been in force since 1 May 2004'.[26]

Although the exact contractual period for which this 'appropriate simulation' has to be conducted is not specified in Article 4(1), the text of the decision indicates that the recovery obligation would continue to run until the PPAs referred to in Article 1(1) are terminated (see, for example, para. 443). In effect, the Commission decision has also required Hungary to recover the aid paid to the various generators from the date of accession to the date of the compulsory termination of their PPAs. The decision does not quantify the amount of aid involved. Instead it requires the Hungarian authorities to conduct the complex market simulation exercise and construct a counter-factual scenario in which no PPAs existed after May 2004 and assess the difference between what each generator received under its contract with MVM and what it would have received had it been required to sell its electricity on a spot market. As a result the Hungarian generators are likely to be confronted with the prospective of recovery of substantial sums and are not likely to receive the generous amounts of compensation enjoyed by their Polish counterparts.

In the following paragraphs, we will explain, first, the background to the contracts, and then turn to the Commission's assessment of the legality of the PPAs. The next section deals with the Commission's analysis of the Polish Act to compensate the generators for termination. In so far as the analysis in the Polish decision is followed in the subsequent Hungarian decision, this too will be pointed out. Indeed, closer analysis suggests that there has been a considerable degree of 'copy-pasting' from the earlier to the later decision. Finally, the Commission's approach to the recovery of the illegal aid in the Hungarian case is examined.

2 AN ANALYSIS OF THE FINAL DECISIONS – KEY ELEMENTS

2.1 State Aid and Tender Procedures

It may be noted that the Commission considered in both the Polish and the Hungarian cases that, despite the interested parties' claims to the contrary, the fact that PPAs were concluded following a competitive tender procedure is not sufficient for them to be deemed as not constituting aid. This reasoning only applies when a member state purchases goods or services for its own use, according to the Commission.

In these cases, the purpose of the competitive procedure was to serve policy objectives such as promotion of foreign investment in Poland and in Hungary, environmental protection and improvements in security of supply, rather than to purchase goods and services required by the state. The fact that a competitive procedure was followed could only lead to the conclusion that the aid involved would be limited to the minimum necessary to achieve the policy objectives; it did not suffice to rule out the presence of state aid.

The power generators argued that any state aid under the PPAs would have been eliminated by the privatization process because the price paid by the companies that purchased the power plants would have taken account of the value of the PPAs. The Commission held that as privatization of the power plants took the form of share deals, it thus referred to case law in which the Court of Justice has analysed how a change in the ownership of a company during a share deal affects the existence of aid and the recipient of unlawful aid granted to the company.[27] It ruled that the unlawful aid remains and stays with the company that benefited from the aid, despite the change in its ownership. The transfer of shares at the market price merely ensured that the buyer did not benefit from state aid either. The change in the ownership of the power plants that benefited from the PPAs did not alter the fact that the PPAs constituted state aid to these power plants. In reality, the power plants benefited from the advantages contained in the PPAs, irrespective of their ownership structure.

2.2 The Relevant Time of Assessment

In its assessment of the question of the relevant time of assessment of the alleged aid measures, the Commission departed from normal practice. In particular, in the Hungarian case it expressly confirmed that it did not have to examine the application of Article 107 TFEU at the time the contracts were concluded. Instead, it took May 2004 – the date of accession – as the relevant time frame. It supported this approach on the basis of the Accession Acts of Hungary and of Poland to the EU, the Procedural Regulation and the court's case law.

Although it conceded that it is true that, when analysing the existence of state aid in a specific case, the Commission would usually, as is required by the courts, assess the situation prevailing at the time when the measure entered into force,[28] it held that this does not mean that the assessment of the measure as potential aid should in all circumstances be limited only to the time at which the aid was granted.

In particular, and relying on Article 1(b) point (v) of the Procedural Regulation, the Commission maintained that there are exceptional circumstances such as the evolution of the common market or the liberalization of a sector, where substantial economic and legal changes take place in a sector or several sectors of the economy and where, owing to these changes, a measure that initially did not come within the scope of Article 107 TFEU will fall under state-aid control. Any other approach would de facto prolong a major part of the pre-competitive market circumstances. This would go against the very intention of putting an end to such uncompetitive situation on a market, that is, to the decision of the member states to liberalize the given sector. The question of whether such state aid is to be classified as existing or new aid, should then only be assessed separately once the Commission has established the existence of state aid.

2.3 The Concept of Advantage in the PPAs

To determine whether the PPAs as a generic system provide an economic advantage to power generators, the Commission had to assess whether, via the PPAs, generators obtain economic advantages that they would not obtain from the market. Power purchase agreements could provide eligible generators with an advantage if the parties to these agreements are placed in a better economic position than other companies. Even though the details of individual PPAs may vary, in the Commission's view, all PPAs are structured around a core, invariable principle: the mandatory purchase by PSE and MVM of most (sometimes all) of the electricity generated by the companies concerned, at a price reviewed periodically in accordance with the principle that the total costs (fixed and variable) of generating electricity, plus a profit margin, are passed on to the consumer.[29]

The core principle is applied for the whole duration of the PPA, which lasts from seven to 20 years from the beginning of operation of the plants, that is, from 10 to 31 years following the conclusion of the PPAs and, in the majority of cases, more than 15 years. This meant that, during this period, the commercial risk associated with operating the power plants was borne by the buyer of the electricity, that is, PSE in Poland and MVM in Hungary. This included the risk associated with fluctuations in electricity generation costs and, in particular, fuel costs, the risk associated with fluctuations in end-user electricity prices, and the risk associated with fluctuation in end-user electricity demand. These are the typical risks that any power generator without a PPA would bear itself. The longer the period is, the greater the value of the guarantee, since it protects against a risk whose occurrence is increasingly unpredictable. In the Hungarian case, the Commission dismissed the impact of the regulatory framework, which divided the Hungarian market into two distinct sectors, so that the generators were not in fact free to sell directly into the 'utility' part of the market, but were required under national law to sell all their output to MVM, and until 2004, at regulated prices.

The Commission considered in the Polish case that the contracts amounted to guarantee, which is the core of the PPAs, and placed the beneficiaries in a better economic situation than other companies on the market and therefore provides an advantage to the relevant power plants. Admittedly, the PPAs were not a traditional form of guarantee but simply provided for payment by the state-owned and state-controlled PSE of the investment costs and the most important (if not all) operating costs of the power plants which are parties to the agreements. In practice, this 'guarantee' meant that, over more or less the full depreciation period or planned lifetime of the plant, and irrespective of any changes in the conditions obtaining on the market, the single buyer buys a fixed quantity of electricity at a price that must ensure the power plant's viability.

In the Commission's view the PPAs as a whole transferred more risks to the single buyers than standard commercial practices (as applicable from May 2004) and prevented both MVM and PSE from diversifying their portfolios and, furthermore, forced both companies to purchase more than they would need in the future.

The Commission further analysed several other aspects of the PPAs – noting that they were concluded only with selected power generators. At the time they were concluded, there were other electricity generators that did not benefit from the PPA rules. More were set up in later years, and new investments were under way without PPA support. On 28 June 2001 a start was made in Poland on eliminating this mechanism and these power generators started selling their electricity at free, market-based prices. None of these mechanisms (price controlled by the state or free, market-based price) enabled generators without PPAs to cover all their costs. They sold their electricity at a price corresponding to marginal costs, that is, a price which only ensures that their variable costs are covered.

The Polish Power Exchange started operating in 1999. From 2001 the average price of electricity on the Polish Power Exchange remained stable and as such confirmed that market prices – that is, the price that generators without PPAs were paid for their electricity on the market – would not suffice to provide the same type of profit guarantee as the guarantee PPAs offer. In liberalized markets, electricity can also be traded via bilateral contracts ('over the counter' or OTC market). The Commission's sector inquiry of 2007 showed that, because of the possibility of arbitrage between power exchanges and bilateral contracts, trading conditions (in particular price and duration of contracts) on the OTC market are similar to those prevailing on power exchanges or spot markets. Under the PPAs, the single buyer undertook to purchase a fixed minimum volume of electricity from power generators at a price covering their full costs until a pre-agreed date. Further, according to the Commission, this decision was imposed on the single buyers by their respective governments.

The Hungarian spot market was considered too marginal to provide a relevant benchmark against which to examine the PPAs in the Hungarian decision. The Commission instead compared the purchase obligation enshrined in the PPAs with the main features of 'standard forward and spot contracts', 'drawing rights' contracts, long-term contracts concluded by large end-consumers, and contracts concluded between generators and transmission system operators (TSOs) for the provision of balancing services at paragraphs 206 to 209 of the decision. Drawing on its analysis in the energy sector inquiry of 2007, it concluded that trade in power on spot market exchanges is always based on marginal pricing, which guarantees only that short-run marginal costs, and not all fixed and capital costs are covered. Furthermore, on spot markets, a power-generating company has no assurance about the level of utilization of its generating capacities. This risk is much higher than for most manufacturing sectors, and is due to the impossibility of storing electricity economically, which is a very specific feature of that industry.

On the basis of this assessment of the Hungarian PPAs, with 'standard practices' elsewhere in Europe, the Commission concluded that:

> the main terms and conditions of the purchase obligation enshrined in the PPAs, i.e. the capacity reservations and guaranteed off-take by MVM under such conditions as to ensure the return on investment of the power plants by shielding them from the commercial risks of the operation of their plant, constitute State aid within the meaning of Article 87(1) of the EC Treaty [now Article 107(1) TFEU]. This State aid is achieved by the combination of the capacity reservations, the minimum guaranteed off-take, the pricing mechanism based on a capacity fee and an energy fee to cover fixed, variable and capital costs, over a long duration beyond normal commercial practice.[30]

Given that it had limited its assessment to the period after May 2004, the Commission did not consider it necessary to establish whether the business case for the PPAs might have been different in the mid-1990s and whether the PPAs would have indeed met the commercial objectives of MVM and PSE at the time they were concluded. Surprisingly, even taking 2004 as the starting point, the Commission failed to consider the disadvantages for buyers relying on spot markets and short-term contracts, that is, the exposure to volatility and liquidity risk. The risks borne by the sellers, in particular the risks involved in investing in economies in transition, were discounted entirely as these risks arose before the relevant time of assessment – that is, May 2004.

2.4 The Market Economy Investor Test (MEIT)

The Commission had not explicitly restricted the relevant time frame of assessment to the period of accession in the Polish case, as it went on to do almost a year later in the Hungarian case. Instead it analysed the application (1) EC Article 107(1) TFEU to the contracts over their entire duration, and it went to some lengths to dismiss the arguments put forward by the generators that the Polish and Hungarian single buyers had acted as normal private investors would have done and hence the MEIT should be applied. It held that the very fact that the Polish government had to decide in PSE's place that new investments would take place and would benefit from PPAs clearly shows that this decision was mainly based on criteria other than market investor considerations. There were two main reasons why PSE could not have had an economic interest in taking this decision without government intervention.

First, PSE purchased a quantity of energy that it already knew might be surplus to its requirements. By awarding the PPAs, PSE undertook to purchase a fixed and significant quantity of electricity (around 50 per cent of Polish electricity production in 2005 and up to 70 per cent in the period in question). The PPAs were signed between 1996 and 1998. It was already clear at the time that Poland was likely to accede to the EU during the life of most if not all of the PPAs. It was known that Poland's accession to the EU would entail integration into the internal electricity market, liberalization of which started with the adoption of Directive 96/92/EC. This meant the opening-up of the market to other competing suppliers and, accordingly, that PSE might not need all the electricity provided for in the PPAs in the light of changes on the electricity market.

The liberalization plans were implemented very rapidly in Poland, with the first customers benefiting from the opening-up of the market in 1999. The Polish Power Exchange opened in the same year. Further changes occurred when the 'second internal electricity market' Directive 2003/54/EC was adopted on 26 June 2003.[31] This Directive provided for the liberalization of the market for all professional consumers by 1 July 2004 and for all consumers by 1 July 2007, thus gradually reducing PSE's captive market share to zero.

Second, even for the share of electricity which PSE actually needed, it made no sense for PSE, as the buyer, to undertake to pay the power plants the full costs of generating power, plus a profit margin established such a long time in advance, even though it was already known that liberalization would allow it to choose between different technologies and prices, including those offered by new market entrants using more efficient technologies.

Buyers have an interest in concluding long-term contracts, argued the Commission, only if these contracts provide them with some hedging against fluctuations in the electricity market and, in particular, against changes linked to fluctuations in fuel costs. For this reason a buyer would have an economic interest in a long-term contract of this type only if the seller offered to take part of the risk associated with fluctuations in fuel costs or if the generating technology ensured stable fuel costs, as is the case with hydropower plants and, in certain conditions, nuclear plants.

The Commission considered that this economic logic was confirmed by the fact that there does not seem to be any example of private buyers taking long-term contracts without state intervention with plants using fossil fuel and covering all production costs for the same duration as the PPAs (more than 10 years). The Commission found none in its 2007 energy sector inquiry, and none of the interested parties submitted an example of such a contract to the Commission.

Similarly, most of the Hungarian generators argued that the PPAs do not confer any advantage to the generators as they correspond to the normal behaviour of any market economy operator in both MVM's and the generators' position. Any private actor in the position of MVM (with a legal obligation of security of supply) would have chosen to enter into the PPAs, and that the advantage of the PPAs do not go beyond what, in the circumstances of the immature energy market of the 1990s in Hungary, was a normal commercial advantage for the parties. Moreover, generators had the legal obligation to enter into an agreement with MVM in order to obtain their operating licence. They emphasized that applying the private investor principle should lead the Commission to take account of the legal requirements and economic reality of the time of conclusion of the PPAs.

With regard to the market economy investor test, in the Hungarian case the Commission clung resolutely to the relevant time of assessment of the existence of state aid in the PPAs – that is, May 2004. The Commission recalled that it did not intend to call into question the necessity of entering into PPAs under the circumstances prevailing at the time of the conclusion of those agreements. This, however, did not in any way mean that the PPAs would not confer an advantage on the generators. None of the interested parties had argued that they would correspond to current market conditions on the internal market.

Hence the Commission considered that in both cases the conclusion of the PPAs was attributable to the state and further, given the policy objectives pursued by the PPAs when assessed against market conditions prevailing at accession, that the market investor test did not apply.

In the Hungarian case, the Commission effectively declined to consider the reasons why MVM would, as a commercial party, have viewed the

PPAs as a reasonable investment at the time the contracts were concluded, as well as a better alternative to vertical integration. Interestingly, in neither case were comments or observations from the single buyers (MVM and PSE) recorded in the final decision. Perhaps the Commission always knows best, but in any event, its approach in the PPA cases certainly represents a departure from the established jurisprudence as summarized and confirmed once more by the court in *West LB*[32] – that the application of the MEIT test should be made at the time when the investment was made, and not with the benefit of hindsight.

2.5 PPAs and Services of General Economic Interest (SGEIs)

The generators, in their observations on the opening decisions had also argued in both cases that the PPAs should be regarded as implementing SGEIs for the purpose of securing electricity supplies and environmental protection and to fulfil the criteria laid down in the *Altmark* judgment,[33] which means that they do not constitute aid within the meaning of Article 107(1) TFEU of the EC Treaty.

The Commission rejected these arguments because, although it acknowledged that member states have a wide margin of discretion to define the scope of SGEIs, the existence of this wide margin of discretion does not mean that just any state intervention with a policy motivation can be characterized as an SGEI. The Commission also held that the member states' wide margin of discretion in defining the scope of SGEIs is restricted in fields where Community legislation exists.

The interested parties also invoked environmental protection as one of the SGEIs to be implemented by the PPAs. More precisely, the PPAs were supposed to support investment designed to allow Polish plants to adapt to EU environmental standards. The Commission considered that the requirement to fulfil environmental standards does not exhibit any special characteristics as compared with the constraints imposed on all companies active in an industrial sector. Furthermore, considering the fulfilment of environmental standards as an SGEI would go directly against the polluter pays principle which is one of the core principles of European environmental law and enshrined in the EC Treaty.

The interested parties further invoked security of supply as one of the SGEIs that the PPAs can fulfil. But the Commission countered that security of supply could be an SGEI, subject to the restrictions provided for in Article 8(4) of Directive 96/92/EC (which corresponds to Article 11(4) of Directive 2003/54/EC), that is, provided that the generators concerned use indigenous primary energy fuel sources, and that the total volume of energy does not exceed in any calendar year 15 per cent of the total primary energy necessary to produce the electricity consumed in the member state concerned.[34] In both cases the PPAs concerned quantities of energy that are largely in excess of the 15 per cent. Furthermore, they did not solely concern generators using indigenous primary energy fuel sources.

Finally, the Commission noted that the power plants concerned by the PPAs did not exhibit any special characteristics that would make them particularly well adapted to meet security of supply objectives. In fact, they were just normal plants connected to the network, and therefore contributed to the overall security of supply in Poland and in Hungary, just like any other power plant in the sector. In view of the above, the Commission concluded that the EC Treaty provisions on SGEIs do not apply to PPAs.

The generators also argued that, even if the PPAs were in fact aid, Article 86(2) EC (now Article 106(2) TFEU) might apply as an alternative basis for the justification of the PPAs but the Commission held that this article can apply only to companies which have been entrusted with providing genuine SGEIs, which was not the case. Finally, compensation for providing the SGEI must be proportionate to the costs incurred; in other words, it must be possible to carry out an assessment of the scope of the SGEIs in order to calculate the associated costs.

The Commission also claimed that the PPAs met the remaining criteria of Article 107(1) TFEU – that is, that they were selective as not every generator benefited from a PPA and not every sector benefited from similar long-term contracts. Trade had been distorted both at the time of the conclusion of the contracts, as well as on accession.

As a result, having rejected both the 'MEIT' and the 'SGEI' tests, the Commission concluded that the PPAs – or at least certain rather ill-defined elements of the PPAs – constituted non-notified aid within the meaning of Article 107(1) TFEU. In the Polish case it went on to assess the proposed Act to compensate the generators.

2.6 Conclusion on the Definition of 'Aid'

The Commission's analysis of the alleged economic benefit which resulted from the Hungarian and Polish PPAs would seem to turn on its assumption that the generators effectively passed the larger share of the risk to the single buyer and, as such, this was not an efficient decision for such a market party. By effectively dismissing the relevance of the economic and financial conditions prevailing at the time the contracts were signed, and the actual constraints facing both parties, the Commission could ignore the sellers' obligations and the risks which they had in turn been prepared to bear when investing in transitional economies. It remains to be seen whether the CFI – now the General Court – will uphold this reasoning. It also remains to be seen whether the Commission would also apply the same approach to analysing the legality of long-term contracts in general. It may well be that the Polish and Hungarian cases presented an exceptional situation in that the PPAs covered large parts of the markets in question and effectively foreclosed new market entrants. That said, the analysis remains highly novel and, as such, highly controversial. As indicated in the introductory remarks to this chapter, the Commission would normally address market foreclosure issues by applying the Treaty competition rules as opposed to the state-aid regime.

The decisions also contain several other novel features that are worthy of analysis. The next section of this chapter turns to an examination of the analysis of the Polish compensation regime and then examine the methodology applied in the Hungarian case to calculate the recoverable aid.

3 COMPATIBILITY OF THE AID MEASURES

In its final decisions in both cases, the Commission dismissed the application of Articles 87(3)(a) and (c) (now Article 107(3)(a) and (c) TFEU) to the PPAs. In particular, it dismissed the potential application of the Regional Aid Guidelines in force when the two countries joined the EU on the grounds that the guidelines only permitted aid for investment costs and not operating aid – which was the type of aid received by the generators.[35] Hence the aid was not eligible for the derogation provided under Article 87(3)(a) EC (now Article 107(3)(a) TFEU). Similarly, it rejected the application of the Environmental Aid Guidelines as these too primarily relate only to investment aid and only authorize operating aid for co-generation.[36] Finally the Commission examined whether the contracts themselves were compatible with its 'Stranded Cost Methodology' and concluded that several elements of the main principles constituting the PPAs do not met the conditions laid down in the methodology. Instead of helping transition to a competitive market, the PPAs had rather created an obstacle to the development of substantial competition. As a consequence they also contradicted the principles laid down in that methodology.

3.1 The Polish Act to Compensate the Generators

The question of whether the proposed compensation for the termination of the PPAs was only relevant in the Polish case as the Hungarian government had not come forward with a proposed compensation mechanism prior to the Commission taking a final decision in that case. In the Polish case, the Commission first established that the four cumulative criteria for the existence of state aid within the meaning of Article 107(1) TFEU were met. First, as to state resources and imputability to the state, the source of the funds to be used for the payments provided for in the Act were derived from the proceeds of a parafiscal levy established by virtue of the same Act.[37] The amount of the levy was to be established by the TSO, and the proceeds of the levy collected by suppliers are to be paid into an account held by a special purpose company, fully owned and controlled by the state. In accordance with the Act, the funds are disbursed to power generators to cover stranded costs in the form of advances for such costs for a given year and in the form of annual adjustments. The formula for calculating these payments enabled the state to cover the losses associated with certain types of cost, plus depreciation and fuel costs, if the revenue collected on the market was not sufficient for that purpose, subject to certain conditions which are likely to be fulfilled in a normal economic scenario. These payments therefore constituted an economic advantage.

The generators argued that the payments did not constitute an advantage because they were only fair compensation for the termination of the PPAs. The generators invoked the *Asteris* judgment,[38] in which the court held that compensation due, as a consequence of harm caused by an illegal state act, did not constitute aid but was on the contrary, a general measure. For the Commission, this reasoning was based on the premise that the PPAs themselves do not constitute an economic advantage, which was not the case. In other words, *Asteris* can only be relied on to claim compensation if the act to which the compensation relates does not itself constitute state aid within the meaning of Article 107(1) TFEU.

3.2 Compatibility of the Compensation

The Commission then proceeded to examine the proposed compensation scheme in accordance with its Stranded Cost Methodology of 2001. The first paragraph of section 3 of the Stranded Costs Methodology explains that stranded costs 'may, in practice, take a variety of forms: long-term purchase contracts, investments undertaken with an implicit or explicit guarantee of sale, investments undertaken outside the scope of normal activity, etc'.[39] In this particular case, and indeed in contrast to the Hungarian case, the aid was deemed to be earmarked for investments in the modernization or expansion of power plants with the PPAs as an explicit guarantee of sale. The Commission therefore held that the aid could fall within the remit of the Stranded Costs Methodology. The Stranded Costs Methodology provides for a two-stage assessment of aid earmarked for compensation of stranded costs. The first stage, which is referred to in section 3 of the methodology, concerns the definition of eligible costs, which involves in particular calculating the maximum compensation that can be awarded. The second stage, which is dealt with in section 4 of the methodology, concerns the mechanism for calculating the actual compensation to be paid for the stranded costs, taking the development of competition in the market into account.

The stranded costs referred to in the Act were closely linked to investments in power plants that cannot be recouped as a result of liberalization of the internal market in electricity. This also applied to take or pay contracts, which were concluded with a view to supplying power plants benefiting from PPAs to an extent consistent with the volume of electricity covered by the PPAs. The Commission noted that the investments in question are investments in power plants. These are particularly long-term investments (from 15 to as many as 30 years), which are very sensitive to electricity price trends that are difficult to predict, in particular during the transition to a fully liberalized market. The costs of these investments cannot be recouped in cases where electricity prices are lower than the prices provided for when the power plants were built.

Hence, the Commission concluded that the Act complied with the criteria laid down in points 3.1 to 3.12 of the methodology. The maximum stranded costs compensation did not exceed the permissible level and could therefore be regarded as eligible within the meaning of the methodology.

The Commission then examined whether the aid fulfilled the conditions laid down in points 4.1 to 4.6 of the methodology. The maximum amounts of compensation were calculated on the basis of clearly defined, individual power plants and take or pay contracts. The compensation actually paid would not exceed these maximum amounts and would take account of actual trends in underlying economic data, in particular electricity prices and volumes of gas purchased under take or pay contracts. For instance, should actual electricity prices differ from the base market price, the amount of actual compensation will be amended accordingly. The actual amounts of compensation for take or pay contracts would also take account of the actual conditions in which the power generators concerned purchase their gas and sell their electricity on the market. If the base market price increased significantly over time, the amount of compensation payable will decrease.

In accordance with point 4.5 the maximum amount of compensation to be paid to a given company is fixed in advance. This takes account of beneficiaries' future profits resulting from productivity gains. The notification of the aid specified in particular how stranded cost calculations would take account of changes in various economic factors (like prices, market shares or other relevant factors indicated by the member states and listed in the methodology).

3.3 Recovery Issues in the Hungarian Decision

As the opening paragraphs of its decision make clear, the Commission and Hungary had failed to agree on a mutually satisfactory approach to the termination of the PPAs and their subsequent compensation. This left the Commission little choice. Having failed unsuccessfully to persuade Hungary to adopt the 'Polish model' the Commission finally condemned the PPAs and ordered recovery. The Commission's approach to determining the amount to be recovered in the Hungarian case is highly unusual. It diverges not just from the earlier stranded cost cases but also from its approach to recovery of illegal state aid in general. Market simulations or the construction of counterfactual scenarios have not been used usually in the past. As the European courts have frequently stressed, the purpose of recovery is a restoration of the status quo *ex ante* – that is, to the situation before the aid in question was granted. How does one fit the aid element in a long-term contract into this approach? Normally the Commission identifies the nature of the advantage at issue – usually a tax advantage or a loan on terms well below market rates or other form of grant or subsidy – quantifies that advantage and requires its repayment, with interest. It does not normally look at the impact of the aid 'on the market' and require a market simulation as if the aid did not exist.

Arguably this approach could be relevant in more 'straightforward' cases where, for example, a major player is given a large subsidy to pursue research and development, thus crowding out potential (or actual) competitors. If the subsidy is illegal, the beneficiary repays it, plus interest. Any anti-competitive distortion and resulting economic damage to other parties would not be 'costed out' and included in the recovery order. That third parties such as competitors could subsequently sue the member state or indeed the beneficiary in separate proceedings for the damage they have suffered, is not ruled out – providing of course that, at the very least, the substantial hurdle of establishing causation can be overcome.[40] Damages awards in state-aid cases before national courts are very rare indeed.

The exact scope and value of the 'purchase obligations' which have been classified as state aid in the Hungarian PPAs in general, is not reflected in Article 1. According to para. 469 of the decision, it would appear that the state aid element in any single PPA could consist of a 'purchase obligation . . . of a certain capacity and a guaranteed minimum quantity . . . at a price covering capital, fixed and variable costs over a significant part of the lifetime of the . . . investments'.[41]

In accordance with Article 4(1) the amount of aid to be recovered by Hungary is to be calculated on the basis of an appropriate simulation of the wholesale market as it would have stood if none of the PPAs as referred to in Article 1(1) had been in force since 1 May 2004. Recovery is not therefore limited to the amount of aid arising from the 'purchase obligations' referred to in Article 1(1) to (3) but is based on a market simulation as if the PPAs did not exist. These two scenarios are by no means identical, either in legal or economic terms, given that the Commission had not condemned the PPAs, as such, as state aid. Nevertheless the Commission required the Hungarian authorities to calculate the difference between the revenues that the generators earned with the PPAs and the revenues that they would have earned by selling their output on a competitive spot market. These counterfactual revenues were to be simulated using a complex 'dispatch' model.

By requiring the Hungarian government to remove all the so-called 'purchase obligations', and to execute recovery as if the contracts did not exist, the Commission effectively required Hungary to ensure the termination of all the PPAs. In the Polish case it also ordered termination of the PPAs. This in turn raises the fascinating legal question of whether the Commission has the power to order the termination of a private contract. It does not have this power in relation to antitrust proceedings. It is up to national courts to determine whether the contracts in question would be void.

4 CONCLUSION

The energy sector has yielded abundant case law on the definition of a state aid within the meaning of Article 107(1) TFEU in the past decades. The two decisions here, however, seem to mark a significantly new direction in the application of the state-aid rules to deal with what is essentially a competition-related problem, that is, market foreclosure caused by long-term vertical contracts. Foreclosure may result from contracts between dominant suppliers and large consumers. But a state-aid analysis pursues a different line of investigation from that followed in an Article 81 EC (now Article 101 TFEU) case. Under the latter article the 'test' is whether the contracts in question would have prevented efficient alternative suppliers from accessing customers. This requires complex market-based analysis. The two state-aid decisions discussed here investigated where it was most efficient to allocate risk in energy markets and to some extent attempted to analyse how different forms of vertical arrangements could deliver this allocation of risk. It is difficult to see how this exercise could be carried out convincingly without taking full account of the market circumstances in which the parties to the contract actually operate and what their actual objectives were when they entered into the contracts, as well as the alternative options available to pursue them at that time. In particular, the actual constraints on pursuing those options have surely to be taken into account in order to understand the business strategy which could or should have been employed. There are many reasons why, even in more liquid wholesale markets, both supplier and purchaser will prefer vertical arrangements. These might take the form of long-term contracts and/or vertical integration. Long-term contracts allow both parties to hedge against market volatility. While it is true that liquidity levels have improved in some markets after market opening, this is neither a guaranteed result nor a conclusive one. Even in liquid markets, vertical arrangements are still necessary to secure investment in new generation.[42] A full examination of the commercial and financial options open to the parties when they exercise the choices they make is therefore vital.

If this analysis is not made then the Commission's attempts to 'second-guess' the reasons why market players entered into a particular set of contracts can lead only to major legal uncertainties for all concerned. If under threat from European state-aid law, longer-term contracts even if commercially attractive are no longer considered a legally valid option, vertical reintegration might be the only choice left. This is, indeed, what has occurred in Poland subsequent to the termination of the PPAs. This does not seem to be the solution to creating liquid markets.

At the same time, it is difficult to predict whether the Commission would apply the same approach to long-term contracts in the future – given that the constellation of circumstances that formed the backdrop to its decisions against Hungary and Poland are unlikely to be replicated elsewhere. The so-called single-buyer system – itself a creature of European energy legislation – has been consigned to the dustbin of history. Long-term contracts to guarantee, for example, investment in nuclear electricity in France and in Finland, have recently been viewed in a positive light.[43] But these two decisions should cause investors to have cause to pause and ponder whether notification to, and clearance by, the Commission should be considered before they enter into long-term supply or purchase contracts with state-owned entities in 'immature' markets.

NOTES

1. DG Competition Report on Energy Sector Inquiry SEC(2006)1724 of 10 January 2007 and Commission Communication (EC) Inquiry pursuant to Article 17 of

Regulation (EC) No. 1/2003 into the European gas and electricity sectors (Final Report) COM(2006) 851 final, 10 January 2007.
2. See Hancher and Hauteclocque (2010).
3. For the Regulations and Directives of the third legislative package on Gas and Electricity see [2009] OJ L 211; for a short account of the package see, Hancher and Hauteclocque (2010).
4. Regulation (EC) No. 1228/2003 of the European Parliament and of the Council of 26 June 2003 on conditions for access to the network for cross-border exchanges in electricity [2003] OJ L 176/1.
5. Directive (EC) 2003/55 of the European Parliament and of the Council of 26 June 2003 concerning common rules for the internal market in natural gas and repealing Directive 98/30/EC [2003] OJ L 176/57.
6. For an overview of policy developments, see Commission (EC) Report on Competition Policy 2008 COM(2009) 374 final, 23 July 2009.
7. See Hancher and Hautecloque (2010).
8. Commission Decision (EC) COMP/B-1/37966 – *Distrigaz* of 11 October 2007 and Commission Press Release IP/07/1487 of 11 October 2007.
9. Hancher (2009).
10. Commission Communication (EC) Inquiry pursuant to Article 17 of Regulation (EC) No. 1/2003 into the European gas and electricity sectors (Final Report) COM(2006) 851 final, 10 January 2007.
11. Commission (EC), 'State Aid Action Plan: Less and better targeted State aid: a roadmap for state aid reform 2005–2009' (Consultation document), COM(2005) 107 final, 7 June 2005.
12. DG Competition, Commission (EC) staff working paper 'Common principles for an economic assessment of the compatibility of State aid under Article 87.3', public consultation closed at 11 June 2009,.
13. See in this respect Case T-55/99 *Confederación Española de Transporte de Mercancias (CETM)* v. *Commission* [2000] ECR II- 3207, para. 102.
14. Case C-222/04 *Ministero dell'Economia e delle Finanze* v. *Cassa di Risparmio di Firenze SpA*, [2006] ECR I-289, para. 140.
15. Case T-156/04 *Électricité de France (EDF)* v. *Commission* (CFI 15 December 2009).
16. Commission Decision N 161/04 *Portugal – Stranded costs in Portugal* [2005] OJ C 250/9.
17. Commission Communication (EC) relating to the methodology for analysing state aid linked to stranded costs – adopted on 26 July 2001, available at: http://ec.europa.eu/competition/state_aid/legislation/stranded_costs_en.pdf (accessed 1 June 2010).
18. Article 18 of Directive 96/92/EC of the European Parliament and of the Council of 19 December 1996 concerning common rules for the internal market in electricity [1997] OJ L 27/20.
19. EC Commission, press release, IP(89) 752.
20. On 31 March 2004, the Hungarian authorities submitted to the Commission – under the procedure referred to in Annex IV, Para. 3, subpara. 1(c) of the Treaty of Accession (the interim procedure) – the notification of the Hungarian Government Decree 183/2002, providing for a system of compensation of costs borne by the state-owned electricity wholesaler MVM (HU 1/2004).
21. Act concerning the conditions of accession of the Czech Republic, the Republic of Estonia, the Republic of Cyprus, the Republic of Latvia, the Republic of Lithuania, the Republic of Hungary, the Republic of Malta, the Republic of Poland, the Republic of Slovenia and the Slovak Republic and the adjustments to the Treaties on which the European Union is founded [2003] OJ L 236/33.
22. Council Regulation (EC) No. 659/1999 of 22 March 1999 laying down detailed rules for the application of Article 93 of the EC Treaty OJ L 83/1, 27 March 1999.
23. Commission decision (EC) of 25 September 2007 on State aid awarded by Poland as part of power purchase agreements and the state aid which Poland is planning to award

concerning compensation for the voluntary termination of power purchase agreements (notified under document number C(2007) 4319) [2009] OJ L 83/1.
24. The Commission subsequently approved this measure in April 2010 (IP/10/470).
25. Commission decision of 4 June 2008 on the state aid C 41/05 awarded by Hungary through power purchase agreements (notified under document C(2008) 2223) [2009] OJ L 225/53.
26. Ibid. Article 4.
27. Joined cases C-328/99 and C-399/00 *Italy and SIM 2 Multimedia* v. *Commission* [2003] ECR I-4035.
28. See also in this respect Case T-98/00 *Linde AG* v. *Commission* [2002] ECR II-3961.
29. The Polish electricity regulator, Urzad Regualcji Energetyki (URE), indirectly retained the right to check whether the costs charged to PSE are justified and reasonable, but the Commission held that in practice URE used this power only to check that the costs were actually linked to electricity generation. Furthermore, URE's checks were only indirect since their purpose is to verify the cost structure of PSE with a view to defining PSE's income from captive customers. In the unlikely circumstance of some of the PPA-related costs charged to PSE being deemed unjustified by URE, it can only prohibit PSE from passing these costs on to its captive customers. This might make it more difficult for PSE to discharge its obligations under the PPAs, but it would not mean they had been legally annulled.
30. Commission decision of 4 June 2008 on the state aid C 41/05 awarded by Hungary through power purchase agreements (notified under document C(2008) 2223) [2009] OJ L 225/53, para. 340.
31. Directive 2003/54/EC of the European Parliament and of the Council of 26 June 2003 concerning common rules for the internal market in electricity and repealing Directive 96/92/EC [2003] OJ L 176/37.
32. Case T-228/99 *Westdeutsche Landesbank Girozentrale (West LB)* v. *Commission* [2003] ECR II-435.
33. Case C-280/00, *Altmark Trans GmbH and Regierungspräsidium Magdeburg* v. *Nahverkehrsgesellschaft Altmark GmbH* [2003] ECR II-7747.
34. See Commission decisions in cases N 34/99 *Austria – Compensation of stranded costs* [2002] OJ C 5/2, NN 49/99 *Spain – Scheme for competition transition costs* [2001] OJ C 268/7, N 6/A/01 *Ireland – Public service obligations imposed on the Electricity Supply Board with respect to the generation of electricity out of peat* [2002] OJ C 77/26 and C 7/2005 *Slovenia – Slovenian electricity tariff* [2007] OJ 219/9.
35. Commission (EC) 'Guidelines on national regional aid' [1998] OJ C74/9.
36. Commission (EC) 'Community guidelines on State aid for environmental protection' [2001] OJ C37/3.
37. See the judgment in Case 173/73 *Italy* v. *Commission* [1974] ECR 709 and Case 78/76 *Steinike & Weinlig* v. *Germany* [1977] ECR 595.
38. Case 106/87 *Asteris AE and others* v. *Hellenic Republic and European Economic Community* [1988] ECR 5515..
39. Commission Communication relating to the methodology for analysing state aid linked to stranded costs – adopted on 26 July 2001, para. 3, available at: http://ec.europa.eu/competition/state_aid/legislation/stranded_costs_en.pdf (accessed 1 June 2010).
40. Case C-39/94 *Syndicat français de l'Express international (SFEI)* v. *La Poste* [1996] ECR I-3547.
41. Commission decision of 4 June 2008 on the state aid C 41/05 awarded by Hungary through power purchase agreements (notified under document C(2008) 2223) [2009] OJ L 225/53, para. 469.
42. See, for example, Roques et al. (2008).
43. See Commission decision on Exeltium, Commission (EC) report on competition policy 2008 COM(2009) 374 final, 23 July 2009 and Commission press release MEMO/08/533 of 31 July 2008. See also Commission press release IP/07/1400 of 26 September 2007 in relation to the French state guarantees for Finnish generator TVO.

REFERENCES

Hancher L. (2009), 'Power plays: the end of the line for long-term energy contracts in Europe?', *Agenda, Advancing Economics in Business*, May, Oxera online publication.

Hancher, L. and A. de Hauteclocque (2010), 'Manufacturing the EU energy markets. The current dynamics of regulatory practice', EUI Working Papers RSCAS 2010/01, Loyola De Palacio Programme on Energy Policy.

Roques, F., D.M. Newbery and W.J. Nuttall (2008), 'Portfolio optimization and utilities' investments in liberalized power markets', in M. Bazilian and F. Roques (eds), *Analytical Models for Energy Diversity and Security*, Oxford: Elsevier, pp. 219–46.

11. The essential facilities doctrine in European competition policy: the case of the energy sector

Adrien de Hauteclocque, Frédéric Marty and Julien Pillot

1 INTRODUCTION[1]

The 2004 US Supreme Court's landmark decision in *Trinko*[2] established a major divide between US and European competition policies. Overall, the larger degree of acceptance of the Essential Facilities Doctrine (thereafter EFD) in European competition policy may induce more frequent mandatory access decisions to dominant firms' strategic assets. If such access-based policies may enhance consumer welfare in the short term, they could compromise dynamic efficiency in the longer term by reducing investment returns and so the incentives to invest. This trade-off is at the heart of many decisions to be taken by regulators and competition authorities in the energy sector. Indeed, the specific characteristics of electricity and gas markets (for example, balancing services in electricity and storage in gas) make them particularly prone to facility foreclosure compared to other network industries such as telecommunications. As a consequence it is generally harder for the regulatory authorities to effectively monitor access. On the other hand investment in the network, in particular in electricity and gas cross-border interconnectors, is crucial for security of supply, the effective development of competitive markets and the massive integration of renewables in energy systems. The fine-tuning of the application of EFD-related principles, either under sector-specific regulation or competition law, is thus an important area of energy regulation.

This chapter reviews and questions the current implementation of EFD principles by European authorities in the energy sector. We analyse in section 2 the origin and the main characteristics of the EFD through the lens of a transatlantic perspective. It will show that several interpretations are possible and that the choices being made inform the observer of the authority's underlying conception of what competition is and what the role of competition policy should be as a result. In section 3, the chapter discusses the implementation of the EFD in the European energy sector and its role within the building of competitive markets. We first consider the links between the EFD and some of the main features of the European liberalization directives such as third party access (hereafter TPA) mechanisms or unbundling requirements. We then discuss a new challenge which arises with the ever pressing need for quick investment in cross-border transportation assets: the regulation of merchant transmission investment. Finally, the application of the EFD on the existing nuclear fleet of EDF by the French Competition Council in the *EDF/Direct Energie* case is analysed.

2 THE ESSENTIAL FACILITIES DOCTRINE IN COMPETITION POLICY: A TRANSATLANTIC PERSPECTIVE

The controversial decision of the Court of First Instance of the European Communities (hereafter CFI) of 17 September 2007 in the *Microsoft* case strongly underlined the differences between European and US competition policies. While the European Courts focus on promoting and/or preserving a market structure of effective competition, US antitrust authorities try to restrain their action to the most important monopolization attempts. From a US standpoint, an intervention of the competition authorities aiming to tackle the exclusion of a dominant firm's rival may be more easily seen as a means to protect competitors rather than the competitive process itself. Mandatory access to an essential resource could also be considered contradictory with the 'freedom of contract' principle. Moreover, such compulsory sharing could be harmful for the competitive process and hence consumers, owing to the potential negative consequences on the incentives to invest.

First, we confront the US and the European implementation of the EFD in the jurisprudence. Then we show that such divergences may reveal the existence of two very different conceptions of competition on both sides of the Atlantic. Based on US and European case law, we successively focus on two dimensions of the transatlantic divergence which is of interest for our analysis in the energy sector: the interface between sector-specific regulation and competition policy and the issue of the socially beneficial level of freedom to be granted to dominant firms.

2.1 The Implementation of the EFD in the USA and in the EU

Coming from US case law, the EFD has always been a controversial concept. Its implementation may lead to compelling a dominant firm to grant access to one of its assets if it is deemed necessary to ensure an effective degree of competition (Cotter 2008). However, the application of this simple principle yields much difficulty in practice. As Waller and Frischmann (2008) noted, the EFD should hold that a dominant firm may incur antitrust liability if it does not provide access to one of its assets (physical facilities and eventually intellectual property rights) even to direct competitors, on a non-discriminatory basis, where sharing is feasible and when the proof is provided that competitors cannot obtain or create any alternative facilities by themselves. Even if the US Supreme Court has never explicitly used the concept in its decisions, the EFD was incrementally built through its case law (Marty and Pillot 2009), especially from its *Terminal Railroad Association* (1912),[3] *Associated Press* (1945),[4] *Lorrain Journal* (1951),[5] *Otter Tail Power* (1973)[6] and *Aspen Skiing* (1985)[7] decisions. As the Supreme Court noted in *Trinko*, the EFD was explicitly used only by some lower US courts. Indeed, the first decision of a US Court of Appeal which has clearly invoked the EFD was the *Gamco Inc* v. *Providence Fruit & Produce Bldg Inc* case in 1952.[8] It was then in 1983[9] that the *MCI* v. *AT&T* case established the four conditions for implementing the EFD in the USA:

- The owner of the facility must be a monopolist.
- It is practically or reasonably impossible to duplicate the facility.[10]
- The use of the facility is denied to competitors.
- Providing the facility is feasible.[11]

According to the US antitrust laws even a monopolist has no general duty to contract or to share one of its assets with its competitors. Nevertheless, in some circumstances, a refusal could violate the section 2 of the Sherman Act.[12] It is especially the case when its decision is susceptible to eliminate competition,[13] either in the upstream or in the downstream markets, as the *Alaska Airlines* decision (1991) of the 9th Circuit Court showed.[14] The case law of the different Courts of Appeal and the ambiguity of the US Supreme Court's jurisprudence then seemed to testify to the implementation of the EFD in the US case,[15] even if it remained one of the most controversial concepts in antitrust (Areeda 1990).

The European use of the EFD has contrasted with the US approach even before the *Trinko* decision. It appears that the EFD underlies many European decisions on unilateral refusal to deals, both in intellectual property (hereafter IP) and in network industries. Both for physical infrastructures and IP rights, the EFD has been used as a means to stimulate (or even create) an effective competition between firms.[16] If the expression 'essential facility' does not directly appear in the European case law, it is also partly because the European Court of Justice (ECJ) uses the concept of 'exceptional circumstances' in which a dominant firm could be forced to grant access to its competitor in order to preserve a market structure of effective competition.

The European acceptance of the EFD is coherent with the case law on unilateral refusals to deal. For example, the *Commercial Solvent* decision (1974)[17] (or the *Telemarketing* decision in 1995[18]) shows that in some circumstances, the refusal to supply a competitor with an essential input (here in the sense of raw materials) could be considered as a violation of Article 82 EC of the EU Treaty. For EFD-related cases, the *Bronner* decision (1998) defines such circumstances:[19]

- The refusal prevents any competition.
- The access is essential for carrying out the applicant's business.
- The access is denied without objective justification.

If *Bronner* was at first interpreted as a limitation of the scope of the EFD, it appears that mandatory access to a dominant firm's asset subsequently received a very large interpretation and became a frequently used remedy. The extensive interpretation of what is an essential facility could be seen both in IP, with the *Magill, IMS* (1994)[20] or *Microsoft* cases and in utilities. The *GVG* decision (2003)[21] is, in this matter, particularly interesting (Stehmann 2004). The Georg Verkeorganisation GmbH (hereafter GVG) is a German railways firm, which wanted to provide an international passenger service from Germany to Milan. It was necessary for GVG to access the Ferrovie dello Stato (hereafter FS) network and to obtain traction to move the train (for example, locomotives and qualified staff) on the Italian infrastructures. As the FS refused to contract with GVG, the latter lodged a complaint before the European Commission on the grounds of the Article 82 of the Treaty. The Commission considered that the *Bronner* test was fulfilled (Castaldo and Nicita 2005): (a) GVG has no alternative than to deal with the FS, (b) the FS refusal is not justified by objective reasons, and (c) the FS refusal eliminates competition. However, as Petit (2004a) notes, if the Commission only explicitly used the expression 'essential facilities' for the railway infrastructure, the same logic was used for the other components of the service (for example, locomotives and qualified staff). Therefore, 'a striking feature of the decision thus lies in the fact that the Commission stretches the "essential facilities" concept beyond the purely non duplicable infrastructures' (Petit 2004a, p. 188).

2.2 A Comparative Perspective of Enforcement in the Post-*Trinko* Period

The divergence between the US and EU acceptance of the EFD became very salient with and since the *Trinko* decision. This US Supreme Court decision highlighted three critical dimensions of the transatlantic divergence on the EFD in particular, and on the conception of competition in general. One dimension concerns the articulation between sector-specific regulation and antitrust policy. A second dimension is linked to the interpretation of the concept of 'competition on the merits' in the USA and in Europe. It leads us to focus on the very specific European conception of the responsibility of dominant firms vis-à-vis the competitive structure of the market.

2.2.1 *Trinko* and the debate *ex ante/ex post* (regulation versus antitrust)

The *Trinko* decision radically circumscribed both the range of claims based on the EFD in the USA and the scope for antitrust intervention in network industries. The *Trinko* case concerns a regulated network industry, telecommunications. The US Telecommunications Act of 1996 requires incumbent local exchange carriers to provide access to their operating support systems to their rival local exchange carriers, without which the latter cannot provide services to consumers. In 1999, the competitors of Verizon filed a complaint to the regulator about the technical conditions of access. A settlement was reached, by which Verizon accepted remedies in order to ensure an effective access to its operating support system. Nevertheless, a claimant filed a class action against Verizon. According to him, the reluctance of Verizon to provide an effective access to its competitors could harm competition and consumer welfare, and could consequently constitute a violation of the section 2 of the Sherman Act. The decision of the Supreme Court was both a radical clarification (and perhaps a turnaround) of previous US case law and a strong differentiation from the European position.

The first aspect of the decision concerns the respective scope of antitrust and sector-specific rules. While the European Commission tends to expand the scope of competition policy on this issue, the US Supreme Court strictly circumscribed antitrust competence. In the case law, *Trinko* contrasts with the *Deutsche Telekom* (hereafter DT) decision taken by the European Commission in 2003.[22] Where the Supreme Court considered that since sector specific remedies are available, the additional benefits of antitrust regulation are likely to be limited, the European authorities considered that competition law has to be enforced despite a previous decision of the regulator. The *Deutsche Telekom* case concerned the prices charged to competitors for accessing the local loop. As the prices exceeded those charged to DT subscribers on the retail market, the DT pricing strategy could be analysed as a margin squeeze. However, DT argued that its pricing scheme could not violate Article 82 of the Treaty because the German regulators had previously approved them. Nevertheless, for the

Commission, even in the presence of sector-specific regulation, EC competition law should be implemented in light of the hierarchy of European institutional norms.[23]

Such paralleled implementation may induce several risks. First, we must take into consideration the risk of parallel complaints before the antitrust authority and the regulator. We should also fear inconsistent decisions, as the *Deutsche Telekom* case showed. Secondly, we have to consider the fact that the rationale and objectives of antitrust and sectoral regulation may significantly diverge. For example, the issue of investment incentives is more important for a regulator than for a court. As Petit (2004a, p. 190) notes, 'since competition authorities are primarily concerned with the elimination of actual restriction to competition, they generally give little importance to the necessity that access conditions ensure sufficient rates of return on investments and do not undercut incentives for innovation'. In other words, antitrust seems to have a bias towards short-term efficiency. In addition, if the regulator disposes of internal highly skilled expertise about the economics of the sector, the Court may be ill-equipped to decide on access matters, especially regarding pricing. In addition, because of information incompleteness and asymmetries, the judge may be more susceptible to take suboptimal decisions.

However, are the respective approaches of the EU and US antitrust policies so clearly opposed to each other after the *Trinko* decision? Things are not so cut and dried. First, the European jurisprudence attests that in several sectors, the Commission gives the priority to sector specific regulation. In the energy sector, the Commission decided in the HFC Bank Plc/British Gas Trading Ltd to abandon its action because the UK gas regulator had concluded that the risk of anticompetitive effect was unlikely (Petit 2004b). Secondly, the *Deutsche Telekom* and *Trinko* cases are not similar in every respect. *Trinko* does not deal with margin squeeze strategy. It is a class action taken by a law firm in order to obtain large financial compensation. Thirdly, the issue of the articulation between antitrust and regulation should be analysed by taking into account the institutional framework and the sector specific regulators' respective capacities and expertises. As Geradin (2004b) argued, a direct comparison is biased because the US antitrust law is mainly a court-based system whereas EC is administrative based. As the Commission both instructs cases and takes decisions, the risk of false negatives or false positives could be considered as more limited (notwithstanding issues of procedural fairness). In addition, because 90 per cent of the US antitrust procedures are followed by private lawsuits, in which the plaintiffs claim for compensatory or punitive damages (Jones 1999), the financial consequences of false positives are not equally important in both systems.

2.2.2 Contrasting views on the competition on the merits and on the dominant firm's responsibility towards competition

A second dimension of the *Trinko* decision deals with the issue of a monopolist's refusal to deal with a competitor. The US Supreme Court reaffirmed in *Trinko* that the antitrust laws should not limit a firm's freedom to contract or not with its competitors.[24] Consequently, there is no systematic duty for a dominant firm to assist a competitor by granting access to the result of previous investments. We have to nevertheless consider that such freedom is not without limit in the USA, especially if a refusal to deal contributes to a monopolization strategy as it was the case in *Aspen* (1985).[25] However, the very specific conditions of *Aspen* are not replicated in the *Trinko* case. The Court did not analyse Verizon's conduct as a predatory strategy which would aim exclusively at achieving an anticompetitive purpose such as the exclusion of a competitor from the market.[26] In *Aspen*, the Court was convinced that the dominant firm attempted 'to exclude its rival on some basis other than efficiency'. For the US case law, a conduct can only be deemed exclusionary when it both harms consumers and makes no business sense, except for its potential to exclude rivals.[27] This is also reflected in the procedure. First, there is the complainant who assumes the burden of proof. Secondly, if the complainant meets this requirement, the monopolist can show a pro-competitive justification for its conduct. Finally, the strategy will be considered unlawful only if the complainant succeeds in demonstrating that the dominant firm could reach the same result in a less exclusionary manner.

The second critical dimension of the *Trinko*, decision concerned the rejection of the EFD by the US Supreme Court. For Waller (2008, p. 364), 'in 2004, the Supreme Court went out of its way to discuss the essential facilities doctrine in the harshest possible words'. The US Supreme Court indeed even considered that the EFD was 'crafted by some lower courts'. The Court also stated that the EFD does not apply in this case (and so in regulated sectors) and, even if such doctrine was recognized, it could only be conceivable where access is unavailable. Therefore, even if the Court would have applied the EFD in the *Trinko* case its decision would be unchanged:

> This conclusion would be unchanged even if we considered to be established law the 'essential facilities' doctrine crafted by some lower courts, under which the Court of Appeals concluded respondent's allegation might state a claim. We have never recognized such a doctrine, and we find no need either to recognize it or to repudiate it here. It suffices for present purpose to note that indispensable requirement for invoking the doctrine is the unavailability of access to the 'essential facilities', where access exists, the doctrine serves no purpose. Thus, it is said that essential facilities claims should . . . be denied where a state or

federal agency has effective power to compel sharing and to regulate its scope and terms.

The US Supreme Court decision illustrates the antitrust concern for the preservation of the firms' investment incentives. In fact, the debates on the implementation of the EFD are very characteristic of a classic trade-off in competition policy between static (or allocative) efficiency and dynamic (or productive) efficiency. Applying the EFD extensively could be analysed as a preference given to access-based policies, which may enhance the consumer welfare in the short term. However, competition policy should also consider that the monopoly position of the infrastructure's owner is, in a Schumpeterian perspective, its first incentive to invest. Even if the monopolist charges supra-competitive prices, its investment is favourable to long-term welfare. Furthermore, when mandatory access is not granted by a court, it would constitute an incentive to invest for both the asset's owner *and* its competitors. Such infrastructure-based policies could favour the development of alternative transportation capacities in the energy sector.

In *Trinko*, the Supreme Court reaffirmed the US preference for infrastructure-based policies. According to the Court a firm has to be free to invest in order to obtain a significant market power and such a purpose is an important vector of competition, innovation, investment and economic growth. We must keep in mind that the Sherman Act does not prohibit dominance or monopoly per se but just the *monopolization* strategies. In *Grinell* (1983),[28] the Supreme Court had already established that it was necessary to distinguish unlawful acquisition – or preservation – of a monopoly rent from a dominant position due to 'superior product, business acumen or historical accident'. In *Alcoa* (1945)[29] the Judge Learned Hand reaffirmed that: 'size does not determine guilt. [In the case of monopolization] there must be some "exclusion" of competitors; the growth must be something else than "natural" or "normal"; there must be a "wrongful intent" or other specific intent, or some "unduly" coercive means must be used'.

This point is of particular interest in understanding the Commission's decision in *Intel*.[30] In this case, the Commission held that fidelity rebates granted by the American undertaking to personal computer manufacturers was likely to foreclose the microprocessor market. In other words, for the Commission, Intel's pricing strategy had to be seen as predatory conduct likely to affect consumer welfare because of the risk to definitely exclude AMD – Intel's only serious rival – from the market. The intervention of the Commission under Article 82 EC revealed also another important difference between US and EU enforcement priorities. While

US institutions tend to focus on acknowledged predatory intent,[31] the EU antitrust authorities only scrutinize the effects the dominant undertaking's behaviour has – or could potentially have – on the competition structure. In this way, European Courts have no special duty to demonstrate that the dominant firm's conduct is *intentionally* harmful.

Trinko may also reveal two very different views of what the word 'competition' means and how a dominant firm must behave on the market. While European competition authorities seem to define competition by an effective rivalry between firms, the US authorities, according to the post-Chicago synthesis, define competition in terms of market performance (Areeda and Hovenkamp 2001). A market can be seen as competitive when firms are incentivized to price their products at the marginal cost. In other words, a competitive market is not automatically characterized by a large number of competing firms because it is contestable (for example, entry and exits are costless). In some markets, 'antitrust intervention to preserve or create a large number of rivals would harm consumer welfare and worsen economic performance' (Kolasky 2004, p. 31). For example, in technological markets a first mover may serve the whole market for a period of time and charge supra-competitive prices in order to recoup its previous investment. In the case of a leapfrogging technological innovation regime, another firm in a second period could replace this first firm. So no dominant position can be considered as definitive (Baumol 2002).

As Kolasky (2004) noted, in newly deregulated sectors also, the development of competition may lead to increased concentration. Therefore, the competitive process can lead to a market structure in which only one firm can entirely serve the market. Such result has long been admitted by the US courts, as the Judge Bailey Aldrich's opinion in the *Union leader* case in 1960 testifies: 'society has an interest in competition even though that competition be an elimination bout'.[32] In other words, antitrust must accept that the (transitional) outcome of the competitive process may be a monopoly. Its control must be exercised in the respect of *the rules of just conduct*, in Hayekian terms. As Kolasky (2004, p. 38) wrote, 'the purpose of antitrust is to assure that the war is fought and the outcome determined on the basis of efficiency'. In addition, the US competition authorities always consider that an undertaking, even a monopolist, remains free to compete aggressively, as dominance is seen as the natural result of market dynamics.

In other words, according to the US case law, a dominant firm has no special duty towards its competitors. As Judge Learned Hand wrote in the *Alcoa* decision in 1945,[33] 'The Act does not mean to condemn the resultant of those very forces which its prime object is to foster. *Finis opus coronat*. The successful competitor, having been urged to compete must not be turned upon when he wins.' For the US antitrust, granting a mandatory access to a facility owned by a 'successful' firm for the purpose of maintaining rivals on the market by limiting its competitive advantage could only produce short-term gains, because of the consequences of such a signal on incentives.

In Europe, a dominant firm has the special responsibility not to impair genuine undistorted competition on the Common Market.[34] Because of its particular position on the market, a dominant firm is not allowed to adopt some strategies, which could be considered as acceptable from other competitors, because their implementation could irremediably compromise the chances of the competitors to succeed on the market (Vesterdorf 2006). A refusal to deal by a dominant firm who controls an essential facility could definitively compromise the competitive structure of the market, even if any undertaking – dominant or not – should have the right to dispose freely of its property and choose its trading partners.

We have also to underline that, in the European framework, the competitive hindrance could be the pure result of a firm's dominant position itself and not of a specific anti-competitive conduct (Boy 2005). Such logic allows restricting the strategic autonomy of the dominant firm more easily and gives more discretion to the competition authority. According to the *Hoffmann-Laroche* decision (1979),[35] a dominant firm must refrain from doing anything that would hinder 'the maintenance of the degree of competition still existing in the market'. In other words, European Competition authorities give the 'special responsibility' to the dominant firm to preserve the competitive structure of the market (Behrens 2006). The *Microsoft* decision concerning interoperability was emblematic of this logic, as Fox (2006, p. 237) wrote: 'The Commission's decision strongly reflects Europe's principle of special responsibility of the dominant firm and the prohibition of using leverage and power to obtain advantages over rivals. These principles overshadow any freedom of the dominant firm to choose with whom and how to deal.'

Therefore, the main risk induced by the European conception of competition is to protect competitors, not competition, whereas the US antitrust is more concerned about false positive errors.[36] False positive cases could chill the competition process. Nevertheless, the difficulty for the US antitrust is to separate the sheep from the goats, that is, to distinguish between competition on the merits and exclusionary or predatory conducts. As a consequence, the US competition authorities run the risk of being excessively tolerant with dominant firms (false negative error) or to intervene too late when the damages to competition are irreversible.[37]

The principles of the EFD now analysed and the differences between Europe and the US stressed, we analyse in the next section how the EFD is implemented in the European energy sectors, what the current trends are and what their possible repercussions will be. We will see that the tendencies depicted above for European antitrust are well reflected by the current practice of competition policy in the energy sector.

3 THE ESSENTIAL FACILITIES DOCTRINE IN THE EU ENERGY SECTOR: TODAY'S APPLICATION AND NEW CHALLENGES

In energy the EFD has rarely been used explicitly, but a broad range of legislative acts and antitrust decisions have been inspired by related concepts. This is the case because the specific characteristics of electricity and gas markets (that is, balancing services in electricity and storage in gas) make them particularly prone to facility foreclosure compared with other network industries such as telecommunications. As a consequence it is generally harder for the regulatory authorities to effectively monitor access.

Back to *British Midland/Aer Lingus* in 1992,[38] the development of the EFD in Europe has largely coincided with the liberalization of network industries (Ashe-Taylor and Moussis 2005) and there is no doubt that, due to their asserted natural monopoly characteristics, the European Commission and its officials consider energy networks, including interconnectors, as essential facilities whose access is required to allow effective competition in related markets (Albers 2001; DG Competition 2007; Lowe 2003; Monti 2003). The principles of the EFD in the European legislation are reflected in the concept of third-party access (hereafter TPA), which refers to a cluster of issues that encompass provisions on unbundling, non-discriminatory access to transmission and distribution grids as well as balancing services (Dziadykiewicz 2007). Mandating access to networks has been one of the most important competition issues in energy since the beginning of liberalization and the recent decisions against E.ON and Rheinisch-Westfälische Elektrizitätswerke (RWE) show that the European Commission is increasingly applying pressure through antitrust enforcement to support the objectives of the sector specific legislation. Essential facilities in energy are thus also falling within the scope of EC Competition law, be it Article 81 and 82 EC or the Merger Regulation (DG Competition 2007).[39] The first part of this section shows that in the current phase of liberalization, legislative acts and competition settlements deriving from the EFD are mostly inspired by the necessity to both open and integrate the markets of European member states. There is thus a focus on short-term market creation. The second part will take a more prospective stance and show that the new needs of the European Union in terms of high-fixed costs investments will increasingly require adaptations in the application of the EFD, sometimes in unexpected directions.

3.1 Today's Challenges: The Building of Competitive Markets

In the European Union, third-party access to essential facilities was considered important enough to justify the enactment of a sector specific legislation and the setting up of national regulatory agencies in charge of its monitoring.[40] The German and New Zealand experiences showed that relying on competition law alone was not sufficient and that a sector-specific regulator in charge of monitoring compliance was needed (Brunekreeft 2002; Small 1999). However, recent competition settlements tend to show that the European Commission and national competition authorities are increasingly taking a more proactive approach under community and national competition law to mitigate the shortcomings of the sector-specific legal framework on that issue.

3.1.1 Secondary EU law: TPA and unbundling as emanations of the EFD

Third-party access grants to economically dependent third parties a right to access and use an infrastructure developed by another company, even against that company's will and business interest except if objective justifications exist. In the second package of Electricity and Gas Directives,[41] TPA concerns the primary market of network operation activities, namely transmission and distribution, which involve physical management of the infrastructure and energy inputs to the system. The different liberalization directives do not provide a clear definition of a TPA right but present the underlying concept. More precisely, TPA refers to the rights granted to (a) gas and electricity producers, (b) energy suppliers and (c) their customers, allowing them to make use of and have their energy traded and transported through electricity grids and gas pipelines that are owned or controlled by other companies. The TPA right thus corresponds with an obligation to contract and a duty to perform on the side of the undertaking in control of the energy transmission system. The Electricity and Gas Directives contain detailed rules on the adoption of homogenous and non-discriminatory access to transmission networks by implementing regulated TPA. Regulated TPA is granted on the basis of tariffs or tariffs methodologies approved and published *ex ante* by national regulatory authorities. This is a significant change compared to the first liberalization directives where member states were given a choice between regulated and negotiated TPA. It is now commonly accepted that regulated TPA is superior to negotiated TPA as a duty to renegotiate prices and conditions for access when contracts end imposing a substantial burden on the access seeker. In addition, short-term transport contracts are often required in energy which increases the frequency of renegotiation, hence transaction costs and price risk for market players. Regulated TPA is thus a more efficient solution.

To achieve an efficient TPA, the different Directives also abolished exclusive rights and gradually imposed accounting, legal and management unbundling of the essential facilities from upstream and downstream activities in order to mitigate the risk of discrimination in the access to the network.[42] Unbundling provisions remain at the heart of the current discussions around the enactment of the third liberalization package. Unbundling not only aims to ensure a non-discriminatory access to the network but also aims at providing the right incentives for the transmission system operators (TSOs) to invest (DG Competition 2007). Unbundling is indeed important as the objectives of the company as a whole may interact with the objectives of the transmission subsidiary in several ways and the transmission subsidiary itself is also harder to regulate if not truly unbundled.[43] Furthermore, TSOs are responsible for the operation, maintenance and, if necessary, development of the transmission system in a given area (interconnectors included).[44] Essential Facility Doctrine principles in energy thus go further than simply preventing a simple refusal to deal. Overall, the Guidelines for Good Practice in relation to TPA services adopted in 2002 at the fifth meeting of the European Gas Regulatory Forum present the bottom line of the European approach on this issue. As in the traditional court case law on the EFD, liberalization directives protect the right of TSOs to deny access for legitimate business reasons. This is unsurprising as they do not restrict the application of EC competition law, as is the case for any European sector-specific legislation or regulatory action (Gatto 2006; Geradin 2004a, 2004b) and as has been recalled in the recent *Deutsche Telekom* case (analysed previously in this chapter). Four main reasons have been included in the legislation. First, is lack of capacity. In this case, any refusal must be justified and TSOs must provide relevant information on measures that would be necessary to reinforce the network. Second is public service obligations imposed by member states within the meaning of Article 86(2) EC. Third is *force majeure*, referred to as 'sudden crises' in the Directives. A fourth criteria concerned eligibility and the reciprocity principle but is no longer relevant since full market opening on the 1 July 2007.

The principles underlying the EFD in secondary EU law also impact the regulation of interconnectors and balancing services. On cross-border interconnectors, the regulations aim to ensure that the existing interconnection capacity is utilized in the most effective and non-discriminatory way feasible. Regulations and guidelines with regard to cross-border tariffs and the allocation of available interconnection capacities have been enacted. The legislation also stipulates compensation mechanisms between TSOs and repeats a number of requirements for non-discrimination, prior publication of tariffs and the fact that they should be aligned with actual costs. These rules had been first agreed upon in the context of the Florence forum and the European Commission made them subsequently legally binding. On the balancing market, the Directives similarly stipulate that rules adopted by TSOs for balancing should be objective, transparent and non-discriminatory. The balancing services are also part of the regulated TPA system. As such, terms and conditions, including rules and tariffs, should be established pursuant to a methodology approved *ex ante* by the national regulatory authority in a non-discriminatory way.

3.1.2 Abuses of dominance by European TSOs and the EFD

The European Commission made clear that provisions on TPA and unbundling in the liberalization directives do not rule out possibilities of discriminatory access and that competition law may be applied to enforce it (DG Competition 2007). Refusal to grant effective TPA could amount to an exclusionary abuse under Article 82(b) EC but Article 81 EC and the merger regulation have also been used. We will see that TPA access has also been an issue in the course of merger proceedings. In EC Competition law, the EFD line of cases is a broad heading covering different refusal-to-supply cases involving an asset which cannot be replicated at reasonable cost. In energy, the European Commission and Community Courts have so far never used the term 'essential facility' as all antitrust actions have ended in informal settlements. However, there is no doubt from informal practice that the European Commission considers energy networks, including interconnectors, an essential facility falling within the scope of Article 82 EC (DG Competition 2007). However, long-distance gas pipelines and gas storage are not always considered essential facilities. Recital 7 of Regulation 1775/2005 on conditions for access to the natural gas transmission networks explicitly acknowledged the existence of pipe-to-pipe competition and the need to take it into account when determining tariffs. As concerns gas storage, it seems that dominance would arise only if the facility is the only or the biggest facility within its service area (Van der Woude 2007). This area would correspond to a geographical circle with a radius of 200 to 250 km around the facility.

For Article 82 EC to be triggered in this line of cases, European and national competition authorities will first have to define the relevant market, substantiate the effect on trade between member states and find proof of abuse of a dominant position. As regards transmission, the

Commission has generally deemed that transmission and distribution were two different relevant markets and should be considered natural monopolies.[45] As concerns balancing services, the Commission estimated in *Sydkraft/Graninge* (2003)[46] that balancing services should be considered a separate product market from the wholesale and transmission markets. In terms of geographical dimensions, the Commission has considered that transmission markets in general are national in scope even if its decisional practice has shown that it can be regional, for instance in Germany where E.ON, Vattenfall, Energie Baden-Wuerttemberg AG (EnBW) and RWE all operate parts of the high-voltage transmission grid. The geographical markets for interconnectors and gas storage are arguably less clear (Dziadykiewicz 2007; Talus and Wälde 2006) but we note that in *Dong/Elsam/Energi* (2006),[47] the Commission has considered a relevant market for 'gas flexibility', including all mechanisms allowing gas operators to balance supply and demand, be it gas storage facilities or flexible supply contracts. In energy, the finding of dominance and its abuse does not markedly differ from the application of these concepts in any other sector. A TSO will generally be considered vertically dominant on the relevant market as it controls a facility with strong natural monopolistic characteristics whose access is required to compete on related markets. An abuse from the TSO to be demonstrated will not require establishing intent. Quite the opposite, if intent can be established, it is established case law in other sectors that abusive intent will be sufficient grounds for abuse even in the absence of any anti-competitive effects. As pointed out by Kotlowski (2006), the Commission confirmed in *Port of Rodby* (1993)[48] that obligations resulting from the ownership of an essential facility may also emerge in a situation of collective dominance. In energy, collective dominance is likely to be found in specific cases such as the German market, even if it has not happened so far except in the old *Almelo* case on long-term exclusive supply contracts.

The EFD and refusal-to-deal cases in general do not have an autonomous legal basis in the EU treaty, EFD cases will therefore have to be qualified according to traditional case law under Article 82 EC, for instance, discrimination (Cowen 1996; Doherty 2001). However, it has been dealt with extensively in the case law of the Commission and Community Courts and it can be said that it has become a category of abuse on its own (Palasthy 2002). Following the case law related to the EFD, the findings of the Sector Enquiry and the interesting classification of the Telecom Access Notice, we now depict the possible grounds for abuse of dominance by European TSOs under Article 82 EC, either on their own national market or on cross-border issues, and show that the application of the EFD in energy is potentially very wide.

To constitute an abuse under Article 82 EC, the behaviour of the dominant company must substantially influence the market structure and thus weaken competition in related markets. Several such abuses can arise from the behaviour of TSOs in their domestic markets. A refusal to give access to an energy network can take many forms and is seldom expressed as an explicit denial; it often manifests itself as willingness to allow access only under disadvantageous conditions. In this sense, the Commission has talked about 'constructive' refusal to deal in the *Deutsche Post* case.[49] The most common forms involve offering unattractive access terms or other unfair trading conditions such as margin squeezes, delaying negotiation tactics or actually dissuasive conditions to use ancillary services such as balancing. A first scenario would thus be a refusal to grant access for the purposes of a service where another operator has been given access by the access provider to operate in that services market, which would amount to discrimination under Article 82 EC. Any prioritizing of customers is then possible but should be objectively justified. It follows that competition law itself does not require universal uniform tariffs for all network users (Kotlowski 2006). In the context of the energy markets the scope for favourable treatment and various rebating practices should be narrow, as significant differentiation is likely to contravene fair competition between economic operators. In this case, the method used to allocate the capacity where demand exceeds supply, such as pro rata rationing, auctions and first come first served, is likely to determine to a great extent whether the application of EC competition law will be triggered (Ashe-Taylor and Moussis 2005; Dziadykiewicz 2007). Following *Sealink/B&I Holyhead* (1992)[50] or *Sea Containers* v. *Stena Sealink* (1994),[51] this would particularly be true when the favoured customers are the established affiliates of the incumbent utilities.

A second approach would be 'pure' refusal to supply, that is to say a situation where no other operator has been given access by a vertically integrated access provider, hence exporting dominance in a related market.[52] A third approach could be a withdrawal of access from an existing customer. Following *United Brands* and *Commercial Solvents*, it is established case law that a firm cannot stop supplying a long-standing customer without objective justification. However, going to a full *rule of reason* on that issue might be problematic as has been seen in the recent *Glaxosmithkline* (2008) line of cases.[53] The last scenario would involve price restraints, namely unfair and excessive prices de facto limiting access to the essential facility (Ridyard 2002). In all these situations, however, the problem remains the same, a vertically integrated operator is dominant on a relevant market constituted by an essential facility and takes advantage of it to become dominant or protect the position of its affiliated arm in a related market by making uneconomic access to that primary market.[54] As a result, it does not appear relevant to establish a stark difference between refusal to supply and essential facilities cases in energy.

Following the criteria depicted in *Bronner*, a consensus emerges in the literature that the first (elimination of all competition) and third (indispensability of the service) criteria will be fulfilled in most cases (Dziadykiewicz 2007; Kotlowski 2006; Palasthy 2002). However, the problem of objective justification remains. As with TPA under sector-specific legislation, a few objective justifications are likely to be accepted. The first kind revolves around technical reasons, for instance, lack of network capacity. This would require the company to justify that the congestions incurred comply clearly with the provisions on capacity allocation enacted by the national regulator and the requirements of the legislation. Under EC competition rules, minimizing the use of the capacity will be considered a limitation of outputs under Article 82 EC. Likewise, an unlawful reservation of cross-border capacities is unlikely to be considered objective justification. Similarly, a refusal to supply linked to a public service obligation might be exempted under Article 86(2) EC[55] as long as the principle of proportionality is complied with.

Even if no formal decisions have ever been taken by the Commission and Community courts, several behavioural and structural remedies concerning conditions on TPA access have been imposed or accepted as commitments during competition investigations. We will now review these cases. As for behavioural remedies, a dozen decisions at the community level have been taken. A first line of decisions concerns the conditions on TPA access itself. The first of such cases concerning access restrictions was the *Marathon* settlement (2004)[56] in the gas sector where the American new entrant filed complaint against Gaz de France (GDF), Thyssengas, Brigitta und Elwerath Betriebsführungs-Gesellschaft mbH (BEB), Ruhrgas and Gasunie for a lack of transparency on access conditions. The gas companies concerned agreed to publish on their websites the contracted and available capacity at all entry and exit points, both for internal and external connections. They also committed to improve balancing services, secondary trade in capacity rights, congestion management and handling of access requests. In *Gazprom/Eni* (2003)[57] and *Gazprom/OMV* (2005),[58] the organization of a better TPA regime was central. It included the introduction of one-month transport contracts, an effective congestion management, the introduction of a secondary market and the regular publication on the internet of the available capacity. In the *Total/GDF* notification (2004),[59] where Total acquired control of gas assets (pipe and storage) in France, the commitment ensured that when a customer changes supplier, the transmission and storage capacities necessary are transferred from the old to the new supplier. In *Disma* (1993),[60] the Commission concluded that oil and gas pipelines are capable of being essential facilities. It applied

Article 81 EC (there were a number of undertakings involved) and the essential facilities doctrine to the jet fuel storage facilities and pipes transferring jet fuel to supply points at Malpensa Airport in Milan.

EC Competition law, and particularly Article 82 EC, similarly applies on cross-border issues (Riis-Madsen and Celli 2002). For already existing and amortized interconnectors owned by dominant firms, the Commission and the European Court of Justice have been particularly harsh with dominant operators and intervened on several occasions to ensure that capacity reservation agreements do not block market access for competing suppliers. They systemically deemed long-term capacity reservations signed before liberalization to be abuse of a dominant position and required that 100 per cent of capacities be freed up (*UK–French submarine interconnector* (2003),[61] *Dutch–German interconnector* (2005),[62] and Norway–Denmark and Denmark–Germany interconnectors following the merger *VEBA/VIAG* in 2001[63]). The relative antitrust tolerance towards risky infrastructure investment seems now impossible to justify for existing amortized infrastructure. Foreclosure effects of new long-term reservations on existing capacity, which will hardly ever be directly linked with new investment in that infrastructure, cannot be counterbalanced by arguments related to the need for investment (DG Competition 2007). The same applies to the prolongation of historical contracts beyond their originally foreseen end date when this possibility was foreseen in the historic transport contract. The Sector Enquiry report refers in instances to agreements relating to the use of capacity gas transit infrastructure. It appears that capacity is not only reserved by incumbent gas suppliers for long durations but also that the reserved capacity is not used. The fact that the gas directive and regulation do not explicitly refer to transit pipelines does not exclude the application of Article 82 EC to that type of infrastructure.

A second line of cases concerns under-investment in the essential facilities. This can be considered as departing substantially from the traditional case law related to the EFD but reflects the importance of essential transmission assets in a market-building context. In *Gazprom/Eni* and *Gazprom/OMV*, the increase of the capacity of the Trans Austria Gasleitung (TAG) pipeline was considered the most important commitment. In *EDF/Hidrocantabrio*[64] and *EnBW/VillarMir*[65] acquisitions, the French and German incumbents committed to increase the capacity of the French/Spanish interconnector to avoid network foreclosure post-acquisition. More recently, Ente Nazionale Idrocarburi (ENI) was convicted by the Italian national competition authority (NCA) for capacity hoarding and strategic under-investment on the Trans-Tunisian Pipeline. The Italian incumbent was fined €290 million and was required to provide 6.5 billion cubic metres of transport capacity to third parties every year by 1 October 2008.

The last line of remedies concerned direct divestitures of an essential facility. This first happened in merger proceedings where ownership unbundling of storage and transport capacities was for instance ordered in *Dong/Elsam/Energi* (storage), *E.ON/MOL* (2005)[66] and *GDF/Suez* (2006)[67] (unbundling of Fluxys). More interestingly, the European Commission started in 2008 to accept commitments of divestiture in the context of Article 82 EC cases. This happened recently in the German market where first E.ON and then RWE negotiated to divest their transmission networks[68] to avoid further antitrust scrutiny whereas the German government was still strongly fighting against ownership unbundling in the context of the discussions around the enactment of the Third Legislative Package.

As Willis and Hughes (2008) rightly pointed out, in all prior EFD cases the owner of the essential facility retained ownership, whereas in *E.ON* (2009)[69] and *RWE* (2009),[70] the Commission managed to obtain divestiture. The extensive application of EFD principles under EU competition law in energy appears as the consequence of the inability of sector specific legislation to truly enforce TPA. Whereas in the USA, following *Trinko*, antitrust jurisdiction became much more limited by the presence of sector regulation, the recent *Deutsch Telekom* case and the divestitures ordered in *E.ON* and *RWE* evidence an opposite trend in the European Union.

Our survey of the current use of the EFD in energy has shown that the special responsibility of dominant firms is clearly a key principle of competition policy in European energy markets. The case law consistently indicates that, if a refusal to deal by a dominant undertaking is not abusive per se, it is particularly hard to objectively justify in energy. As a result, the competition enforcement of EFD principles in energy is not limited to the pure refusal-to-supply case and extends to discrimination, transparency requirements, adequate investment and the like.

3.2 New Application of EFD-related Principles in Energy: Merchant Transmission Investment and Nuclear

A duty to supply may create perverse incentives for the owner of an essential facility. Between extending and restricting the application of the EFD principles in energy, we will show in the last part of this section how European energy regulators try to arbitrate between building competitive markets in the short term and achieving other, often conflicting, goals such as the preservation of long-term investment incentives. We will in turn analyse two opposing trends: the narrowing of the EFD to allow merchant transmission investment and the possible widening of the EFD to some incumbents' existing generation capacities in view of maintaining low retail tariffs for equity reasons.

3.2.1 The case of merchant investment in transmission[71]

Developing interconnection encounters difficulties of several kinds. Some are well known such as the opposition of local population to high-voltage power lines and others are not specific to interconnection, such as a lack of harmonization of application procedures and planning processes. This has for instance led the European Commission to appointing European coordinators[72] to pursue identified priority projects or try to accelerate the harmonization of market designs, for instance through the European Network of Transmission System Operators (ENTSO)-E initiative. In its guidelines for trans-European energy networks (the TransEuropean Energy Networks-Electricity [TEN-E] Guidelines), projects of 'common interest' have been defined and might be supported through loans from the European Investment Bank.[73] A Directive to safeguard security of electricity supply has also been enacted but has hardly been followed by any concrete effect. These initiatives, though useful, have not yet enabled the required increase of interconnection capacity.

According to the Sector Enquiry, the internal conflicts of some vertically integrated companies holding essential facilities is the main obstacle to the satisfactory development of the European cross-border transmission network through regulated investments. However, the failure of the European policy on ownership unbundling is not the only reason for this outcome. The lack of an EU-wide energy regulator with effective power to monitor and regulate market developments *ex ante*, especially cross-border trade issues, is particularly detrimental to the integration and the well-functioning of European energy markets (Glachant and Lévêque 2009). As a result, the regulation of cross-border investments in the network remains within the ambit of national regulation and the national tropism of regulators contributes to impair cross-border investment.

Merchant transmission investment is increasingly being seen in the European Union as a possible way forward. They are private investment partly or fully exempted from TPA and the use of the congestion rent, which thus conflicts with the EFD principles underlying much of European competition policy in energy markets. Prior to 2003, the UK/Belgium gas interconnector and the Viking Cable between Norwegian and German electricity markets had already obtained exemptions from TPA and the use of the congestion rent by the European Commission under the Merger Regulation but the procedure needed streamlining. A new regulatory mechanism was thus needed to better arbitrate between short- and long-term efficiency criteria in the development of the network and to provide legal certainty.

Since the second legislative package in 2003, private parties can obtain exemptions from national regulatory authorities to develop merchant transmission investment for the most risky interconnection projects. For example, the electricity interconnector BritNed between Great Britain and the Netherlands that should be in operation in 2010 will be a merchant line owned by a subsidiary of both the British and the Dutch TSOs. For an exemption to the rules on TPA and the use of the congestion rent to be granted by national regulators, the project must fulfil a set of conditions concerning among others, the impact of the project on competition and network externalities, the level of risk involved or its legal form. The objective of merchant line regulation is explicitly to arbitrate between short-term competition through TPA and long-term efficiency gains through increased investment to facilitate the coming over of a truly integrated energy market. From an EC law perspective, the exemption test is nothing more than the effect test pursued under EC competition rules carried out *ex ante* to provide sufficient legal certainty to potential investors. The dozen decisions in the gas sector and the three decisions in the electricity sector already give some indications of the current difficulties in implementing an effective regulatory regime on merchant transmission investment.

In the gas sector, the lack of consistency among decisions taken in different member states (Van der Vijver 2008) led the Commission to publish an interpretatory note with a view to help both regulators enforce the law and market players to anticipate it. This document shows the difficulties in streamlining a regulatory regime able to ensure both predictability and accuracy in the balancing between short- and long-term efficiency criteria. This lack of methodology to interpret the regulation is a source of regulatory uncertainty. It could be mitigated by the presence of a single enforcer. This is however far from being the case as each national regulatory authority retains jurisdiction on its own national territory, and cross-border infrastructure must be regulated by consensus between the regulators involved. In addition, national regulatory authorities have tended to be very lenient with the granting of exemption in the gas sector. In fact, all exemptions have been granted with very long durations, except in *Gate* in which the exemption was limited from 25 to 20 years. Some commentators have been speaking about a 'regulatory competition' and its inherent risk of a 'race to the bottom' which means that regulators would grant the TPA exemption with too lenient conditions to avoid having the project relocate to a competing country (Van der Vijver 2008).[74]

In electricity, the main current problem concerns the right of incumbent TSOs and dominant generators to build their own merchant lines. As concerns TSOs, the BritNed and NorNed projects showed that incumbent TSOs will be granted exemptions with no difficulties, provided they meet the requirements laid down in the legislation. Merchant transmission investments by TSOs are, however, known to lead to under-sized transmission investment with capacity of around half the optimal level (Pérez-Arriaga et al., 1995). NorNed which links the Netherlands with Norway is an example of such a situation. It was initially thought to have a 1200 MW capacity, which was the optimal capacity from the social point of view. However, the regulators (respectively Directie Toezicht Energie [DTe] and Norges Vassdrags og Energidirektorat [NVE]) and the TSOs (respectively Tennet and Statnett) chose a 600 MW capacity for the project to be commercially feasible though socially suboptimal (Bugten 2004). In addition, there may be possible substitution between optimal regulated and suboptimal merchant investments. The incumbent TSOs are also likely to have incentives to manipulate dispatch so as to increase profits on the merchant line and decrease revenues on the unregulated line (Brunekreeft 2005). Besides this, incumbent TSOs may have fuzzy incentives to deal with possible network externalities due to merchant lines for the best interest of society, despite legal unbundling. Indeed, transmission investment can potentially generate negative externalities and then be detrimental to the whole power system (Bushnell and Stoft 1996). However, this criterion is not clear and its application is tricky as only TSOs have the expertise to measure negative effects of any transmission investments. Since this measure consists of the TSOs evaluating competitors in transmission-building, they may have a conflict of interest with, and discrimination against, new entrants in merchant lines.

If allowing incumbent TSOs to build merchant lines is a problem, allowing merchant transmission investors by incumbent generators might also raise some forms of anti-competitive behaviour. The first market abuse concerns pre-emptive investment and anti-competitive retention of capacities. This relates to the idea that a dominant generator may be willing to build a merchant line for strategic reasons and not because it seeks to maximize profits. Pre-emptive investments mean that the dominant generator may build a merchant line so as to avoid a competitor doing it first and thus with a view to control cross-border capacities. There is therefore a true first-mover advantage in merchant transmission investments if discretionary withholding of capacities is possible post-investment. Of course, the risk of pre-emptive investments will lower if high diseconomies of scale occur in the future. The second competition problem may arise if the price differential between the home and the destination markets reverse. In this case, the dominant generator may use the merchant line to block competitors importing from the former destination market. This thus allows the dominant generator to protect its domestic market position in case it made a wrong investment decision in the first place. Investing in a merchant line in this case becomes a defensive investment *ex post*. Both problems amount to a problem of foreclosure of an essential facility. The last competition problem relates to the opportunity given to the merchant line owner to manipulate wholesale spot prices in the destination market, especially in the peak period (Kuijlaars and Zwart 2003). This will be possible if the size of the merchant line is substantial compared with the size of the destination spot market and if the merchant investor is present as a major producer in the destination market.

Overall, three key factors currently lead to reconsidering the application of the EFD on interconnectors. First, the politics of liberalization and the resulting shortcomings in the allocation of regulatory powers in the European Union once again influence the policy choices being made and the way these choices are enforced. The tropism of national regulators, unsatisfactory unbundling and the lack of an EU-wide regulator lead to structural under-investment in the cross-border transmission network. These investments are highly capital-intensive and risky. To provide enough incentives for private parties to invest, a sound and predictable regulatory framework is needed and the principles of the EFD must be narrowed and applied with more flexibility. Second, the evolution of the technology naturally leads to reconsidering the natural monopoly characteristics of the transmission network, also in electricity, but mostly in gas. Essential Facility Doctrine principles cannot be enforced with the same strength if essential facilities can be duplicated. Third, a narrowing of EFD principles in this case leads to new forms of market abuses and the need to rethink the articulation between regulated and unregulated investment in the network.

3.2.2 An extension of the EFD to nuclear facilities? A new discussion opened by the *EDF/Direct Energie* case in France

In late 2007, a decision of the French Competition Council in the *EDF/Direct Energie* case opened new doors for the application of EFD principles in energy markets: their application to nuclear generation capacities. Direct Energie was a new entrant in French retailing with no production capacity who signed a five-year contract with EDF (in December 2005) at a price comparable to that of forward contracts with the longest maturity (three years) on Powernext at that time. Direct Energie nevertheless decided to sue EDF for an infringement of the French rules on abuse of dominance mainly because the compromise on the price of the five-year contract did not eventually allow it to maintain a stable customer base in the professional market segment.

The situation cannot be understood without underlining the non-application of the European 2003 Directive in France, which imposes retail price liberalization. The French retail market was at that time divided into two segments mainly for political reasons: a regulated retail market where prices were based on the historical cost of EDF (amortized) nuclear capacities and a free market where prices were de facto aligned and hence disconnected from competitive wholesale prices. In practice, the inability to compete with EDF in the professional free retail market was linked to the very existence of the 'EDF Pro' offer, which did not reflect wholesale market prices but was broadly aligned with the regulated tariffs that the successive government decided to maintain after the opening up of this market segment in July 2004. Électricité de France argued that it had to set its retail prices to match the competing regulated tariffs, so that the free market could flourish. The root of the problem was therefore the existence of regulated tariffs which did not even cover the long-run marginal cost of a new nuclear capacity, but more or less the historical cost of existing nuclear equipment. We also note that this situation was particularly problematic from a competition point of view because France, contrary to the UK or Italy, had not split up generation and distribution assets following liberalization.

The Competition Council interpreted this situation by ignoring the determining effects of regulated tariffs, considering the EDF's Tariff Pro offer as predatory pricing. Owing to the overwhelmingly dominant position of EDF, restraints on interconnectors and a still limited spot market, the Council deemed there was no alternative for a pure supplier to bilaterally contract with EDF for a substantial part of its baseload demand. Following this contract, Direct Energie remained unable to compete with the French incumbent retail subsidiary in the free market for professional consumers. It therefore decided to sue EDF for an infringement of the French rules on abuse of dominance mainly on three grounds: price discrimination on this market (between Direct Energie and the EDF retail subsidiary), margin squeeze and discriminatory access to nuclear baseload capacities. This case thus has relevance within the context of the EFD.

Concerning the margin squeeze aspect of the case, the Council recognized that Direct Energie was probably squeezed out between the EDF retail offer for professionals (EDF Pro) and the price paid in the five-year long-term contract. The Council was, however, only able to conclude on a *presumption* of margin squeeze. Regarding price discrimination, the Council stated that it could not conclude due to missing evidence and that further analysis was required. Similarly, on discriminatory access to nuclear baseload capacities, the Council stated that there was no evidence that EDF refused to sell electricity to Direct Energie. Just before Direct Energie decided to sue EDF, the latter had indeed agreed to contract with the former for long-term access to nuclear production at prices based upon generation costs.

To remedy the presumption of margin squeeze, EDF proposed giving access to its nuclear capacities (by the mean of auctions – the so-called virtual power plants [VPPs]) at a price reflecting the production costs and therefore allowing the non historic suppliers to compete with the incumbent on the free market. The Council accepted this proposal. This decision thereby granted access to an asset considered as 'essential' to effectively compete in the downstream market, which was thus very specifically structured by the persistence of the regulated tariff and the EDF competing price offer. The *EDF/Direct Energie* case thus fits a priori well in the EFD line of cases, provided that the essential facility character is related to the critical role of a regulated tariff broadly aligned on the historical cost of existing nuclear equipments. However, it is not so because EDF is overwhelmingly dominant in one market where it would hold a specific asset allowing it to be largely dominant in a related market, but because successive governments have been imposing on it, as the historic supplier, to maintain tariffs related to historical costs. This decision must thus be assessed against the criteria defined in the EFD line of cases to examine its wider relevance.

First, are nuclear facilities duplicable in the context of the French market? The Council cites evidence that EDF has a de facto monopoly on nuclear investment in France and that it is too capital-intensive for most players as grounds for concluding that Direct Energie was not able to invest on its own in this technology. All independent suppliers interviewed testified that they were only able to invest in mid-merit and peaking fossil-fuel plants under current conditions. In addition, it is true that foreclosure of suitable nuclear sites do exist in practice. As a result, it is fair to accept that this condition is fulfilled to a large extent, but not without emphasizing that it depends on the size of competitors. In 2007 GDF Suez (Suez at the moment of the Council decision) announced its ambition to invest in new nuclear capacities in the French territories in the future. We also note that small producers or even retailers without production capacities could invest in nuclear by taking ownership participations in incumbents' projects or in consortia. Overall, despite the obvious difficulties related to the size of the investment, it remains that the only conclusive argument concerns the foreclosure of existing nuclear sites.

Second, is access to the EDF's nuclear capacities indispensable to carrying on the requesting party's business, inasmuch as there is no actual or potential substitute of the service? The Council ruled out the possibilities that VPPs, and especially imports, could fit the needs of alternative suppliers. As pointed out by the National Economic Research Council (NERA 2007), this argument is far from entirely convincing. Imports, baseload and peak-load VPPs represented about 61 TWh for a consumption of individual suppliers of about 37 TWh, which left 24 TWh available for growth. It is, however, possible that congestion at the border prevents

Direct Energie from obtaining enough imports when it needs them most; for example, during peak periods. However, in that case, investment in mid-merit and peaking plant may provide Direct Energie with an effective alternative. In addition, we note that this argument does not take into account the fact that there is often an oversupply of VPPs in the French market and that EDF often end up re-purchasing them from primary buyers without a sufficient customer base.

Finally, is the refusal of the service likely to eliminate all competition in the relevant market on the part of the person requesting the service? This is where the analysis of the Council is least convincing. Indeed, access to nuclear is required only when nuclear is marginal in the merit order, which happens only in very few hours during the year, even in the French market (never in Belgium for instance). More fundamentally and as shown above, the existence of regulated tariffs and the way they are set out may qualify existing nuclear capacities as 'essential' assets. As a result, even though this French case does not demonstrate that all nuclear investments should be considered as 'essential facilities', it does show that EFD principles may be relevant in certain specific political and regulatory contexts. This case has had important and ongoing repercussions in the French market. Following the ruling of the French Competition Council, the Chamsaur Commission report was made public in April 2009 to provide guidance to French lawmakers on how to structurally remedy that situation. The report advocated the withdrawal of regulated retail tariffs for companies, but not for households, and the introduction of administered wholesale tariff on electricity from nuclear power generation (for a full comment see Crampes et al. 2009). A project for new legislation, partly based on that report, was proposed by the French government in October 2009. We note that the project for the so-called 'loi NOME', currently under discussion, explicitly refers to the concept of essential facilities.

4 CONCLUSION

In a sense, the current application of EFD principles in EU energy markets appears as an extension of the duty for the Commission to monitor under Article 86 EC 'public undertakings and undertakings to which Member States grant special or exclusive rights' to a duty for every regulatory and competition authority to monitor undertakings with a *quasi* veto right on the market-building process. In the new market context, EFD principles cannot be strictly limited to pure refusal to deal with cases but must be adapted to the objectives of the European Union. The very existence of a TPA regime applied *ex ante* shows the specificity and importance of the application of the EFD to open markets in energy. This is due to the risk of facility foreclosure which is arguably higher in energy than in other sectors such as telecommunications. As a result, EFD principles in EC energy law go as far as including an *obligation* to invest.

We have seen that the implementation of the EFD by the European competition authorities, which constitutes one of the main bases of TPA and unbundling policies, is now at the crossroads in energy. An extensive application of the EFD is almost natural in Europe. As Fox (2005, p. 953) was arguing, 'the United States is now wedded to a principle of non-interference with unilateral decisions and especially abhors affirmative duties, even if a rule of law imposing such duties would increase competition, and the EU has neither a principle of non-interference nor an aversion to affirmative duties'. Ridyard (2004, p. 670) indeed noted that mandatory access was in some circumstances imposed not only to essential facilities but also to 'convenient' ones, for example, to some 'asset without access to which it would be jolly inconvenient for rivals because they would need to offer customers a better product in order to overcome the advantages of the incumbent'.

An extensive conception of the EFD could be a useful device in order to accentuate and accelerate the liberalization process of utilities in the European context. In this sense, antitrust is neither a substitute for regulation nor a subsidiary device but complementary. For example, in the gas sector, it could be considered that the implementation of competition rules in parallel to sector-specific regulation can tackle the remaining barrier to effective competition more aggressively and more rapidly (Ashe-Taylor and Moussis 2005). But, if the ambiguity of the EFD could be a chance for the liberalization process, we have also to consider both the risks induced by false positive decisions (OECD 1996), the unintentional encouragement given to strategic lawsuits brought by rivals and the reduction of investment incentives for the competing undertakings. Judicial review will thus be crucial to ensuring that the enforcement of EFD principles by European regulatory and competition authorities truly promotes consumer welfare in energy markets.

NOTES

1. We wish to thank Dominique Finon and Christophe Defeuilley from GIS Larsen for their support and very helpful comments. All errors remain ours of course. This chapter reflects the state of the law as it stands in July 2009.
2. *Verizon Communications Inc* v. *Law Office of Curtis Trinko*, LLP, 540 US Supreme Court 398 (2004).
3. *US* v. *Terminal railroad association*, 224 US Supreme Court 383 (1912).

4. *Associated Press* v. *US*, 326 US Supreme Court 1 (1945).
5. *Lorrain Journal Co* v. *US*, 342 US Supreme Court 143, 146 (1951).
6. *Otter Tail Power Co* v. *United States*, 410 US Supreme Court 366, 377 (1973).
7. *Aspen Skiing Co* v. *Aspen Highlands Skiing Corp*, 472 US Supreme Court 585 (1985).
8. *Gamco Inc* v. *Providence Fruit & Produce Bldg Inc*, 194 F.2d 484, 1st Circuit (1952).
9. *MCI Communication Corp* v. *AT&T Co*, 708 F.2d, 1081, 1132, 7th Circuit (1983).
10. 'To be "essential" a facility need not be indispensable, it is sufficient if duplication of the facility would be economically infeasible and if denial of its use inflicts a severe handicap on potential markets entrants'. *Hecht* v. *Pro Football Inc*, 570 F.2d, 982, 992, DC Circuit (1977).
11. 'The Antitrust Laws do not require that the essential facility be shared if such sharing would be impractical or would inhibit the defendant's ability to serve its customers adequately'. Hecht (ibid.).
12. *Caribbean Broadcasting Sys. Ltd* v. *Cable & Wireless PLC*, 148 F.3d, DC Circuit (1998).
13. *City of Anaheim* v. *S. Cal. Edison Co*, 955 F.2d, 1373, 1380, 9th Circuit (1992).
14. *Alaska Airlines Inc* v. *American Airlines* 948 F.2d, 536, 9th Circuit (1991).
15. 'It is an illegal restraint of trade to foreclose the scarce facility', *Hecht* v. *Pro Football Inc*, 570 F.2d, DC Circuit (1977).
16. 'Over the last fifteen years, the Commission has made extensive use of EFD to stimulate downstream competition in a range of markets' (Geradin 2004b, p. 1526).
17. Cases 6, 7/73 *Istituto Chemioterapico Italiano Spa and Commercial Solvents Corp.* v. *Commission* (1974).
18. *Telemarketing* v. *CCT and IPB*, case 311/84 (1995).
19. *Oscar Bronner* v. *Mediaprint*, C-7/97, ECJ (1998).
20. *IMS Health GmbH & Co. OHG* v. *NDC Health GmbH & Co. KG.*, C-418/01, [2004] ECR I-05039, ECJ.
21. *GVG/FS*, COMP/37.685, EC 64, 27 August 2003.
22. Commission decision of 21 May 2003 – Deutsche Telekom.
23. We have to consider the fact that the US Telecommunication Act of 1996 also explicitly mentions that the Act does not prevent the implementation of antitrust laws to regulated sectors.
24. *US* v. *Colgate Co*, 250 US 300, 307 (1919).
25. *Aspen Skiing Co* v. *Aspen Highlands Skiing Corp*, 472 US 585 (1985).
26. We also note that another difference between *Trinko* and *Aspen* lies in the fact that in the latter case the access was initially granted. In *Aspen*, the court observed a disruption of a previous level of supply.
27. *Advanced Health Care Serv.* v. *Radford County Hospital*, 910 F.2d 139, 148, 4th Circuit (1990).
28. *Barry Wright Corp* v. *ITT Grinnell Corp*, 724 F.2d 227, 1st Circuit (1983).
29. *US* v. *Aluminum Co. of America*, 148 F.2d 416, 430, 2nd Circuit (1945).
30. *European Commission/Intel*, Case COMP/C-3/37.990, 13 May 2009.
31. In the US, two conditions have to be jointly met to characterize a predatory conduct. First, the dominant undertaking has to settle its sale prices below its own costs. Second, the dominant firm must have reasonable expectation to recoup its previous investments (losses) in the long-run.
32. *Union Leader Corp* v. *Newspaper of New England Inc*, 284 F.2d 582, 590, 1st Circuit (1960).
33. *US* v. *Aluminum Co. of America*, 148 F.2d 416, 430, 2nd Circuit (1945).
34. *Nederlansche Baden Industrie Michelin NV* v. *Commission*, aff C-322/81.
35. *Hoffmann-Laroche* v. *Commission Européenne*, aff – 85/76, ECJ, 13 February 1979.
36. 'If you are hunting for a predator and mistakenly shoot a competitor, you injure consumers' (Elzinga and Mills 2001, p. 2479)
37. On the contrary, according the US case law, 'In order to assure that the bout is determined by the market and not by the referee, it is also important to not intervene too often and too soon' (Kolasky 2004, p. 44).

38. See commentary of the case by the Commission in European Commission, 22nd Report on Competition Policy, 1992, point 219.
39. We can note that these objectives are already present in primary EU law. Indeed, according to the Treaty, the internal market can be characterized as an area without internal frontiers in which the free movement of electricity is ensured across the Community (Article 14(2) EC). Most importantly, the Community must not merely pursue the abolition of obstacles to trade between Member States (Article 3(1)(c) EC), but also ensure that competition is not distorted (Article 3(1)(g) EC), which justifies antitrust enforcement on this issue.
40. Articles 23 of the Electricity and 25 of the Gas Directives.
41. Directives 2003/54/EC, OJ 2003, L176/37, and 2003/55/EC, OJ 2003, L176/57.
42. Articles 10 and 15 of the Electricity Directive; Articles 9 and 13 of the Gas Directive
43. The Commission even thinks that a minority stake in a transmission or distribution networks may create the same kinds of externalities, see Case COMP/M.4180 *Gaz de France/Suez*, decision of 14 December 2006, par. 631–3.
44. Article 2(4) of the Electricity Directive.
45. Case M.3696 *E.ON/MOL* (2005).
46. Case M.3268 *Sydkraft/Graninge* (2003).
47. Case COMP/M.3868, DONG/Elsam/Energi E2 (2006), see also IP/06/313 of 14 March 2006.
48. *Port of Rødby* Commission Decision 94/119/EC of 21 December 1993 concerning a refusal to grant access to the facilities of the port of Rødby, OJ 1994 L55/52 [1994] 5 CMLR 457.
49. *Deutsche Post – Interception of cross-border mail*, OJ 2001 L 331/40, para. 103.
50. *Sealink/B&I Holyhead*, 29 [1992] 5 CMLR 255, at para 41.
51. *Containers Ltd/Stena Sealink*, OJ 1994, L15/8.
52. This is referred to as essential facilities case in the Telecom Notice.
53. *Glaxosmithkline* (C-468/06 to C-478/06) presented 1 April 2008.
54. Areeda (1990) has argued that the term essential facility should only be applied in the case of vertically integrated incumbents present in related markets.
55. Electricity supply has for instance been accepted as a service of general economic interest by the ECJ in *Municipality of Almelo and Others* v. *Energiebedrijf IJsselmij NV* (C-393/92, [1994] ECR I-1477, ECJ) and *Ijsselcentrale* (IV/32.732, O.J. 16.1.1991, L 28/32).
56. *Marathon*: IP/04/573 of 30.4.2004, IP/03/1129 of 29 July 2003, IP/03/547 of 16 March 2003; IP/01/1641 of 23 November 2001.
57. Case COMP/38.308, *Gazprom/ENI*. See also IP/03/1345 of 6 October 2003.
58. Case COMP/38.085, *Gazprom/OMV*. See also IP/05/195 of 17 February 2005.
59. M.3410 *Total/GDF* (2004).
60. See the Commission's XXIIIrd Report on Competition Policy (1993) at pp. 141–3.
61. UK/France Interconnector, informal settlement, IP/01/341 of 12 March 2001.
62. Case C-17/03 *Vereniging voor Energie, Milieu en Water, Amsterdam Power Exchange Spotmarket BV, Eneco NV* v. *Directeur van de Dienst uitvoering en toezicht energie* [2005] ECR I-4983. See Commission Staff Working Paper on the decision C-17/03 of 7 June 2005 of the Court of Justice of the European Communities, SEC (2006) 547, 26 April 2006.
63. Case M.1673 *VEBA/VIAG* (2001).
64. M.3187 *EDF/Hidrocantabrio*.
65. M. 2434, *EnBW/Villar Mir*.
66. Case COMP/M.3696, 21 December 2005.
67. Case COMP/M.4180, 14 December 2006.
68. However, E.ON still retains ownership of its gas network and RWE of its electricity network.
69. Case COMP/39.388–389, *E.ON*, O.J. 13 February 2009, C 32/08; MEMO/08/396 of 12 June 2008.

70. Case COMP/39.402, *RWE*, O.J. 5.12.2008, C 310/23; IP/09/410 of 18 March 2009.
71. This sub-section is based on Hauteclocque and Rious (2009), 'Reconsidering the Role of Merchant Transmission Investment in the Light of the Third Energy Package: the Role of Dominant Generators', EUI Working Papers RSCAS 2009/59.
72. A coordinator has for instance has been appointed for the Germany/Poland/Lithuania, Denmark/Germany/Poland and France/Spain interconnections.
73. However, the TEN-E funds only amount to about EUR 20 mns and are mainly used for feasibility studies.
74. Ofgem even states in *Dragon LNG* that it is trying to establish 'the most favourable regulatory scheme'.

REFERENCES

Albers, M. (2001), 'Energy liberalization and EC Competition Law', *Fordham International Law Journal,* **25** (4), 909.

Areeda, P. (1990), 'Essential facilities: an epithet in need of limiting principles', *Antitrust Law Journal,* **58**, 841.

Areeda, P. and H. Hovenkamp (eds) (2001), *Antitrust Law: an Analysis of Antitrust Principles and their Application*, New York: Aspen.

Ashe-Taylor, J. and V. Moussis (2005), 'EU Competition Law on third-party access to gas transmission networks', *Utilities Law Review*, **14** (3), 105–10.

Baumol, W.J. (2002), *The Free Market Innovation Machine: Analysing the Growth Miracle of Capitalism*, Princeton, NJ: Princeton University Press.

Behrens, P. (2006), 'Controlling dominance or protecting competition: from individual abuses to responsibility for competition', in H. Ullrich (ed.), *The Evolution of European Competition Law: Whose Regulation, Which Competition?*, Cheltenham, UK and Northampton, MA, USA: Edward Elgar, pp. 224–32.

Boy, L. (2005), 'L'abus de pouvoir de marché, contrôle de la domination ou protection de la concurrence', *Revue Internationale de Droit Economique*, **19** (1), 27–50.

Brunekreeft, G. (2002), 'Regulation and third-party discrimination in the German electricity supply industry', *European Journal of Law and Economics*, **13** (2), 203–20.

Brunekreeft, G. (2005), 'Regulatory issues in merchant transmission investment', *Utilities Policy*, **13** (1), 175–86.

Bugten, T. (2004), 'Investment planning in practice: NorNed', European Transmission Investment Conference, Copenhagen, Denmark, 18–19 October.

Bushnell, J. and S. Stoft (1996), 'Electric grid investment under a contract network regime', *Journal of Regulatory Economics*, **10** (1), 61–79.

Castaldo, A. and A. Nicita (2005), 'Essential facility and efficiency in European antitrust: some lessons from GVG /FS in the railway sector', European Association of Law and Economics, Ljubljana, September.

Cotter, T.F. (2008), 'Essential Facilities Doctrine', University of Minnesota Law School, *Legal Studies Research Paper* No. 08-18.

Cowen, T. (1996), 'The essential facilities doctrine in EC competition law: towards a "matrix" infrastructure', in B. Hawk (ed.), *Annual Proceedings of the Fordham Corporate Law Institute*, London: Sweet and Maxwell, pp. 521–8.

Crampes, C., J.-M. Glachant, C. Hirschhausen, F. Lévêque, D. Newbery, I.

Perez-Arriaga, P. Ranci, S. Stoft and B. Willems (2009), 'Where the Champsaur Commission has got it wrong?', *The Electricity Journal*, **22** (7), 81–6.
DG Competition (2006), *Report on Energy Sector Inquiry*, SEC(2006) 1724 final of 10 January 2007.
Doherty, B. (2001), 'Just what are essential facilities?', *Common Market Law Review*, **38** (2), 397–436.
Dziadykiewicz, E. (2007), 'Refusal to grant third-party access by an electricity transmission operator – overview of competition law issue', *Journal of Energy and Natural Resources Law*, **25** (2), 114–49.
Elzinga, K.G. and D.E. Mills (2001), 'Predatory pricing and strategic theory', *Georgia Law Journal*, **89**, 2475–94.
Fox, E.M. (2005), 'A tale of two jurisdictions and an orphan case: antitrust, intellectual property, and refusals to deal', *Fordham International Law Journal*, **28** (4), 952–66.
Fox, E.M. (2006), 'Abuse of dominant position: the Americanization of European competition law', in H. Ullrich (ed), *The Evolution of European Competition Law: Whose Regulation, Which Competition?*, Cheltenham, UK and Northampton, MA, USA: Edward Elgar, pp. 233–7.
Gatto, A. (2006), 'Governance in the European Union: a legal perspective', *Columbia Journal of European Law*, **12** (2), 487–516.
Geradin, D. (2004a), 'The development of European regulatory agencies: what the EU should learn from US experience', *Columbia Journal of European Law*, **11** (9), 1–75.
Geradin, D. (2004b), 'Limiting the scope of Article 82 of the EU treaty: what can the EU learn from the US Supreme Court's judgment in Trinko in the wake of Microsoft, IMS and Deutsche Telekom?', *Common Market Law Review*, **41** (6), 1519–53.
Glachant, J.-M. and F. Lévêque (2009), 'Electricity internal market in the European Union: what to do next?', in J.-M. Glachant and F. Lévêque (eds), *Electricity Reform in Europe: Towards a Single Energy Market*, Cheltenham, UK and Northampton, MA, USA: Edward Elgar, pp. 3–32.
Hauteclocque, A. de and V. Rious (2009), 'Reconsidering the role of merchant transmission investment in the light of the third energy package: the role of dominant generators', *EUI Working Papers RSCAS*, 2009/59.
Jones, C. (1999), *Private Enforcement of Antitrust Law in the EU, UK and USA*, Oxford: Oxford University Press.
Kolasky, W.J. (2004), 'What is competition? A comparison of US and European Perspectives', *The Antitrust Bulletin*, **49** (1), 29–53.
Kotlowski, A. (2006), 'Third-party access rights in the energy sector: a competition law perspective', *Utilities Law Review*, **16** (3), 101–9.
Kuijlaars, K.-J. and G. Zwart (2003), 'Regulatory issues surrounding merchant interconnection', Dienst uitvoering en Toezicht Energie (Office for Energy Regulation), The Netherlands.
Lowe, P. (2003), 'Applying EU competition law to the newly liberalized energy market: likely antitrust enforcement issues important to an emerging private sector', speech at the Mentor Group Forum for EU-US Legal-Economic Affairs, 13 May.
Marty, F. and J. Pillot (2009), 'Stratégies juridiques et théorie des facilités essentielles', in A. Masson (ed.), *Les stratégies juridiques des entreprises*, Brussels: Larcier, pp. 317–37.

Monti, M. (2003), 'Applying EU competition law to the newly liberalized energy markets', communication to the World Forum on Energy Regulation, Rome, 6 October.

National Economic Research Council (NERA) (2007), 'French Conseil de la Concurrence finds EDG guilty of charging market prices', *Energy Regulation Insights*, **34**.

Organisation for Economic Co-operation and Development (OECD) (1996), *Abuse of Dominance and Monopolisation, Policy Roundtables, OECD/GD(96)131,* Paris, September.

Palasthy, A. (2002), 'Third party access in the electricity sector: EC competition law and sector specific regulation', *Journal of Energy and Natural Resources Law*, **20** (1), 1–13.

Pérez-Arriaga, I., J. Rubio-Oderiz, J. Puerta, J. Arceluz and J. Marin (1995), 'Marginal pricing of transmission services: an analysis of cost recovery', *IEEE Transactions on Power Systems*, **10** (1), 546–53.

Petit, N. (2004a), 'Circumscribing the scope of EC competition law in network industries? A comparative approach of the US Supreme Court ruling in the Trinko case', *Utilities Law Review*, **13** (6), 185–91.

Petit, N. (2004b), 'The proliferation of national regulatory authorities alongside competition authorities: a source of jurisdictional confusion', Collège européen de Bruges, Global Competition Law Centre Working Paper Series, no. 02/2004.

Ridyard, D. (2002), 'Exclusionary pricing and price discrimination abuses under Article 82 – an economic analysis', *European Competition Law Review*, **23** (6), 286–303.

Ridyard, D. (2004), 'Compulsory access under EC competition law – a new doctrine of "convenient facilities" and the case of price regulation', *European Competition Law Review*, **25** (11), 669–73.

Riis-Madsen, C. and R. Celli (2002), 'New developments in EU legislation and application of competition rules to interconnectors', *The International Energy Law and Taxation Review*, **8**, 177–83.

Small, J.P. (1999), 'Regulation and competition law for networks in New Zealand', Centre for Research in Network Economics and Communications working paper, University of Auckland.

Stehmann, O. (2004), 'Applying essential facility's reasoning to passenger rail services in the EU – the Commission decision in the case GVG', *European Competition Law Review*, **25** (7), 390–94.

Talus, K. and T. Wälde (2006), 'Electricity interconnectors: a serious challenge for EC competition law', *Competition and Regulation in Network Industries*, **1** (3), 353–87.

Van der Vijver, T. (2008), 'Exemptions to third party access for new infrastructures in the European community gas sector – the exception that defies the rule?', *European Competition Law Review*, **29** (4), pp. 229–37.

Van der Woude, M. (2007), 'Article 102 TFEU – abuse of a dominant position', in C. Jones (ed.), *EU Energy Law Volume II: EU Competition Law and Energy Markets*, Leuven: Claeys and Casteels, pp. 271–342.

Vesterdorf, B. (2006), 'Considérations sur la notion de concurrence par les mérites', in G. Canivet (ed.), *La modernisation du droit de la concurrence*, Paris: LGDJ, pp. 163–77.

Waller, S.W. (2008), 'Areeda, epithets and essential facilities', *Wisconsin Law Review*, **3** (2), 359–86.

Waller, S.W. and B. Frischmann (2008), 'Revitalizing essential facilities', *The Antitrust Law Journal*, **75** (1), 1.
Willis, P. and P. Hughes (2008), 'Structural remedies in Article 82 energy cases', *The Competition Law Review*, **4** (2), 147–74.

PART IV

Conclusion

12. Efficiency, competition and long-term contracts in electricity markets: summary and conclusions of the workshop organized by the GIS LARSEN and the Loyola de Palacio Program of the European University Institute, Florence, 15–16 January 2009

Adrien de Hauteclocque

The current financial crisis will only slow down the long-term trend of rising world electricity demand but might significantly hamper investment decisions in the short term and lead to a supply crunch once the economy recovers. Overall, $1 trillion a year of investment worldwide would be needed by 2030 to meet consumer needs. The timing of investment decisions is therefore a key aspect, reinforced by the ageing of baseload capacities (essentially coal, fuel, oil and nuclear). The fulfilment of climate policy commitments might also require a massive wave of investment in high fixed-cost technologies such as carbon capture and storage (CCS), nuclear and large-scale renewables units. Investment in the next decade will thus be critical to a low-carbon future in the longer term and long-term supply contracts might be needed to achieve these goals under current investment conditions. The workshop aimed to explore the institutional ways to allow investment in different technologies and make the average prices reach their optimal level in the long term.

The workshop, co-organized by the European University Institute and the Laboratoire d'Analyse économique des Réseaux et des Systems Energétique (LARSEN), on the issue of long-term supply contracts in European decentralized electricity markets gathered together 42 experts to discuss current problems and possible solutions under the Chatham House rules. The first session discussed the contribution of long-term supply contracts to the fulfilment of different policy objectives such as long-term generation adequacy, security of supply and sustainably low prices for energy-intensive industries. The second session addressed the effects of these contracts in an imperfectly competitive market setting and their relative strengths and weaknesses as compared to vertical integration from a more academic perspective. The last session focused on the current action of national and community competition authorities vis-à-vis these contracts, both under the antitrust or state-aid rules, and in comparison with US jurisprudence. The main elements discussed during the workshop and the key conclusions from the debate among regulators, competition authorities, the International Energy Agency (IEA), lawyers, industry, financial and academic delegates are reported here.

1 THE NECESSITY OF VERTICAL ARRANGEMENTS

There has been a fairly wide consensus among participants on the fact that the current willingness of market players to resort to more durable vertical arrangements such as vertical integration and long-term contracts stems from the current shortcomings of the liberalization process. In particular, the under-development of liquid and stable forward contract markets, available at time horizons matching the life span of new investments, yields risks of anti-competitive market abuse and does not allow for an optimal allocation of investment risks. This has tended to lead market players to invest in combined cycle gas turbine (CCGT), given high correlation between gas and electricity prices and low capital intensiveness, because financial investors impose project financing. Power generation technologies indeed have different risk and return characteristics which yield different needs in terms of secure dispatch. Without long-term contracts, the operational and contractual flexibility of CCGT has tended to make it the preferred technology for new entrants. The availability of long-term contracts therefore seems to greatly improve incentives to diversify away from CCGT by investing in coal and nuclear and facilitate project financing. However, it has been recalled that contractual arrangements might often be less important determinants of investment decisions than the local state of supply and demand conditions or risk-aversion profiles.

From the buyer side, the volatility of organized spot and forward markets limited the viability of the pure supplier model and undermined the competitiveness of energy-intensive users. In view of these concerns, long-term bilateral supply contracts could help producers and large buyers to mutually hedge price and quantity risks, and reduce transaction costs from repeated spot contracting, especially when contractors are averse to risk.

However, producer and buyer interests do not completely converge. Suppliers and large consumers needs contractual flexibility, which is against producers' interests. Moreover producers willing to contract for 15 or 20 years to sink high fixed-costs investments face problems of counterparty credibility and a misalignment of contracting incentives with some potential buyers. Facing the risk of new retail entry, electricity resellers without a consumer franchise do not appear credible counterparties for such very long-term, fixed-price, fixed-quantity contracts owing to the difficulties encountered when managing their downstream retail commitments. Resellers thus tend to favour hedging through call options, indexed price contracts or tolling contracts, probably complemented by a portfolio of generation assets. A natural response to the misalignment of contracting incentives between producers and retailers has been vertical reintegration in several markets (for example, the New Zealand, UK, Australia and regional US markets). Vertical reintegration occurs when the costs and risks of contracting (transaction costs, contractual incompleteness and bounded rationality, costs and risks of hold-up, regulatory risks, market power costs) exceed those of ownership (agency costs, costs of collective decision-making, costs of risk-bearing). The virtues of vertical integration are plenty for individual market players. It improves not only investment and risk management but also provides a natural and self-sustaining hedge against wholesale prices and quantity risks, as well as market power and asymmetric information costs, as it internalizes these risks and costs to the firm. It enables better matching of load profiles and supply security preferences. It also enhances scale differences between integrated firms and retail entrants, thereby reducing integrated firms' exposure to predation.

Energy intensive industries appeared more suitable counterparties for long-term contracting. Their need to access baseload electricity at the lowest cost possible through long-term contracts with nuclear producers was highlighted. Competing on a global scale, energy-intensive users may face worldwide competitors with largely lower and less volatile fuel prices, which is detrimental to the competitiveness of European industries. It has been recognized that long-term contracts cannot solve all problems as fixed-price contracts may also create margin risks for energy-intensive users, but the current state of organized wholesale markets and the need to mitigate CO_2 price risks make them willing to share limited amounts of risk with producers for investments in new hydropower and nuclear plants.

On the flip side, long-term supply contracts and innovative contractual structures such as producer/consumer cooperatives, though useful for individual market players, may have ambiguous effects on market-building and these effects crucially depend on the structuring of contract clauses (for example, duration, exclusivity or destination). Moreover contracts create customer foreclosure, limit the development of spot markets and prevent the development of transparent price mechanisms, as has been indicated by the Sector Enquiry. Traditional long-term contracts include take and pay contracts, take or pay contracts and virtual power plants. They all impact liquidity levels in spot markets in different ways. If all these contracts lead somehow to varying degrees of foreclosure, they also have diverse effects on consumer surplus, investment, risk management, and entry and spot prices.

2 FROM THE COMPETITION'S POINT OF VIEW

Contract clauses regarding duration, flexibility mechanisms, exclusive dealing and use restrictions are particularly relevant. Anti-competitive effects of long-term contracts are linked with the market position of contractors and it has been widely agreed upon that the dominant position of certain contractors is a bigger problem that the duration of supply contracts itself. As a result, long-term contracts should not represent more than a certain percentage of the market, to allow for efficient entry, this percentage remaining open for discussion.

In a similar vein competitive foreclosure effects are possible. It has also been highlighted that long-term bilateral contracts could crowd out the development of bilateral financial forward contracts which appear to have the same effects on risk mitigation but without creating anti-competitive foreclosure effects, although this was highly debated because of the weak feasibility of such contracts. State-aid problems may also arise for certain purchasing consortia and stranded power purchase agreements, especially in Eastern Europe.

As to vertical integration, it tends to mitigate wholesale market power and support retail competition among incumbent players but limits retail entry and regulators' ability to monitor wholesale prices as such prices are marginalized and other relevant variables such as generation costs are less easily observable.

A useful parallel with international liberalized gas markets showed that the relationship between liberalization processes and long-term contracts is not straightforward. With an increased number of market participants and the concurrent cost reduction in the liquid natural gas (LNG) value-added chain, asset specificity of investments has decreased and firms which face fewer hold-up risks tend to move from long-term contracts towards short-term trading. No inherent conflict between liberalization and infrastructure investments was depicted in this industry, except for the most risky investment in interconnectors or imports and transit infrastructure, which might need fine-tuning of the (partial or total) exemption rules from third-party access to provide adequate incentives to invest. Nevertheless, the current situation supports the idea that the forecasts of sustainable high wholesale and CO_2 prices allow for high fixed-cost generation investment without long-term contracts if a higher level of liquidity is quickly brought on to electricity markets. Overall, long-term contracts thus appear both as a barrier to competition and market liquidity, and as a cure from the shortcomings of restructuring in European energy markets. Long-term contracting, vertical integration and spot trading should thus be seen as natural complements to support both investment and competition in decentralized electricity markets, though some delegates thought that investment should be favoured over competition in the forthcoming period.

National and EU competition authorities must thus balance pro- and anti-competitive effects of long-term supply contracts taking into account the extent of vertical integration, spot trading and retail competition. At the beginning of liberalization, long-term contracts were often part of liberalization packages to smooth the transition towards competitive electricity markets and facilitate competitive entry in generation. In the European Union, stranded power purchase agreements, for instance in Portugal, Poland and Hungary, have been or are still being reviewed under the state-aid rules, the issue being around the compensation schemes for the operators which suffered from liberalization owing to their long-term commitments or guarantees. As concerns anti-competitive foreclosure effects attached to new long-term contracts reviewed under the antitrust rules (especially Article 82 EC), a methodology of analysis seems to be emerging. A multiple-step approach is increasingly used to reduce regulatory costs and balance anti-competitive effects with potential efficiency gains, in particular if it does not foreclose entry of more efficient players.

However, if some insights from the competition economics of long-term contracts in energy seem to be included in the analysis, European competition policy is constrained by the procedural aspect of the legal process (for example, burden and standard of proof) and the remedies imposed remain open for discussion. Furthermore, the regulation of long-term contracts should not add legal uncertainty to the problem of contracting inherent in decentralized electricity markets. Some delegates viewed as suitable the publication of non-binding guidelines on acceptable contract forms.

Indeed, considerable uncertainties still remain on the treatment of energy-intensive users and incumbent generators investing in new high fixed-cost capacities. The challenges now also lie in the devising of new indicators to truly quantify and then balance pro- and anti-competitive effects of long-term contracts. Some delegates showed concerns that competition authorities could use competition policy as an industrial policy tool, especially with the use of remedies that would be more than proportionate to the infringements committed.

Also highlighted were the more lenient treatment of long-term contracts in the USA compared with the European Union, and the different positions on the application of the 'essential facility' doctrine on electricity transmission networks, revealing different conceptions of competition on merits and responsibility of dominant incumbents.

3 NO DEFINITIVE CONCLUSION ABOUT THE TENSION BETWEEN SECURITY OF SUPPLY AND MARKET COMPETITION

Finally, the link between security of supply and long-term contracts appeared somewhat unclear. By facilitating investments in high fixed-cost projects, long-term contracts contributed to fuel-mix diversity and infrastructure development. It has been pointed out that competition so far has not provided the incentives for investments in Europe to cope with a severe disruption in gas supplies on a market basis. In theory, some generators could specialize in redundant capacities and sell security of supply in the same way as an insurance company, but the systematic involvement of governments during these random events seems to preclude market players and financial intermediaries from developing appropriate market-based mechanisms. Other delegates thought that only planning could fulfil security of supply and that European mechanisms should be established. But another group of delegates defended the idea that improvement of market designs are just as much needed as a smart competition policy for ensuring security of supply.

Index